Vandals in the Bomb Factory:

The History and Literature of
the Students for a Democratic Society

edited by

G. LOUIS HEATH

The Scarecrow Press, Inc.

Metuchen, N.J.   1976

Other Scarecrow books by G. Louis Heath:

The Hot Campus: The Politics that Impede Change in the
   Technoversity (1973)

The Black Panther Leaders Speak (1976)

Off the Pigs! The History and Literature of the Black Panther Party (1976)

Mutiny Does Not Happen Lightly: The Literature of the
   American Resistance to the Vietnam War (1976)

Library of Congress Cataloging in Publication Data

Heath, G   Louis.
   Vandals in the bomb factory.

   Bibliography: p.
   Includes index.
   1. Students for a Democratic Society.
2. Students—United States—Political activity.
I. Title.
LA229.H4   322.4'2   75-40266
ISBN 0-8108-0890-0

Copyright © 1976 by G. Louis Heath

Manufactured in the United States of America

For my summer students
at the University of British Columbia in 1973,
especially Dick Hamakawa,
Colin Hybridge and Ian Flemming

CONTENTS

I. A NOTE ON THE EDITING

Vandals in the Bomb Factory: The History and Literature of the Students for a Democratic Society draws upon a decade of research. The documents incorporated into the book were selected from a set of almost 2,000 items collected by the compiler on ninety-five campuses throughout the United States. The items included were chosen as being most representative of and informative about SDS thought and activities through the sixties and into the early seventies. The date and location of collection and the source of each document are indicated. The history section draws heavily upon government research reports and testimony before government committees, especially the House Committee on Internal Security, referred to herein as HCIS. All sources of materials edited and written into the history section are recorded in the footnotes.

The bibliography was begun at the University of California at Berkeley in 1969 and finished at Illinois State University in 1974. It focuses in detail on materials about SDS and related campus radical activity during the years of SDS' prominence as a New Left group.

The full meaning of the title, Vandals in the Bomb Factory, becomes apparent as one reads. "Vandals" refers to SDS'ers and their penchant for confrontation and terrorism directed toward the Establishment. "The Bomb Factory" is, of course, the Establishment, the American garrison state that efficiently mass-produced violence in Vietnam and poverty (another sort of violence) at home. Thus the image is one of a gigantic war machine that a very small group of dissidents attempts to disrupt but cannot.

G. L. H.

II. CHRONOLOGY

<u>1905</u>. Upton Sinclair, Walter Lippmann, Clarence Darrow, and Jack London found Intercollegiate Socialist Society (ISS), precursor of SDS.

<u>1917</u>. Sixty ISS campus chapters become dormant during World War I, rallying around the flag in response to President Wilson's appeal to make the world "safe for democracy."

<u>1921</u>. ISS reorganized as League for Industrial Democracy.

<u>1930s</u>. During the Depression the League for Industrial Democracy consigns its campus activity to the Student League for Industrial Democracy (SLID). Numerous student and youth movements emerge. The revolutionary National Student League, founded January 1932, is most militant.

<u>Summer, 1934</u>. National Student League membership peaks at 800.

<u>December, 1935</u>. NSL and SLID merge to form American Student Union.

<u>1936</u>. American Student Union sponsors peace strike. Thousands sign Oxford Pledge not to fight in wars. American students favor non-involvement and isolation as Adolf Hitler emerges.

<u>1939</u>. American Student Union achieves membership of 12,000.

<u>June, 1941</u>. ASU adopts pro-war position to involve U.S. against Hitler to save communist Russia.

<u>December, 1941</u>. U.S. enters World War II.

<u>World War II period</u>. Little campus radicalism. American Youth for Democracy organized in 1943 in support of the

Alliance of the U.S.S.R. and the West.

1946. League for Industrial Democracy revives and reorganizes its student subsidiary, SLID. SLID had lost much of its identity in the 1935 merger with NSL.

1948. American Youth for Democracy helps to organize the Youth Progressives, youth arm of the Progressive Party. Vice President Henry Agard Wallace fails to become President and the Progressives all but disappear.

Early 1950s. The period on campus known as the "silent fifties." Students mostly concerned with careers and marriage.

February, 1957. Labor Youth League, the communist youth organization, dissolves. Revelations of Stalinist atrocities collapse it.

Late 1950s. Young white college students join the black civil rights movement. They support black sit-ins, marches, and voter registration drives in the South.

1959. League for Industrial Democracy reorganizes its youth arm, SLID, as SDS, the Students for a Democratic Society.

February 1, 1960. Four black college students conduct a lunch-counter sit-in in Greensboro, North Carolina. This sit-in catalyzes mass non-violent civil disobedience by other black college students to desegregate lunch counters in the South.

April, 1960. The Student Non-Violent Coordinating Committee (SNCC) is organized.

June 17-19, 1960. SDS convenes first convention in the Barbizon-Plaza Hotel, New York.

Early 1960s. Events, especially in the South, raise the political consciousness of youth to a highly idealistic concern for social justice. Montgomery bus boycott, murder of Emmet Till, etc. expose the inequities and violence of the society. Radical white activity in the South, largely through SNCC, is brought to the college campuses of the North. The techniques applied in the South are taken to the North. Shop-ins and picketing are used against stores, and sit-ins and, later, teach-ins against the universities. The focus of the activity switches rapidly from civil rights to Vietnam in the summer and fall of 1965. Student political activity on campus proliferates and intensifies.

1962. Tom Hayden writes "The Port Huron Statement," a manifesto of the New Left. SDS members travel south to help SNCC in voter registration campaigns. SDS advocates disarmament and disengagement and opposes nuclear testing and civil defense preparations. SDS demonstrates against apartheid in South Africa.

1963. SDS activity largely limited to off-campus walks (preliminary to marches) and rallies supporting a foreign policy of disarmament and withdrawal from Vietnam and the North Atlantic Treaty Organization (NATO). SDS uses conventional methods such as educational programs, leafleting, and conferences. SDS annual convention convenes at Camp Gulliver near Pine Hill in upstate New York. Richard Flacks of the University of Chicago prepares the main document entitled "America and the New Era." The document becomes known as the "Son of Port Huron Statement." Economic Research and Action Project (ERAP) begins.

1964. Political Education Project (PEP) initiated. ERAP sponsors community organizing projects in Newark, Trenton, Boston, Baltimore, Cleveland, Chicago, Chester (Pa.), Philadelphia, Louisville, and Hazard (Ky.). SDS cooperates with the Appalachian Economic and Political Action Conference, and the Committee for Miners in Kentucky and Tennessee. It supports Citizens United for Adequate Welfare (CUFAW) in Cleveland. Peace Research and Education Project (PREP) launched. Newark Community Union Project begins. SDS supports Mississippi Freedom Democratic Party at August 1964 Democratic National Convention. Hundreds of northern college students travel south for civil rights activities. Civil rights legislation passes on July 2. Vietnam War escalated dramatically after the August 2-4 Gulf of Tonkin incident. Free Speech Movement at Berkeley. SDS has 27 campus chapters and 1,200 members.

1965. Vietnam War escalates. SDS membership increases to 125 campus chapters with 4,000 members. SDS sponsors a series of nationwide demonstrations against Vietnam War. SDS President Paul Potter demands American withdrawal from Vietnam. SDS sponsors "March on Washington to End the War in Vietnam" on April 17. SDS deletes Communist-exclusion clause from its constitution. It sponsors mass demonstration on August 6-9 called the Assembly of Unrepresented People. The draft becomes the target of anti-war protests. SDS supports SANE-sponsored March on Washington for Peace and a Negotiated Settlement in Vietnam on November 27. Radical Education Project (REP) created.

1966. SDS sponsors sit-ins, teach-ins, fasts, vigils, meetings, leafletings, and picketing in opposition to the Vietnam War. It organizes half the 100 "free universities" established during the year. Commitment to a decentralized SDS with no interest in electoral politics and no organizational ideology. Movement away from community organizing as a focus of activism. SDS publishes pamphlet, "High School Reform: Toward a Student Movement."

1967. SDS membership about 30, 000 in 227 chapters. SDS organizes around "student power" issues and allegations of university complicity with the military. Commitment to "university reform" and a politics of "resistance." SDS President Carl Davidson publishes "Toward a Student Syndicalist Movement." SDS sponsors North American Congress on Latin America (NACLA) and a demonstration against Defense Secretary Robert McNamara at Harvard University. Large SDS-sponsored march against CIA recruiters on Columbia University campus. SDS encourages draft resistance. Many SDS'ers participate in Vietnam Week, April 8-15. Many read Ché Guevara's Guerrilla Warfare. SDS rupture with SNCC begins; relations develop with the National Mobilization Committee to End the War in Vietnam (Mobe) and the Black Panther Party (BPP). Several SDS leaders visit North Vietnam. SDS leaders attend conference in Bratislava, Czechoslovakia sponsored by the Czechoslovakian Peace Committee. SDS representative attends 50th anniversary of the Bolshevik Revolution held in Moscow during July.

1968. SDS urges members to get summer jobs in factories to establish closer ties with workers. It sponsors trip of students to Cuba. Mark Rudd leads violent takeover of Columbia University in April. Vietnamese Communists launch ferocious Tet offensive against thirty South Vietnamese provincial capitals. SDS representatives confer with representatives of North Vietnam and the National Liberation Front of South Vietnam in Budapest during September. American SDS representative attends annual conference of the West German SDS (League of Socialist German Students) and Japanese atomic and hydrogen bomb conference. SDS sponsors International Assembly of Revolutionary Student Movements in New York City during September. SDS publishes pamphlet, "The New Radicals in the Multiversity, An Analysis and Strategy for the Student Movement." It sponsors "Weeks of

Resistance" in spring.   The assassination of Martin Luther
King on April 4 sets off a chain of rioting in the ghettos of
more than eighty cities.   Robert F. Kennedy assassinated
June 6.   SDS heavily involved in demonstrations at Democratic National Convention in Chicago during August.   All
bombing raids on North Vietnam end October 31.

1969.   SDS representatives led by Rennie Davis travel to
Hanoi to take custody of two American fliers and a U.S.
Navy seaman held prisoner of war by the North Vietnamese.
SDS sends a delegation to the tenth anniversary of the Cuban
revolution, celebrated January 2 in Havana.   SDS'ers join
black workers in a wildcat strike at the Ford plant in Mahwah, New Jersey in April.   SDS involved in a number of
campus disruptions.   SDS'ers force cancellation of a March
appearance by San Francisco Mayor Joseph Alioto at Georgetown University.   Confrontation with Dr. S. I. Hayakawa at
the University of Colorado.   Opposition to ROTC, defense
research, and law enforcement officers' training on campus.
SDS supports "black liberation" struggles on campus and "confrontation politics."   It supports the Black Panther Party's
program for "liberation" of the black colony within the U.S.
SDS severs "fraternal" ties with Southern Student Organizing
Committee.   It helps raise bail funds and builds a program
to defend Panther leader Fred Hampton.   SDS National Council pledges support to the Vietnamese Communists and Ho
Chi Minh.   In-fighting among splinter groups at SDS national
convention at Chicago Coliseum, June 18-22, begins the rapid
decline of SDS as the major New Left student organization.
Pro-Progressive Labor Party elements are expelled from SDS,
but remainder of membership splits into a Revolutionary
Youth Movement I faction--known as the Weathermen--and a
Revolutionary Youth Movement II faction.   Weathermen faction
dominates national SDS.   Violent mass anti-war demonstrations in Chicago, October 8-11.   SDS'ers participate in a
"work-in" in private industry and help man picket lines in
trade union disputes.   Violent student strike at San Francisco
State College during 1968-69 academic year.   One of the
largest anti-Vietnam War demonstrations on November 15 in
Washington, D.C.   SDS delegation visits Cuba for meetings
with representatives of the National Liberation Front of
South Vietnam.

1970.   SDS organizes Venceremos Brigade of Americans to
help harvest Cuban sugar crop.   Three SDS members killed
in a Greenwich Village townhouse in New York City while
putting together the component parts of a bomb.   Justice Department indicts thirteen Weathermen for conspiracy to bomb

police and military installations and carry out assassinations. Weathermen send various communications media their "Declaration of a State of War." Bomb planted by SDS explodes in the Bank of America in New York City. American troops invade Cambodia on April 30. Four Kent State University students shot dead on May 4.

1971. Vietnam War winds down rapidly. SDS ceases to be a viable national organization. Many SDS members turn to the conventional channels of society. A few small splinter factions live on, emphasizing anarchy and violence.

III

HISTORY OF THE STUDENTS FOR A DEMOCRATIC SOCIETY

Chapter 1

ORIGINS AND ANTECEDENTS:
ISS TO LID/SLID TO SDS

We are people of this generation, bred in
at least modest comfort, housed now in
universities, looking uncomfortably to the
world we inherit. [1]

In name, Students for a Democratic Society was born
in 1959, but its genesis occurred in 1905 when the most important early 20th century student movement in the United
States took root on various college campuses.

In that year, novelist Upton Sinclair and newspaper
correspondent and columnist-to-be Walter Lippmann, together
with defense attorney Clarence Darrow and adventure writer
Jack London, helped found what was called the Intercollegiate
Socialist Society (ISS). The ISS has been described as a
socialist and labor-oriented middle-class movement. [2]

By April 2, 1917, when President Woodrow Wilson
asked a cheering Congress to declare war on Kaiser Wil-
helm's Germany, with the ringing declaration: "The world
must be made safe for democracy," the ISS boasted it had
60 campus chapters.

Students of every political persuasion melted under the
appeal of Wilson's call and, for all practical purposes, student movements declared a moratorium on activity until
World War I ended.

In 1921, ISS reorganized under a new name--League
for Industrial Democracy--and vowed to strengthen its so-
cialist-oriented, educational venture in colleges and among
the general public. [3]

Some historians have commented that a post-World War I

3

disillusionment sent many youths in Europe into tough-minded, anti-humanitarian, nihilistic, and revolutionary movements such as fascism and communism. However, in the United States in the 1920s, campus radicalism was reportedly conspicuous by its absence. The prime factor in a politicalization of U.S. college campuses was the depression at the end of the decade.

Thus, in the 1930s student and youth movements proliferated--the most militant being the revolutionary National Student League and the largest in adherents being the American Student Union. Both were dominated by the Communist Party of the United States. [4]

By the 1930s, the campus activity of the League for Industrial Democracy had been consigned to a student department--the Student League for Industrial Democracy (SLID).

NATIONAL STUDENT LEAGUE

In January 1932 the National Student League was organized on a platform which contended that capitalism and representative government had failed the American working man and concluded that the USSR and its state-planned economy were the only solution. The NSL, described as the only militant student movement ever to exist in America prior to the emergence of the New Left, exploited anti-war sentiment, held demonstrations and marches, and attempted physical disruption of campus activities which led to arrest, suspensions and expulsions of its members from colleges.

In the summer of 1934, its membership allegedly peaked at 800.

Previous competition on campuses between NSL and SLID ended in December 1935, with a unity convention which found socialists and communists forming a "united front"--the American Student Union. ASU would achieve a paid-up membership of 12,000 by 1939.

The student generation of the mid-1930s had been born during, or immediately after, World War I and had grown up through the boom-to-bust years of the "roaring twenties" and the great depression. Many of them had become disillusioned by post-mortems on the Great War and particularly by the disclosures made by the Nye committee investigations of mu-

nitions makers, the development of international cartels, the
increasingly aggressive and repressive nature of Nazism and
Fascism in Western Europe, and the rising threat of another
"war to end wars."

The International Encyclopedia of the Social Sciences
(New York: Macmillan, 1968) notes that disillusionment over
World War I was most clearly demonstrated by the passage
of a resolution in 1933 by the Oxford Union Society in England, declaring the refusal by students of the Oxford Union
to fight in any future war for King or country. Thousands
of English students reportedly took the so-called Oxford
Pledge and it later was circulated in the United States where
it became an official part of the student peace strike which
the American Student Union sponsored in 1936.

The spirit of non-involvement and isolationism was
sweeping across America at the very time when Adolf Hitler
was reoccupying the Rhineland and carrying out the Anschluss
of Austria, Italy was destroying the independence of Ethiopia,
and Japanese militarists were using China as a "proving
ground" for later and wider aggressions in the Far East.

According to the ASU's Student Union Bulletin of April
10, 1936, and its The Student Advocate of May of that year,
the April peace strike among students was designed to show
that American students were opposed to war, opposed to
Nazism, opposed to Japanese militarism where it threatened
the Soviet Union's Far Eastern territories, and--with a seeming impracticality not unlike some of the attitudes of today's
campus radicals--opposed to American budgetary expenditures
for armaments. ASU insisted that U.S. students would support no war that the U.S. Government might become involved
in and they opposed any loans, credits, or supplies to bel-
ligerents, including those trying to defend themselves against
the mounting threat of German, Italian, and Japanese aggression.

ASU publications also indicated that they felt the ROTC
should be abolished as a means of preventing the alleged militarization of American youth. However, the "non-interven-
tionist" line of "neutrality" and "anti-war" declarations by
campus radicals in the 1930s was comprised at a meeting of
the ASU national executive committee in September 1937,
where ASU gave support to anti-Franco Loyalists in the
Spanish civil war. [5]

Interestingly enough, the international communist movement had been warning against Nazi and Fascist aggression and had been calling for collective security since 1934. The communist position was anything but "isolationist" from 1934 until the Hitler-Stalin peace pact of August 1939.

However, Iversen points out that socialists in this same period, once the Reds abandoned the militance of their National Student League against war and once they were gripped by fear of the rising power of Nazi Germany, were actually the most militant in that they regarded capitalist America as just as great a threat to peace as the Fascists were. Socialists and pacifists, communists and non-communists were all found in the student "peace" movement of the 1930s, but most seem to have been influenced by the view that being _for_ peace and _against_ war would somehow deter aggression by totalitarian states.

Through this period ASU was anti-Nazi until the Hitler-Stalin Pact was approved. Then ASU was simply anti-war and against any U.S. involvement. However, once the pact was abrogated and Hitler opened a second front against the Soviet Union in June of 1941, ASU followed the Communist Party lead in becoming actively pro-war--to save communist Russia, not Western countries with their concepts of freedom. With the attack on Pearl Harbor in December of 1941, ASU's wish was fulfilled and the United States became allied with the war of resistance to totalitarian expansion both in Europe and Asia.

The World War II period saw little campus radicalism although a new communist front, the American Youth for Democracy, was organized in 1943 in support of the Alliance of the U.S.S.R. and the West.

In 1946, the League for Industrial Democracy managed to revive and reorganize its student subsidiary, SLID, which had lost much of its identity in the earlier merger with NSL into ASU.

In 1948, the American Youth for Democracy helped organize a youth affiliate of the then budding Progressive Party, to be known as the Young Progressives, with the prime objective of advancing the political fortunes of Vice President Henry Agard Wallace. The Progressives--young and old--jumped on the Wallace bandwagon only to ride into near oblivion with the dismal failure of his presidential aspirations.

What was left of the communist youth movement in the United States in the 1950s virtually collapsed after Soviet Premier Nikita Khrushchev's annihilating revelations about Joseph Stalin, followed by Khrushchev's own Stalinist-style suppression of the brief but heroic Hungarian revolution of 1956. The communist youth organization--Labor Youth League --operated from May of 1949 until events led to its dissolution in February 1957. SLID, like its aging parent, LID, continued to operate in support of its social-democratic traditions through the 1950s, but it never recovered its pre-war eminence.

CONCERN FOR CIVIL RIGHTS

Youth's natural idealism and concern for change, however, were finding a new outlet in the late 1950s. Triggered by World War II experiences in which Negroes demonstrated an increased determination to seek equality with white men, and fired by the 1954 Supreme Court decision to require the end of racial segregation in public schools, young America found a cause around which to rally.

White students used spring vacations, Christmas holidays, and weekends to support Negro sit-ins, marches, and voting registration drives in the Southland. It was a period of emancipation and it brought results, helping the Negro to flex some political muscle while tearing down many of the walls of racial segregation.

Sporadic and unpublicized sit-ins graduated to mass action after four Negro college students conducted a lunch-counter sit-in in Greensboro, N.C., on February 1, 1960. This stimulated a mass action by other Negro college students in non-violent, civil disobedience techniques to desegregate lunch counters in the South and resulted in the formation of SNCC the following April. [6]

C. Clark Kissinger, national secretary of SDS in 1964-65, wrote about the awakening of student concerns in the second half of the 1950s, observing:

> The Montgomery bus boycott and the murder of Emmet Till brought again to the public mind the inequities of the South in a manner reminiscent of the Scottsboro trials. Questions of basic morality and political philosophy were shoved upon students

by such events as the execution of Caryl Chessman.
And students in small numbers began to respond,
at first through such events as the annual Youth
Marches for Integrated Schools.
    With the coming of the Sixties, student politi-
cal action broke out on every front and in every direction. Most important, of course, were student
sit-ins in the South. For the first time in decades,
students were participating directly in social change
--and the effect was electrifying. The Student Non-
Violent Coordinating Committee was formed, and
SNCC support emerged in the North. [7]

Nick Egleson, as president of the Students for a Democratic Society, writing in New Left Notes on January 6,
1967, declared:

> The idea, the possibility of protest in the south as
> well as the experience of it, was an important part
> in sparking campus protests. Dissent in one place
> created the possibility for dissent elsewhere, and
> dissent materialized on the campus.

In 1959--some 54 years after its founding--the League
for Industrial Democracy agreed to regroup, revitalize, and
rename its youth arm, shifting from SLID to SDS, Students
for a Democratic Society. [8]

SDS and SNCC came into close association at a conference on "Human Rights in the North," organized by SDS
founder Al Haber and held at the University of Michigan in
the late spring of 1960. The conference was actually a series of workshops designed to encourage students on northern
campuses from New York to Chicago to become active in
their own communities in behalf of improved race relations
and against racial discrimination and segregation.

Among the participants in the conference was James
Farmer, SLID national secretary in the fifties and at this
time associated with the Congress of Racial Equality. CORE
had been engaged in sit-ins and other activity against various
forms of racial discrimination since the 1940s. Although its
primary concentration was in the North, CORE members at
this time were also supporting and participating in the mass
demonstrations in the South.

Prior to the SDS conference, SDS chapters and other

predominantly white student groups in the North were register-
ing their sympathy with the Negro student sit-ins in the South
by donating money, picketing northern outlets of national chain
stores subject to sit-ins in the South, and sending petitions
to Congress. [9]

SDS held its first convention June 17-19, 1960, in the
Barbizon-Plaza Hotel, New York. As with SNCC, the birth
of SDS came soon after the Greensboro and Nashville sit-ins.

The constitution of the new organization proclaimed it
to be "an association of young people on the left" and invited
"liberals and radicals, activists and scholars, students and
faculty" to join.

Haber, field secretary of SDS and "the person most
responsible for the birth of the modern SDS," was elected
both president and national secretary. [10] Jonathan Weiss of
the University of Chicago Law School was elected vice president, and Eric Walter of Yale, its international vice president.

SDS met again for its national convention at Hudson
Guild Farms near New York City on September 8-10, 1961.
In announcing the meeting, Haber noted that SDS had passed
through a year of reorganization and reorientation. Campus
movements, he said, would be developed and deepened. Either campus chapters or campus political parties would be
developed depending on what was most appropriate to the situation. Where an SDS chapter was not possible, a loose
association would be worked out with other established groups
in order to create a national communications network. The
convention was billed as the first major attempt by politically
interested students to define the points of controversy on the
student left. [11]

Haber was reelected president and Robert Ross of the
University of Michigan was chosen vice president for the
1961-62 school year. [12]

Ross was instrumental in a project in 1961 that gave
SDS visibility in the United States National Student Associa-
tion (NSA). Many SDS members were listed on the rolls of
NSA which was established in 1948 at Madison, Wisconsin.
Some 300 colleges and universities became affiliated with
NSA through their student governments. At NSA's 1961 na-
tional congress in Madison, Ross and other SDS members

organized a Liberal Study Group, to provide an "informal
meeting place" where NSA delegates could discuss ideas of
particular importance to liberals and radicals of the student
intellectual community. [13] A subsequent SDS convention bulletin asserted that SDS members at the NSA meeting were the
spokesmen "for liberal and democratic ideas. "[14]

HUAC ATTACKED

The SDS-NSA study group held daily forums during the
national congress on such topics as university reform, civil
rights, peace, and abolition of the House Committee on Un-
American Activities. Collaborating with SDS in setting up the
NSA study group were representatives of student members of
the Americans for Democratic Action (ADA), Young Democrats, the Young People's Socialist League, and the Student
Peace Union. [15]

The value to the infant SDS of associating with NSA,
an organization that would eventually be accused of being a
youth front for the U. S. Central Intelligence Agency, was
summed up by Clark Kissinger:[16]

> And, strange as it may seem to the post-CIA stu-
> dent generation, it was the regional and national
> meetings of NSA which first brought together North-
> ern white radicals. [17]

In December 1961, the SDS national executive committee met in Ann Arbor, Michigan, to develop a new ideological definition for the youth movement in the North. It
commissioned Thomas Hayden, a University of Michigan student, to prepare a draft of a manifesto which would have
relevance in view of the new student activism in the United
States and which would be presented to delegates at the forthcoming June 1962 convention.

In the interim, efforts to expand membership were
generally nonproductive, and by the time the 1962 convention
was held at an AFL/CIO camp at Port Huron, Michigan,
only 45 delegates showed up. The most influential of those
present came from the University of Michigan, Cornell,
Swarthmore, and New York University.

Tom Hayden delivered "The Port Huron Statement"
which he and Haber had prepared and it was so well received

by the participants that Hayden was promptly elected president of SDS, having been field secretary of the organization in 1961 and having organized the SDS chapter at the University of Michigan in 1960. Paul Booth of Swarthmore was elected vice president and James Monsonis of Yale--a SNCC civil rights worker--was appointed national secretary to replace Al Haber.

When SDS held its first convention in 1960 it could point to a membership of only 200. It had enjoyed no spectacular growth, but thanks largely to the Port Huron manifesto, SDS could claim a following of nearly 1, 000 by the end of 1962.

Over the next five years, more than 100, 000 copies of the 60-page Port Huron Statement were allegedly distributed. It has been described as constituting the first manifesto of the so-called New Left movement in the United States. [18]

Although both SDS and SNCC are considered prototype "New Left" organizations in the United States, the New Left itself has generally been defined as an amorphous movement of individuals and groups, mainly on the campuses, lacking unity but sharing a common outlook which 1) seeks radical or fundamental reconstruction of American institutions; 2) opposes existing social institutions as "exploitative" or "dehumanizing"; 3) favors decentralized "direct action, " violent or non-violent; and 4) initially rejected rigid doctrines such as those espoused by the Communist Party, U.S.A., and other "old left" groups.

Space does not permit any extensive reference to The Port Huron Statement, but this volume would be incomplete without the inclusion of the introduction of that manifesto entitled "Agenda for a Generation" (see Section IV).

The Port Huron Statement took note of the thousands of students in the past few years who had been breaking the "crust of apathy" by moving "actively and directly" against racial injustices, the threat of war, and other issues. Young Americans, according to the statement, were distressed by the paradox--even hypocrisy--revealed when American ideals were contrasted with such realities as racial discrimination, war, and poverty.

The convictions and analysis presented in The Port Huron Statement signified that SDS was committing itself to

"the search for truly democratic alternatives" to the present
circumstances and that its effort would involve social experimentation. SDS, the statement admitted, had "no sure for-
mulas, no closed theories. " The use of violence "in social
change or interchange, " however, was "abhorrent, " the
statement declared. While it did not find the American political system to be the "model" of which its glorifiers spoke,
SDS nevertheless expressed itself as being in "basic opposition to the communist system" which, as in the case of the
Soviet state, has led to the denial of basic liberties and human dignity.

SDS avowed its concern over the realization of human
potentials and satisfying human relationships in the deperson-
alized, technological society. It pledged to work for a "social system" which it described as "a democracy of individual
participation" or "participatory democracy. " The principle
of participatory democracy should prevail in political, economic, and other major institutions of American society, the Port
Huron Statement maintained. The central aims of such social
changes were "that the individual share in those social decisions determining the quality and direction of his life; that
society be organized to encourage independence in men and
provide the media for their common participation. "

SDS viewed the universities as a "potential base" and
"agency" for a movement for social change. On the campuses, a "new left of young people" would hopefully some
day produce a synthesis of liberal and socialist views and
establish alliances with other elements in American communities which would make them a force to be reckoned with in
the political arena. The strategic role of the university was
explained in The Port Huron Statement in these words:

> Social relevance, the accessibility to knowledge, and
> internal openness--these together make the univer-
> sity a potential base and agency in a movement of
> social change.
>   1.   Any new left in America must be, in
> large measure, a left with real intellectual skills,
> committed to deliberativeness, honesty, reflection
> as working tools. The university permits the polit-
> ical life to be an adjunct to the academic one, and
> action to be informed by reason.
>   2.   A new left must be distributed in sig-
> nificant social roles throughout the country. The
> universities are distributed in such a manner.

3. A new left must consist of younger people who matured in the post-war world, and partially be directed to the recruitment of younger people. The university is an obvious beginning point.
4. A new left must include liberals and socialists, the former for their relevance, the latter for their sense of thoroughgoing reforms in the system. The university is a more sensible place than a political party for these two traditions to begin to discuss their differences and look for political synthesis.
5. A new left must start controversy across the land, if national policies and national apathy are to be reversed. The ideal university is a community of controversy, within itself and in its effects on communities beyond.
6. A new left must transform modern complexity into issues that can be understood and felt close-up by every human being. It must give form to the feelings of helplessness and indifference, so that people may see the political, social and economic sources of their private troubles and organize to change society. In a time of supposed prosperity, moral complacency and political manipulation, a new left cannot rely on only aching stomachs to be the engine force of social reform. The case for change, for alternatives that will involve uncomfortable personal efforts, must be argued as never before. The university is a relevant place for all of these activities. [19]

Thus did Students for a Democratic Society set the stage for a decade of activism on the campuses of the Nation and ten years of remarkably rapid growth for the New Left and radicalization of a significant proportion of today's youth.

NOTES

1. "The Port Huron Statement"--manifesto of Students for a Democratic Society--opening paragraph of "Introduction: Agenda for a Generation, " published by SDS, 119 Fifth Avenue, New York, N. Y.

2. Socialism and American Life, eds. Donald Egbert and Stow Persons (New Jersey: Princeton University Press, 1962), vol. I, p. 312; Robert W. Iversen,

The Communists and the Schools (New York: Harcourt, Brace & Co., 1959), p. 121

3. Iversen, op. cit., p. 123; and John Dewey et al., Thirty-Five Years of Educational Pioneering (New York, League for Industrial Democracy, 1941), p. 10.

4. Daniel Bell, "The Background and Development of Marxian Socialism in the United States," in Socialism and American Life, pp. 360, 382; Iversen, op. cit., p. 123.

5. The Student Advocate, October 1937.

6. SNCC (Student Nonviolent Coordinating Committee) was originally conceived by its organizers as an instrument for coordinating the different groups participating in the sit-ins in the South earlier in 1960 and as an informal source of aid for independent direct-action groups, according to Massimo Teodori's historical study of the New Left, "America and the New Era" in The New Left: A Documentary History, p. 14.

7. C. Clark Kissinger, Students for a Democratic Society: Organizer's Handbook (New York: Students for a Democratic Society, the Student Department of the League for Industrial Democracy, 1964), p. 1.

8. Hearings, Investigation of Students for a Democratic Society, pt. 1-A (Georgetown University), House Committee on Internal Security, June 3-4, 1969, p. 127.

9. Venture, published by Students for a Democratic Society, vol. 1, No. 4, April 1960, and New Left Notes, June 10, 1968, p. 16.

10. New Left Notes, June 10, 1968, p. 16.

11. Announcement, National Conference, Sept. 8-10, 1961, Students for a Democratic Society, no date, p. 2.

12. SDS pamphlet, January 1962.

13. "Students for a Democratic Society!" (promotional flyer circulated by SDS, 1965).

14. SDS Convention Bulletin, No. 1, April 25, 1962.

15. Op. cit.

16. New Left Notes, June 10, 1968.

17. SDS literature habitually referred to its membership as
    including liberals and radicals, without definition of
    those terms.
    An article in the SDS newspaper, New Left Notes,
    of Feb. 3, 1967, indicated that the term "radical" was
    subject to various definitions by radicals themselves.
    The article noted that the word, which in its simplest
    form meant getting at the root of things, was used by
    many to indicate an opposition to a fundamental part of
    the status quo. Some radicals preferred to emphasize
    the very act of opposition, while others promoted some
    specific program such as anti-capitalism, the article
    asserted.
    A sympathetic foreign historian has observed
    that the word "radical," as used in the United States,
    designates any leftist position and is not tied to any
    specific political or intellectual tradition as in Europe.
    The term was applied to show "a position of opposi-
    tion to the system, in contrast to the term 'liberal,'
    which designates the moderate attitude taken by some-
    one who wishes to reform and correct the system
    while accepting its values and basic structures," ac-
    cording to this observer. Radicals in the United
    States, he found, included socialists of all tendencies,
    communists, pacifists, non-violent revolutionaries,
    Marxists, and libertarians. The New Left: A Docu-
    mentary History, ed. Massimo Teodori (New York,
    Indianapolis, and Kansas City: Bobbs-Merrill Co.,
    1969), p. 5.

18. Teodori, op. cit., p. 163.

19. "The Port Huron Statement" of SDS, June 1962, pp.
    51, 52.

Chapter 2

WORKING WITHIN THE SYSTEM:
SDS AND THE NEW LEFT, 1962-65

> We regard men as infinitely precious and
> possessed of unfulfilled capacities for rea-
> son, freedom, and love.... We see little
> reason why men cannot meet with increas-
> ing skill the complexities and responsibili-
> ties of their situation, if society is organ-
> ized not for minority, but for majority,
> participation in decision-making. [1]

Advocating what they proudly called participatory de-
mocracy and armed with enthusiasm, idealism, and The Port
Huron Statement, SDS set out in the summer of 1962 like St.
George en route to slay the dragon.

For them, the first dragon was racial inequality and
segregation. Though SDS lacked an action program it could
rightfully call its own, it heartily championed the cause of
SNCC in the active pursuit of civil rights.

SDS established numerous organizational contacts in
line with its 1962 constitution. [2]

In its formative years, according to C. Clark Kis-
singer, SDS maintained a "close relationship" with the Young
People's Socialist League (YPSL), youth arm of the Socialist
Party.

It also established an identity within the United States
National Student Association (NSA), which was made up of
representatives of student governments of most of the nation's
leading colleges and universities. At the same time, SDS
activities held some attraction for some of the members of
the Student Peace Union which, at its zenith, had a membership of some 6,000. SPU was beginning to lose some of its

16

appeal to students because its principal concern had been an end to nuclear testing. When the nuclear test ban treaty was approaching approval, some of the SPU membership drifted toward SDS and new issues of a more pressing nature.

Knowing what SDS was not in its formative years is as important as knowing what it was. It was an organization, rather loosely drawn, with relatively limited objectives. It was not tightly disciplined and made no pretense of controlling a large following. It was anxious to use the democratic process to bring about changes in a society which SDS felt needed to develop new priorities and reform. It was not a revolutionary movement seeking to take charge of or otherwise dominate other organizations and individuals. It was socialist-inclined, but it was not favorably disposed toward communism. It was often critical of the way in which government, business, and the decision-makers in America operated, but it was not--at the outset--anti-Establishment.

CIVIL RIGHTS STRUGGLE

The civil rights movement, North and South, gained in intensity in the 1962-63 academic year. By their own accounts[3] SDS members were among the students who traveled south to help the SNCC in voter registration campaigns. SDS and other student organizations also helped to raise funds and collect clothing in the North for SNCC's southern efforts and volunteered themselves for "tutorial" projects in northern Negro ghettos.

Shortly before the November elections of 1962, SDS, NSA, the Northern Student Movement (NSM), Young People's Socialist League[4] (YPSL), and the campus ADA (Americans for Democratic Action) teamed up for election day leafleting against racial discrimination during the voter registration period in the South. Donations for this project were solicited by these groups and the proceeds, amounting to some $3,000, went to SNCC.[5]

SDS member Betty Garman and others worked in SNCC's Atlanta headquarters and one SDS flyer described the organization as "a Northern Arm" for SNCC and for the Mississippi Freedom Democratic Party.

Over the Thanksgiving weekend in 1962, the new national secretary, James Monsonis, attended SNCC's Leader-

ship Training Seminar in Nashville. The purpose of the
meeting was to learn new techniques and "concerns in the
movement, " and to draw strength from each other. Other
SDS staffers maintained "close touch with the Northern Student Movement (NSM) as it grows into the major student civil
rights movement in the North. " SDS offered NSM "whatever
assistance possible" and specified such aid as helping at NSM
conferences and supplying personnel whenever necessary.

On the international front, SDS in 1962 was calling
for U. S. initiatives toward disarmament and disengagement
and abandonment of a so-called policy of deterrence.   SDS
also urged U. S. support of anti-colonial and "progressive"
nationalist movements, free trade, and expanded foreign economic aid.   The organization was a co-sponsor in February
1962 of a march on Washington, along with such youth groups
as the Student Peace Union.   The avowed aim of the march
was to register opposition to any arms race, nuclear testing,
and civil defense preparations by the United States.   Marchers
allegedly opposed the cold war policies of both the Soviet bloc
and Western democracies.

SDS also co-sponsored Easter peace marches on similar themes in April.   During the Cuban missile crisis the
following October, SDS members joined in debates, rallies,
picket lines, and leafletings.   An SDS publication described
events of this period as an indication of a need for "drastic
changes" in America's international policies. [6]

Further evidence of SDS' international interest was
provided on December 10, 1962, a date proclaimed to be
Human Rights Day.   Led by the American Committee on
Africa (ACOA), an organization to support the "liberation" of
the black majorities in white-run southern Africa, SDS helped
to organize a series of demonstrations opposing apartheid,
the racial separation policy of the Republic of South Africa,
and calling for economic sanctions against that state.

In New York City, for example, a picket line action
was planned against the main office of the First National City
Bank, then alleged to be a major source for investment financing in South Africa, according to SDS. [7]

The year ended with SDS asking its members to send
SNCC headquarters in Atlanta a Christmas card enclosing a
dollar bill.

In January 1963, SDS moved in a new direction.   It
urged members to contact an organization called Youth to
Abolish HUAC (House Committee on Un-American Activities,
HCUA) in New York City, charging that HCUA suspected communists to be at the root of all evil, to the extent that today's
"acceptable" person was "tomorrow's Communist."

At the same time, SDS began promoting a monthly
student journal called Common Sense and plugged a War Resisters League "Peace Calendar"--which contained some biog-
raphies of New Left heroes.   SDS warmly supported a sale
of holiday cards by the Congress of Racial Equality since the
proceeds were to be used for CORE's civil rights campaign. 8

Otherwise, SDS activity seems to have been largely
limited to off-campus walks (the preliminary to marches) and
rallies urging a redirection of American foreign policy toward
disarmament and disengagement from the growing struggle in
Vietnam and from the North Atlantic Treaty Organization
(NATO).

Most campus activity was restricted to so-called educational programs by means of SDS-backed conferences and
the distribution of literature which either was published by or
reflected the viewpoint of SDS.

In June 1963, the SDS annual convention was held at
Camp Gulliver, near Pine Hill in upstate New York.   Richard
Flacks of the University of Chicago prepared the main document for the session, entitled "America and the New Era."
His thesis became known as the "Son of Port Huron Statement" and formed the backdrop to a convention which attracted
several hundred delegates who adopted a policy declaration defining and attacking "the establishment."

C. Clark Kissinger, a subsequent national secretary
of SDS, has stated that the convention drew youths attracted
by the slogan of "participatory democracy" and also those
stimulated by the writings of the late C. Wright Mills.   Kissinger notes that the term "New Left" was imported into this
country from Britain.   Some American youths were sub-
scribers to the British New Left Review, he stated, and in
1961 they had read Mills' "Letter to the New Left."   Mills
had called attention to unrest among students and young intellectuals in advanced capitalist, communist, and under-developed countries and urged innovative and imaginative efforts
by a "New Left" in the United States based on the possibility

that they--and not the "workers" of Marxist tradition--would
be the agency for radical changes in society. Mills described
worldwide student unrest as a kind of "moral upsurge," but
noted: "Much of it is direct non-violent action" and "we
must learn from their practice" and work out "new forms of
action."9

COOPERATIVE RELATIONSHIPS

The Port Huron spirit had envisioned "cooperative"
relationships between a "New Left" of students on campus and
labor, civil rights, and "other liberal forces outside the campus."10 The 1963 convention statement, "America and the New
Era," reiterated the Port Huron formulation that men deserved more of a share in decision-making which affected
their lives. The position paper deplored a lack of militancy
by labor and liberal forces. It also attacked the inability of
President John F. Kennedy's New Frontiersmen to solve social ills. The Kennedy administration practiced "corporate
liberalism" which allegedly strengthened the power of large
corporations in American society while instituting only "token"
reforms from above in an "undemocratic" elitist manner,
SDS charged.

Those whose job it was to preserve the allegedly unsatisfactory "system" and "existing power arrangements" in
America were the "Establishment," the SDS statement asserted. The term was applied not only to the President and
officials of the executive branch of Government, but also to
many corporate leaders, foundation officials, some labor
leaders, and those in the Republican Party who had roles in
policy-making.

Among those outside the Establishment, the SDS
warned, were the "new insurgents" who were increasingly
active on the local level in behalf of civil rights, unemployment problems, peace efforts, university reform, and political reform. "The outcome of these efforts at creating insurgent politics could be the organization of constituencies
expressing, for the first time in this generation, the needs
of ordinary men for a decent life," SDS declared. [11] While
Negro protest was identified as the "most crucial" upsurge
of the times, SDS maintained that the "most pressing needs
of our time" included not only complete racial equality, but
also disarmament and "abundance with social justice."[12]

An SDS official acknowledged that few SDS'ers five
years later were even aware of "America and the New Era."[13]
That document has been described as an illustration of the
two-way direction of SDS in the early sixties: dedicated to
an autonomous search for new constituencies yet also a coali-
tionist policy aimed at pressuring existing political parties
for change.[14]

Elected president at the convention was Todd Gitlin of
Harvard's Peace Club and SDS affiliate, Toxin. Paul Booth
was reelected vice president and Lee Webb of Boston University was subsequently named national secretary by the SDS
National Council. The 200 authorized convention delegates
contributed $1,700 to the SDS treasury and agreed to seek
closer ties with the American labor movement. During the
summer, the United Auto Workers did give SDS a grant of
$5,000 for use in trying to interest students in programs
backed by the UAW.

SDS FORMATION OF ERAP

The SDS National Council allocated half the funds to
the establishment of the organization's first national project--
ERAP--the Economic Research and Action Project. By fall
ERAP was headquartered in Ann Arbor, Michigan, and former
SDS president Al Haber was put in charge. The balance of
the UAW money was turned over to Joseph Chabot of the University of Michigan. Chabot was field secretary of SDS and
he was given the task of organizing unemployed youth in Chicago in the fall of 1963.[15] Later, this program was named
JOIN (Jobs or Income Now) Community Union. ERAP ultimately expanded to eight other cities with a combined staff
of 125 organizers.[16]

Meanwhile, in August of 1963, the march on Washington by some 200,000 people, mostly Negro, to petition the
Federal Government for "jobs and freedom," impressed SDS
leaders because it related civil rights to economic opportunity;
it convinced many SDS members that unemployment was the
most critical social ill in American society and that automation was a major contributor to the job shortage for many
Negroes.

An ERAP "action" program--in which SDS members
undertook community organizing projects mostly located in
poor black and white neighborhoods in northern cities--was

stimulated by the experience of a number of SDS activists
from Swarthmore College. In September 1963, these activists, fresh from summer civil rights struggles in Maryland,
went into the black ghetto in nearby Chester, Pennsylvania,
on the premise that problems of unemployment and poverty
beset the Negro in the North as well as in the South; and
students on northern campuses could participate in a movement for Negro freedom without migrating south. The SDS
members conducted house-to-house surveys in an effort to
determine the community's views of its most pressing needs,
joined with local residents in demonstrations in November
against school overcrowding, and allegedly were helpful in
bringing residents into block organizations under local leaders
to present complaints to local authorities about inadequacies
in housing, public services, schools, and police practices. [17]

When the National Council met in December, Tom
Hayden persuaded SDS that such community organizing work
should be given top priority in the coming year. Haber took
the opposing view, arguing that SDS should always consider
the organization of a college campus movement as its primary
responsibility. This schism eventually led to Haber's resignation from his ERAP assignment. It marked the beginnings
of a dispute which SDS never completely resolved--namely,
whether to concentrate on campus or off campus. (In 1966,
for instance, campus organizing received top priority, but
in 1969 SDS shifted its emphasis back to the streets.)[18]

The June 1964 SDS convention returned to the Pine
Hill location and 360 delegates were accredited. A former
vice president of the National Student Association, Paul Potter
of Oberlin, was elected president. Vernon Grizzard of
Swarthmore became vice president and Charles Clark Kissinger of the University of Chicago, who had been given an
interim appointment as national secretary at an earlier national council meeting, was continued in that office.

The convention endorsed Hayden's insistence that
ERAP receive prime attention. The SDS delegates also authorized a second national program, which they labeled the
Political Education Project (PEP), to deal with partisan
electoral politics in the 1964 election campaign. SDS leaders
were urged to arrange for instruction of members in the
techniques of political campaigning. James Williams was
appointed director of PEP, assisted by Steve Max and Doug
Ireland. [19]

By the summer of 1964, ERAP claimed to be the
sponsor of community organizing projects in Chester, Philadelphia, Newark, Trenton, Boston, Baltimore, Cleveland,
Chicago, and in Louisville and Hazard in the State of Kentucky. [20]   Around 150 SDS student organizers were estimated
to be at work in urban communities that summer, and some
40 of them chose to continue with their projects rather than
return to the campuses in the fall of 1964. [21]

SDS cooperated with the Appalachian Economic and
Political Action Conference, and the Committee for Miners
in areas of Kentucky and Tennessee. [22]   In Cleveland, Ohio,
SDS supported a Negro and white welfare mothers organization, Citizens United for Adequate Welfare (CUFAW).   ERAP
promoters pledged that as they formed new community organizing projects, efforts would be made to create coalitions
of participating groups among them.   In New Brunswick,
N. J. , SDS cooperated with the Community Action Project
which ERAP described as an organization run by people from
the ghetto and the State university.   An ERAP report detailed
many of the urban action programs, but did not specify
whether college or urban SDS'ers coordinated or participated
in the groups with which ERAP cooperated.

Organizers sometimes lived at poverty levels in the
black or white communities where they often began by survey-
ing communities to determine priorities of local problems.
There was a variety of issues and a great variety of organizing styles.   Organizing unemployed youth was discovered to
be too large a problem for SDS'ers in a project undertaken
in Chicago late in 1963 with the help of UAW funds.   The
project was shifted to a new location in the city and given
a new emphasis on local welfare and housing problems and
community services for the poor. [23]

ERAP has been described by the historians sympathetic
to the New Left as a process of pragmatic testing and ex-
perimentation--guided by some activists' hopes for institutional changes achieved through a grassroots interracial movement of the poor.   A populist, "participatory democracy"
approach was discerned in the way SDS community organizers
sought to activate ghetto residents in behalf of their needs as
they themselves perceived them, and to exert pressure from
independent bases of power in the community or as reform
movements in political or labor organizations. [24]

The SDS move into community organizing was initially

stimulated by moral concerns over the plight of the Negro,
it has been noted by these historians, and SDS also tended
to emulate, tactically, its southern New Left counterpart, the
Student Nonviolent Coordinating Committee. [25]   Originally a
campus civil rights organization pledged to non-violent direct
action tactics, SNCC had been reorganized after the summer
of 1961 into an association of full-time organizers, many of
them former students, who chose to live among the southern
poor at subsistence wages. [26]   Both SNCC and SDS activists
frowned on permanent leaders, hierarchical relations, and
parliamentary procedures and worked to encourage local initiatives through community groupings which were unstructured
and had no programs formulated in advance. [27]

ERAP's leadership in 1964 was composed of Rennie
Davis, director, and an executive committee of eight: Robb
Burlage, Joseph Chabot, Todd Gitlin, Tom Hayden, Sharon
Jeffrey, Ken McEldowney, Paul Potter, and Lee Webb.   This
committee was accountable to the SDS National Council. [28]
The SDS president and its national secretary had automatic
representation on the committee.

Another national project created by SDS was the Peace
Research and Education Project (PREP), a program designed
to link its peace and international relations programs to economic and other domestic issues.

PREP was administered by two coordinators appointed
by the National Council and an executive committee responsible to the Council which consisted of the coordinators, the
president and national secretary of SDS, seven at-large members elected by the Council, and the directors of all PREP
community projects. [29]

PREP undertook to produce handbills urging an end
to U. S. intervention in Vietnam for distribution at election
rallies in the autumn.   Some of the announced issues on
which PREP focused were conversion of the defense industry
to meet social needs, abolition of the peacetime draft, abolition of the compulsory nature of ROTC, and America's involvement in the Third World. [30]

In 1964 SDS was still quite active in the civil rights
movement.   In a "Dear Friend" letter explaining SDS purposes and programs, SDS staffer Barbara Steinberg wrote:[31]

We organize independently or in cooperation with

other local and national organizations such as the
Northern Student Movement, SNCC, and the Southern
Student Organizing Committee (SSOC) in the estab-
lishment of community and campus projects....

Chapter reports to the national office in 1964 revealed
that there was considerable local, collaborative activity. A
University of Washington chapter correspondent reported that
SDS, the local unit of the Socialist Workers Party (SWP), a
Trotskyist communist group, and others joined together to
form an Ad Hoc Committee for Peace in Vietnam. [32] Later,
University of Washington SDS members aided local CORE
members by joining its picket line and a sit-in at a realty
company whose owner, according to SDS, was a "racist."

A Reed College (Portland, Oregon) SDS correspondent
wrote that its chapter was in "close contact with the Young
Democrats," and that its membership overlapped considerably
with campus civil rights activists. The SDS chapter also had
made plans to help the UAW in its fall organizing work in
1964.

The New University (uptown New York City) SDS chapter became part of the Heights Freedom Movement which had
organized "Project Mississippi." A Books-for-Birmingham
(Alabama) project was also started on behalf of SNCC community centers.

The San Francisco Bay area SDS correspondent reported that the members there were cooperating in campaigns
dealing with urban renewal and low-rent housing. Spearhead-
ing this activity were groups including black representatives
from the International Longshoremen's and Warehousemen's
Union. SDS was also active in the Oakland area with other
groups on school boycott and welfare projects. In Oakland,
SDS participated in the programs of the Welfare Rights Committee (WRC) whose members reportedly had had their welfare checks withheld until the head of the house went to work.

ERAP director Rennie Davis reported in the June 1964
SDS Bulletin that the Packinghouse Workers had assigned
Leon Beverly, its international representative, to work with
JOIN, the ERAP community action project in Chicago.

ERAP's summer project members in Louisville, Ky.,
worked with the established West End Community Council
(WECC), primarily a housing and desegregation program.

In Newark, SDS, in conjunction with the National and
Newark Committees for Full Employment (COFE) and the
Clinton Hill Neighborhood Council (CHNC), sponsored the
"Newark Community Union Project, " a movement based on
the issues of employment, housing, and education. SDS provided 12 workers; CHNC housed them, Newark COFE provided a director and an office, and National COFE, a research consultant. [33] Tom Hayden was leader of ERAP's
"Newark Project. "

    In Philadelphia, ERAP's project goals were not dis-
similar to its urban projects elsewhere. ERAP teamed up
with the Independent Citizens Committee--a quasi-political
group--and several local unions to co-sponsor a Labor Day
"March for Jobs. "

    In Trenton, SDS co-sponsored its summer project with
the League for Equality and Opportunity, self-described as a
direct-action civil rights group. ERAP's eight-man staff was
aided, part-time, by the league, as well as by high school
students. SDS also worked with the South Ward Civic Association on voter registration in the predominantly black South
Ward. ERAP's chief interest there was the housing issue
and also the development of a local grassroots organization
which, it hoped, would in turn influence local and national
governments. [34]

    On another front, Paul Booth, SDS vice president, re-
ported that PREP had started to integrate its campus programs with the Universities Committee on Peace and War,
a faculty group directed by Otto Feinstein of Wayne State.

    Booth also noted the dissolution of the Student Peace
Union at its 1964 convention, and wrote that PREP was now
the "sole service" for campus peace groups. SDS' peace
literature would be made available to former SPU chapters,
as well as to the Young Democrats, and church-related associations.

TRADITIONAL "POLITICKING" IN 1964

    Although community organizing continued to hold top
priority in SDS during 1964, many within the organization
preferred concentration, and involvement in, the forthcoming November national elections, while still others advocated
working toward establishment of a socialist third party.

The SDS 1964 convention had authorized establishment of PEP to satisfy those who favored partisan political activity and lobbying. While the SDS national office issued a button with the slogan "Part of the Way with LBJ," the SDS political action arm paid considerable attention to so-called political insurgents running on reform and peace platforms in the fall of 1964. [35] The national convention had also pledged the organization's support to efforts by the Mississippi Freedom Democratic Party which was challenging the regular party organization in the State and seeking seats at the August 1964 Democratic National Convention. [36]

An SDS Bulletin, issued in July 1964, announced that the SDS commitment to electoral politics was important in realizing the organization's goal of participatory democracy. In addition to working for realignment within the Democratic Party and for the MFDP, which it described as a "political mobilization of dispossessed groups," the SDS Bulletin said its community organizers would continue to seek to develop new institutions at a grassroots level, outside of existing political institutions, with a future possibility of political candidates emerging from such community organizations. [37] Community organizing failed to produce new political forms; the Mississippi Freedom Democratic Party bid for national party recognition failed; and the December 1964 National Council meeting of SDS refused any further support to the Political Education Project. PEP expired shortly thereafter.

Several major developments in the summer of 1964-- which reportedly helped set the stage for student activism in the following academic year--included:
1) A journey to the South by hundreds of northern college students for a summer of civil rights activity; [38]
2) Enactment of civil rights legislation on July 2, 1964;
3) Escalation of the Vietnam war after the August 2-4 Gulf of Tonkin incident in which two U.S. destroyers were attacked by North Vietnamese torpedo boats and U.S. forces engaged in retaliatory attacks.

Adult historians of the New Left, and student activists themselves, have credited continuous northern student involvement in "direct actions" in behalf of desegregation and Negro voter registration in the early sixties with inspiring the "direct mass action" techniques which were formally introduced to U.S. college campuses with the Free Speech Movement at the University of California at Berkeley in the fall of 1964.

A number of historians also expressed the opinion that many of the immediate aims of the southern sit-ins, marches, and community organizing efforts had been achieved by the summer of 1964, and adult "co-optation" of student activists' efforts, symbolized by the passage of Federal legislation, encouraged the students to veer toward other targets in American society. [39] A new issue was in the making after the Gulf of Tonkin incident, which was destined to lead to increased calls on American youth to serve in a foreign war. [40]

Various student groups had been engaging in campus "educational"-type activity during the early sixties on pacifist issues, as well as on university reform, in the sense of seeking a loosening of "paternalistic" administrative restrictions on students. SDS was itself involved in promoting the latter efforts. [41]

The school year of 1964-65 is a significant one in many respects for SDS. It proved to be a year in which a major gain was made in membership. When colleges and universities opened in September, SDS had just 27 chapters and 1,200 members on its rolls. By the end of the school year, 1965, the figures had increased to 125 chapters with some 4,000 members listed by the national organization, according to Kissinger.

SDS leaders acknowledged that they were caught unprepared when direct action techniques arrived on campuses in the form of the much-publicized Free Speech Movement at the University of California at Berkeley. [42] Mass demonstrations and strikes, involving confrontations with administrative and law enforcement authorities, erupted at the university beginning in September 1964. FSM pursued shifting objectives, but initially the protest movement had the support of a broad range of campus groups from left wingers to conservatives, all of whom wanted the right to advance either political or civil rights causes within the boundaries of the campus. A number of the activists in the university demonstrations had been active in southern organizing during the preceding summer. [43]

SDS members at Berkeley and in chapters in other parts of the country supported the Free Speech Movement, national secretary C. Clark Kissinger stated. [44] Kissinger, who had assumed the national secretary's post in June 1964, later that year wrote an Organizer's Handbook which the SDS national office mimeographed and circulated for the use

of students interested in organizing a campus SDS chapter.
While not an official policy document of the organization and
not intended for general circulation by SDS members, the
handbook nevertheless offered an insight into national office
views of the values of direct-action tactics on campus.

"Direct action, " the handbook explained, had come to
the fore most recently "in the civil rights and peace movements and involved such forms as the picket line, leafleting,
sit-ins, demonstrations, marches, strikes, and many forms
of civil disobedience. " It is "the quickest road to a lot of
publicity (good or bad) fast, and this is one of its main
uses, " Kissinger wrote. Other reasons for direct action, he
said, were to have an effect, not only on the object of the
action, but also on the "participants" in the action. A pacifist organization's manual was recommended for those who
contemplated civil disobedience, with the advice from Kissinger that "There are times and places where one has no
choice but to deliberately break the law. " All participants
in such action must nevertheless be aware of legal consequences in advance and must have consulted legal counsel,
Kissinger warned. He outlined various steps organizers
could take--including advance notification to press, radio,
and TV if publicity were the object of the direct action. [45]

The first step for would-be founders of campus units
of SDS, he wrote, was the formation of a "paper chapter, "
that is, organizing a few persons and completing the few
essentials required by SDS for the recognition of a chapter.
Recruits should be sought, first among the organizer's
friends, secondly among activists in local peace, civil
rights, and church groups, and thirdly, following an inquiry
to the national office, by contacting individual national members of SDS who attended the same college.

Secondly, the organizer should forthrightly explain the
whats and wherefores of SDS to interested individuals. This
would require some homework by the organizer. In addition
to distributing copies of SDS' constitution, the chapter leader
should explain to students who run SDS, where its money
comes from, what its issues are, and how it differs from
other organizations. Kissinger suggested that the organizer
begin by first reading the SDS constitution, The Port Huron
Statement, "America and the New Era, " and several recent
SDS Bulletins.

In short, the organizer should approach prospective

members with 1) a few answers and 2) an idea for a beginning program. Although a visiting SDS official, such as a
traveler or regional organizer, would prove helpful during the
initial period, a chapter could not be created by an outsider.

The local organizer was then to sign up a few members, using the membership cards provided by the national
office. By mailing at least five stubs from the SDS cards
and their corresponding dues, a copy of the chapter's local
constitution, and a list of officers to the national office, the
new chapter would become recognized provisionally by the
president pending the next meeting of the National Council.

The next step for the local organizer was to go to the
offices of the dean of students and the student government
and request that the chapter be officially recognized by the
administration. Follow the regulations carefully, Kissinger
cautioned, because "this is not the time nor the place to get
into a squabble with the university. " Moreover, the school
might contribute money to the campus organizer's infant chapter and then later, the author candidly stated, the chapter
could choose the issues and be more effective.

In preparing its constitution, the new chapter should
strive to make it short, touching only upon the main points.
The simplest way, Kissinger stated, was to copy another constitution, and the national office had sample copies readily
available.

The first meeting of the chapter should be structured
in advance so that participants did not sit around "staring at
each other. " The draft constitution should be presented by a
competent chairman, and someone should be prepared to
serve as provisional president. Definite program suggestions
should be made and a date set for the next meeting. SDS
literature should also be readily available at the meeting.

The principal concept for the chapter organizer to
remember, he said, was that chapter members should not
view the rest of the campus as a passive body, because that
is where the recruits are found. The chapter was encouraged
to keep in constant contact with the national organization and
to send representatives to its convention and National Council
(NC) meetings. The chapter leader was also advised to contact personnel in SDS' ERAP and PREP projects if such were
located near his campus.

Recruitment, Kissinger counseled, came about as a result of having a good, "exciting" program which would make students want to become part of the activity. New chapter leaders were warned, however, that membership in SDS should never be a prerequisite for participation in its program. Recruitment should start at the beginning of the semester, he said, because the students' time for extra-curricular activity diminished as the term progressed. (Georgetown SDS chapter leaders set up literature tables to attract freshmen during the registration in early September.)

Kissinger pointed out that several of SDS' "finest" chapters had begun as other organizations and subsequently became the nucleus for the SDS unit on the campus. Again, at Georgetown University, this was observed to be true when members of its Student Peace Union chapter became, for all practical purposes, the initial members of SDS on that campus. Anti-war groups at other universities also converted their organizations into local SDS affiliates. At the University of Michigan, Voice, although retaining its name, became the SDS chapter, as did a Peace Club at Harvard University. Kissinger wrote that groups which wished to retain their original name could do so. If they wished to remain independent, however, they could choose to affiliate with SDS as an "associate group" and send a non-voting representative to the NC. (Article III, section 4 of the SDS constitution, as amended in 1967, made provision for such affiliation.)

Kissinger's handbook covered other pertinent organizational aspects of interest to beginning chapters. Chapter dues should be established, but new members were to be reminded also of their financial obligation to the national office. Two ERAP projects, he said by way of example, were financed by $2,696.81 raised by the Swarthmore chapter of SDS through faculty concert projects and from student body contributions.

The college's own resources should be reviewed, namely movie and slide projectors, tape recorders, meeting rooms, film libraries, mimeograph machines, ditto machines, graphic arts labs, dark rooms, etc. Mimeograph paper, he said, could be purchased below list price from the school if the organization had been officially recognized by the college. The handbook also offered advice on other equipment, and the use thereof, such as cameras, picket signs, banners, handbills, and posters.

Kissinger did not overlook high schools in his

organizer's manual, as he pointed out to the college organizer
that SDS had (in 1964) high school chapters and "many high
school members. " Moreover, SDS had no minimum age for
membership, he added.   High School students did not have to
wait until they went to college to become involved.   Secondary
schools did face problems, however, first, because they did
not live on campus as did college students, and secondly,
because high school administrations disapproved of "political
clubs. "

SDS ZEROES IN ON VIETNAM WAR

The 1964-65 academic year found SDS operating on a
small scale on many different fronts.   SDS officers acknowledged that the many-faceted program was accompanied by internal wrangling among elements of the membership preferring some particular line of action.   SDS community organizers, for example, competed successfully against the politi-
cal-action oriented members for a larger share of the organization's efforts and resources in 1964.   Those SDS'ers, convinced that the main role of the organization was on-campus
education and recruiting, also took a back seat in this period,
although the aforementioned SDS Organizer's Handbook, written late in 1964, suggested issues for those chapters most
concerned with on-campus matters. 46

Among the possible on-campus activities itemized in
the handbook were protests against dormitory hours and other
regulations; a contest for control of the student government;
demands for curricular reform and the setting up of extra-
curricular courses which the university refused to teach; investigation of property holdings of the university and the degree to which it depended on defense contracts; and organizing
unions of university employees.

Wrangling over SDS programing dominated the SDS
National Council meeting which convened in New York City,
December 28-31, 1964, participants reported.   The Berkeley
Free Speech Movement was endorsed, and the importance of
SDS community organizing also was affirmed.   Political activity was downgraded, allegedly because many activists were
disenchanted with the idea of promoting social change by
working through traditional Democratic Party organizational
channels and favored grassroots organizing which could lead
to independent political action. 47

The December 1964 National Council session approved a program of "direct actions" to protest investments in the Republic of South Africa by American business and financial institutions, on the grounds that they helped to sustain that government's system of apartheid. A series of nationwide demonstrations was envisioned, beginning in March 1965 with a visit and possible sit-in at the office of Chase Manhattan Bank in New York. Demonstrations occurred in at least six cities, including New York, where Kissinger reported that the sit-in at Chase Manhattan involved some 600 people and led to 40 arrests. An individual describing himself as an unpaid coordinator in the SDS national office for the national anti-apartheid program said efforts to build additional demonstrations, teach-ins, and the like during the following year of 1966 failed.

He blamed the failure on the organizational weaknesses of SDS which meant that a local individual determined the fate of such a program. The intent of the direct actions on this issue was described as an effort to focus the "mass media" on South Africa and to create a sense of purpose and solidarity on the part of the demonstrators. [48]

Divisions within the organization on tactics and programs almost killed a mass march proposal at the December 1964 National Council meeting, which was destined to convert SDS into the major student organization on the so-called New Left.

A proposal that SDS sponsor an anti-Vietnam war march on Washington, D. C. was actually defeated and only after prolonged debate was it reconsidered and passed. SDS officials have explained that SDS'ers traditionally rejected organizing around a single issue such as the Vietnam war and were oriented to pursuing influence over national affairs, including foreign policy, by a "bottom-up," grassroots campaign (i. e., the participatory democracy outlook). Thus many SDS community organizers, then and in the future, resisted "ineffective" marches on the war. [49]

The "March on Washington to End the War in Vietnam" was set for April 17, 1965, to coincide with the Easter recess at colleges and universities. An official "Call" issued by SDS declared that the Vietnam war injured Americans and Vietnamese alike and stated that the national protest march was intended to publicize opposition to "the dangerous, illegal, useless, and immoral war in Vietnam." [50]

The position of some of the SDS leaders on the war was illustrated by the speech subsequently delivered by SDS president Paul Potter before the marchers in Washington, D. C. on April 17.   In the Port Huron mimeographed State- ment of 1962, SDS had declared that hopes for peace in a world polarized by an East-West power struggle depended upon establishing neutralist or non-aligned regimes in all "trouble zones, " which would include South Vietnam.   Speak- ing in Washington in the spring of 1965, the SDS president demanded the withdrawal of American troops from Vietnam even though the action could possibly lead to the imposition of a communist regime in South Vietnam.   Potter asserted that Vietnam would find no freedom through the existing gov- ernment in South Vietnam and continued U. S. bombings of the country.   The best course for the United States to follow, he declared, was to seek to influence nations falling under communist control to an independent posture with respect to the international communist movement. [51]

The SDS president also advised that SDS did not intend to attack the problem of war simply by a statement of pro- test, but rather sought to help create a "massive social movement" which would challenge and fundamentally change "the system" in America which made possible a Vietnam war, poverty, and discrimination.   Building such a movement in American communities, he told the thousands of youth gath- ered near the Washington Monument, would be difficult in a society which doesn't tolerate "fundamental challenges. "   Pot- ter maintained that the American "system" or "institutions" had still to be named, analyzed, and understood before they could be changed to permit "ordinary men" to assume control rather than to be manipulated by "faceless bureaucracies. "

The movement for change, he was nevertheless cer- tain, would rely on "new and creative forms of protest" in- cluding civil disobedience.   As he stated in the conclusion of his speech,

> that means that we build a movement ... based on
> the integrity of man and a belief in man's capacity
> to tolerate all the weird formulations of society
> that men may choose to strive for; a movement
> that will build on the new and creative forms of
> protest that are beginning to emerge, such as the
> teach-in, and extend their efforts and intensify
> them; that we will build a movement that will find
> ways to support the increasing numbers of young

men who are unwilling to and will not fight in Vietnam; a movement that will not tolerate the escalation or prolongation of this war but will, if necessary, respond to the administration war effort with
massive civil disobedience all over the country,
that will wrench the country into a confrontation
with the issues of the war; a movement that must
of necessity reach out to all these people in Vietnam or elsewhere who are struggling to find decen-
cy and control for their lives. [52]

SDS had retained sole sponsorship of the Washington
march, but invited participation by all individuals and organizations opposed to American "intervention" in Vietnam.   National secretary Kissinger noted that: "This meant that for
the first time since the Cold War began, real live communists
(of all shades and descriptions) were accorded equal status
with the old-line pacifist and liberal anti-communist peace
groups.   Naturally the LID (which was still paying the National Secretary's salary) went through the roof, and SANE
flatly refused to participate. "[53]

SDS leaders admittedly expected only a few thousand
demonstrators to turn out for a protest against the escalating
U. S. military effort to beat back an increasingly aggressive
Vietnamese communist assault on the Republic of South Vietnam.   The long-drawn-out conflict entered a new phase early
in February 1965, however.   U. S. forces inaugurated daily
bombing raids over North Vietnam in an effort to force the
North Vietnamese communist government to the conference
table.   It also appeared at this time as if U. S. troops would
very shortly be formally committed to combat on Vietnamese
soil. [54]

Growing campus interest in the Vietnam war issue was
demonstrated by a rash of "teach-ins" on the war.   SDS
members were reportedly among the organizers of the first
teach-in in March 1965 at the University of Michigan at Ann
Arbor. [55]   Draft cards were burned on some campuses.

When the SDS march finally came off on April 17,
1965, masses of young people--mostly students, and in numbers variously estimated at anywhere from 15, 000 to 25, 000
--showed up in the Nation's Capital to demonstrate against
U. S. intervention in Vietnam.

As a result of the turnout, then national secretary

Kissinger maintained, SDS became "nationally known and recognized as the main force on the white New Left. "

NOTES

1. "The Port Huron Statement, " p. 4.

2. "Section 4: ASSOCIATED GROUPS: Independent groups
    can affiliate as associates of SDS by vote of their
    membership and designation of a liaison representative
    to sit on the National Council with consultative vote.
    The representative shall be a member of SDS.   Such
    association is provisional until the approval of the Na-
    tional Council.   The form of the relationship shall be
    worked out in each case between the group and the
    National Council.
        "Section 5: FRATERNAL ORGANIZATIONS:
    National or regional organizations whose programs
    and purposes are consistent with the broad aims and
    principles of SDS can be invited by the National Coun-
    cil to be fraternal with SDS and have a fraternal vote
    on the National Council.   Such organizations shall ap-
    point a liaison representative who shall be a member
    of SDS.
        "Section 6: SDS welcomes the opportunity to
    co-operate with other individuals and organizations in
    jointly sponsoring specific action programs and joint
    stands on specific issues.   The National Council shall
    be empowered to determine specific co-operative ac-
    tivity.   (Co-operation does not imply endorsement.)"
        In point of fact, most of SDS' organizational
    contacts fell within section 6.

3. Histories of SDS in SDS magazine, Radical America,
    May-June 1968; New Left Notes, June 10, 1968.

4. Youth arm of the Socialist Party.

5. SDS Membership Bulletin, No. 1, 1962-63, p. 8.

6. SDS Membership Bulletin, No. 2, 1962-63, p. 2; SDS
    Convention Bulletin, No. 1, Apr. 25, 1962, p. 6;
    Student Peace Union Bulletin, January 1962.

7. SDS Membership Bulletin, No. 2, 1962-63, p. 6.

8. Ibid., p. 4.

9. C. Wright Mills, "Letter to the New Left," originally in New Left Review, London, 1961, reprinted in The New Left, a Collection of Essays, ed. Priscilla Long (Boston: Extending Horizon Books, 1969), p. 25.

10. "The Port Huron Statement."

11. "America and the New Era," in The New Left: A Documentary History, ed. Massimo Teodori, p. 181; definition of "Establishment" appears on p. 175.

12. Ibid., pp. 178, 182.

13. Kissinger in New Left Notes, June 10, 1968.

14. Teodori, op. cit., pp. 43-47.

15. New Left Notes, June 10, 1968, p. 20.

16. New Left Notes, June 24, 1968, p. 2.

17. Teodori, op. cit., pp. 26-29; Carl Wittman (leader in first ERAP community action project in Chester, Pa.), "Students and Economic Action," in Teodori, op. cit., pp. 128-133; Todd Gitlin (leader in Chicago community action project), "The Radical Potential of the Poor," in Teodori, op. cit., pp. 136-149; Tom Hayden (leader of Newark project), in Teodori, op. cit., p. 135; Richard Rothstein, "Evolution of the ERAP Organizers," in The New Left, a Collection of Essays, pp. 272-288; Staughton Lynd, "Introduction," op. cit., p. 7; New Left Notes, Feb. 26, 1968, pp. 5, 8.

18. Kissinger in New Left Notes, June 24, 1968, p. 1.

19. SDS Bulletin, January 1965, vol. 3, No. 4.

20. SDS Bulletin, July 1964, vol. 2, and New Left Notes, June 24, 1968. However, Teodori's documentary history of the New Left lists the 10 locations as follows: Cleveland, New Haven, Appalachia, Baltimore, Oakland (Calif.), Boston, Cairo (Ill.), Hazard (Ky.), Newark, and Chicago. Teodori calls them community organizing projects coordinated by ERAP (p. 487).

21. SDS Bulletin, January 1964; Todd Gitlin, "Vietnam, A
     Selected Bibliography" (printed by SDS, March 1965).

22. "A Movement of Many Voices," Economic Research and
     Action Project, SDS, pp. 12, 13.

23. Teodori, op. cit.; Kissinger in New Left Notes, June
     10, 1968.

24. Rothstein in The New Left, a Collection of Essays.

25. Carl Davidson in Guardian, Mar. 22, 1969, p. 13;
     Staughton Lynd and James O'Brien in The New Left,
     a Collection of Essays, pp. 7, 8; Michael Kazin in
     American Scholar, Autumn 1969.

26. James Forman, a SNCC history in Exhibit 4 to HCIS
     Hearings on SDS, pt. 6-A, October 1969.

27. Teodori, op. cit., pp. 53, 54; Radical America, May-
     June 1968; James P. O'Brien, "The New Left's Early
     Years," in Radical America, May-June 1968.

28. SDS' Summer Projects of the ERAPs, flyer, 1964, Ann
     Arbor, Mich.

29. Kissinger, Organizer's Handbook, p. 25.

30. Idem; Kissinger in New Left Notes, June 10, 1968;
     SDS Bulletin, July 1964.

31. SDS letter, published undated, but received for HCIS
     files in 1964.

32. SDS Bulletin, vol. 2, No. 9, June 1964, p. 2.

33. Ibid., p. 25.

34. Ibid., p. 26.

35. Kissinger, Organizer's Handbook, issued by SDS na-
     tional office, 1965; SDS recruiting leaflet, 1964; SDS
     leaflet "Vietnam...," March 1965.

36. SDS Bulletin, July 1964.

37. Ibid.

38. Estimates ranged up to 600 and 800, the latter in
     Teodori, op. cit.

39. Lewis Feuer, The Conflict of Generations (New York:
     Basic Books, Inc., 1969); James Forman, op. cit.

40. "J. Edgar Hoover lists Tonkin incident as important de-
     velopment in Fordham Law Review article," Congres-
     sional Record, Feb. 17, 1970.

41. Kissinger, Organizer's Handbook, p. 3.

42. Kissinger in New Left Notes, July 8, 1968, p. 6.

43. Michael Kazin in American Scholar, Autumn, 1969.

44. New Left Notes, July 8, 1968, p. 6.

45. Kissinger, Organizer's Handbook, pp. 9, 10, 20.

46. Kissinger in New Left Notes, July 8, 1968.

47. Kissinger in New Left Notes, July 8, 1968, p. 6; SDS
     Bulletin, January 1965; National Guardian, Jan. 9,
     1965, p. 4; Staughton Lynd in The New Left, a Col-
     lection of Essays, pp. 8, 9; Studies on the Left,
     Spring 1965, pp. 61-70; Progressive Labor, January-
     February 1965.

48. Kissinger, New Left Notes, July 8, 1968; National
     Guardian, Feb. 13, 1965, p. 9, and Feb. 27, 1965,
     p. 5; literature from California SDS organizations,
     1966.

49. Kissinger, New Left Notes, July 8, 1968, Los Angeles
     Times article to The Washington Post, Sept. 9, 1965.

50. Call to the march.

51. SDS leaflet on the March on Washington to End the War
     in Vietnam, published in New York, May 1965; The
     Port Huron Statement, pp. 33 and 36.

52. Potter, SDS leaflet on March on Washington. Potter
     had stated that the American "system" was frustrating
     movements for change in Vietnam as well as in the
     U.S.

53. Kissinger in <u>New Left Notes,</u> July 8, 1968, p. 6; see
     also <u>National Guardian,</u> Jan. 9, 1965, p. 4.
         LID refers to the League for Industrial Democ-
     racy, parent organization of SDS, whose policy toward
     communists was reflected in the SDS constitutional op-
     position to "authoritarian movements, both of Commu-
     nism and the domestic Right." SANE is the popular
     abbreviation for the National Committee for a Sane
     Nuclear Policy.

54. O'Brien in <u>Radical America,</u> May–June 1968.

55. Richard E. Peterson in <u>Students in Revolt,</u> eds. Sey-
     mour M. Lipset and Philip Altbach (Boston: Houghton-
     Mifflin Co., 1969), p. 208.

Chapter 3

DIKES UNPLUGGED: FROM DISSENT TO
ACTIVE RESISTANCE, 1965-1967

> 'Boring from below'--this is the program
> of SDS. In the community, on the campus,
> and in the halls of the mighty, SDS seeks
> to counter 'top-down' control and manipula-
> tion with 'bottom up' insurgency and par-
> ticipation. We are radicals--radical dem-
> ocrats; and in America, democracy is a
> radical notion. [1]

The "March on Washington" represented a critical departure for SDS--one that may have had much to do with the
ultimate rise and fall of the organization.

An assortment of groups with a mixture of ideological
credentials was persuaded to join in the effort. Participating
were such organizations as Committee for Nonviolent Action
(CNVA); Women Strike for Peace (WSP); Student Peace Union
(SPU); Women's International League for Peace and Freedom
(WILPF); War Resisters League (WRL); Bronx Reform Democrats; Local 1199--Hospital Workers (AFL-CIO); District
65--Retail Workers (AFL-CIO).

Other groups endorsing the march included: The Com-
mittee on Christian Peace Concerns of the National Student
Christian Federation (NSCF); Young People's Socialist League
(YPSL); W. E. B. DuBois Clubs of America (DCA); Young Socialist Alliance (YSA); May 2nd Movement (M2M); American
Socialist Organizing Committee (ASOC); and Youth Against
War and Fascism (YAWF). Many local chapters from both
CORE and SNCC supported this SDS demonstration which included picketing the White House and a march to the Capitol
for the presentation of a statement on the war to the Con-
gress.

FBI Director J. Edgar Hoover testified on February

10, 1966, before a House Appropriations Subcommittee, that communists from throughout the Nation participated in the demonstration, and that over 70 past or present Communist Party members from New York City alone, including several national leaders, were observed among the participants. [2]

Attending SDS' June 1965 convention at a camp near Kewadin, Michigan, according to Mr. Hoover, was practically every subversive organization in the United States, including the Young Socialist Alliance (YSA), youth arm of the Trotskyite Socialist Workers Party (SWP), the CPUSA, Spartacist (a Trotskyite splinter group), the pro-Peking Progressive Labor Party (PLP) (a Marxist-Leninist group), and its front, the May 2nd Movement.

By the time the National Council of SDS met on Labor Day weekend in 1965, Hoover would later testify, 20 of the approximately 100 participants had past or present affiliations with the Communist Party or other subversive groups.

Thanks to the success of the rally, local chapters increased in number and the SDS annual budget skyrocketed to $60,000, enabling an increase in the national office staff to twelve and the acquisition of SDS' first printing press.

During the June national convention outgoing secretary Kissinger observed that SDS "consciously rejected leadership of the anti-war movement at a time when everyone was looking to SDS to call the next big national hoo-hah." The convention reaffirmed instead the SDS'ers' preference for trying to organize local power bases and for a multi-issue orientation.

END OF COMMUNIST-EXCLUSION CLAUSE

Kissinger reported that the convention nevertheless marked a transition from an old to a new SDS. Beards and ponchos replaced the traditional clean-shaven appearance of delegates, some of whom were "turned on." A decentralization was authorized in SDS' organizational structure, and virtually all former national officers declined to continue in any capacity in the national leadership of SDS. It had been suggested that possibly national officers were unnecessary. The president's role was downgraded and the staff office of the national secretary was reduced in keeping with the convention's reaffirmation to its commitment to develop local power

bases on campus. Finally, SDS removed from its constitution the long-ignored communist-exclusion clause. [3] LID had
initially put this passage into the document to prevent a second communist united-front-style take-over of its youth arm,
as had happened during the mid-thirties.

The constitution adopted by the convention in June
1962 had stated in its preamble that SDS had felt the urgency
to put forth a radical, democratic program counterposed to
authoritarian movements both of communism and the domestic
right.   Also Article III, section 2, had stated that SDS was
clear in its opposition to any totalitarian principle as a basis
for government or social organization, and that advocates or
apologists for such a principle were not eligible for membership. [4]   These passages were struck.

The delegates elected Carl Oglesby of Antioch College
as president, [5] Jeff Shero of the University of Texas as vice
president, [6] and Paul Booth, former SDS vice president, as
national secretary.

On August 6-9, 1965, a mass demonstration was held
in Washington, D.C., called the Assembly of Unrepresented
People.   Thirty-one persons, representing the following organizations, issued the call: SDS, DCA, PLP, M2M, WSP,
CORE, SNCC, National Committee to Abolish the House Un-
American Activities Committee, Southern Conference Educational Fund (SCEF); War Resisters League, Women's International League for Peace and Freedom, and the Council of
Federated Organizations (COFO).   The August 6 portion of
the three-day program, promoting draft card burning, was
sponsored by SDS. [7]

The overall issue of association was raised at the
September 1965 National Council meeting in Bloomington,
Indiana, in preparation for SDS' first national membership
conference in December.   One of the key issues which would
be taken up dealt with the subject of forming coalitions.   One
campus SDS newsletter, in a section entitled "Coalition With
Whom?" asked its members to consider what SDS' "attitude
should be toward the DuBois Clubs, the May 2nd Movement,
the Progressive Labor Party, on the one hand, and the LID,
the AFL-CIO, the Socialist Party, the ADA, and the re-
formed Democrats on the other." It asked if "our attitude"
needed to be clear on such coalitions, and also in what respects SDS differed from other groups. [8]

SDS had been active during the mid-sixties in an anti-war coalition called the National Coordinating Committee to End the War in Vietnam, also known as the National Coordinating Committee (NCC). SDS members went to NCC's convention, attended by 1,500 anti-warriors, in Washington, D.C., November 25-28, 1965, and reported later on the "viciousness of the factional fights." SDS members tried to "steer clear" of the "brawls" which revolved around two proposals. One involved whether or not NCC should be a single-issue organization.

The second squabble involved preparations for an anti-war march sponsored by SANE. SANE's supporters fought with the younger YAWF members over the slogans to be used during the march, with YAWF pressing for more militant themes. An SDS member who appeared surprised at these NCC factional disputes wrote that "the anti-war movement is suffering from delusions of grandeur."9 The SDS'er pointed out that at the SDS National Council meeting in September, "everyone agreed that more educational rather than more demonstrative action was our major hope."

SDS' parent group, LID, noted in its news bulletin that SDS' unpleasant experience with leaders of NCC--particularly at the stormy convention mentioned above--disillusioned many of the more sophisticated SDS'ers.10 Following NCC's conference, SDS'ers voted against endorsing NCC programs and, instead, agreed not to seek the immediate withdrawal of American troops from Vietnam.

LID CONCERN WITH SDS FRATERNIZING

LID was becoming concerned at this time about its highly active youth arm, because its own tax-exempt status might be placed in jeopardy. But the league was more concerned about the communist groups with which SDS had increasingly been fraternizing. Paul Feldman, a LID board member, wrote that the cautious attitude exhibited by SDS toward association with communists was under attack from within the organization as well as from outside groups such as the DuBois Clubs, the NCC, PLP, and M2M. LID objected to NCC principally on the grounds that it "practiced 'united front' demonstrations" with pro-communists.11

Carl Oglesby, who was SDS president at the time of the LID-SDS split-up, insisted that SDS was still headed "in a very healthy direction. "[12]   This assessment became questionable as SDS rejected the peaceful protest format of the early sixties for one of increasingly violent demonstrations and head-on confrontations in the second half of the decade. Mr. Feldman's warning to SDS was on the mark concerning its organizational associates on the outside and their allies within the student group, as events later were to demonstrate dramatically.

(Because of SDS' open-door policy toward communists, as evidenced during its April march on Washington, as well as its deletion of pertinent passages concerning totalitarianism from its constitution and membership cards; and secondly because its tax-exempt status could be jeopardized as a result of SDS' increasing militance, LID and its student affiliate parted ways in October 1965. The two groups reached an "amicable severance" which took effect on January 1, 1966. [13])

The year 1965 provided a new national policy decision which SDS was able to exploit. In June, U.S. field commanders were authorized to commit U.S. troop units to combat in Vietnam. Prior to this, the only American soldiers engaged in fighting were those acting as advisers to the South Vietnamese army. In the face of this development, the draft became the focus of anti-war protests by the fall of 1965 as students returned to campus.

New radical student groups, traditional religious and pacifist groups, and what has been described as a de facto underground simply unwilling to perform military service were drawn together in the draft protest.

PLAN FOR ANTI-DRAFT CAMPAIGN

As the 1965-66 academic year opened, SDS national officers unfolded a plan for a nationwide, SDS anti-draft campaign. The plan--outlined at a press conference held in Washington, D.C., in late October by SDS national president Carl Oglesby and national secretary Paul Booth--would commit SDS to encourage all draft-age youth to file for exemptions as conscientious objectors. [14]   A Quaker organization was quick to criticize such proposed misuse of draft exemption based on genuine conscientious objection. The proposal was withdrawn by the new SDS national leadership in November 1965 only after a referendum of the SDS membership turned thumbs down on the project. [15]   One chapter reported

that most of its members opposed the proposal out of concern over its possible illegality. [16]   Another chapter stated
it would encourage avoiding the draft but only in legal ways. [17]
A regional SDS organization fired off a telegram to national
secretary Booth, objecting not so much to the anti-draft proposal as to the implication that the SDS national office had
any right to attempt to establish a national policy for SDS in
view of the local autonomy of SDS chapters. [18]

National secretary Booth, in announcing abandonment
of the original anti-draft campaign, said the national SDS
would promote alternative ways of fulfilling military service
requirements--such as service in domestic civilian projects.
"I want to build, not burn," was the national secretary's
avowed aim. [19]

A September 1965 National Council meeting had reaffirmed SDS prejudices against mass demonstrations, but the
organization nevertheless issued a national call urging support
for a SANE-sponsored March on Washington for Peace and a
Negotiated Settlement in Vietnam.   The SDS call in support
of the march, scheduled for November 27, 1965, urged a
cease-fire and withdrawal of American troops from Vietnam
plus a guarantee of political amnesty.   SDS declared that
America's main problems were with racial injustice and poverty at home, not a fight with communism abroad.   The
student organization, according to the appeal, wanted to see
an end to "oligarchic rule" and "privileged power" in both
the U.S. and Vietnam, and their replacement with "popular
democracy" in which "the people" make the decisions. [20]

Statements by SDS national leaders late in 1965 and
throughout 1966 often attacked U.S. foreign policy as a built-
in defect of a "system" which they labeled "corporate liberalism."   According to this view, no matter what men were
elected in an allegedly "liberal"-led American government,
existing institutional arrangements resulted in a foreign policy
based on expanding and protecting private economic investments abroad; people and politicians were either instruments
or protectors of this "system."

As SDS president Carl Oglesby expressed it in a
speech at an anti-war conference in Washington, D.C., in
the fall of 1965, "liberal" Government leaders were protectors of an American corporate system which exploited foreign
countries for profit and sought to give moral sanction to
these efforts by describing them as anti-communist.   Oglesby

acknowledged the "bitter ugliness" of Soviet tanks invading
Hungary and conceded that communist revolutions had been
and would continue to be "bloody and tyrannous." He deplored, however, an American foreign policy aimed at suppressing such revolutions and expressed himself as being
more concerned over "more vicious" right wing tyrannies
which would be aided in the course of such a foreign policy. [21]

A modified anti-draft program promoted by the SDS
national leadership and some of the locals during the 1965-66
academic year included 1) publication and sale of some 15, 000
copies of a handbook on conscientious objection to the draft,[22]
and 2) a campaign to persuade college professors not to turn
in class rankings used by Selective Service boards in reviewing student draft deferments. [23] A national membership conference and national council meeting held December 27, 1965
to January 2, 1966 at the University of Illinois, produced a
resolution to circulate among potential draftees so-called
freedom draft cards stating, in line with the national secretary's aforementioned policy statement:

> I want to work for democracy. I do not want to
> fight in Vietnam, because the war is destroying
> our hopes for democracy both there and at home.
> I want to build, not burn. The work done by many
> young Americans in Alabama and Mississippi is a
> prime example of what I want to do. [24]

CREATION OF RADICAL EDUCATION PROJECT

One of the purposes of the national membership conference was to talk about various internal problems of a
greatly enlarged student organization committed to a variety
of different activities. Subjects announced for discussion,
for example, were a definition of the "Establishment" and
the U. S. "power structure"; an anti-"imperialist" foreign
policy stance as opposed to an anti-interventionist one; attitudes toward communist and national liberation movements;
and organization, ideology, and strategy. [25]

A conference workshop on ideology included Marxists
and anarchists in the debate. Reportedly as part of an effort to overcome confusion in SDS ranks on ideological matters, a Radical Education Project was created to engage in
research and publication in the field.

The merits of organizing among students, the poor,
or workers were also debated. A paper by present and
former national officers foresaw the SDS role as building a
movement for social changes based on demands of the poor
and the Negro in the communities and, on campus, around
a student and faculty demand for control over their own universities. [26]

SDS community organizers reportedly appeared dispir-
ited at the conference and indicated their growing belief that
the poor were not the most approachable element of the population for SDS purposes. [27] One of the organizers subsequently observed that frustration over the failure of community
organizing efforts had induced in at least some of the organizers a hostile view of labor and liberal groups and a readiness to follow ERAP leader Rennie Davis' idea of advancing
demands not likely to be met by the local power structure in
order to teach people that American society denies them opportunities and rights (i. e., primary emphasis was placed on
the radicalization effect of organizing work rather than an
achievement of reforms). Some community organizers, from
their own accounts, were now viewing the U. S. system as an
"imperialist" one and supporting domestic goals of "collectiv-
izing" economic decision-making and "democratizing" and "decentralizing" every political, economic, and social institution
in America. [28]

In late 1965, an ERAP spokesman reported, most
SDS community organizers had already abandoned original
hopes of achieving social reforms, inspiring mass protest
(or "populist upsurges") from the ranks of labor and liberal
organizations, and enlisting poor whites in the Negro freedom movement.

The SDS leader offered the following pessimistic views
of ERAP gains:

> Although ERAP projects developed a facility for
> winning specific welfare (public aid) grievance
> cases and for forcing, by rent strike, an occasion-
> al landlord to fix up, in all ten ERAP projects only
> two concessions were gained from the 'power struc-
> ture.' In Cleveland, a free lunch program was
> granted to the children to aid recipients who at-
> tended public school; and in Newark, a locally
> elected war on poverty board was able to appro-
> priate funds for a recreation center. [29]

While SDS organizers reportedly found the "power structure" unresponsive to demands from below, and masses of persons unwilling to swing into action on the strength of the SDS example, some organizers noted that they themselves became involved in internal disagreements as well as conflicts with welfare and other local authorities, labor and liberal groups which tended to jeopardize contributions to solving grievances of the poor. The young organizers were quickly frustrated by the slow and difficult nature of community organizing, and constantly shifted direction in their community organizing efforts, it was also acknowledged. [30] Those involved in the organizing were not clear as to the intent of the community organizations they were seeking to build in an effort to transform American society. [31] An observer noted that the refusal of the young activists to consider alliances or coalitions with local representatives of the "Establishment" tended to forestall the achievement of goods and services the poor wanted. [32]

Jonathan Eisen, an observer at the December conference, wrote his own critical views regarding what he thought was SDS' problem during this hectic growth period.

> The SDS has had a hard time coming to terms with its new importance on the national scene, and ... is groping around trying to reduce the hiatus between necessity and its rather inadequate structural capabilities. One of the tasks of the conference was to grapple with the hard fact that unless the SDS can overcome its organization limitations, its influence and magnetism are likely to fade rapidly. And Vietnam is the hangup. [33]

The conference, wrote Eisen, was "a morass, a labyrinth, a marathon of procedural amendments, non-sequiturs, soul-searching, maneuvering, partying and arguing, plenaries which went nowhere, and proposals which were unheeded and undebated. "[34]

COMMUNIST INFILTRATION OF SDS

The problem of affiliation by SDS with other organizations continued to gnaw at internal organization harmony in the early part of 1966. Members of two communist satellites --the W. E. B. DuBois Clubs and the M2M (May 2nd Movement)--entered SDS and vied for influence and ultimate

control.   Pressures from both groups provided disputes within SDS chapters on the propriety of collaborating.

For instance, the DuBois Clubs contacted a Midwest
SDS chapter to request support for a "peace" demonstration
in January 1966.   SDS members considered whether or not
it was wise to "affiliate ourselves in name and membership."[35]
The chapter's newsletter carried two articles, one pro, one
con, for the consideration of its members who would subsequently vote on the issue.   The pro-participation member
stated that without the broadest organizational representation,
the demonstration "could flop," thereby making the local
peace movement look ridiculous and the non-participating SDS
"look like splitters or organization sectarians or worse."
Proponents of collaboration pointed out that the demonstration
was sponsored not only by the DuBois Clubs but also the college chapter of the Young People's Socialist League and the
local chapter of the National Coordinating Committee to End
the War in Vietnam.   The "pro" view held that SDS, the
ADA, Quakers, and other anti-war groups should back the
proposal.

The opponents of such participation argued that SDS
should work in the university dormitories, not in the streets
and not in front of the Post Office or the draft board.   The
author of the "con" view opposed allocating SDS financial and
physical resources to a project which "we have never been
asked to discuss.   I feel that we should keep our name out
of it," he added.   Because of past anti-war activities, this
opponent of working with the DuBois demonstration said there
were already "too many people on this campus who are
afraid to even talk to us.... Our effectiveness has been cut
sharply and I would hate to see it cut further by focusing
again on demonstration tactics," he added.[36]

Gerald Wayne Kirk, FBI informant, CPUSA member,
recognized leader of the SDS chapter at the University of
Chicago, chairman of that school's DuBois Club chapter, and
later Midwest director of DCA, informed HCIS that CPUSA
influence in SDS--via its DuBois Club--was significant.   According to this witness, the Communist Party initially condemned SDS-led campus disorders as ineffective and premature.   In May of 1968, however, the party decided to try to
win over SDS members to the Communist Party's ideology
and tactics and to recruit SDS'ers into the DCA or the party
itself.

The party's wooing of SDS included gifts of money through individual party members. Party members in SDS also did their assignments well, which made SDS'ers more dependent upon them, according to Kirk. When SDS members actually invited party members into SDS to help stem the growing influence of the pro-Peking PLP faction in SDS, the party had a better opportunity to exploit the factional infighting for its own purposes.

In addition to offering ideological guidance, the party reportedly worked to develop SDS contacts with "socialist" nations and for SDS cooperation with the party and other organizations in "united front" actions against the Establishment.

Just as the DuBois Clubs were active in promoting penetration of SDS, so were the leaders of the Progressive Labor Party, the pro-Peking wing of American communists. PLP disbanded its youth group, M2M, in February of 1966 and ordered its members to join SDS. In thus seeding the student group with M2M infiltrators, PLP laid the groundwork for the eventual blowup of SDS at its 1969 convention.

Meanwhile, SDS grew and thrived on issues growing out of the Vietnam war.

An SDS member, reviewing SDS history, has maintained that the growth of the organization closely paralleled an increase in opposition among the American population to the American military effort in Vietnam. Regardless of the validity of his broad assessment, the writer observed that anti-draft activity--by young people acting individually or through various organizations--escalated at the beginning of 1966 as the Vietnam war, for the first time, affected the lives of college students. [37] The Selective Service Director had announced that draft boards were going to examine class rankings of students for the first time since the Korean war. Special Selective Service written examinations were also devised and set for May 14, 21, and June 3, 1966, at examination centers throughout the country, as an additional method of determining which students would lose draft deferments. College students would have to obtain a certain score on the exams or remain within the top ranks of their class to retain deferment.

Protests against use of class rankings in determining draft deferments were reportedly initiated by several faculty

groups in eastern colleges and picked up by the SDS and other
student activists.

SDS, it should also be noted, was neither the first
organization nor the only one to engage in various types of
anti-draft actions. (In the case of SNCC, for example, a
policy statement issued in January 1966 had declared the
organization's intention not only to oppose the war effort but
also to encourage draft resistance. SDS, whose recruiting
literature at this time portrayed itself as the "northern arm"
of SNCC, did not reach a similar official position until December 1966. [38])

In May of 1966, class rankings provided an issue for
1, 000 students to occupy a University of Wisconsin building
for almost a week; for a sleep-in at Hunter College in New
York; for a sit-in at Brooklyn College; picketing at the City
College of New York; and many other demonstrations at colleges throughout the nation. In some cases, SDS chapters
were publicized as a leading force in campus anti-draft actions. For example, after propagandizing since March 1966
against an agreement of the University of Chicago administration to furnish class rankings to Selective Service, the local
SDS chapter called a mass meeting in May at which some
300 students formed an ad hoc, anti-recruiting committee and
sponsored a sit-in at the administration building from May
11 to 16, 1966. Within three days after the end of that sit-
in, some 200 students at nearby Roosevelt University sat-in
at their own administration building until they were dispersed
by police. The action followed a local SDS chapter's anti-
draft campaign, but the demands of the demonstrators were
broadened to include not only opposition to submission of
class rankings and grades to Selective Service and use of the
campus for administering Selective Service tests, but also
an appeal for a student role in the university decision-making
processes. [39]

SDS "NATIONAL VIETNAM EXAM"

An SDS National Council meeting on April 10, 1966,
devised a "counter-examination" which would be printed and
circulated in an effort to reach some of the nearly half-mil-
lion college students expected to take the first Selective Service draft deferment test on May 14. This SDS "National
Vietnam Exam" was designed to publicize the organization's
opposition to the American military effort in Vietnam as well

as its view that the draft was "unfair" and "undemocratic"
because it discriminated against youth who cannot go to college. An additional SDS National Council proposal to urge
college students not to take advantage of their privilege and
not to take the deferment exam was defeated by a referendum
of the SDS membership.   SDS national secretary Booth reported that 350,000 of the SDS exams were distributed at
some 820 of the campus centers at which the first Selective
Service test was being administered. [40]

In addition to sit-ins, other local SDS activity in the
spring of 1966--all apparently peaceful--included teach-ins,
fasts, vigils, meetings, leafletings, and picketing on the subject of the Vietnam war in general, or the draft in particular,
according to press reports.

Other campus-related activities in which SDS'ers were
reportedly involved in the 1965-66 academic year were the
formation of so-called free universities.   Often held in private homes at little or no cost to students, and taught by
anyone from professors and students to community representatives, "free universities" specialized in courses which universities did not, or would not, offer.   Courses might range
from yoga or beginning guitar to Marxism and anarchism,
and about half of the estimated 100 free universities set up
around the country that year were reported to have been
formed through local SDS efforts. [41]   In some localities, during the same year, SDS members concentrated on purely
campus issues such as the quality and price of cafeteria food
and the rents for university housing.   As was the case at
Indiana University, SDS worked within a broad coalition, including conservative youth groups and student government
leaders in the field of university reforms. [42]   Some SDS
chapters sponsored campus speaking appearances by official
representatives of the Communist Party, U.S.A., or its
Maoist split-off, the Progressive Labor Party.   In the same
period, SDS chapters sponsored campus rallies or petitions
protesting the arrest and trial in the Soviet Union of writers
daring to speak critically of communism in practice.

In August of 1966, some 350 delegates from 140
chapters met in convention near Cedar Lake, Iowa. [43]   Discussion and debate included the matter of working with liberals, communists, and blacks. [44]

With respect to "liberals," one speaker said SDS
should work with rank and file citizens of "liberal" persua-

sion rather than with their avowed leaders because "liberal"
leadership was often much too conservative and tended to be
easily frightened by their own followers.   Another speaker
reportedly insisted that the white middle class was the most
"radicalizable" group in American society.   These views
are interesting when compared to the communist contention
that the middle class is too bourgeois and that only the working class can be depended upon as the backbone for revolutionary change.

Regarding communists, convention discussion centered
on whether or not members of communist groups who were
also members of the SDS should be required to reveal their
dual affiliation before running for office.   PLP members
showed no hesitation in doing so, though members of CPUSA
refrained, and following the convention the SDS National
Council voted 41-3 against a proposal to require identification of "dual members. "

Communist Party, U.S.A. member Bettina Aptheker
--whose father, Herbert Aptheker, is the designated theoretician of CPUSA--addressed the convention in an effort to enlist support for a student strike against the war in Vietnam.
She urged the delegates at the SDS convention "to accept
Communist Party members freely into their ranks.   We feel
that SDS can help us, but it is not a one-way street.   We
feel that we can also help them in arguing certain positions, "
she added.

On black power, a convention panel included Anne
Braden, who appeared on behalf of the Southern Conference
Educational Fund, Charles Cobb of SNCC, and Bill Higgs, a
lawyer for CORE and SNCC.   They discussed SDS' relations
with the white and black poor.   SNCC had been reorganized
in the spring of 1966 under new chairman Stokely Carmichael
and thereafter discouraged white participation as it pursued
its equally new "black power" line.   SDS support of the reorganized SNCC was expressed earlier in a resolution passed
at the June 1966 meeting of the SDS National Council. [45]

What came out of the discussions was the concept that
an interracial movement of the poor can have validity only
after the black community has organized equal power with
the white radical community and the white community is
purged of racism.   SDS' responsibility, Cobb said, was to
organize the white community along these lines. [46]

The convention elected Nick Egleson, president; Carl
Davidson, vice president; and Gregory Calvert, national secretary.   Dee Jacobson became the assistant national secretary. [47]

Some of the delegates wanted SDS to concentrate on
organizing resistance to the draft, but the majority present
decided that organization emphasis should be placed on campus activities and that individual chapters should organize
their own anti-draft and other programs for action.

The convention passed a resolution stating that neither
the convention nor the SDS National Council could take a position making the membership liable for conviction on felony
charges arising from draft resistance unless a majority of
SDS members approved the policy in a referendum. [48]

As a seeming compromise, those who recommended
that the SDS national office take more of a leadership role
and give more attention to draft resistance were appeased
when the convention named Jeffrey Segal as national anti-
draft organizer. Segal, who had been indicted in 1965 for
draft evasion, received a four-year prison sentence for the
offense in November 1966, but actually did not begin serving
time until 1968.

There were delegates at the convention who wanted to
create powerful student unions and there were still others
who wanted to turn SDS away from the campus by changing
it into a group of full-time organizers, modeled after the
SNCC organization rather than a collection of campus chapters. [49]

The newly elected national leadership, however, reflected the consensus of the convention in their commitment
to a decentralized SDS organization with no interest in electoral politics, no agreed upon ideology, and a new focus on
campus activism. [50] For the first time the SDS convention
delegates heard no reports dealing with community organiz-
ing--formerly the area of SDS concentration. [51]

The Radical Education Project, which was reported
to have become relatively autonomous, was instructed to integrate with SDS for the purpose of providing a kind of internal education program for the local SDS chapters.

Observers noted that the trend in SDS was toward

organizing a campus movement for social change on university reform issues as well as for anti-war causes.

NEW LEFT VERSUS OLD LEFT

The National Guardian, reporting on New Left and old
left developments in this period, observed that insiders considered the term "New Left" to apply to organizations and
individuals developing new ideological and tactical approaches
to radical social change and consciously rejecting the approaches of existing old left parties and youth groups. Style,
vocabulary, and even a "mystique" also distinguished groups
such as SDS, the National Guardian commented, calling attention to their commitment to direct action, abstention from
any ideology compatible with old left forms, attacks on a
"system" broader than just the "capitalism" attacked by the
old left; and the search for new areas in which to organize
for social change--based on a grassroots "let-the-people-de-
cide outlook" characterized as "participatory democracy."
Particularly noteworthy to the National Guardian was the New
Left propensity for asking questions, for experimentation,
rather than for preaching or providing answers. [52]

The lack of a clear-cut program for specific goals
was deplored by the retiring national president, Carl Oglesby,
at the SDS national convention in August 1966. "In SDS
there is a deep concern that something is wrong with America and that certain institutions are responsible," he declared in his convention speech. "We need to develop greater clarity about what we think the world ought to be like."
The youth organization offered no political platform for
change, he noted at another point. [53]

"What we seek," one of the convention participants
declared, is "something new, very American and revolutionary. This takes time. "[54]

The convention instruction to the Radical Education
Project to service local chapters with "educational" materials
was described by SDS activists as an attempt to stimulate
analyses of the nature of American society and ideas about
the most important type of social change the organization
should work towards. [55] Endless, even chaotic discussions
at SDS meetings convinced some observers that the organization was in this period an apolitical, anarchistic, activist
group. [56]

Recruiting literature issued by SDS at this time, quoting from the preamble to the SDS constitution, spoke of its vision "of a democratic society, where at all levels the people have control of the decisions which affect them and the resources on which they are dependent" and of SDS interest in programs necessary "to effect change at the most basic levels of economic, political, and social organizations." Not bound by organizational discipline, SDS was building a "movement" rather than an organization, its literature asserted, in a society it described as being beset by power politics and war, political manipulators, and poverty amid concentrations of wealth.

The application of this approach was illustrated by the Northern California regional office of SDS in explaining to liberal and left groups why the SDS refused to become involved in a political campaign of a local independent, anti-war candidate. Use of established electoral molds, the SDS office said, would have forced upon SDS activists the "very high structure & organization" of a political party, offered no opportunity for involving people of the community in decision-making, and encouraged manipulation by an elite few. SDS'ers were not interested in a style of politics which takes over either organizations, communities, or people, the regional office added. 57

SDS IN THE 1966-67 ACADEMIC YEAR

The principal focus of activity by national and local SDS organizations in the 1966-67 academic year was organizing on college campuses around "student power" issues and issues charging university complicity with the military. 58

By mid-term, national officers were proclaiming the commitment of SDS to a politics of "resistance" as compared to its previous confinement to politics and "protest." Disruption was called for by at least one national officer and was occasionally carried out on a local chapter level.

Discussion of SDS tactics and activities is complicated by differences in viewpoints existing among national and local SDS activists and what national officers conceded to be almost anarchic individualism on the part of local chapters.

Within SDS ranks, according to the newly elected national vice president, Carl Davidson, were different varieties

of communists and socialists, three or four different kinds
of anarchists, syndicalists, social democrats, humanist liberals, former libertarian laissez-faire capitalists, and hippie
types. 59

Reporting on a survey of some sixty SDS chapters,
early in 1967, Davidson found each was "doing its own thing"
and was composed mainly of anti-intellectual activists attracted by slogans, not theories. Differences also existed at
the local level, Davidson reported, as activists coexisted in
a chapter with smaller percentages of intellectuals (usually
graduate students) and "organizing" types (who carried out
time-consuming chores of keeping the chapter going). He observed that the "organizers" were on campus in part to obtain student deferment from the draft.

The independence of local units was emphasized by
the new national secretary, Greg Calvert, in an interview
late in 1966:

> The minute we start sending anything that looks
> like an order, the periodic debate about abolishing
> the national office starts up again.
>   You have to let the local chapters decide
> their course on the basis of whatever their situa-
> tion is--let them organize their lives from where
> they happen to be. 60

UNIVERSITY REFORM AND "STUDENT POWER"

SDS recruiting literature for 1966 emphasized SDS interest in "university reform," which it said was illustrated
by SDS chapter efforts to inaugurate "counter-courses," and
campaigns against "Cold War" research grants to universities,
"paternalistic" social rules, free speech restrictions, rising
education costs, irrelevant curricula, and the like. 61

Some additional on-campus tactics in the name of
"university reform" were proposed at the August 1966 national convention in a working paper by Davidson. Although
the convention failed to approve the document, Davidson was
elected to the first of two terms in a national SDS office and
his ideas were disseminated in a pamphlet printed by the
Radical Education Project under the title "Toward a Student
Syndicalist Movement. "62 Davidson urged that SDS campus
chapters push for a student syndicalist goal which he defined

as student control over the rules that governed them on campus. He urged working through a campus political party to seize control of the student government or through a student union of all the students.

Davidson's attack on the university as a knowledge factory for corporations was admittedly not original with him, and the campus political party had been successfully used at Berkeley to gain a voice in student government some years before. [63] The tactics recommended by the new SDS national officer for radicalizing students into opposition to the present American "system" are worthy of note, however. These included constant harassing and disruption of meetings of existing student governments; sit-ins in administration buildings, faculty parking lots, and maintenance departments; boycotts of classes; organizing and sponsoring violations of existing rules such as dormitory sleep-outs, freedom parties in restricted apartments, non-violent seizure of IBM cards, disruption of oversize classes, and non-violent occupation of student newspapers and radio stations. Although grade abolition was recommended as a main issue on the basis of its impact upon all students, other popular campus issues urged upon SDS organizers were student participation in planning course content, reduction in class sizes, and student-made dorm rules. [64]

The SDS chapter at the University of Michigan operated in the fall of 1966 as a political party named "Voice." However, the issue of student rankings for draft use had stirred into action the university's student government and a broad coalition of student groups which held a brief and orderly sit-in on campus in November 1966. The local SDS reportedly held its own sit-in when it failed to achieve any influence over the larger student coalition, which by the way also agitated for a greater student voice in the university decision-making process. [65]

In November 1966, SDS' REP, self-styled "intellectual center for the New Left Movement in America," and part of an "international intelligence network," helped to initiate and co-sponsored the North American Congress on Latin America (NACLA). [66] Other co-sponsors included the University Christian Movement, the Fellowship of Reconciliation, and SNCC. NACLA would coordinate research and maintain contacts in the hemisphere. In point of fact NACLA would prepare papers showing alleged U.S. complicity in influencing Latin American political affairs, and it also would develop a program "geared towards throwing military work off campus."[67]

Another "student power" publication printed and circulated by SDS in 1966 dealt with organizing in high schools and junior high schools. Originally printed in February 1966, the pamphlet, High School Reform: Toward a Student Movement, was written by a California high school student who took note of the growing conflict in high schools over everything from long hair to the Vietnam war. The pamphlet offered organizing techniques for high school students who might agree with the writer that a "decent society" would more readily be achieved if high schools had student-teacher councils to draw up rules; student-teacher conferences to plan course offerings and methods of study; no compulsory courses; no attendance office or student police; small classes and completely free and undisciplined discussion.[68]

ACTIVITIES ON THE CAMPUSES,
FALL OF 1966

Press coverage of campus activism indicated that students were protesting in the fall of 1966 on various "student power" issues as well as war-related issues such as the appearance of military recruiters on campus, university cooperation with the draft, and secret defense research projects at universities.[69] SDS was not credited with primary responsibility for many of the protest movements, such as the University of Michigan anti-draft sit-in and a student strike at Berkeley in the late fall of 1966.[70] At the University of Wisconsin, anti-war and communist groups were more militantly active and in some cases scornful of the disorganized SDS operation.[71]

SDS had participated--with other groups--in autumn sit-ins on anti-ranking and student power issues at both the University of Michigan and City College of New York. Queens College SDS joined other groups in a campus sit-in protesting the presence of a recruiter from the Marine Corps. SDS locals sponsored picketing of CIA recruiters at the University of California at Davis and picketing of recruiters from Dow Chemical Company at San Fernando Valley State College in California. On ten campuses, SDS chapters engaged in campaigns to get the university to withhold class rankings from draft boards, in some cases succeeding in getting a referendum on the issue.[72]

The most publicized and serious confrontation engi-
neered by SDS late in 1966 appeared to have occurred the
day before the national elections in November 1966 when a
crowd of 800 demonstrators and spectators ringed Defense
Secretary Robert McNamara as he attempted to depart from
Harvard University. Seeking to dramatize its opposition to
the Vietnam war, the local SDS tried to force the Defense
Secretary into a debate he had formally declined in advance.
As demonstrators lay down in front of his car and delayed
his departure, a Harvard dean declared them guilty of the
dangerous policy of "taking physical charge" of another person. [73] The SDS chapter had voted to hold a disruptive demonstration if McNamara refused to engage in a debate on the
Vietnam war and, following his refusal, had promised re-
straint only if the Government official departed via an agreed
upon exit, which was also refused. [74]

Press coverage failed to reflect the full range of activity by SDS chapters in the winter months of 1966-67, vice
president Davidson's aforementioned inspection tour revealed.
He found some chapters just beginning to organize their first
teach-in and one or two chapters which considered the setting
up of a literature table as "extreme" behavior. In some
places, SDS'ers had active unions of draft resisters while
other chapters felt that publicizing a conscientious objector's
handbook was too radical. On "student power" issues, some
chapters favored student strikes while SDS'ers in other localities were trying to liberalize dress regulations by having
weekly luncheon-talk sessions with a college dean. [75]

In November 1966, the SDS local at Columbia University managed to attract several hundred students for a march
and peaceful petition to the administration protesting the
presence on campus of recruiters from the Central Intelligence Agency. When CIA interviewers returned in February
1967, Columbia faced its first sit-in and first physical disruption as eighteen members of a minority faction in campus
SDS blocked doors to the interview rooms. The action has
been cited as an example of the division even within SDS
chapters over politics and tactics, since the chapter leadership and majority issued a formal statement disapproving the
sit-in. [76]

"Confusion" and "individualism" on the local chapter
level--as typified by the Columbia University chapter--in-
dicated to many observers that no "cohesive" national program was likely to appear in SDS for some years, despite

policy resolutions at national meetings giving an appearance
of coherence and purpose. [77]

Diversity was the keynote of other chapter activity reported in the press in the early part of 1967, although SDS
on some campuses acted with rising militancy. Demonstrations, including a sit-in against Dow recruiters at the University of Wisconsin in February 1967, reportedly led to the arrest of a number of students and a ban against SDS by the
student senate. [78] Dow recruiters were allegedly forced off
the campus of San Francisco State College as a result of
SDS efforts in March 1967. [79] On some campuses, SDS'ers
signaled opposition to the Vietnam war through literature
distributions, teach-ins, peace "walks, " and petition campaigns. In other localities, campus SDS sponsored "student
power" rallies or distributed leaflets protesting U. S. business
investments in the Republic of South Africa.

The national SDS organization officially declared it was
moving from the tactics of protest to those of resistance,
starting with the issue of the draft.

FROM "PROTEST TO RESISTANCE"

The SDS National Council, after nineteen hours of debate at a session at the University of California at Berkeley,
on December 28, 1966, passed a resolution on the draft,
which it subsequently distributed in pamphlet form under the
title, SDS and the Draft, From Protest to Resistance.

The resolution committed national SDS to the task of
providing staff, finances, and supplies for the organization
of "unions of draft resisters. " Youths from high schools,
colleges, and communities were to be solicited to join these
unions, which would engage in demonstrations during pre-induction physicals, inductions, at draft boards and recruiting
stations, and also to do "educational" work against the draft
or war among potential inductees and men already in the
military. The SDS resolution called upon all young men to
resist the draft, urged college youth to quit the campus to
organize draft resistance in the communities, and promised
to publish literature to aid resistance to the war effort among
men in the armed forces. The resolution appealed to local
SDS chapters to implement the program. [80]

An acknowledged advocate of a "resistance" strategy,

national vice president Davidson, explained his view of how
SDS should operate in the future in printed Essays on Draft
Resistance distributed by the organization's national office, [81]
as well as in the official SDS publication, New Left Notes.

Davidson had described himself in the SDS official
newspaper as an advocate of "revolution" as compared to
some other political views within SDS which preferred working toward "sweeping reform" or "radical social change."
However, as a revolutionary who believed that no revolutionary
situation existed in the United States, Davidson wrote in New
Left Notes of February 3, 1967, that SDS should concentrate
on stimulating a "radical or revolutionary consciousness" in
other persons.   SDS organizers, he went on--

> should be creating permanent local centers of rad-
> ical opposition with the capacity for becoming the
> foundation of an American resistance movement.

Even though SDS and similar groups had only limited power,
Davidson added, it had the power to "disrupt" which could
be "significant," and he hoped SDS members would work to
develop "techniques of creative disruption "[82]

Davidson touted the advantages of a resistance movement built around the draft in one of the Essays on Draft Resistance.   The prime purpose of draft resistance, he noted
at the outset, was to reach young Americans of draft age
with SDS complaints against the draft, the Vietnam war, U.S.
foreign policy, and domestic policies.   A secondary purpose
was to encourage and assist young men to get out of the
draft or the military by both legal and "illegal" methods, he
asserted.

In Davidson's view, which called for resistance in
preparation for eventual revolution, draft resistance also had
the virtue of putting

> people into battle with the government itself.   Anti-
> draft organizing moves from protest activity to
> activity that takes on more and more of the charac-
> teristics of a seditious resistance movement.   Di-
> rect action at induction centers and courtrooms
> begins to de-sanctify those traditional American
> institutions oppressing people both at home and
> abroad.   The people reached by the anti-draft or-
> ganizers (young men of draft age or those already

in the military) soon begin to translate their personal anxieties about the war and the draft into
political dissent and opposition. 83

Direct action at pre-induction or induction points, according to Davidson, also hit the Government and the military
where they were "most vulnerable, in terms of disruptive
tactics. "84

Davidson's essay disclosed that his views were predi-
cated on an escalating and expanding war involving the American military in actions throughout Southeast Asia, in a confrontation with China, and in action in Latin America. He
praised draft resistance as an issue not readily "co-opted"
by the Establishment and as a method of broadening the SDS
base to include high school students and working youth.

This concern about maintaining a radical position not
easily co-opted by the Establishment was also expressed by
SDS national secretary Greg Calvert when he joined representatives of some eighteen national student organizations in
a conference on the draft held February 5, 1967, in Washington, D.C. Most of the organizations, which included conservative and religious youth groupings, endorsed a statement opposing the draft but recommending an alternative voluntary service. SDS joined in a minority statement against
the voluntary service that also noted the organization's com-
plaint with more than just the draft policies of the American
Government. As Calvert explained, the "corporate-liberal
establishment" was seeking to "co-opt" student alienation and
dissent and channel it into positive action and forms acceptable to the Establishment, but:

> Radicals like ourselves argue that dissent and the
> new forms of social commitment are expressions
> of the alienation of students from the meaningless
> alternatives of this society and that this alienation
> can only find meaningful expression through involve-
> ment in activities which will build a movement for
> revolutionary change in this society and which will
> reorient America towards a creative interaction
> with revolutionary movements in the Western-dom-
> inated Third World. 85

National secretary Calvert, like Davidson, was also
publicly advocating at this period the development in others
of a "radical or revolutionary consciousness" in order to

build a revolutionary movement allegedly for freedom from a "brutal" and "dehumanizing" system known as American corporate capitalism and its corollary, aggressive imperialism. If no agency for truly radical, revolutionary change could be found in the United States, he maintained, SDS must pin its hopes on external "peasant" (Third World) revolutions. [86]

Calvert endorsed draft resistance as a method of involving people in actions which would help build "revolutionary cadres." [87]

In a speech at a Wisconsin statewide SDS meeting in March 1967, Calvert cited the Nuremberg war crime trials after World War II as justification for the SDS national office proposal to resist the draft. An SDS chapter president at the University of Wisconsin, however, preferred as his authority, Henry David Thoreau's essay on civil disobedience. [88]

Davidson claimed that active draft resisters' unions were already operative as a result of some SDS chapters' efforts early in 1967. A Berkeley SDS Anti-Draft Union was active in April and May 1967 with forums and rallies advising draft-eligible youth on forms of draft resistance, picketing of Army and Navy recruiters on the University of California campus as well as a nearby induction center, and helping to form an anti-draft union at a nearby high school. Union spokesmen indicated that its activity was designed to show that the draft was only indicative of an alleged sickness in American society at large. [89]

Other publicized anti-draft activity in the spring and summer of 1967 included SDS solicitation at Cornell University of pledges to destroy draft cards at a future mass demonstration, and petitioning at the University of Colorado in which signers would affirm opposition to the Vietnam war and to military service. A meeting called by the SDS chapter at Northern Illinois University in February 1967 was postponed when only one person turned out in response to an appeal to establish a student draft resisters' group. [90]

GROWTH AND THE EXERCISE OF POWER

SDS continued its rapid growth from 1966 into 1967. [91] Davidson wrote in February 1967 that he and Nick Egleson had visited about sixty chapters and compared notes on the size of SDS. They estimated that local and national mem-

bership rolls combined numbered about 30,000 members, of
whom 6,000 were carried as national members. [92] The two
SDS officials had underestimated the group's size, he said,
and pointed out that the group had grown tenfold during 1965-
66.   Admitting that SDS organizers were not all "that good,"
Davidson deduced that far more people had sought out SDS
than SDS had consciously contacted. Almost every week, he
said, the national office discovered an active chapter somewhere that no one had known existed. [93] John Veneziak, national chapter correspondent, had stated that some chapters
waited for months before contacting the national organization
and that there were "probably a lot" (of chapters) in existence
that the national office did not know about. [94] One observer
of SDS activities put the number of chapters during this period
at 227. [95]

In the spring of 1967 SDS employed nine traveling organizers who were paid from $10 to $30 per week. The national office staff, paid at the same scale, employed ten persons. Because of SDS' increased radicalism and its explicit
attacks against so-called left liberalism, "liberal conscience
money" no longer pumped into SDS coffers. It operated on
an annual budget of about $80,000, one-tenth of NSA's budget,
which meant that the student group was usually "broke. "[96]

The major leftist activity for 1967 was Vietnam Week
(April 8-15) which included in part a proposal for a nationwide student strike--a project which was later scuttled--pro-
posed by CPUSA member Bettina (Aptheker) Kurzweil, and
secondly, demonstrations on April 15 in New York and San
Francisco, which, although falling short of the hoped-for
1,000,000 demonstrators, did muster a total of over 150,000
marchers. The April 15 demonstration had been sponsored
by Spring Mobilization Committee to End the War in Vietnam
(one of several predecessors to the New Mobilization Committee), a united front in which communists played a dominant role. [97]

SDS' national administrative committee objected to
Mrs. Kurzweil's student strike project, although it was not
opposed in principle to the idea of such a strike. SDS objected to the student strike on three grounds, one of which,
significant to this report, was simply the question of leadership in the strike.

"SDS members must realize, " Greg Calvert wrote,
"that their organization is the largest of the radical student

groups and therefore has the responsibility of leadership and active direction of the radical student movement. "[98]

As had been noted above, SDS leaders were becoming aware that they were being used by other groups, in this instance, the Student Mobilization Committee, which the House Committee on Un-American Activities characterized[99] as an organization in which "Communists are playing a dominant role. "

Calvert wrote that SDS had been providing most of the troops for everybody else's demonstrations. In effect, he said, SDS had been used to make other people's political points and to help others build their organizations.

Although Mrs. Kurzweil spoke on behalf of her April 1967 strike project at the SDS August 1966 convention, the delegates failed to endorse it.

At a Chicago conference in December 1966, sponsored by a coalition of the communist and radical youth groups who were promoting the student strike, SDS proposed that the groups support SDS' opposition to the 2-S draft status, but DCA, YSA, and CPUSA delegates rejected SDS' proposal. An SDS delegate jumped over a row of chairs and shouted that he felt "used." Subsequently, a leader of the SDS chapter at Roosevelt University was to write:

> I'd just like to say that SDS should be careful in the coming period about just who and what it enters into coalitions and united actions with. [100]

SHIFTING TACTICAL LINE ON THE CAMPUSES

Statements and literature from the SDS national headquarters urged college students to leave the campus to organize draft resisters, yet at the same time called for redoubled efforts to take advantage of new opportunities for on-campus organizing.

Thus, SDS president Nick Egleson announced in New Left Notes, immediately after the passage of the draft resistance program, that "a campus based student movement is increasingly possible. "

The SDS president explained that in recent months

the organization's leadership had changed its thinking about the conditions existing in the universities and, as a result, put "new substance" in strategy and tactics for a student movement. Increasing numbers of student strikes and other demonstrations on campuses since the spring of 1966, Egleson said, opened up the possibilities that continued student dissent could lead students into a new view of the alleged "misuse" of power and political processes in American society and thus help to build a larger "movement" for social change.

"Courage" to raise such issues as tuition rates and cafeteria food prices was the "new condition" on campuses which grew naturally out of recent developments in the country. Egleson asserted:

> The war was an easy thing to protest against, because the issues were so clear, the inhumanity so overpowering. The war became an issue on the campus (ranking, germ research, police training, testing) and the protest was easily brought within the campus. And once the issue of control was raised on war-centered issues, like ranking, it could be raised in other areas as well.

Contributing to this changed situation, according to Egleson, was fear on the part of college administrators which either led to their making mistakes in response to student demands and increasing student support for an issue or impelled them to give in to student demands and offered students an incentive to raise additional demands in the future.

Based upon the knowledge that "we have the power which stems both from student willingness to act and from administrative unease," the SDS leader said, the organization had its first idea of a strategy and tactics which he described as follows:

> Our strategy is still simple, but at least it is there: take a small issue and immediately raise the question of student control. Take the draft exam, as at Buffalo or Madison, and ask for a vote and structure to make future decisions. Take rankings, as at Chicago, and ask for a referendum. Take the price of food, as at SF State College, and ask for student control of the corporation which runs the lunch room and book store.

The "student power" actions, in Egleson's view, would politicalize the students involved by showing them they lacked power to shape their own lives as a result of the "authoritarian" structure in which they were expected to live out their lives under the present American "system."[101]

Despite his own personal penchant for draft resistance and building for eventual revolution, SDS national vice president Davidson declared that there was no single answer available to those opposing foreign American military involvements. Therefore, there was a need for a continuation of a variety of tactics such as demonstrations, teach-ins, fighting for student power, organizing the poor, organizing the so-called working class, running radical candidates in elections, and turning hippies into "Provos."[102]

STATEMENTS ON OVERALL SDS AIMS

As previously indicated, SDS encompassed varying views of the degree of social "change" required in America and the method for achieving such changes. Reformists and avowed revolutionists both appeared geared to an action program without too much consideration of possible alternatives to the ills they complained of in existing American institutions.

Greg Calvert's National Secretary's Report in January 1967 declared that:

> At its present stage of development, SDS cannot be understood in terms of traditional political organization. Neither ideological clarity (as political analysis) nor organizational stability are fundamentally important to SDSers. What counts is that SDS be where the action is. What counts is that SDS be involved in the creation of a cutting-edge in the freedom struggle.[103]

The SDS national organization supported draft resistance, Calvert said, without apologies for having only a program of struggle and resistance with no clear path to power.[104]

SDS president Nick Egleson, in a speaking tour of various SDS chapters in November 1966, had described the major role of SDS as that of a "catalyst" for change in society as a whole. Dismissing national elections as irrele-

vant, Egleson reportedly told the University of Illinois chapter
that SDS hoped to create a genuine revolution in American society which would decentralize government and bring about
"viable popular control of the institutions of power--the economic institutions. "105

Speeches and writings by vice president Davidson and
national secretary Calvert included references to a need for
"revolutionary struggle" to achieve social change. 106 After
a weeklong visit to SDS national headquarters in the spring of
1967, a writer for the newsweekly, National Guardian, reported that virtually the entire leadership thought they could
build a broad movement based on a radical rejection of American life and culture and on resistance to the demands of society. SDS leaders operated, he observed, on the premise
that a significant minority of Americans under age 26 were
alienated from schools or jobs, bewildered over problems of
racism, poverty, and the Vietnam war, and were in cultural
revolt; it was allegedly SDS' job to unlock this basic rejection
of American society and propose a revolutionary alternative.
Secretary Calvert talked of reaching youth by involving them
"on the gut level, " of getting students to confront the university administrator and youth to confront the draft board.
Such confrontations would allegedly produce both a collective
resistance and revolutionary consciousness. 107

As some in SDS theorized at this time, the campus
protest movement had developed over a conflict between the
ideology and the realities of American society, and not as a
rejection of society. However, participation in demonstrations did result in partial radicalization of protest movements. 108

Secretary Calvert, who as previously noted was denouncing American corporate capitalism and American "imperialism" in this period, told an SDS conference that some
of America's new radicals were moving from romantic pos-
tures to an analysis of America which began to relate the
anarchist demand, "I want freedom, " to that of a revolutionary socialist analysis providing for a kind of "collective liberation. " Calvert himself suggested that SDS might look for
mass support from a so-called new working class, a vast
new group of technical and professional workers, including
teachers and social workers, who were necessary to but not
necessarily satisfied with modern "supertechnological capitalism. " Students are future members of this new working
class and their demands for "student control" in their uni-

versities will become revolutionary demands when they graduate and demand economic control, Calvert argued. [109]

The minority of "super-intellectuals" within SDS, referred to by Davidson, argued in the pages of New Left Notes
about a new working class and other theories. The National
Guardian writer claimed that many in SDS, as of early 1967,
were interested in Marxism and that Ché Guevara's Guerrilla
Warfare vied with Herbert Marcuse's One-Dimensional Man
as required reading for those in SDS who were "seriously"
interested in social change. [110] New Left intellectuals were
described by other observers as dissatisfied with nineteenth
century Marxist answers, however, and searching for new
approaches potentially tending toward socialism.   They were
also usually disinterested in State control and distrustful of
authority and bureaucracies.   New Left intellectuals could
be understood, in the view of some, only by reading the
works of numerous psychologists and philosophers, writing
on everything from alienation to anarchism, who influenced
them to some extent. [111]

NOTES

1. Two-page recruiting leaflet, Students for a Democratic
    Society, received by the compiler on May 12, 1967.

2. Communist Origin and Manipulation of Vietnam Week
    (April 8-15, 1967), Report, House Committee on Un-
    American Activities, March 31, 1967, p. 37.

3. SDS Bulletin, July 1964, p. 21.

4. Kissinger, Organizer's Handbook, p. 25.

5. New Left Notes, July 8, 1968, p. 6.

6. New Leader, September 27, 1965, p. 13.

7. Congressional Record, August 4, 1965, pp. 18709-
    18716; Speeches by Hon. E. E. Willis, Hon. J. Ash-
    brook.

8. SDS Chapter Report, Indiana University, December 6,
    1965, p. 2.

9. Idem.

10. LID News Bulletin, Winter 1966, p. 8.

11. Idem.

12. National Guardian, September 17, 1966, p. 6.

13. National Guardian, December 4, 1965, p. 4.

14. Chicago Tribune, October 21, 1965; The Washington
     Post, October 20-21, 1965; New York Times, October
     19-20, 1965.

15. Newsletter, SDS chapter, Indiana University, Blooming-
     ton, Indiana, November 17, 1965.

16. Ibid.

17. Daily Californian, University of California, Berkeley,
     SDS, October 19-20, 1965.

18. SDS West Coast Region, November 20, 1965, meeting.

19. New York Times, November 19, 1965, p. 5. SDS
     policy some years later would be altered in line with
     a national officer's alteration of Booth's slogan: "I
     want to build not. Burn."

20. Call attached to Indiana University SDS Newsletter,
     November 17, 1965.

21. Carl Oglesby, "Trapped in a System," The New Left:
     A Documentary History, pp. 182-188. Manipulative
     "corporate liberalism" was also the system attacked
     by SDS vice president Carl Davidson in New Left
     Notes in September 1966.
          The official news bulletin of the League for In-
     dustrial Democracy, which severed connections with
     SDS at the end of 1965, complained that the youth
     organization failed to judge American and communist
     policies by the same standards and was indulging in
     a kind of "reactive anti-American establishmentarian-
     ism." (News Bulletin, LID, Winter 1966).

22. National Guardian, November 27, 1965, p. 7; New York
     Times, April 19, 1966.

23. The Washington Post, October 20, 1965.

24. National Guardian, January 15, 1966, p. 5.

25. Newsletter, SDS chapter, Indiana University, December
     6, 1965.

26. National Guardian, January 15, 1966, p. 5.

27. New America, September 30, 1966.

28. Rothstein, in The New Left, a Collection of Essays,
     pp. 279, 282.

29. Ibid. Rothstein is described as an SDS member who
     participated in formulating plans for the ERAP projects
     and from August 1964 to summer of 1967 worked with
     the JOIN community project in Chicago.

30. Ibid.

31. Staughton Lynd, "The New Radicals and Participatory
     Democracy," in Teodori, op. cit., p. 229.

32. Irving Howe in Dissent, Summer 1965, p. 313; see also
     James O'Brien in The New Left, a Collection of Es-
     says, p. 7, and Andrew Kopkind, New Republic article
     reprinted by SDS around 1966.

33. The Activist, March 1966, p. 6.

34. Ibid., p. 8.

35. Newsletter, SDS chapter, Indiana University, January
     10, 1966.

36. Ibid.

37. Kazin in American Scholar, pp. 646-649.

38. SDS recruiting leaflet; Kazin, op. cit.; Lynd in The
     New Left, a Collection of Essays, p. 8; Detroit News,
     December 26, 1966.

39. National Guardian, May 21, 1966, p. 9, and May 28,
     1966, p. 9.

40. National Guardian, May 7, 1966, and May 21, 1966;
     copy of one-page SDS leaflet, Call for an Examina-
     tion of Conscience.

41. School and Society, October 26, 1968.

42. Newsletter, SDS chapter, Indiana University, December
     6, 1965.

43. Chicago Daily News, September 3, 1966.

44. National Guardian, September 17, 1966, pp. 7, 8.

45. National Guardian, July 2, 1966, p. 4.

46. National Guardian, September 17, 1966, pp. 7, 8.

47. National Guardian, April 8, 1967, p. 8.

48. Northern California Regional SDS Newsletter, September
     13, 1966; National Guardian, September 17, 1966;
     Mason City, Iowa, Globe-Gazette, September 3, 1966;
     Kansas City Times, September 5, 1966; New America,
     September 30, 1966.

49. Ibid.

50. Ibid.

51. The Worker, September 20, 1966, p. 6.

52. Michael Munk, "New Left: The ideological bases,"
     National Guardian, September 26, 1965, pp. 3, 4.

53. Mason City, Iowa, Globe-Gazette, September 1, 1966.

54. National Guardian, September 16, 1966, p. 7.

55. Northern California Regional SDS Newsletter, September
     13, 1966.

56. Frank Joyce, "Letter to the New Left," Liberation,
     February 1966, p. 48. In his Organizer's Handbook
     of 1965, then National Secretary Kissinger had also
     called for SDS members to start concerning them-
     selves with "ideology" or some "radical philosophy of
     politics." He made the observation that students be-
     come disillusioned and start to consider such ques-
     tions as ideology "when they first discover that the
     personal and social values which they were taught
     and which they hold are not expressed by contempo-

rary social values and organization." Kissinger held
it was necessary for SDS to steer such youth away
from cynicism and toward developing a coherent theory
of social change.

57. Northern California Regional SDS Newsletter, September
     13, 1966, pp. 1-3, 7.

58. Washington Free Press, July 21, 1967, p. 5.

59. New Left Notes, February 3, 1967, p. 4.

60. Detroit News, December 27, 1966, pp. 1, 10.

61. Previously cited SDS recruiting pamphlet, footnote 1,
     above.

62. Carl Davidson, pamphlet, Toward a Student Syndicalist
     Movement, and Detroit News, December 26, 1966,
     pp. 1, 16.

63. Davidson, op. cit.; Detroit News, December 29, 1966,
     pp. 1, 10.

64. Davidson, op. cit.

65. New York Times, November 30, 1966; Detroit News,
     December 26, 1966, pp. 1, 16.

66. REP letterhead; Guardian, January 28, 1967, p. 5.

67. New Left Notes, September 11, 1967, p. 2.

68. Mark Kleiman, High School Reform: Toward a Student
     Movement, February 1966.

69. Detroit News, December 28, 1966, pp. 1, 10.

70. Idem and issue of December 27, 1966; National Guard-
     ian, December 3, 1966, p. 4.

71. Detroit News, December 28, 1966.

72. National Guardian, April 1, 1967, p. 10; Spark, June
     1967; "PL Boston News," January 1967, pp. 3, 4.
     Students reportedly voted against university submission
     of class rankings in a referendum at San Francisco
     State College.

73. Harvard Alumni Bulletin, November 30, 1966.

74. Detroit News, December 26, 1966, p. 16.

75. Carl Davidson, "National Vice-President's Report--Has
     SDS Gone to Pot?" New Left Notes, February 3, 1967,
     p. 4.

76. New York Columbian Spectator, March 6, 1967; Crisis
     at Columbia, Report of the Fact-Finding Commission
     Appointed to Investigate the Disturbances at Columbia
     University in April and May 1968 (New York: Random
     House, Inc., 1968), pp. 64, 65.

77. Ibid.

78. Madison State Journal, March 5, 1967.

79. National Guardian, March 18, 1967, p. 5.

80. SDS and the Draft, From Protest to Resistance, pam-
     phlet.

81. Our Fight Is Here, Essays on Draft Resistance, printed
     pamphlet containing an essay on "Praxis Makes Per-
     fect," by Carl Davidson, pp. 2-4.

82. Davidson in New Left Notes, February 3, 1967, pp. 4,
     5.

83. Davidson, "Praxis Makes Perfect," p. 3.

84. Ibid., p. 2. The SDS Essays on Draft Resistance in-
     cluded a detailed description of the history and tactics
     of an underground resistance movement of youth in
     France who took the side of the Algerian rebels during
     their long war against French rule, 1958-1962.

85. New Left Notes, February 13, 1967, pp. 2, 11; see
     also National Guardian, February 11, 1967, pp. 1, 9,
     and New York Times, February 6, 1967.

86. Speech at SDS conference at Princeton University, Feb-
     ruary 17-19, 1967, printed in National Guardian,
     March 25, 1967, pp. 3, 4.

87. National Secretary's Report from New Left Notes,

January 13, 1967, reprinted as foreword to pamphlet with text of SDS National Council resolution on draft resistance.

88. Milwaukee Journal, March 6, 1967; Wisconsin State Journal, March 5, 1967.

89. Daily Californian, February 20, 1967, and May 22, 1967.

90. Cornell Sun, March 23, 1967; Colorado Daily, July 26, 1967; Rockford, Illinois, Star, February 22, 1967.

91. New Left Notes, February 3, 1967, p. 4.

92. Ibid.

93. Ibid.

94. The Nation, May 22, 1967, p. 656.

95. National Guardian, April 8, 1967, p. 1.

96. National Guardian, April 15, 1967, p. 5.

97. Communist Origin and Manipulation of Vietnam Week (April 8-15, 1967), Report, House Committee on Un-American Activities, March 31, 1967, p. 53.

98. Ibid., p. 40.

99. Ibid., p. 53.

100. Ibid., p. 41.

101. Nick Egleson, "Changes in our thinking," New Left Notes, January 6, 1967, pp. 2, 4.

102. Davidson, "Praxis Makes Perfect"; Frank A. Pinner, "Western European Student Movements through Changing Times," Students in Revolt.
        "Provos" apparently refer to a Dutch quasi-anarchist youth group which staged theatrical "Happenings" on the streets of Amsterdam and won international publicity in March 1966 when it disrupted the marriage of the Netherlands Princess Beatrix to a German diplomat. It spoke of "resistance" and "provoking" society whenever an opportunity presented itself.

103. New Left Notes, January 13, 1967.

104. Ibid.

105. Illini, Champaign, Illinois, November 11, 1966.

106. National Guardian, April 8, 1967, p. 8.

107. Ibid.

108. New Left Notes, theoretical section, February 13,
      1967, p. 6.

109. Calvert speech at SDS conference, Princeton Univer-
      sity, February 17-19, 1967, in National Guardian,
      March 25, 1967, pp. 3, 4; see also Teodori, op.
      cit., p. 82.

110. National Guardian, April 8, 1967, p. 8; New Left
      Notes, February 3 and 13, 1967.

111. Teodori, op. cit., pp. 80-82; Columbian Spectator,
      March 6, 1967; David Greenfield, Ideology of the New
      Left, quoted in Los Angeles Times, December 22,
      1968.

Chapter 4

AND HOW THE TORRENT ROARED:
SDS IN THE MAINSTREAM OF PROTEST, 1967-69

> Many of our people hoped, somewhat ma-
> nipulatively, that the situation of this coun-
> try would deteriorate with increasing rapid-
> ity. We looked for the ghettos to blow, for
> more wars of national liberation to start,
> and for repression to start. We realized,
> although we never said as much, that the
> essential ingredient of our survival was
> conflict. As long as there was conflict,
> there would be a reason for us to act, and
> room for us to act.[1]

Restless and frustrated in the search for "instant
change" and perhaps over-inflated with a sense of student
power, SDS leadership opened its 1967 national convention
in Ann Arbor, Michigan, June 25-30.

The positions of president and vice president were
abolished and the top offices became those of national secretary, national education secretary, and interorganizational
secretary. Michael Spiegel of Harvard was chosen national
secretary. Robert Pardun of the University of Texas, who
had organized both his campus chapter and the regional
Texas-Oklahoma SDS unit,[2] became education secretary.
Former SDS vice president Carl Davidson was named interorganizational secretary.[3]

The 300 participating delegates to the convention established an 11-member national interim committee (NIC) as
a "central committee" composed of eight elected members
plus the three national officers. NIC would convene monthly[4] and play an important role between meetings of the National Council which met quarterly. The convention also authorized the employment of 36 full-time campus organizers
to radicalize and "educate" students.

In the course of the convention and the national council meeting which immediately followed it and ended July 2, delegates voted for civil disobedience and disruption of the Selective Service System and a harsher view of the U.S. and South Vietnamese military efforts against the Vietnamese communists.

A convention resolution on anti-war activities opposed mass anti-war marches on Washington as being less effective than organizing a movement through local demonstrations, referendums, draft resistance, and issues not specifically connected to the war. Only by organizing an on-going movement from below--which will actually have power to cause changes--can Vietnams be ended, the organization resolution declared. The war, SDS found, was "not a mistake of an essentially good government, but the logical result of a government which oppresses people in the U.S. and throughout the world." SDS would not support anything less than immediate withdrawal of U.S. forces from Vietnam, according to the resolution, because demands for a bombing halt or negotiations implied a U.S. right to intervention in Vietnam which SDS would not concede.

The convention reaffirmed SDS opposition to conscription in language which accused the U.S. of using the draft for "an aggressive and imperialist foreign policy." The resolution renewed SDS' encouragement of the formation of draft resisters' unions and urged that draft resistance move beyond individual protest to collective action. "Tactics such as civil disobedience and disruption of the Selective Service System are among those advocated when they complement the overall strategy of resistance to the draft and to other forms of oppression," the resolution stated. Delegates who argued in favor of the attack on Selective Service stated it "was tied into the authoritarian and imperialist nature of American society," for which SDS had no alternative other than its previous commitment to some system involving "participatory democracy." Delegates also overrode a minority who objected to making an "explicitly illegal statement" such as the following in the anti-draft resolution:

> SDS encourages chapters and draft resistance unions to aid servicemen in opposition and disruption within the Armed Forces. We also urge aid to servicemen who wish to terminate their association with the Armed Forces by going underground. [5]

Convention resolutions took note of ghetto rebellions which flared up in the summer of 1967 in many American cities. SDS attributed the violence to rebellions against alleged police abuse and general social and economic exploitation. SDS delegates promised to seek to create organizations of whites to serve as allies of what it called the "black liberation movement." At the time of rebellious outbreaks, such organizations would be expected to plead the cause of black activists, organize sympathy demonstrations around police precinct stations and on campuses, and engage in "direct action, including civil disobedience if called for."[6]

The SDS convention featured a workshop on women's liberation which was responsible for a resolution pledging the SDS to help liberate women from the discrimination produced by male supremacy. The SDS national council, following the convention, voted to work for abolition of the United States National Students Association on the grounds that it was a "CIA-manipulated tool of the U.S. government and as such serves its oppressive domestic and imperialistic foreign policy."[7] Certain ties between the NSA and CIA had been publicized by Ramparts magazine the preceding March.

During this period SDS' national officers came to the conclusion that many SDS members were not politically sophisticated, and it was decided that the students' "revolutionary consciousness" should be raised. Field organizers were to undertake an educational role.

A Radical Education Center was created in the Chicago headquarters as the "internal education arm of SDS" and it had several tasks:[8]

1) Support teacher-organizers (T-O's), who had been trained by SDS and assigned by the national administration committee (NAC) to do organizational work for SDS.
2) Produce literature of an analytical nature on: corporate involvement on the campus; military training and the GI; the draft; American society from its political, social, and economic aspects; labor, community organizing and ethnic groups.
3) Coordinate and transmit data from other radical research groups to chapters and organizers; compile "information packets" on major American corporations involved in either war production or heavy foreign investments.
4) Maintain a speaker's bureau and film collection.
5) Collect material produced by chapters and the

T-O's and circulate data on their experiences as well as that
from other organizations; collect radical publications of foreign insurgent movements and digest the significant ones for
printing in New Left Notes.
       6) Establish a research library.

       The convention defeated a proposal that SDS formally
affiliate with certain foreign youth groups in Western Europe
and Japan on grounds that SDS lacked information about the
groups adequate to overcome dissenting views within SDS.
However, the organization did vote to send an observer to
Havana, Cuba, in July to attend the (LASO) Latin American
Solidarity Organization conference. 9   After much debate,
SDS also voted to send an observer to the Moscow celebra-
tion of the 50th anniversary of the founding of the Soviet
Union, with the qualification that the move in no way indicated
SDS considered the Soviet Union to be either democratic or
socialist.   The subsequent National Council session further
clarified the SDS stand by passing a resolution stating the
SDS delegate would go to Moscow to publicize the fact that
SDS condemned the U. S. S. R. "for its role as a party to
American aggression against the Vietnamese people and reaf-
firms its stand that the U. S. government, with the help of
the Soviet government, is responsible for that war. "10

       SDS former and current national officers had displayed
an interest in the North Vietnamese communist cause during
foreign travels just prior to the convention.   An SDS national
council member reportedly had been in Stockholm, Sweden,
in May 1967 when Bertrand Russell's International War
Crimes Tribunal had found the American Government guilty
as a result of its intervention in Vietnam.   SDS president
Nick Egleson toured communist North Vietnam only weeks
before the SDS national convention opened. 11

       The year 1967 was a period of increasing contacts be-
tween New Leftists and representatives of what were referred
to as "Third World" revolutionary movements; namely the
Vietnamese communist insurgents and Castroite guerrilla
movements in Latin America.

       The LASO conference called upon revolutionaries in
all Latin American nations to prepare for armed struggle
against their governments and against U. S. "imperialist"
influences in their countries.   Considerable publicity already
had been focused on guerrilla movements in Latin America
as a result of distribution in the U. S. of translations of

French leftist journalist Regis Debray's detailed outline of
how Castro and Ché Guevara intended to carry out communist
subversion and revolution. The outbreak of guerrilla warfare
in Bolivia in March 1967, later disclosed to be under the
leadership of Ché Guevara, and Ché's April 1967 "from somewhere in the world" message to revolutionaries to follow the
"Vietnamese road" and create many Vietnams in Latin America excited the imagination of would-be revolutionaries in
SDS. [12]

In early 1967, it is noteworthy that both SDS national
secretary Greg Calvert and vice president Carl Davidson declared they saw something to emulate in the tactics of Cuban
communist guerrilla forces in Guatemala. They spoke not
of armed struggle, however, but they did point to the mass
appeal of guerrilla tactics. They noted that the guerrillas
asked about people's problems and longings and then demonstrated that they all shared similar problems and had only to
"unite and resist."[13]

A New York Times correspondent covering the SDS
national convention proceedings in June 1967 was struck by
the way delegates talked freely about "guerrilla warfare,"
"counterinsurgency techniques," and the "guerrilla mentality."
The peculiar application of the terms in what was primarily
a gathering of college students was noted by the Times' correspondent:

> But what these words meant was often questionable.
> To some, for example, guerrilla warfare simply
> meant giving the wrong answers in surveys in an
> attempt to disrupt a computer-oriented economy.
> To others, it meant older college students entering
> freshmen courses and disrupting classes.[14]

An annual congress of the National Student Association,
held in August 1967 in the Maryland suburbs of Washington,
D.C., brought out 25 SDS activists from the Washington area
and New York to implement the SDS National Council decision to attempt to destroy that organization of student governments. The SDS members held a kind of counter-congress
in what was actually an attempt to disaffect any radicals attending the NSA congress. SDS'ers derided NSA as a CIA
front and a bureaucratic institution which the U.S. Government
relied upon to keep campus politics within bounds agreeable
to "corporate liberalism."

An account of these efforts in New Left Notes by Jeff
Jones of the New York regional SDS office demonstrated the
increased militance of some SDS activists at this time.   One
of the headings to Jones' article was "Build not, Burn!"--
an incendiary adaptation of the SDS slogan of an earlier period, "We Want to Build, Not Burn. "   In outlining methods
by which SDS members on campuses might succeed in the
task of destroying NSA, Jones took a destructive approach
toward both NSA and the U. S. Government:

> NSA is only one of many liberal institutions in a
> liberal society.   The destruction of the NSA is
> clearly not as desirable as the destruction of the
> CIA, the Selective Service System--the corporate
> capitalist form of government itself. [15]

In the summer of 1967, SDS urged its chapters to support by means of demonstration, defense committees, fund-
raising, and other actions the 16 members of the Revolutionary Action Movement (RAM) charged in New York City
with conspiracy to commit murder (two members) and conspiracy to advocate criminal acts (14 members) against Negro
leaders Roy Wilkins and Whitney Young. [16]   In the same action, SDS recommended similar support for 11 SNCC members arrested for criminal anarchy following a police raid
against the Philadelphia SNCC office, where dynamite had
been found.

SDS IN THE 1967-68 ACADEMIC YEAR

Carl Davidson, the SDS interorganizational secretary,
went back to his alma mater, the University of Nebraska,
early in September 1967 to lambast the student government
and promote SDS.   Stating that the black power movement
had led the way by recognizing riots as a "legitimate form
of protest and disobedience, " Davidson reportedly advocated
that the white student left should pursue comparable attempts
to break down the system in the academic community.   If
negotiation failed, Davidson was quoted as saying, every
student leader should keep the idea in the back of his head
that when nitty gets down to gritty, he should go to the administration and say, "Either give us what we're asking for,
or we'll shut this school down. "[17]

The director of the SDS' new Radical Education Center
at the same time was advocating a slightly different kind of

militancy for SDS, in a speech before SDS'ers at the University of Illinois. Parades, petitions, and draft card burning were not accomplishing any change in the course of the Vietnam war, he reportedly declared, and he felt the time had come to move SDS efforts into the streets, to organize in urban centers for a U.S. liberation front, whether it took ten or more years as it had in Cuba. [18]

During the spring and summer of 1967 a great number of organizations had been engaged in various types of anti-war or anti-draft work and were committed to varying philosophies ranging from acceptance of democratic processes to advocacy of domestic political revolution and support of the Vietcong. The myriad groups making up the so-called anti-war movement had projected another of the perennial marches on Washington, D.C., on October 21, 1967. It was also to be a kind of climax to various local anti-war actions scheduled for October 16-21, which some groups labeled Stop the Draft Week. [19]

More militant elements became involved in a rash of disruptive and frequently violent demonstrations at induction centers and college campuses during that week. Demonstrations by thousands of persons at the Oakland, California, Army induction center on October 17, 1967 led to clashes with police, the use of tear gas, and arrests. Demonstrators were also arrested at an induction center in Chicago.

SDS members from the University of California at Berkeley and the University of Chicago were admittedly involved with other activist groups and individuals in the respective induction center actions. Berkeley SDS spokesmen announced in advance their plan to support massive civil disobedience at the nearby induction center which would involve a sit-in and blockade of buses and, while allegedly nonviolent, was admittedly obstructive in intent. [20]

Serving as an issue for demonstrators on the campuses was the appearance of recruiters from Dow Chemical Company or the military. Hundreds of students sat-in against Dow recruiters at the University of Wisconsin on October 18, at the call of an ad hoc committee. There was rock-throwing when police ended the disruption. Injuries to 65 demonstrators and policemen resulted. [21] Disruption of a different style was the story two days later at Brooklyn College in New York, where 8,000 students boycotted classes (went "on strike") to protest police intervention and arrests on campus

the previous day in disturbances connected with a protest
against U. S. Navy recruiters. The Brooklyn College SDS
chapter, reputedly dominated by elements sympathetic to the
Maoist Progressive Labor Party, served as a catalyst in the
incident when the administration refused the chapter permission to set up its literature table near the recruiters'
booth. 22

    Among the many campus actions on anti-war themes
reported in the press in October and November, the following
were credited specifically to the impetus provided by local
SDS chapters: in October, local SDS'ers sat-in at Harvard
and physically interfered with campus recruitment by Dow
Chemical Company; blocked interviews by CIA representatives
at the University of Colorado; and instituted a blockade of a
Princeton military research building in a protest against university relations with the Institute for Defense Analysis.

    In November, SDS'ers were involved in a sit-in
against the CIA at Stanford University in California; a sit-in
against Marine Corps recruiters at the University of Iowa
which led to arrests and occasional violence; and an anti-
Dow sit-in at the University of Rochester in New York which
was followed by a student strike protesting disciplinary suspensions imposed as a result of the sit-in.

    Campus SDS activities in the 1967-68 academic year,
related to the Vietnam war, fell into three general categories,
some members observed in the organization's official publication, New Left Notes: 1) draft resistance; 2) protests
against recruiting by military and other Government agencies,
or private firms such as Dow Chemical which manufactured
napalm; and 3) campaigns against war research on the campus.

    SDS'ers were reportedly activated on such issues for
mixed motives. Some merely sought to register a moral
protest against war, the writers in New Left Notes observed,
while a lesser number of true "radicals" saw protests as a
means for radicalizing students into agreeing there was a
need for basic changes in society. 23

    Differences within the membership over legal versus
obstructionist tactics were demonstrated by the SDS chapter
at the University of California at Berkeley where SDS'ers in
November 1967 were promoting all three phases of anti-war
activity--anti-draft, anti-recruiters, and anti-defense re-

search, in addition to a campaign to remove ROTC from the
campus. SDS members split into two groups to confront recruiters from CIA and Dow Chemical Company--one group
pledged to peaceful and legal behavior and the second to obstruction. [24] Anti-war actions took an entirely different tack
on other campuses in the fall. SDS'ers at the State University of New York at Binghamton worked to raise funds for a
Thanksgiving for children in North and South Vietnam, working through recognized international relief agencies. An SDS
chapter spokesman at Southern Methodist University at Dallas
expressed opposition to the arrival of a paid anti-draft organizer from the SDS national office because the local chapter
preferred to rely on peaceful and political methods of effecting change. [25]

Local campus issues continued to involve some SDS
chapters such as the chapter at Pennsylvania State College
which announced it would begin protests in November 1967
over the price of student football tickets.

Off-campus actions were reemphasized in some chapters, particularly those where members of the Progressive
Labor Party were effective in promoting their idea that students should try to strike up an alliance with workers (the
so-called worker-student alliance strategy). Thus, SDS'ers
at Queens College joined picket lines with striking New York
City transit workers in December 1967, Boston SDS'ers later
opposed transit fare increases in their own area; and SDS'ers
in the Midwest and West were trying to establish contact
with steel workers, copper workers, and farm workers. [26]

While SDS'ers pursued different tactics over a variety
of issues on campuses, proponents of more off-campus activity also differed over the details of such work. In contrast to the ties-to-labor school, a group of SDS'ers from
Columbia and City College of New York started a West-Side
Community Draft Resistance Project in a Puerto Rican neighborhood of New York City in the summer of 1967. A hand-
ful stayed on in the fall although their demonstrations and
draft counseling admittedly had "very little effect" on the
community. [27]

A contingent of SDS'ers had also participated in the
mass anti-war march on Washington, D. C., on October 21,
1967, despite the specific disapproval of the project voiced
in SDS national convention resolutions. An SDS National
Council meeting on October 6-8 had voted to encourage SDS

participation in ways each saw fit despite SDS' continued disagreements with the sponsoring National Mobilization Committee to End the War in Vietnam over its tactics and line.
SDS'ers were among the groups which broke away from the
larger body of marchers to engage in an unauthorized sit-
down at the Pentagon which ended only after mass arrests
and numerous injuries to soldiers and demonstrators alike. [28]

DISCUSSIONS OF THE TACTICS OF "RESISTANCE"

SDS leaders at the Pentagon were reportedly turned
off by the passive, wait-to-be-arrested line of many demonstrators, and some arrests while engaging in "resisting"
America's so-called war-making strategies being enunciated
by Ché Guevara, Regis Debray, and even Mao Tse-tung. [29]
After militants confronted the defense establishment at the
Pentagon with what an observer described as "new tactics
inspired both by guerrilla warfare and by aggressive non-
violence, "[30] a member of SDS from the University of Chicago
discussed in New Left Notes the lessons taught by the Pentagon episode. He allegedly showed that demonstrators should
break up into small mobile groups to confront various American institutions and the police in the future. To this enthusiastic "guerrilla," possible SDS tactics of the future were
portrayed as follows in a passage that also casts interesting
light on SDS'ers' desire for maximum publicity:

> Tactically, it is conceivable that we may decide
> that disruptions with large groups of people in one
> place are unfeasible. For example, if we wanted
> to shut down a major city, Newark, say, we might
> divide into 50 groups of 20, some of the groups
> doing very public things (e.g., blocking intersec-
> tions), while others committed inconspicuous acts
> of sabotage (e.g., cut wires), while still others
> provided drama and color (e.g., hippies flying over
> the city in big balloons throwing peanuts to police-
> men). People will undoubtedly come up with more
> realistic schemes. We must also face the problem
> of publicity and coverage in the mass media. Meth-
> ods must be devised which trick them into giving
> us the publicity we want, and here, provo tactics
> are probably what's called for. [31]

SDS national interorganizational secretary, Carl David-

son, was the avowed mastermind of a resistance strategy he
was calling institutional resistance at this time.   He claimed
that the three national secretaries of SDS agreed on the same
strategy despite some other national officers' preference for
other tactics including the worker-student alliance type activity.

Although he claimed to disapprove of "supermilitants"
who had abandoned patience and non-violence, Davidson said
the idea of "institutional resistance" looked toward "the disruption and dismantling of the institutions of power."[32]

In a speech on October 27, 1967, outlining the strategy, Davidson expressed the view that the Pentagon demonstration, ghetto rioting, and campus demonstrations all indicated that "the possibility for peaceful change in America
has died" and, while conditions did not justify armed struggle, they did call for a day-to-day strategy of resistance.
The strategy involved a "deobfuscation" process by which the
radicals sought to propagate their own conviction that there
was a lack of freedom in American society, and radicals
were not constrained by liberals' "free speech" rhetoric from
such actions as stopping military recruiting on campuses "by
whatever means we have to do it."   The strategy of resistance further involved the process of "desanctification of authority," which, as Davidson explained it, involved defiant
radical confrontations at induction centers and other institutions which would ostensibly reveal the powerlessness of people in relation to their institutions and reduce respect for
these institutions.   Once disengaged from existing institutions, radicals should seek to create new structures based
on new values, as was already being attempted, he said,
through free universities and the underground press.

Daily resistance aimed at eventual disruption and dismantling of the institutions of power, Davidson said, was beginning with the university.   The university, in Davidson's
view, was a "service station," a developer of manpower for
corporate capitalism, and shutting down the institution was
completely justifiable:

> When we talk about institutional resistance what we
> say is not only that our system is bad but the ends
> to which it puts our manpower is rotten and that
> we're going to stop that flow of manpower.   We're
> going to build a resistance within the institution.
> And the recruiters will be stopped, and the war

researchers will be stopped or be seriously disrupted to the point where that institution cannot
function at all.

Davidson conceded that the strategy of "institutional
resistance" was a negative one and offered no better alternatives to the existing system.   However, "... the times tell
me that what we have to do at this time is to destroy, " he
declared. [33]

The policy of resistance was also described and supported by Tom Hayden, SDS' first president, who had remained in frequent touch with the SDS national office and was
often a guest speaker before campus chapters.   The Pentagon
confrontation made resistance the official watchword of the
anti-war movement, he maintained in testimony before a
Presidential commission inquiring into the causes and prevention of violence.   In blocking doors and engaging in other
forms of resistance, activists admittedly went beyond that
form of civil disobedience in which an individual broke a law
to test its legality and then accepted the right of authorities
to punish him, with jail if necessary.   Many demonstrators
involved in confrontations since October 1967, Hayden said,
were challenging the "legitimacy" of existing authorities because they viewed the U. S. system as a "sick" one, in which
law was based on power, not justice.   The demonstrators,
accordingly, did not accept the right of any authorities to
punish them for doing what the demonstrators felt to be "morally" right. [34]

In the fall, campus confrontations between students and
college administrations picked up from the point where they
had ceased at the end of the previous school year.

The December 1967 National Council meeting discussed
organizational plans for the summer of 1968.   SDS urged its
members to get summer jobs in factories, to establish closer
ties with workers, [35] and to continue their anti-war, anti-
draft organizing efforts.   The effort to identify with workers
reflected PLP's view of the importance of enlisting support
for the radical revolutionary movement from the ranks of
organized labor.   The Council delegates debated revolutionary
possibilities in America--namely, was revolution necessary,
and if so, when, and how? [36]

For SDS, 1967 marked the beginning of a rupture
with another longtime ally and "fraternal" group--SNCC.

SDS had stated that it recognized SNCC's right to develop its
own international position and program independently, but it
noted "with deep concern and regret" SNCC's recent inclina-
tion toward racism in general and anti-Semitism in particular.
SDS called upon SNCC to engage with SDS in a dialogue on
these two issues. 37

While SDS was having its difficulties with NSA and
SNCC it was establishing new relations with the National
Mobilization Committee to End the War in Vietnam (Mobe),
now called the New Mobilization Committee (New Mobe), and
the Black Panther Party (BPP). In December 1967, SDS'
NC authorized a representative to attend meetings of Mobe
to keep the student group advised of Mobe's plans for demonstrations at the August 1968 Democratic Convention. 38 Nationally SDS withheld its official endorsement of the Mobe-
proposed mass mobilization for the following August, on the
basis that such a confrontation would project no clear political
message and, secondly, that participation by SDS might be
construed as an attempt to influence the Democratic Party.
The fact is, SDS had an aversion to both major political
parties.

On December 11, 1967, SDS at Harvard University
and the American Institute of Marxist Studies (AIMS), in
"fruitful intellectual co-operation, " co-sponsored a symposium
on "Marxism and the Theatre" in Cambridge, Mass. 39 The
institute was directed by Herbert Aptheker, acknowledged
theoretician of the CPUSA. Seven forums on "Marxism and
Contemporary Problems" were held at Harvard between
March and May 1967 under the joint sponsorship of AIMS
and SDS. 40

On February 21, 1968, SDS national education secretary Robert Pardun delivered a speech in Houston about the
"resistance movement" the organization was building in America. He stated that the National Guard manual defined a resistance movement as a popular movement against legally
constituted authority to withdraw people's support from such
authority. By "involving an ever increasing number of people in struggles which show them that major institutions of
this country--the police, the universities, the Army, the
Government, and the economic base that they serve--are
their enemies and must be fought, " he said, SDS was building a popular resistance movement.

Pardun declared that these "establishment" institutions

were to be fought on the grounds that they were allegedly used to keep people in their place by rulers who, contrary to the teachings of schools and the mass media, exploited and regimented people while pursuing racist and imperialist policies. Pardun was imprecise about exactly what SDS resistance was to achieve, but he insisted it was a kind of struggle for "freedom," "human dignity," and a "new society free from racism and exploitation."[41]

In connection with "resistance," SDS leaders were rather obviously influenced and inspired by communist revolutionary activities on the international scene.

In a speech outlining SDS strategy for "institutional resistance"[42] national interorganizational secretary Carl Davidson acknowledged indebtedness to the teachings of the then recently deceased prophet of guerrilla warfare to promote Red revolution--Ché Guevara. Davidson was also an admirer of the political arm of the Vietcong in South Vietnam --the so-called National Liberation Front--with whose representatives he had recently conferred.

SDS had learned a lot from "Third World" revolutionaries, said Davidson, as well as from SNCC and other black militant groups on the domestic scene.[43]

As far back as December 1965, SDS leader Thomas Hayden had accompanied CPUSA's Herbert Aptheker and Yale professor Staughton Lynd on a "fact-finding mission to Hanoi." Aptheker had received an invitation from the Ho Chi Minh regime for himself and two non-communists to visit North Vietnam. Thus, SDS made contact with the hierarchy of international communism as well as with the theoretical leader of the CPUSA. Upon his return from Hanoi, Hayden--as an SDS founder and its tactical chief--toured the United States, lecturing on his trip to North Vietnam, on the sins of American policy in Southeast Asia, and on the virtues of communist revolution in that area.

During testimony December 3, 1968, before the former House Committee on Un-American Activities, Hayden stated he traveled to North Vietnam again in October 1967.

He also traveled to Paris in July of 1968--just prior to the attempted disruption of the Democratic National Convention in Chicago--to confer with the North Vietnamese delegation at the Paris peace talks. While in Paris, Hayden testified, he met with Colonel Ha Van Lau, one of the Hanoi officials with whom he had met on his trips to North Vietnam. In fact, he said he had conducted extensive discussions with the colonel during his 1966 and 1967 journeys to the North Vietnamese capital.

Other accounts of SDS travel and dealing with Hanoi over recent years may be summed up as follows:

North Vietnam

Nicholas M. Egleson, while serving as SDS national president, visited North Vietnam during the summer of 1967 at the invitation of the Peace Committee of North Vietnam. Committee (HCIS) witness Douglas Hegdahl, U. S. Navy petty officer and former prisoner of war in North Vietnam, testified on December 11, 1969, that Egleson had visited the prison camp in Hanoi where Hegdahl was incarcerated. Hegdahl recalled that this was on June 8, 1967, and that Egleson had been accompanied by Dave Dellinger, of the Spring Mobilization Committee to End the War in Vietnam. [44]

Jeff Jones, Cathy Wilkerson, and Steve Halliwell, SDS national organizers, were invited to visit Hanoi by the North Vietnam Student Union. However, after they reached Cambodia in December 1967, they were unable to complete their trip to North Vietnam as all foreign visits had been cancelled by the Hanoi government due to the intensity of the bombings. [45]

In late 1967, a former member of the SDS National Council and former head of ERAP, Rennard Cordon Davis, attended a conference in Bratislava, Czechoslovakia, along with 40 other Americans. At that conference an invitation was extended to him to make a trip to North Vietnam. He accepted the invitation and traveled to North Vietnam in October 1967. [46]

Davis returned from North Vietnam in October 1967. In April 1968 he spoke at a function sponsored by the Socialist Workers Party at Debs Hall in Detroit, Michigan. His topic concerned his trip to North Vietnam and conferences held with Vietcong representatives. While in North Vietnam in October 1967, Davis visited some American prisoners of war. [47]

Vernon Grizzard, an SDS regional official in New England, traveled to Hanoi in July 1968 along with two other Americans, Ann Scheer and Stewart Meacham, to receive three American pilots who had been prisoners of war in North Vietnam. [48]

Rennard Davis left the United States on July 15, 1969, en route to Hanoi to take custody of two American fliers and a U. S. Navy seaman being held prisoner of war by the North Vietnamese. Davis was accompanied by Linda Evans, SDS national interim committee member, Norman Fruchter, Robert Kramer, and John Douglas of Newsreel. The original goal of the group, of merely receiving the prisoners of war and escorting them back to the United States, was changed when the Vietnamese realized that most of the delegation represented segments of the movement that were not pacifists, but had actively joined in the struggle of the Vietnamese and were fighting in the United States to end the war. Instead of spending all of their time talking to the prisoners to be released, Linda Evans and other members of the delegation were taken on a 18-day tour of North Vietnam, seeing that country and talking with the North Vietnamese people. Upon returning to the United States, Evans reported on the impressions she received during the 18 days of traveling about the countryside of North Vietnam. [49]

North Vietnam was just one of several countries where SDS activists met with communist delegations and received "inspiration" for promoting the openly revolutionary goals later adopted by SDS.

Cuba

Cuba was a particularly strong magnet for visits by SDS representatives. SDS continued to demonstrate an interest in Cuba after its previously described decision to send an observer to a Havana conference in the summer of 1967. In February 1968, at the invitation of the Cuban Government and the Cuban Federation of University Students, the SDS sponsored a trip of 20 students to Cuba. The group arrived in Havana on February 9, 1968, and subsequently traveled through Cuba for a three-week period. They departed from Cuba en route to the United States on March 2, 1968. Dena Clamage, a leader of the SDS chapter at Wayne State University in Detroit, was one of the 20 students who made the trip. After returning from Cuba, Clamage wrote articles

about her visit in Cuba in the Fifth Estate, an underground
newspaper published in Detroit.   These articles in general
described the revolutionary fervor in Cuba and her favorable
reaction to conditions in that country. [50]

Mark Rudd was also a member of the above-mentioned
SDS-sponsored delegation to Cuba.   When Rudd returned to
the United States he gave his impression of the trip to the
Guardian.   He had special praise for Ché Guevara, the slain
Cuban guerrilla fighter who has become one of the SDS heroes.
Rudd also noted that he had returned from Cuba more en-
thusiastic than ever about the Cuban revolution.

A short time after Rudd returned from Cuba he led
the uprisings at Columbia University in April 1968, which
caused property damage in excess of one-half million dollars.
The takeover of Columbia University was the first major incident involving the use of violence by SDS to accomplish its
objective. [51]

In early 1968, when Tom Hayden traveled to Cuba, he
attended the International Cultural Congress in Havana.   Delegates were also in attendance from various parts of Asia and
Latin America.   European representatives included delegates
from France, Great Britain, Italy, Spain, and the Soviet Union.   The congress was billed as one which would awaken the
consciousness of a cultural identity.   At the congress, some
500 delegates from 70 countries condemned the United States
for its role of worldwide "imperialist aggressor" and support
was pledged to the Vietnamese people in their struggle against
the United States.   The congress closed with an appeal to all
intellectuals to boycott United States' academic and cultural
programs.   It was reported that perhaps the maximum benefit
resulting from the Cultural Congress was the informal exchange of information between the various delegates. [52]

At an SDS national interim committee meeting held
on June 15, 1968, in Chicago, it was announced that the
Council had accepted an invitation from the Cuban people to
send from three to five official representatives to the July
26th (1968) celebrations in Havana. [53]

A group of 34 SDS members traveled to Cuba by way
of Mexico on August 26, 1968.   Upon arrival in Cuba, the
group was provided with guides and given a conducted tour
of farms, hospitals, power plants, and other installations.
During these tours, the differences between pre-revolutionary

and post-revolutionary accomplishments were continually
stressed.   Part of the group met with a representative of the
National Liberation Front of South Vietnam who identified
himself as Huynh Van Ba.   This representative told the group
that more and more demonstrations against the war in Vietnam should be conducted in the United States and should emphasize the number of United States soldiers being killed, the
number of planes being shot down, and the cost of the war.
He also told the group that it should not only organize draft
resistance, but should also have people volunteer for service
in the Armed Forces in order to perform resistance-type
activity from within.   The SDS members were cautioned to
shy away from the use of the word "communism," just as
did the revolutionary movements in both Cuba and South Vietnam during the initial periods of their revolutions.   Ba explained that communism connotes something evil to many people in the West.   Therefore, he instructed that they talk
about the new life that will be available after the revolution.
In this connection, he suggested that such things as free
medical care and better living conditions be stressed.   In
conclusion, Huynh Van Ba urged the SDS members to solicit
funds in the United States for the National Liberation Front.[54]

        At an SDS national interim committee meeting held on
August 30, 1968, there was a discussion on the value of the
trips to Cuba by SDS representatives.   The council felt that
the Cuban trips should be continued, but were valuable only
when the people who traveled there learned information of
value to the development of the SDS.   It was emphasized that
small groups of no more than ten with comprehensive training in the Spanish language and a study of the Cuban revolution would be more effective.[55]

        The SDS, at the invitation of the Cuban Government,
sent a delegation of four members to the 10th anniversary
of the Cuban revolution which was celebrated in Havana,
Cuba, on January 2, 1969.[56]

        In late 1968, the SDS national interim committee an-
nounced a week of solidarity with Cuba was to be celebrated
by SDS in the United States from January 2 to 10, 1969,
since this particular week included the date on which the
United States severed diplomatic relations with Cuba.   It was
indicated that the solidarity week would consist mainly of an
education program, with posters and educational materials
being prepared by the SDS national office.[57]

An illustration of local chapter observance of Cuba week is offered in HCIS committee hearings on activities of the SDS unit at George Washington University. The observance, which did not get underway until late January 1969, included a film and lecturer extolling conditions under the Cuban communist regime and attacking American policy towards Cuba. [58]

Czechoslovakia

A conference was held at Bratislava, Czechoslovakia, from September 6 through 13, 1967, which was sponsored by the Czechoslovakian Peace Committee. The conference was arranged by Dave Dellinger, anti-war activist from the United States. Among the 41 persons from the United States who attended the conference were SDS leaders Nicholas Egleson, Thomas Hayden, and Steven Halliwell, who headed an SDS delegation of nine. Both North Vietnam and the National Liberation Front of South Vietnam sent delegates to the conference. The North Vietnamese representative, Mrs. Nguyen Thi Binh, later represented her government at the Paris peace talks. The purpose of the conference was to create solidarity and mutual understanding between revolutionaries from North and South Vietnam and their supporters in the United States. [59]

Christopher Jencks, one of the members of the delegation from the United States that attended the Bratislava conference, asserted that the United States delegation saw the Vietnam war as an inevitable byproduct of a sickness in the American system which would only be cured by radical political remedies. Jencks stated that the common bond between the New Left and the National Liberation Front of South Vietnam was not a common dream or a common experience, but a common enemy--the United States Government, the system, the Establishment. [60]

Hungary

Vernon Grizzard, New England regional SDS official, and Bruce Dancis, a former president of the SDS chapter at Cornell University, were among a group of some 20 American anti-war activists who traveled to Budapest, Hungary, in September 1968 to confer with representatives of North Vietnam and the National Liberation Front of South Vietnam.

The conference, which convened on September 6, 1968, centered on the Paris peace talks and on prospects for further
student unrest in the United States as well as on plans to increase draft resistance and to create discontent among American GIs. Grizzard reported that the North Vietnamese and
Vietcong were pleased and interested in the plans of the
United States delegation. Grizzard noted that one of the
plans mentioned was the holding of a national GI week just
before the national elections in the United States in November 1968. Also included in the plans discussed with the
North Vietnamese communists were plans to establish additional coffee houses outside of Army camps in the United
States, where an intensive effort was to be made to propagan-
dize the GIs. [61] The first coffee house had been set up in
January 1968 and more had been started under Mobe's auspices during the summer.

An article by Bruce Dancis captioned "American Radicals Meet Vietnamese Revolutionaries" appeared in the September 27, 1968, issue of The First Issue, an underground
magazine at Cornell University, edited by Dancis. In this
article, Dancis noted that he was a member of a delegation
of activists from the United States who traveled to Budapest,
Hungary, to meet with five representatives of the National
Liberation Front of South Vietnam and four representatives
of the North Vietnamese Government. He stated that the
United States delegation consisted of "twenty SDS and resistance types" and two United States Army deserters who were
working with the American Deserters Committee in Sweden.
According to Dancis, the purpose of the meeting was to provide the Vietnamese an opportunity to report on their struggle
for self-determination and to provide the delegation from the
United States an opportunity to tell the Vietnamese about the
draft-resistance movement on college campuses and in high
schools, about organizing among the military, and about the
black movement in the United States. Dancis reported that
the Vietnamese were knowledgeable concerning the anti-war
movement in the United States and felt close to those in the
movement, particularly those who were engaged in resisting
the draft.

John Willard Davis, brother of SDS official Rennie
Davis and the SDS leader at Marietta College, Marietta,
Ohio, was a member of the delegation from the United States
that attended the September 1968 conference in Budapest.
Immediately following the conference, John Davis traveled
to Prague, Czechoslovakia, and then to Stockholm, Sweden,

where he visited with American deserters.   His next stop
was in Germany for an annual congress of the West German
SDS (Sozialistischer Deutscher Studentenbund, or League of
Socialist German Students), a militant leftist-oriented student
organization in West Germany.   There he met and held discussions with Danny Cohn-Bendit, also known as Danny the
Red, leader of a radical French student movement.   Before
returning to the United States, John Davis stopped in Paris
for discussions with the North Vietnamese negotiators at the
Paris peace talks. [62]

Germany

At an SDS national interim committee meeting held on
August 30, 1968, in Chicago, Sigrid Fronius, from West
Berlin gave a talk on her organization, the German SDS. [63]

Karl Dietrich Wolff, a professed Marxist and an official of the German SDS, made a tour of the United States in
early 1969 for the purpose of raising funds for the legal defense of the German SDS.   During February and March 1969,
Wolff appeared at some 13 colleges and universities in the
United States.   Many of his appearances were sponsored by
the American SDS.   Wolff told his listeners at the University
of Michigan in Ann Arbor that there was a need to build an
international revolutionary alliance, as a victory for the
movement in one country is a victory in another.   He criticized students in the United States for not working together
as they were in Germany, and said that the time had passed
for just sitting around discussing matters--they must act. [64]

Hearings by the House Committee on Internal Security
showed that Wolff declared before the SDS chapter at George
Washington University that it was allegedly necessary for
radical students in West Germany to graduate to more forceful means of expression.   More recently, Wolff reported,
students no longer ran away when police came to break up
demonstrations.   They set up barricades and "clubbed back."
Wolff also talked of parallels between the situations in West
Germany and the United States. [65]

After speaking at a rally sponsored by the SDS at
George Washington University on March 12, 1969, Wolff was
subpoenaed to appear before the United States Senate Internal
Security Subcommittee.   Spokesmen for the SDS in this country denounced the subcommittee's action and termed it official

harassment of "our brother from West Germany." In his
appearance before the Subcommittee on March 14, 1969,
Wolff launched an obscene tirade against the subcommittee
and refused to answer questions concerning his activities.

According to the August 23, 1969, issue of New Left
Notes, American SDS members, including students, workers,
and former soldiers, had been publishing an anti-war paper,
Where It's At, in West Berlin for more than a year. The
group was also reported to be planning to open a GI coffee
house. Threats of prosecution had been made against this
paper for calling for American GIs to desert from the Army.

Yugoslavia

At an SDS national interim committee meeting held on
August 30, 1968, in Chicago, it was announced that SDS interorganizational secretary Bernardine Dohrn was in Yugoslavia. There was no indication as to the purpose of her
trip or the proposed length of her stay in Yugoslavia. [66]

Soviet Union

Jeff Shero was the SDS representative from the United
States at the celebration of the 50th anniversary of the Bolshevik revolution held in July 1967 in Moscow. [67]

Communist China

At the June 1969 SDS national convention held in
Chicago, Christopher Z. Milton told the delegates that he
had spent three years in Communist China where he was a
member of the revolutionary Red Guard. SDS also printed
in pamphlet form a long interview with the 18-year-old American who was attending high school in Red China when Mao
decided to unleash the destructive energies of Chinese youth
to help purge the Communist Party, government and institutions of persons lacking a proper revolutionary outlook.
Milton recounted in his interview the stoning of school officials and other hoodlum acts by the young Red Guards.
Milton said his experiences made him optimistic that if the
Chinese could "build socialism," the Americans could also. [68]

Sweden

At a meeting of the SDS national interim committee held October 11-13, 1968, at the University of Colorado at Boulder, there was a discussion on "New Left internationalism." On this occasion, SDS national interorganizational secretary Bernardine Dohrn spoke of traveling in Europe and holding meetings with United States military deserters in Sweden. She also mentioned having held meetings with the German SDS and with members of the National Liberation Front of South Vietnam. Dohrn told the delegates they must develop a consciousness against imperialism. [69]

France

Eric Gordon, president of the SDS chapter at Tulane University in New Orleans from October 1967 to February 1968, wrote an article in New Left Notes of July 8, 1968, entitled "A Letter from Paris." In this article, Gordon related his contacts with French revolutionaries in Paris.

Japan

At an SDS national interim committee meeting held in Chicago on August 30, 1968, a discussion on internationalism began with a report from Ken Cloke on his trip to Japan as the SDS representative at the Japanese atomic and hydrogen bomb conference held on August 3, 1968. [70]

Cloke, a Los Angeles SDS regional member, is the author of an article which appeared in the September 16, 1968 issue of New Left Notes entitled "Japan and the Japanese Left," which gives an account of the complex politics of Japan, the splits and factions of the various radical movements, and describes certain resistance organizations in Japan.

It should be noted that unlike the old-line communist groups in this country which have clear ties with the international revolutionary movement, the SDS is not known to be directly linked with any foreign organization. However, as indicated, SDS representatives in the United States established and maintained contacts with representatives of communist and other radical organizations abroad through meetings, conferences, and written communications.

In turn, radical students from a number of Western democracies journeyed to the United States to attend an SDS-sponsored International Assembly of Revolutionary Student Movements, held in New York City in September 1968.

It should be remembered that in 1968, student protest movements had become a global phenomenon. When Columbia University buildings were forcibly occupied by students in the spring of 1968, students were also demonstrating in many highly industrialized as well as underdeveloped nations, and in communist as well as non-communist societies. While students were motivated by a variety of issues and varying goals, their tactics were often strikingly similar. Students mass-marched in the streets, occupied buildings, and engaged in bloody clashes with police in some 20 countries that year.

SDS' National Council and its official publication had demonstrated its own affinity with such communist revolution-ary movements as the Cuban and Vietnamese communists and with New Leftists in Western European nations idolizing the same revolutionaries. [71]

A call for an International Assembly of Revolutionary Student Movements, to be held in September 1968, was issued jointly by the Columbia University Strike Coordinating Commit-tee and SDS of Columbia. The call noted that the assembly would deal with two main topics. One would be the stage of the class struggle and the potential of new revolutionary forces in individual countries. The other would be prospects and possible formation of an international revolutionary move-ment. According to the call, the insurrection at Columbia University, the "Easter Actions" in Germany, and the student revolution in France in May 1968 all pointed toward the for-mation of social anti-capitalist forces within the various countries. It was stated that the time had come for the creation of a revolutionary theory and this promoted the is-suance of the call for an International Assembly of Revolu-tionary Student Movements. The call also noted that the assembly would allow for the presentation of an international perspective to youth in the United States. It was indicated that representatives from England, France, Canada, Germany, Italy, Japan, Spain, Yugoslavia, Czechoslovakia, Mexico, and the United States were expected to attend the assembly. [72]

The International Assembly of Revolutionary Student Movements was held as scheduled at Columbia University and New York University during the week of September 18-23,

1968. Over 500 students from Italy, Germany, France, Great Britain, Mexico, and Canada as well as the United States took part. Among the foreign groups represented were the German SDS and the outlawed French JCR (Revolutionary Communist Youth), a Trotskyite group. Carl Davidson, one of the SDS representatives from the United States at the assembly, reported in the Guardian of September 28, 1968, that the assembly was a "flop." Davidson based his characterization of the assembly on general disagreement on plans and programs. He reported that practically every session of the assembly degenerated into a shouting match.

EXPLOITING "STUDENT POWER" 1967-68

SDS organizers expressed dismay that mass demonstrations were underway on campuses in the 1967-68 academic year without radical leadership and without proper "political" guidance that would have made protest part of a fight against the entire American "system." Angered at a mass march at a New York university which allegedly "co-opted" the radicals' tactics for "liberal" ends, then New York SDS organizer Jeff Jones labeled the student protest an example of "mobilized fascism."[73] Another conflict in late 1967 at San Francisco State College which actually led to a shutdown of an administration building was denounced in an issue of New Left Notes for failing to involve "political targets."[74]

Student radicals some years earlier had considered struggle for student participation and control a "radicalizing" process which would continue after students graduated into society at large, Davidson has explained. Finding themselves actually working for "reform," many radicals chose to support only student power issues with some relation to an "oppressed" group outside the campus and to launch a resistance campaign against military or corporate uses of universities, Davidson said.[75]

In line with a national SDS strategy to confront and disable military and paramilitary power on certain campuses, SDS announced it was joining with several other organizations in a conference in Chicago, November 10-12, 1967, to attempt to map programs of action against campus military operations and research.[76] At the conference, SDS interorganizational secretary Carl Davidson reportedly advanced the merits of "destruction, dislocation and obstruction" to deny to the military access to the manpower, intelligence and resources of universities.

By pursuing escalating tactics on campuses, radicals would "desanctify" the university, which Davidson described as stripping it of moral, intellectual, and political pretexts.[77]

An effort to influence the growing "student power" movement on campuses was made by SDS in the printing and distribution in May 1968 of a lengthy handbook on campus organizing. The pamphlet, written in 1967 by Davidson and titled The New Radicals in the Multiversity, an Analysis and Strategy for the Student Movement, was an updating of his 1966 working paper, "Toward a Student Syndicalist Movement."

Davidson continued to promote the formation of campus political parties and free student unions, and added a discussion of the possibilities of future student strikes on the model of an action at the University of California at Berkeley in December 1966. The new pamphlet also came out against students struggling for reforms of the university simply for the sake of reform. SDS organizers should work with university reform-minded students, however, Davidson said, on the principle espoused by Ché Guevara in Guerrilla Warfare to the effect that organizers must work with people in the institutions the people have faith in, even if the organizer himself does not think such forms of actions lead anywhere.

Student radicals were urged to avoid student power issues which gave students only a partial voice in university decision-making processes. They were to concentrate either on trying to control those processes or abolishing them. Campaigns to abolish student courts and other disciplinary tribunals, campus police, military influences on campus, and the grading system were recommended by Davidson, who suggested that a handy rule of thumb for a useful issue was whether or not it would have the effect of weakening aspects of "corporate capitalism."

Protests allegedly had value to the degree that they produced a "revolutionary class consciousness" among members of a future new working class who would one day hopefully organize a larger movement for social changes based on principles of "participatory democracy" and "worker control."[78]

SDS HAS SOMETHING FOR
THE HIGH SCHOOL STUDENT TOO

The extension of the student power movement down to

the high school level was welcomed by SDS organizers in the fall of 1967. New York SDS organizer Jeff Jones claimed that new self-organized high school chapters, contacting his office in New York, proved that many in the 14- to 16-year-old group were rejecting American society and had only to be turned on to SDS perspectives. [79]

A new, revised edition of Mark Kleiman's pamphlet, High School Reform: Toward a Student Movement, was printed by SDS in March 1968. The change in tactics and outlook of the SDS national leadership in the two years since the original printing of the pamphlet in February 1966 was demonstrated by the major change in proposed issues and purposes for the high school activist. The original edition proposed that high school organizers steer clear of anti-war, civil rights, and other "political" issues in working for student participation in high school decision-making processes. This language was deleted in 1968 in favor of a new statement declaring that a high school reform movement could never radically alter an educational institution and, at best, could "radicalize" the high school students themselves through their mutual struggles. It was necessary to change the way people related to each other--to build them into a "community of resistance"--without expecting to change the "authoritarian" educational institutions, the 1968 pamphlet stated. [80]

"Only in rare instances," wrote J. Edgar Hoover in the PTA Magazine in January 1970, "has SDS been able to organize by attempting to create a nucleus of SDS members or sympathizers to work inside the school as catalysts for radical action. Outsiders tried to organize high school students by contacting them initially in the immediate vicinity of their schools by an activity called leafleting." Invitations were extended to the younger students during this time to attend SDS-sponsored seminars, conferences, or demonstrations. In one instance, Mr. Hoover wrote, some 50 high school students assisted SDS in an attempt to seize a college building. Another SDS method of reaching the high school student en masse was by eliciting an invitation to speak from a high school club or student government. SDS might also penetrate a high school by aiding its students to publish an underground newspaper, and by assisting them in this endeavor with funds, equipment, and editorial guidance.

"RESISTANCE" IN THE SPRING OF 1968

National SDS secretaries such as Carl Davidson and

Robert Pardun sought to promote "Weeks of Resistance" in
the spring of 1968, which Pardun explained as a continuation
of SDS resistance activity on a "formally planned basis, "
with coordinated confrontations on campus against targets selected in advance.

Davidson advanced the proposal as preferable to peri-
odically proposed, symbolic student strikes, which he said
were defensive rather than offensive in nature, and often dif-
fused the issues because radicals lost complete control of the
action.   (Davidson saw a student strike as having value only
if many universities were on strike at the same time and
confronted the academic community with a major crisis.)
Advocates of "institutional resistance, " such as Davidson and
Pardun, held up as a model the physical confrontation between
police and demonstrators against Dow Chemical recruiters at
the University of Wisconsin in October 1967. [81]

Pardun argued that the new militancy on campuses was
not going to disappear and that it was up to a national SDS
organization to try to give it "direction" and "political content. "   Concentration on student confrontations on campus was
necessary, according to Pardun, because SDS was not yet
capable of working in communities or among workers.   National coordination and planning for SDS student activity was
urged by Pardun with the observation that, "The process of
bringing this country to a halt is not an easy one. "[82]   Pardun
defined the national leadership's concept of "resistance" as
follows:

> Resistance is a way of looking at yourself and the
> movement which comes when you finally lose all
> faith in the ability of those in power to make any
> meaningful change.   It defines a resistance to that
> power's manipulation of your life, but also it de-
> fines an understanding that liberation can only come
> through collective struggle.   Taken in that way the
> resistance movement is one of positive action toward
> reaching new people, exposing the nature of power
> in this country, and raising people's consciousness
> about the kinds of struggle which must be waged if
> that liberation is to be accomplished. [83]

Other elements within SDS objected to "institutional
resistance" as a tactic which put bodies on the line to slow
down "the machine" yet often served to scare off sizable
numbers of students from support of a radical-initiated cause.

Another result was the downgrading of other approaches such
as working with off-campus groups, whether the concentration
was on the disadvantaged or the so-called working class. [84]
Many in the organization took a "softer" approach, viewed reforms in the universities as valuable in themselves, in addition to helping build a radical movement, and tended to support less militant actions, according to debates reported in
New Left Notes. But all factions agreed national-level argument was academic because the SDS membership ignored national council resolutions when it did not suit local leadership
or a local campus situation.

ESCALATION OF CAMPUS DISORDERS
IN THE SPRING OF 1968

The first few months of 1968 were filled with domestic
and international events which have been credited with affecting to some degree the course of SDS.

Events related to the Vietnam war included the January
30, 1968 launching of a ferocious Tet offensive by the Vietnamese communists against 30 South Vietnamese provincial
capitals. President Johnson declared that the offensive had
ended in complete military failure by early February, but
the episode was credited with giving the Vietnamese communists a temporary psychological advantage and having an adverse impact on that part of the American public which had
been optimistic about the course of the war.

On February 15, 1968, the National Security Council
decided to abolish draft deferments of youths enrolled in
graduate schools. National SDS responded with an appeal in
New Left Notes for stepped up anti-draft activity by SDS
members. The main product of the SDS National Council
meeting in Lexington, Kentucky, March 28-31, 1968, was an
anti-draft resolution calling upon members to organize collective resistance to the draft on college campuses, in high
schools, communities, and factories.

SDS national officers were mandated to try to establish
a summer alliance with SNCC and various anti-draft organizations to pursue these same objectives. The council also
voted support for anti-war groups engaged in resistance inside the Army. SDS opposition to the draft and war should
emphasize "the imperialist" nature of American foreign policy
and "raise basic questions about the capitalist system, " the
council declared. [85]

Coincidentally, on the last day of the national council session, March 31, President Johnson announced that the U.S. was unilaterally halting the bombing of 90 per cent of the North Vietnamese territory. When deescalation of the war effort was followed by the opening of preliminary peace talks on May 10, 1968, some SDS activists prematurely talked about types of programs feasible for SDS when the war was over. [86]

Violence and civil disorders, not related to the Vietnam war, still stalked the land on both sides of the Atlantic. The assassination of civil rights leader Martin Luther King on April 4, 1968, set off a chain of rioting in the ghettos of more than 80 American cities. Within days, a number of Black Panther Party officials were engaged in a shootout with Oakland, California policemen which resulted in death for one member of the militant black nationalist group. The SDS national office dispatched a telegram to a rally, supporting release of Black Panther leaders from jail and denouncing the Oakland police for what the radical youth group labeled as "systematic efforts to destroy" the BPP. The SDS' New Left Notes immediately publicized the platform of the Black Panther Party, which was now replacing SNCC as an exemplary kind of organization in the eyes of many SDS activists. [87]

(Only two months later, on June 6, the American people would be stunned to learn that an assassin's bullet had taken the life of presidential candidate Robert F. Kennedy, less than five years after a similar fate befell his brother, President John F. Kennedy.)

Meanwhile, in February and March 1968, students were reported to be engaged in acts of rebellion, in both non-violent and disruptive ways, not only in the United States but also in the technologically advanced societies of Europe, both communist and non-communist.

A press roundup of student activism in Europe in March of 1968 disclosed that

--in Madrid, Spain, police ejected a thousand students after a three-day sit-in at the University of Santiago de Compostela;

--Rome University was closed after student clashes with police left 200 wounded;

--English students tried to overturn the car of a government official;

--Warsaw, Poland, was the scene of street demonstrations by students aroused over government control of cultural affairs;

--Czech students demanded TV time to demonstrate their solidarity with the Polish youth. [88]

In France, continuous agitation and strikes during 1967-68 over overcrowded university classes, bans on political activity, and the like culminated on March 22, 1968, in an occupation of a building of the University of Paris branch in the Paris suburb of Nanterre. The occupation, led by the anarchistic Daniel Cohn-Bendit, sparked a spreading student rebellion which led to mass protests at the Sorbonne in May, street fighting, workers' strikes involving millions of Frenchmen, and a French Government crisis. [89]

In Western Germany on April 11, a leader of the New Leftist German SDS, Rudi Dutschke, was shot and seriously wounded by a young man who told police he was inspired by the assassination of Martin Luther King and who slept under a portrait of Hitler. [90] The national office of the American SDS organization fired off a telegram of outrage and solidarity, and New Left Notes of April 15 was filled with the details of German students' retaliation by window smashing, burning trucks, and plans to occupy a technical college in downtown West Berlin to serve as headquarters for their "immediate revolution. "[91]

Among the domestic episodes in which SDS members were specifically reported to be involved during February 1968 were an occupation of buildings in cooperation with a black nationalist student group at Eastern Michigan University, and a similar joint occupation of the president's office at Seattle Community College in the State of Washington. The local SDS opened its spring offensive at Columbia University in New York on February 27 by joining in a brief sit-in and temporary disruption of an administrative office to publicize its plans to "smash the military" at Columbia and expansion of the university into the nearby black community. Street theatre tactics were part of Columbia SDS' announced program to "build to 'shut it down'. "[92]

The SDS' New Left Notes claimed that the organiza-

tion's "desanctification of the week" also took place at Columbia University in March 1968 when the New York City director of Selective Service was struck in the face by a lemon
meringue pie as he addressed several hundred students in the
university auditorium. 93

New Left Notes reported in early March that SDS'ers
were demonstrating against university associations with the
Institute for Defense Analysis at Penn State, Princeton, the
University of Michigan, and the University of Chicago. 94

SDS' "FINEST HOUR"--
THE CLOSING OF COLUMBIA UNIVERSITY

On April 23, 1968, the local SDS chapter sponsored
a rally on the Columbia University campus to protest the
university's relation to the Institute for Defense Analysis,
the school's alleged "racist" policies in relation to the nearby community of Harlem, and disciplinary probation in effect against some of the SDS leaders.

The rally by some 150 students on the outdoor campus
escalated that same day into an invasion of a university building where three school officials were held hostage for 24
hours. On the following day, additional buildings were occupied by a growing mass of rebellious students, estimated to
be 700 to 1,000 strong and extending beyond the original core
of members of the SDS and the Students Afro-American Society. The university president's office was ransacked and
a total of five buildings were under occupation before more
than 1,000 policemen entered the campus on the sixth day of
the disorders and cleared the buildings in a violent and chaotic student-police encounter. Classes came to a virtual stand-
still at the university for the rest of the academic year. 95

A subsequently appointed fact-finding commission of
scholars and lawyers found that a minority of members within the local SDS chapter, motivated by a desire to "subvert
and destroy the university because it was a tool of an 'evil
society', " should be held partially responsible for the events
of April 23-30. Their role was described as that of a catalyst. 96 The SDS chapter membership as a whole did not exceed 50 to 100 members, the commission found, and they included a wide range of views from reformers to revolutionaries.

The SDS national office immediately sent out telegrams urging students to "create two, three, many Columbias." An issue of New Left Notes was put out with a photograph of a Vietcong flag waved by students from the tower of a Columbia University building and a simple bold caption: "Two, Three, Many Columbias..." The SDS publication acknowledged receiving phone calls asking for an explanation of the national office telegram and the meaning of the slogan. The publication qualified its action by alleging that the telegram was sponsored by "Columbia strikers" who also coined the slogan "two, three, many Columbias." New Left Notes limited its own specific advice to the terse statement: "We should respond."[97]

SDS' interorganizational secretary Carl Davidson was less reticent after the academic year came to a close. He said the Columbia University rebellion marked a new plateau for SDS, was the best expression of the possibilities of a strategy of "institutional resistance," and should be a model for campus organizing efforts by SDS members in the 1968-69 academic year.[98]

SDS organizers' enthusiasm for an immediate repetition of Columbia University events on other campuses was also acknowledged by Davidson. The Columbia rebellion, he said,

> has successfully summed up and expressed the best aspects of the main thrust of our national political efforts in the last two years. Even with little conscious effort on the part of our national organizers, dozens of student activists responded to the call 'Create two, three, many Columbias' by initiating similar, though less dramatic, struggles on their own campuses.[99]

For SDS'ers and other advocates of a "resistance" strategy, Tom Hayden observed, Columbia University opened a "new tactical stage"--

> From the overnight occupation of buildings to permanent occupation; from mill-ins to the creation of revolutionary committees; from symbolic civil disobedience to barricaded resistance.

Hayden expressed confidence that the future would find even more militant tactics in use, including smaller hit-

and-run operations on offices of professors doing weapons
research, for example.   Students, he said, were moving
toward use of their power "to stop the machine if it cannot
be made to serve human ends," to the beginning of what
Columbia University rebels called "bringing the war home."[100]

          In May of 1968, SDS'ers participated with other campus
activists in brief sit-ins at university offices at Brooklyn College and Northwestern University in Chicago, in what may
have been unsuccessful efforts to imitate their comrades at
Columbia.   Tom Hayden, later that year, informed the President's Commission on Violence that students who tried and
failed in efforts to mimic the Columbia demonstrators had
failed to take into account the need for broad popular support
for their cause.[101]

          SDS officer Carl Davidson expressed the opinion that
SDS needed to pay more attention to developing "allies" in its
struggles.   The activists at Columbia, in his opinion, were
motivated to some extent by the concurrent French and German student uprising, to show an "audacity" and "inspiration"
which went beyond what seemed possible.[102]

          SDS PROGRAM DESCRIBED AS "NEGATIVIST"

          By the conclusion of the 1967-68 academic year, a
number of SDS activists were arguing that the traditional
tendency of SDS'ers to engage in a negative or nihilistic "action for action's sake" around the issues of the day should
be converted into commitment to some specific long-range
objectives.   Others protested against the autonomous nature
of local SDS chapters and the lack of a strong central organization, a view reputedly rejected by most members because
of an anti-authoritarian spirit and a distrust of "top-down"
bureaucracies.

          An interviewer of SDS activists, in the wave of pub-
licity accorded to the organization as a result of the Columbia
riots, reported finding that most SDS'ers were socialists ap-
plying the principle of participatory democracy in such a way
that they advocated a worker's share not only in a corporation's profits but also in the selection of the managers, the
selection by students and faculty of university administrators,
and neighborhood control of schools.[103]

          One college senior interviewed by the press in this

period described himself as a "philosophical and moral anarchist," which allegedly did not mean absence of law and
order but elevation of the individual over the state.   In a society with a complete adherence to participatory democracy,
the SDS member maintained, men did not delegate powers to
representatives but were personally involved in decision-making. 104

A long New Left Notes dissertation by SDS activist
Cathy Wilkerson in March of 1968 complained that students
were trained to serve as "non-creative" functionaries in a
highly technological system controlled by the "power elite."
She expressed her dissatisfaction with the criteria and values
of the so-called "ruling class," and "alienating" working conditions, all geared to economic needs and ignoring "social
and human drives."105

One of the most militant voices in SDS, Carl Davidson, liked to defend resistance tactics on the basis of our
"revolutionary critique" of the "institutions and society" which
"we are trying to destroy." Davidson and those of like mind
argued that the social order they rebelled against was totalitarian, manipulative, repressive, and antidemocratic, and
therefore--on the basis of the Nuremburg decisions, which
expected Hitler's opposition to oppose him, not debate him--
the SDS militants felt it their "duty" to "suppress" anti-democratic activities of the dominant order in the United States.
These militants insisted they could thus not be held accountable on grounds of denial of civil liberties when they physically disrupted campus recruiters from the military, for example. 106

An advocate of instilling more organization and purpose
in SDS summarized SDS' existing "crisis"-oriented operation
as follows:

> Ironically, we have always had a tacit reliance upon
> the system to keep us alive.   As agitators, our
> work depended primarily on the development of
> crises.   We did not have much of a perspective,
> largely because we did not really need one.
>   We were saved for a while by the Black
> Power movement, and by the emergence of the
> Third World as a revolutionary force, if for no
> other reason than that those movements gave us
> more to sink our teeth into.   By allying ourselves
> on paper with those movements, we began to be

able to develop a whole body of theory which defined
us in their terms. We were now supporters of the
NLF, dedicated antiimperialists, and active allies
(via militant street actions such as STDW) of the
Internal Black Power movement.

Many of our people hoped, somewhat manipu-
latively, that the situation of this country would de-
teriorate with increasing rapidity. We looked for
the ghettos to blow, for more wars of national liberation to start, and for repression to start. We
realized, although we never said as much, that the
essential ingredient of our survival was conflict.
As long as there was conflict, there would be a
reason for us to act, and room for us to act. [107]

That student interest in SDS was still growing was evi-
dent from the number of delegates and observers--500--who
attended its June 9-15, 1968, convention at Michigan State
University at East Lansing. The following national officers
were elected by the delegates: Michael Klonsky, of San
Fernando Valley State College and of the Los Angeles regional
office, national secretary; Bernardine Dohrn, University of
Chicago Law School and former member of the National Lawyers Guild, interorganizational secretary; Fred Gordon of
Harvard and a teaching assistant at San Diego State College,
education secretary. The eight other elected members who
composed the upgraded national interim committee were:
Carl Oglesby, former SDS president, Antioch College, Ohio;
Mike James, JOIN organizer in Chicago, University of California; Eric Mann, organizer for the Newark Community
Union Project; "Chip" Marshal of Ithaca, N.Y.; Jeffrey Jones
of New York; Michael Spiegel of Washington, D.C.; Morgan
Spector of San Francisco; and Bartee Haile of Dallas, Texas. [108]

Officers at the convention reported an income for the
previous year of $115, 094 and expenses of $114, 642. Pledged
contributions of $51, 773, dues and subscriptions of $19, 059,
and funds from miscellaneous activities constituted the sources
of income. [109]

The student group estimated that it had a total membership of 30, 000 supporters on 300 college campuses.

Delegates argued over a plethora of proposals for a
revised organizational structure and new tactics and strategy.
After days of intense debating, all restructuring proposals

were defeated and "nothing concrete was resolved" on the
subject of strategy, New Left Notes reported. [110]

As a proponent of a more formal organization described it, SDS remained a "confederation of localized con-
glomerations of people held together by one name and a spi-
der-web network of comrades with informal connections who
act as a roughly-constructed cadre group, " and rather than
carrying out national programs planned in advance, SDS was
confined to a series of local actions tied together either
spontaneously or by word spread by the press. [111] The 500
who appeared at the convention, therefore, were also in no
sense "representatives" (i. e. , they were not authorized spokesmen for all the chapters and brought no "instructions" down
from a national level). [112]

SDS membership at this time was described as a mass
of some 30, 000 loosely connected alienated activists, mostly
students, with a couple of hundred or so persons, mostly
former students, "who have been around for a while and are
committed to a long-term movement for revolutionary change
as well as radical action. " One defeated proposal for restructuring was aimed at reducing existing friction between
these "cadre" or organizer types and the mass SDS membership through a system of national organizers. [113]

The loose organizational structure of SDS was defended
by proponents as an application of the group's own principle
of participatory democracy. Among the viewpoints represented
at the convention which helped retain the local autonomy feature of the SDS organization were those of the anarchist elements and members or supporters of the disciplined, Maoist
organization which had split off from the Communist Party,
U. S. A. , some years earlier and operated under the title,
Progressive Labor Party. [114]

Among the various strategies debated and rejected by
inaction of the convention were proposals that SDS: 1) change
its emphasis from building a radical movement to the work
of "making" revolution; 2) create a revolutionary political
party; 3) establish alliances with industrial workers; and 4)
enter into the military to organize from within against the
system. [115] The Columbia University rebellion was not the
focus of convention discussions it was expected to be, the
newly elected national secretary, Michael Klonsky, complained
later.

Some of the old and new national leaders expressed dismay that the convention could not act on ways SDS could expand and grow through "new constituencies." SDS lost thousands of members each year because they left school or dropped out of a basically student movement, Klonsky averred, and some of the new officers were anxious to experiment with organizing on a citywide basis and among young professionals in what they called a "new working class."

It was left to the national interim committee meeting, following the convention, to agree with Klonsky that the causes and effects of the Columbia University uprising must be studied "in order to create more Columbias." To the new national secretary, "Columbia was a classic example of student power being used the way we have often discussed in the past. Is there revolutionary potential in this kind of power? How must that power develop?" he asked in comments on the convention in New Left Notes. The French student experience of propelling workers into civil disobedience was also being studied by SDS leaders for lessons it might offer the American New Left. 116

One of the reputed reasons for the inability of the convention to agree on a single major resolution was the en masse attendance and disciplined voting by SDS'ers who were also affiliated with the Progressive Labor Party. Shouting matches were frequent as some SDS activists, also representing the viewpoint of the newly elected national leadership, charged PLP supporters with trying to "use" SDS by treating it as a mass base to be manipulated by a small, Marxist-Leninist vanguard.

The PLP faction in SDS, known as the Worker-Student Alliance (WSA) faction, had shown its resentment toward SDS' leadership at the previous 1967 convention, but it was not strong enough to secure positions of leadership legitimately. Although WSA was well organized, disciplined, and adhered generally to a classic Marxist ideology, these features were not the principal reasons that SDS delegates disliked the faction. The main objections to WSA were that it held closed caucuses, voted as a bloc, and had interests which differed from those of SDS. 117

A PLP-WSA take-over did not materialize at the 1968 convention, although the faction had a unified delegation of 60-70 delegates. However, WSA did nearly secure a seat on the national interim committee. 118 Some SDS regulars believed that PLP was using SDS as a recruiting ground for members.

The dispute between the SDS leadership, sometimes called the national office faction or the national "collective," and the WSA during the 1968 convention also involved racial issues. WSA held that racism was based upon economic class exploitation, while the SDS leadership tended to support the claims of black nationalist groups that blacks were subject to a special kind of colonial oppression as a result of white racism.

The dominant "new left" leadership of SDS was reported to be turned off further by the PLP's old left line that revolutionaries had to depend upon the "industrial working class" for strength enough to make a revolution, and by the PLP'ers' "worker-student alliance" line for SDS, which stressed college students marching on picket lines and other action around "economic" issues. SDS activists just back from trips to Cuba and Hanoi, as well as visits with the French and German student movements, were also repelled by rigid PLP adherence to the Chinese communist line. New Leftists of theoretical bent wanted to work out their own analyses of modern-day capitalism, without simply adopting theories which some believed were applicable only to czarist Russia half a century ago.

During a bitter floor debate between PLP supporters and their opponents, as the convention prepared to elect national officers, a PLP'er accused the opposition of "red-baiting." A supporter of a "new" left approach reportedly responded with incredulous anger: "Red-baiting! I'm the communist here, not PLP."[119]

A hastily organized "new Left" caucus on the morning of the election of officers supported the candidacy of the new national secretary, Mike Klonsky, and new interorganizational secretary, Bernardine Dohrn. Fred Gordon, unknown to the caucus, offered himself for the third secretarial post dealing with internal education and was elected along with Klonsky and Dohrn.

Asked after her nomination if she considered herself a socialist, Miss Dohrn told the delegates she considered herself a "revolutionary communist." Klonsky also described himself as a communist during the convention proceedings as well as in a subsequent speaking appearance at the University of Florida.[120]

The weekly Guardian, which regularly covered events
on the New Left, including SDS, commented after the convention that SDS in the last year had evolved from its anti-imperialist and anti-capitalist perspective and was on the "preci-
pice" of embracing socialism, or in the terminology of a considerable number of SDS members, "revolutionary communism."121

The editors of the official SDS publication, New Left
Notes, confirmed that within the movement there was talk
about "communism, the principles of communism, with a
small c." The newspaper had this to say on the point in its
issue of June 24, 1968, summarizing its recent national convention:

> Apart from our anti-imperialist analysis of the
> (Vietnam) War, the rebellions, and the university,
> we are most known to folks by something called
> 'participatory democracy.'
>   At the same time, within our movement, we
> talk more and more about 'acting as a collective,'
> 'being responsible to a collective,' even 'fighting
> against elitism' or 'fighting against institutionalized
> individualism.' We are beginning to talk about
> class consciousness. In short, talk inside the
> Movement is about communism, the principles of
> communism, with a small c. Our task this sum-
> mer is to develop those beginnings of an ideology
> in terms that make sense to Americans. That
> can't be done out of a book. 122

Two SDS activists publicly issued warnings, stimulated
by the differences at the convention over tactics and objectives, which appear prophetic in the light of developments in
the student organization in subsequent years. 123

The new national secretary Mike Klonsky declared in
a summary of the convention proceedings that, "Our internal
contradictions can serve to make us strong, or they can destroy us unless we develop methods of resolving them while
they are still internal."124

During the bitter debate on the convention floor between
PLP sympathizers and their opponents, 125 the Guardian recorded an accusation by Jeff Gordon, a PLP member in the
New York SDS, to the effect that the real problem facing SDS
was not "differing political views" but "terrorist disruption."

Gordon warned that such disruption would destroy SDS and
that the national office of SDS would be to blame. [126]

One of the workshops at the June 1968 national convention had dealt with the subject of "sabotage and explosives, "
Federal Bureau of Investigation's Director J. Edgar Hoover
disclosed during his appearance in September 1968 before the
President's Commission on Violence. Mr. Hoover described
the suggestions made at this workshop for the stated purpose
of disrupting Selective Service facilities and law enforcement.
They included: flushing bombs in toilets to destroy plumbing;
using sharp, tripod-shaped metal instruments to halt vehicles;
firing Molotov cocktails from shotguns; jamming radio equipment; and dropping thermite bombs down manholes to destroy
communications systems. [127]

SDS TRAVELING ORGANIZERS

In an article in New Left Notes, in June 1968, Alan
Spector, SDS New England Regional Organizer, took issue
with Jeff Segal's proposed constitutional amendment calling
for the replacement of the NIC by 19 full-time staff members,
including the three secretaries, and a 15-man national organizing committee. [128] The main thrust of his argument
against Segal gave some insight into the nature of the SDS
traveling organizer. Spector objected to Segal's proposition
on the grounds that full-time N.O. staff personnel, like full-
time SDS travelers or organizers, ceased to be responsible
to any specific constituency (i.e., urban or college chapter).

Being removed from the daily experience and problems
of campus organizing distorted one's viewpoint, and an organizer, he said, who did not understand the problems of his
constituency could not serve it. The traveling organizer, who
carried around films and literature and who helped to set up
meetings and politically strengthened campus chapters, should
be aware of the problems existing on the campus. Usually,
however, he could not afford to wait around for weeks to experience these student problems personally. He could, however, learn enough about situations, both good and bad, existing on one particular campus, and relay his analysis to other
chapters, "engaging in a give-and-take process whereby the
campus organizer and the traveling organizer both teach and
learn from each other." [129]

Basically, the "travelers" conducted three interrelated

functions: mechanical, experience and strategy exchange,
and ideological, stated Spector.   National officers should be
closely linked to the campus and, therefore, the professional
traveler, in time, was not a suitable candidate for national
office.   Moreover, warned Spector, to be a "professional
radical" too long may create "another movement bureaucrat"
rather than an organizer.   In his opinion, Spector said, full-
time travelers should either go back to an unorganized campus, enroll, and build a movement there, or go into the professions or factories to carry out organizing activities.

SOME SDS ACTIVITY IN THE SUMMER OF 1968

More than 2, 000 SDS members were engaged in "summer projects" in 1968, according to the SDS publication,
which said this was an SDS effort to "build and deepen our
movement" by finding new constituencies (groups of persons
willing to support the SDS efforts to bring about radical
changes in American society). [130]

SDS members were reported to be working during the
summer on anti-draft projects in various communities or
trying to interest high school youths in the SDS cause.   Several hundred members found jobs in industrial plants and
shops as part of a "work-in" program. [131]

Work-ins had been sponsored on a small scale by
various SDS locals in the California area in 1967 and operated
on a larger scale only in the summers of 1968 and 1969.   A
major promoter of the industry work-in was the Progressive
Labor Party which had produced a handbook in 1967 to advise
college students how to obtain jobs in private industry in order to bring a radical political message to workers and help
students build a bond with the only class powerful enough to
achieve revolutionary change in America.   The PLP'ers' instruction pamphlet was reprinted by the SDS national office
for use by SDS members during the 1969 summer work-in,
although the December 1968 National Council of SDS pointedly
disclaimed any agreement with the PLP tactical line. [132]

A number of the more militant SDS activists, including
the SDS' new national secretary, Mike Klonsky, were involved
in the street fighting which erupted on the streets of Chicago
in August 1968 in the course of a mass anti-war demonstration staged by the National Mobilization Committee to End
the War in Vietnam to coincide with the Democratic National
Convention.

The December 1967 national council meeting of SDS
had refused to endorse the mass demonstrations for reasons
which included SDS disinterest in seeking to influence existing
political parties in the United States. [133]   The newly elected
11-man SDS national interim committee met in late July, and
decided, nevertheless, that SDS organizers should travel to
Chicago and engage in "recruiting" activity for SDS among the
demonstrators.   The Chicago SDS office promised that SDS'ers
would be organizing support demonstrations if Chicago police
"start rioting" in the streets.

After the actual outbreak of rioting by police and demonstrators, Radio Havana conducted a telephone interview
with Klonsky on August 28.   Klonsky was quoted as stating:
"We have been fighting in the streets for four days.   Many
of our people have been beaten up, and many of them are in
jail, but we are winning. "[134]

NEW NATIONAL LEADERSHIP
SUGGESTS A FALL PROGRAM

The first national council meeting after the Democratic
National Convention convened at the University of Colorado
at Boulder, October 11-13, 1968, and voted for a fall program which reflected the views of the new national leaders.

The main resolution, with a pun for the title--"Boulder
and Boulder"--declared that SDS believed (at least on the national level) that:

1)   elections were a fraud because they fostered an
"illusion" that people have democratic power over their major
institutions, whereas only "a ruling class" controls the
schools, factories, courts, jail, Army, and electoral processes, and the correct answer was organization of the people
to engage in "direct action";[135]
2)   the U.S. should immediately withdraw from Vietnam because SDS "supports the people's war in Vietnam"
(an indirect expression of support for the Vietnamese communist cause, to be expressed more frankly in later SDS resolutions);
3)   "racism" should be ended and, in addition, SDS
affirmed "the right of black people to defend and liberate
themselves by any means necessary" and the necessity for
police to be "disarmed. "

The council resolution called for organization of strikes
by high school and college students throughout the nation on
November 4 and 5, 1968, [136] to publicize the view that elections are a "fraud" and for regional demonstrations in major
cities.

The strike was also seen as a means to organize high
school students, in addition to providing them with a gesture
of defiance. [137] Another resolution of the national council had
singled out the high schools for a special SDS organizing effort by approving the hiring of a national high school coordinator and appealing to regional organizations and chapters of
SDS to make organizing among these younger students a large
part of their programs. The SDS would approach the high
school student, according to the resolution, with the line that:

> Knowing that the school cannot change to the extent
> we want unless we change the system which uses it,
> we will organize in the high school to move students
> to overthrow that system by confronting the issues
> that directly affect them. [138]

The strategy behind SDS' anti-electoral program was
described as a hope to build up radical strength as a result
of an increasing political "polarization" process. The resolution described the SDS intent in this way:

> In the present pre-election period, that crisis [be-
> setting capitalism at home and abroad] is manifested
> by an increasing political polarization: the center
> has proven its failure--just as it can't either get
> out of or win in Vietnam, so it can't successfully
> change or preserve the status quo at home.
>   The failure of the center is irreversible;
> it remains for the left not to cling to liberal myths,
> but to build its own strength out of the polarization,
> to build the left pole. The growth of the right is
> a reaction to the threat of the left's real and po-
> tential strength here and internationally; it remains
> for us to make the threat real. [139]

Support on the local level was also urged for a GI
Week being staged by various anti-war groups for the week
prior to the elections.

INCREASED TALK OF
VIOLENCE AND ARMED STRUGGLE

Investigations by the House Committee on Internal Security established that a 19-page pamphlet titled "Sabotage" was made available at the October sessions of the SDS National Council. The pamphlet contained instructions and drawings on the preparation of Molotov cocktails and other incendiary devices, auto and tank traps and various explosive materials for the specific purpose of sabotage. This literature actually consisted of reproductions of pages from a booklet, 150 Questions for a Guerrilla, which had been published in 1963. The author of the published booklet was General Alberto Bayo, self-advertised as "The man who trained Castro."

National secretary Mike Klonsky's speech to the October national council session contained references to the threat of repression and to an eventual necessity for "armed struggle," according to Carl Davidson, recent SDS national officer who "covered" the national council as a staff correspondent for the radical newsweekly, the Guardian. [140]

Shortly thereafter, on October 21, 1968, Klonsky spoke before students at Western Michigan University and reportedly advocated tearing down the power structure to replace it with "people power," by which Klonsky meant that students would control the universities and workers would operate the factories. Klonsky expressed the belief that personal liberation would not be achieved, however, without an armed struggle. [141]

Among those pleading the cause of various tactical lines for SDS in New Left Notes in September 1968 was an SDS chapter on New York City's Lower East Side whose members were sometimes described as "anarchists" or "crazies." The group maintained that the street fighting in Chicago at the time of the Democratic National Convention the preceding summer had shown the value of hit-and-run street fighting tactics by groups emerging from a crowd and disappearing back into it. The chapter urged SDS to begin to rely on dropouts, working youth and blacks who were the disaffected "outsiders" in American society, and to base an SDS action program on the premise that the American revolution has already begun. [142]

The militant language also cropped up at rallies held on some of the nation's campuses as an apparently common

substitute for the so-called strike urged by the SDS National
Council around the issue of the national elections on November 5, 1968.   The four universities in the area of Washington, D.C., had rallies on November 4 attended by a total
estimated turnout of no more than 700 students.   Each was
addressed in turn by SDS national interim committee member,
Carl Oglesby.   Oglesby's advice to the students at the George
Washington University rally, as recorded by the press, was
that "going to the streets" was the student's only alternative
because the "system" had shut off all possibility of peaceful
change. 143

A special leaflet issued by the SDS national office on
the election day campaign expressed hope that actions by
SDS members on November 4 and 5, 1968, would escalate
to the level of "occupying schools to turn them into a forum
for SDS: CLOSING THEM DOWN. "144

A review of radical activities actually occurring on
that date, appearing in the Guardian, stated that the SDS-
called student strike failed to interrupt education at a single
high school, college, or university and must be classified as
a "bomb. "

On election day, however, a number of Washington
area campus SDS leaders were arrested by police for their
role in a protest march by some 1,000 persons which invaded an area near the White House where demonstrations
are barred. 145

SDS ACTIVITY ON COLLEGE CAMPUSES
IN THE FALL OF 1968

Committee investigations and hearings revealed that
campus SDS chapters were relatively pacific at the beginning
of the 1968-69 academic year, which produced expressions of
disappointment from some of the more militant SDS activists
but concurrence of local chapters committed to non-violent
policies.

The militant SDS chapter at Columbia University
sought to halt fall registration, from which suspended SDS'ers
were barred, but found they were unable to recapture the
student support necessary for a successful disruption of the
university processes. 146

The Harvard branch of SDS, which attracted 500 youth
to its first meeting in September 1968, agreed to work on
issues of draft resistance, university complicity with war-related agencies, and expansion of the university into slum
areas, but specifically rejected tactics of obstructionism. [147]
(By December 1968, however, at least some of the chapter
members had second thoughts about this pledge because they
launched a sit-in against ROTC which forced cancellation of
a faculty meeting on the issue.) In early November, the
SDS chapter at City College of New York was involved with
other activists in a week-long non-disruptive anti-war sit-in
which was finally broken up by police. [148]

Rallies, marches, leaflets, and petitions were the
more common SDS chapter methods in the fall of 1968, committee investigations and hearings disclosed. SDS members'
protests fell into one or more of four broad categories of
issues: 1) war-related issues such as opposition to ROTC,
military or CIA recruitment on campus, and military research on campus; 2) student power issues, which included
requests for a pass-fail grading system, beer sales on campus, no dormitory curfews, better student housing, or a
voice in hiring and firing of professors; 3) labor issues,
which found students supporting improved wages for university
employees or marching off campus on union picket lines; and
4) support of black student demands. Spokesmen for chapters
announced their commitment to a variety of techniques--some
geared to a non-violent pursuit of reforms of the university
through legitimate channels and others openly committed to
policies of intimidation and disruption.

Some observers of campus activism reported that in
the fall of 1968 white students were less active in confrontations than during the preceding academic year, but black
students were leading sit-ins, demonstrations, and sometimes
disruption at numerous universities in the same months. The
black militants tended to cooperate with radical whites only on
occasion, and then only when expedient. [149]

In keeping with what historians to the New Left observed as the tendency of white radicals to follow the lead
of their black brothers, the December meeting of the national
council declared that fighting racism was one of its primary
tasks and that its duty was to ally itself with and support
"black liberation" struggles on campus and in the communities.

The new emphasis of the national leadership gave to war-related issues a secondary priority and placed even lesser stress on once important issues of student power, although the organization embraced youths who still preferred to remain active around those broad categories. A number of SDS activists were reported to feel at this period, however, that the Vietnam war no longer offered much potential for mobilizing support for SDS actions. This attitude resulted from a seeming de-fusing of the issue brought on by the Paris peace negotiations between the U.S. and North Vietnamese Governments and the end to all bombing raids over North Vietnam on October 31, 1968. Some activists also expressed fear of what they called "repression" by the new administration which was scheduled to take office in the new year. 150

The December national council meeting of SDS was most noteworthy, however, for its decision marking a new effort by SDS to move off the campus and become something more than a student organization, and for the revolutionary objectives the council spelled out for SDS in neo-Marxian terms.

SDS VOTES TO BUILD A
REVOLUTIONARY YOUTH MOVEMENT

Amid rumors of plots and counterplots for control of SDS, more than 1,200 persons showed up at the five-day national council session held at the University of Michigan at Ann Arbor, December 26-31, 1968. Only about 170 of them were voting delegates, representing some 100 chapters out of a reputed 300-chapter total. Since the number of delegates from a chapter depended upon the number of dues-paying "national" members, reports circulated that the Progressive Labor Party had encouraged its SDS chapter members to also become "national" members in order to "stack" the council meeting. Regardless of the truth of the rumor, supporters of the PL line had a near majority in intense floor battles, as close votes disclosed, and in one instance succeeded in getting through a "Fight Racism" resolution written by the PLP-WSA faction. 151

A majority of the national leadership and regional staffs nevertheless maintained control of the proceedings and pushed through the principal policy resolution written by national secretary Klonsky and titled "Toward a Revolutionary Youth Movement." The resolution proposed that SDS expand

beyond the confines of the college campus and seek to create
a revolutionary youth movement. It would search for its
new recruits among young workers, high school students, the
Armed Forces, community colleges, trade schools, dropouts,
and the unemployed.

Delegates loyal to the national office majority and
those sympathetic to the Maoist PLP quoted Marx, Lenin,
and Mao Tse-tung in support of their contrary positions.
The revolutionary youth movement resolution committed the
SDS leadership to an anti-capitalist "working-class" analysis
which agreed with traditional Marxists that workers were the
main motive force for revolution, but added the conviction
that revolutionary youth, by "exemplary actions," could incite
others to the need for struggle to "bring about the downfall
of capitalism, the system which is at the root of man's oppression."[152]

The revolutionary youth movement would consider itself engaged in the same struggles as those of the Vietnamese
(communists) and fighters for black liberation. SDS would
make fighting racism a primary task on the premise that it
was a useful tool of the capitalists, but also because SDS
agreed with black nationalists who considered themselves to
be a "colony" fighting a kind of anti-colonial struggle within
the United States.

Offered merely as "suggestions" for implementing the
new off-campus orientation of SDS were: organizing in
schools outside the regular college level and among dropout
youth; attacks on universities that serve corporations exploiting "Third World" countries; attempts to stop universities
from functioning for "racist and imperialist" purposes by
opposing police institutes, counter-insurgency centers, university slum holdings; calling for increased college admissions of black and brown students, etc.

Other national council actions taken over the opposition of pro-PLP forces included condemnation of male supremacy as an idea and a practice (a "women's liberation"
resolution) and scheduling of a solidarity-with-Cuba week during the January anniversary of Fidel Castro's assumption of
power. Films from Cuba and Hanoi were shown during the
council sessions, and when factional rivalry became intense,
supporters of the national leadership majority reportedly
chanted "Ho, Ho, Ho Chi Minh" and PLP members and sympathizers responded with "Mao, Mao, Mao Tse-tung."

These divisions were to lead to increasingly bitter internal battles, on a national and also on a local chapter level, by early 1969. Some chapters were split into two separate organizations as a result of such rivalry over tactics, and others were immobilized on campuses where PLP enjoyed a substantial following. This festering dissension was destined to come to a head six months later at the next SDS national convention.

Signs of yet another internal faction destined to grow and assume a dominant influence by the time of the next national convention were contained in the proposal made at the December council meeting by Mark Rudd, who had been chairman of the Columbia University SDS chapter at the time it sparked the Spring 1968 rebellion at the school. One of the usual national mobilizations against the Vietnam war was scheduled for Washington, D.C., on the occasion of the inauguration of President Nixon in January 1969, and Rudd proposed that SDS people make "a strong, militant presence felt" by engaging in its own demonstrations at the International Police Institute and the South Vietnamese Embassy. The actions--rejected by the council--were recommended as an expression of non-support to the President and support to the pro-communist National Liberation Front. [153]

Rudd appeared to reflect a position of quite another group of SDS activists whose interests were not satisfied by the existing leadership. As an Ohio regional SDS organizer put it, many SDS "kids" had been attracted to the movement on the basis of the so-called vitality and militancy of SDS actions at Columbia University and on the streets of Chicago at the time of the Democratic National Convention. To keep and to get new members, according to this view, SDS had to show it was a "fighting movement," and an action during the President's Inaugural on January 20, 1969, was to this group a perfect opportunity. [154]

Another group of SDS activists operating on regional and local levels produced a working paper with another militant line at the December council meeting. No action was taken on it there, but was revived at a regional SDS conference several months later, and its content reflected that some organizers were prepared to back a more aggressive anti-Vietnam war effort via SDS attacks on campus ROTC programs, on the stated justification that it was no longer proper to think of "resisting" imperialism, but time to mobilize people to "combat it." The activists argued that actions

such as occurred at Columbia University or the long violent
struggle at San Francisco State College might be "isolated
actions," but they were useful in shocking the entire anti-war
movement into greater militancy.[155]

Some clue to the outlook of the majority of the SDS
national leadership in the 1968–69 academic year may be contained in a speech by Carl Oglesby, member of the national
interim committee, at a rally on December 5, 1968. "We're
not waiting for something called the proletariat,"[156] he reportedly declared. "We're making history."[157]

NOTES

1. Morgan Spector in New Left Notes, May 20, 1968, p.
   2.

2. Movement Speakers' Guide, compiled by Eric Goldfield,
   Spring 1967; revised by Janet Dowty, Fall 1967, REP,
   Ann Arbor, Mich., p. 14.

3. Report on elections in New Left Notes, July 10, 1967,
   Committee Exhibit No. 21-B in House Committee on
   Internal Security hearings on SDS, pt. 3-B (George
   Washington University), p. 1013.

4. SDS constitution as revised at 1967 convention, printed
   in New Left Notes, June 10, 1968, Committee Exhibit
   No. 42 in HCIS hearings on SDS, pt. 6-B.

5. New Left Notes, July 10, 1967, pp. 4, 5.

6. Ibid., p. 5.

7. Ibid., p. 8.

8. Ibid., p. 7.

9. A conference called by Fidel Castro and dominated by
   him with the aid of leaders or would-be leaders of
   Castroite guerrilla movements in other Latin American nations. The sessions were held July 31-Aug.
   10, 1967.

10. New Left Notes, July 10, 1967, p. 8.

11.   Chicago Peace Council leaflet, May 1967; HCIS hearings
      on SDS, pt. 7-A, December, 1969.

12.   Communist Commitment to Force and Violence, Report,
      House Committee on Un-American Activities, Mar. 2,
      1968.

13.   Calvert, speech at SDS conference at Princeton Univer-
      sity, Feb. 17-19, 1967; Davidson, quoted in National
      Guardian, Apr. 8, 1967, pp. 1, 8.

14.   New York Times, July 3, 1967, p. 15.

15.   New Left Notes, Sept. 11, 1967, pp. 1, 4. Jeff Jones
      was elected two years later to one of the three top
      national secretary posts in SDS.

16.   New Left Notes, July 10, 1967, p. 2.

17.   Daily Nebraskan, Sept. 13, 1967.

18.   Daily Illini, Oct. 4, 1967.

19.   The New Left: A Documentary History, ed. Massimo
      Teodori, p. 57; National Guardian, Sept. 2, 1967.

20.   New York Times, Oct. 18, 1967; Daily Californian,
      Aug. 18, 1967; Berkeley SDS leaflets.

21.   Washington Evening Star, Oct. 19, 1967.

22.   New York Times, Oct. 20, 21, 1967; Challenge, Nov.-
      Dec., 1967, p. 17; Phillip A. Lure in New Guard
      Dec. 1967, p. 10; National Review, Jan. 30, 1968,
      p. 86.

23.   New Left Notes, Feb. 5, 1968, pp. 1, 3.

24.   Daily Californian, Nov. 8, 1967; leaflets of Berkeley
      SDS.

25.   Dallas, Tex., Times-Herald, Oct. 6, 1967.

26.   New Left Notes, Feb. 5 and 26, 1968.

27.   New Left Notes, Feb. 5, 1968, p. 5.

28. Liberation, November 1967, p. 11; National Guardian, Oct. 21, 1967, pp. 1, 6; New York Times, Oct. 22, 23, 1967.

29. Liberation, November 1967.

30. Teodori, op. cit., p. 57.

31. "Power at the Pentagon, " New Left Notes, Oct. 30, 1967, pp. 1-3. See previous reference to provoking tactics used by Dutch Provos.

32. Davidson in New Left Notes, Feb. 12, 1968, pp. 3, 7, 8; National Guardian, Nov. 11, 1967, p. 9.

33. Davidson in National Guardian, Nov. 11, 1967, p. 9.

34. Tom Hayden, testimony, Oct. 24, 1968, National Commission on the Causes and Prevention of Violence.

35. The Worker, Jan. 28, 1968, p. 9.

36. Guardian, Jan. 6, 1968, p. 9.

37. New Left Notes, Sept. 11, 1967, p. 4.

38. "Subversive Involvement in Disruption of 1968 Democratic Party National Convention, " pt. 1, HCUA hearings, Oct. 1, 3, 4, 1968, p. 2255.

39. New Left Notes, AIMS Newsletter, January-February 1968, p. 1.

40. AIMS Newsletters, May-June 1967, September-October 1967, January-February 1968.

41. Pardun in New Left Notes, Mar. 11, 1968, p. 7.

42. Davidson speech, Oct. 27, 1967.

43. In the summer of 1967, Stokely Carmichael, in a new SNCC post of field secretary, had engaged in foreign travels which included Havana and Hanoi. Some militant SNCC leaders were not only talking of the need for revolutionary struggles in the U.S., where they viewed the black population as a kind of "colony," but were also asserting that blacks had a responsibility

to give revolutionary direction and leadership to all persons domestically engaged in anti-war or resistance activities. The position was taken, for example, by James Forman of the New York SNCC operation, in a letter reprinted in New Left Notes, Mar. 4, 1968, in which Forman also declared the long-term objectives of anti-war activists should be "antiracist," "anticapitalist," and "antiimperialist."

44. Guardian, June 24, 1967, p. 12; Douglas Hegdahl, testimony, Dec. 11, 1969, HCIS hearing on SDS involvement in POW release, p. 2265.

45. Cathy Wilkerson recounted this journey and the delegation's contacts with Vietnamese representatives in Cambodia in New Left Notes, Dec. 18, 1967, Committee Exhibit 21-D in HCIS hearings on SDS, pt. 3-B (George Washington University), pp. 1015-1020. See also The Movement, December 1967, p. 11.

46. Rennard Davis, testimony, Dec. 3, 1968, HCUA hearings, "Subversive Involvement in Disruption of 1968 Democratic Party National Convention," p. 2630.

47. Idem. The Worker, Nov. 27, 1967; "Riots, Civil and Criminal Disorders," pt. 18, hearings, Senate Permanent Subcommittee on Investigations, June 16, 1969, p. 3633; Douglas Hegdahl, testimony, Dec. 11, 1969, HCIS hearings on SDS involvement in POW release, p. 2271.

48. Guardian, July 13, 1968, p. 6.

49. HCIS hearings on SDS, pt. 7-A, Dec. 9-11 and 16, 1969; New Left Notes, Sept. 12, 1969, pp. 5, 37.

50. Fifth Estate, Feb. 6, 1968; Hearing before the Permanent Subcommittee on Investigations, Committee on Government Operations, U.S. Senate, on riots, civil, and criminal disorder, June 16, 1969, pt. 18, pp. 3489, 3623.

51. Guardian, Mar. 23, 1968, p. 13; New York Times, May 19, 1968; Chicago Daily News, June 14, 1968; Anthony Bouscaren and Daniel Lyons, Left of Liberal, p. 281.

52. Guardian, Feb. 3, 1968, pp. 1, 6, Jan. 27, 1968, and
     Dec. 30, 1967; Hearings before Permanent Subcommit-
     tee on Investigations, U.S. Senate, pt. 18, p. 3495;
     Thomas C. Hayden, testimony, Dec. 3, 1968, HCUA
     hearings, "Subversive Involvement in Disruption of
     1968 Democratic Party National Convention, " pp. 2552-
     2554.

53. New Left Notes, June 24, 1968, p. 8.

54. Reader's Digest, October 1969, p. 121f.

55. New Left Notes, Sept. 9, 1968, p. 3.

56. Life, Feb. 14, 1969, pp. 62-68; Illini, Jan. 11, 1969;
     New Left Notes, Nov. 19, 1968, p. 7.

57. New Left Notes, Nov. 19, 1968, p. 7.

58. Committee Exhibit No. 20, HCIS hearings on SDS, pt.
     3-B (George Washington University), pp. 964-966.

59. Guardian, Sept. 23, 1967, pp. 1, 10; Ramparts, No-
     vember 1967; San Francisco Chronicle, Nov. 5, 1967.

60. New Republic, Oct. 7, 1967, and Oct. 21, 1967.

61. San Francisco Chronicle, Sept. 23, 1968, p. 9; The
     Washington Post, Sept. 21, 1968, p. A-3.

62. The Marcolian, May 1-16, 1969.

63. New Left Notes, Sept. 9, 1968, p. 3.

64. New York Regional SDS Newsletter, Mar. 12, 1969,
     p. 8; speech by Assistant Director William C. Sulli-
     van, Federal Bureau of Investigation, before U.S.
     Chamber of Commerce, Apr. 27, 1969.

65. Committee Exhibit No. 20 in HCIS hearings on SDS,
     pt. 3-B (George Washington University), pp. 966-968;
     The Washington Post, Mar. 15, 1969, p. A-4.

66. New Left Notes, Sept. 9, 1968, p. 3.

67. New Left Notes, July 10, 1967, p. 8.

68. SDS pamphlet, Committee Exhibit No. 6 in HCIS hear-
     ings on SDS, pt. 6-A, pp. 1867-1890. See also The
     Movement, February 1969, and Reader's Digest,
     October 1969, p. 121.

69. U. S. A. magazine, Oct. 25, 1968.

70. New Left Notes, Sept. 9, 1968, p. 3.

71. "Report on Student [sic] in the University and Society
     of Today," reports from national group members to
     a committee of the Interparliamentary Union, Congres-
     sional Record, Mar. 16, 1970, pp. E 2029-2042;
     Time, May 3, 1968, pp. 24, 25; Atlas, July 1968,
     pp. 18-21; Monthly Review, September 1968, pp. 14-
     37.

72. New Politics, August 1968.

73. National Guardian, Oct. 21, 1967, p. 6.

74. New Left Notes, Dec. 18, 1967, pp. 7, 8.

75. Davidson in Guardian, Dec. 14, 1968, p. 5.

76. New Left Notes, Sept. 11, 1967, p. 2; National Guard-
     ian, Nov. 4, 1967, p. 4.

77. National Guardian, Nov. 18, 1967, pp. 1, 7.

78. Carl Davidson, The New Radicals in the Multiversity,
     May 1968.

79. National Guardian, Oct. 21, 1967, p. 6.

80. Mark Kleiman, High School Reform: Toward a Student
     Movement, March 1968, p. 14.

81. Robert Pardun in New Left Notes, Dec. 18, 1967, pp.
     2, 3; Carl Davidson in New Left Notes, Dec. 18,
     1967, pp. 2, 5, 6; and New Left Notes, Dec. 18,
     1967, p. 3.

82. Pardun in New Left Notes, Dec. 18, 1967, p. 3.

83. Ibid., p. 2.

84. New Left Notes, Dec. 4, 1967, p. 5.

85. Later in the year, a recruiting pamphlet issued by SDS
     under the title "SDS, An Introduction" described the
     organization's stand on Vietnam as follows: "SDS
     completely opposes the U.S. Government's immoral,
     illegal, and genocidal war against the people of Viet-
     nam. We urge and will organize all young men to
     wage a collective struggle in resistance to the Draft
     by refusing to serve in the Military. We also seek
     to break the barriers placed between us and our
     brothers in uniform. When forced by threat of im-
     prisonment or exile, some of us will organize within
     the Armed Forces, advocating desertion and other
     forms of resistance to U.S. foreign policy." (Com-
     mittee Exhibit No. 8, HCIS hearings on SDS, pt. 5
     (American University), pp. 1107-1114.) See also
     New Left Notes, Apr. 8, 1968, pp. 4, 5.

86. Mike Spiegel, SDS national secretary, in New Left
     Notes, Apr. 8, 1968.

87. New Left Notes, Apr. 15, 1968, pp. 1, 5.

88. "Roundup" in National Review, Mar. 26, 1968, pp.
     278, 279, in which the commentator expressed the
     opinion that everywhere students seemed to be re-
     belling against some manifestation of what they saw
     as a stifling, bureaucratic mass system that leaves
     them powerless and is unresponsive to their needs
     and desires. A columnist in the National Review of
     Apr. 28, 1968, p. 391, observed that youth now
     overflowing the universities seemed to be kicking
     against the dominant authority and ideology, which
     pitted them in a democracy on the side of fascism,
     socialism, or anarchy, and in a communist society,
     on the side of freedom.

89. Students in Revolt, eds. Lipset and Altbach, pp. 129-
     131, 142.

90. National Review, Apr. 30, 1968.

91. New Left Notes, Apr. 15, 1968, p. 1.

92. New Left Notes, Mar. 7, 1968, p. 8.

93. New Left Notes, Mar. 25, 1968, p. 3.

94. New Left Notes, Mar. 4, 1968.

95. Crisis at Columbia, Report of Fact-Finding Commission
     Appointed to Investigate the Disturbances at Columbia
     University in April-May 1968 (New York: Vintage
     Books [Random House], 1968).

96. Ibid., p. 58.

97. New Left Notes, May 6, 1968, pp. 1, 5. Tom Hayden,
     writing in Ramparts, June 15, 1968, declared the
     slogan "Create two, three, many Columbias"--after
     Ché Guevara's appeal to revolutionaries to create two,
     three, many Vietnams--had been written on Columbia
     University walls by the occupying students. Hayden
     translated the demand to mean expand the strike so
     that the U.S. "must change or send its troops to oc-
     cupy American campuses." Hayden felt the goal re-
     alistic at that time in view of the "explosive mix"
     present on dozens of campuses.

98. Davidson in New Left Notes, June 10, 1968, and the
     Guardian, Dec. 14, 1968, p. 5.

99. Davidson in New Left Notes, June 10, 1968, pp. 6,
     11.

100. Hayden in Ramparts, June 15, 1968, p. 40.

101. Hayden, testimony, Oct. 24, 1968, before National
     Commission on the Causes and Prevention of Vio-
     lence.

102. New Left Notes, June 10, 1968, pp. 6, 11.

103. Henry DeZutter, "SDS: Thunder from the Campus,"
     Chicago Daily News, June 4, 1968.

104. Appleton, Wis., Post-Crescent, June 30, 1968.

105. New Left Notes, Mar. 11, 1968, pp. 1-4.

106. Davidson in New Left Notes, Nov. 13, 1967, p. 4.

107. Morgan Spector in New Left Notes, May 20, 1968,
     p. 2.

108. Guardian, Sept. 28, 1968.

109. HCIS hearings on SDS, pt. 1-A, p. 144.

110. New Left Notes, June 24, 1968.

111. Jeffrey Segal in New Left Notes, June 10, 1968, p. 8.

112. New Left Notes, June 24, 1968.

113. Segal, in New Left Notes, June 10, 1968.

114. Pitt News, June 28, 1968; Madison, Wis., Daily
     Cardinal, June 25, 1968.
          Out-going internal education secretary Robert
     Pardun explained the loose organizational style and
     growing conflict between politically conscious cadre
     and local chapters as due to the fact that "SDS was
     built and is still being built to a large extent out of
     the rebellion of certain segments of American Youth
     against the ideology--that is, parents, schools, cops,
     the draft, et al. The fact that that rebellion takes
     the form of rebellion against all authority, against
     discipline, and against ideology is one of the objec-
     tive conditions which we have had to deal with. "
     (New Left Notes, June 10, 1968, p. 6.)

115. Ibid.; New Left Notes, June 24, 1968; Guardian, June
     22, 1968, p. 5.

116. New Left Notes, June 24, 1968, p. 3.

117. HCIS hearings on SDS, pt. 1-A, p. 144.

118. Guardian, June 22, 1968, p. 1.

119. Guardian, June 22, 1968, pp. 4, 5; see also The Mili-
     tant, July 12, 1968, p. 9.

120. Confirmed by New York Times correspondent on scene,
     later testifying at House Committee on Internal Secu-
     rity. Klonsky's statements were described by a wit-
     ness from the Gainesville, Fla., Police Dept. (See
     HCIS hearings on SDS, pt. 1-A, June 3, 4, 1969.)

121. Guardian, June 22, 1968, p. 4.

122. New Left Notes, June 24, 1968, p. 3.

123. Ibid.

124. Ibid.

125. Ibid.

126. Guardian, June 22, 1968, p. 5.

127. Hoover, testimony, Sept. 18, 1968, before National Commission on the Causes and Prevention of Violence.

128. New Left Notes, June 10, 1968, p. 13.

129. Ibid.

130. New Left Notes, June 24, 1968, p. 3.

131. Ibid.

132. See work-in handbooks inserted in Congressional Record, July 20, 1967, pp. H 9102-9105, and Congressional Record, Apr. 23, 1968, pp. F3282-3283, and New Left Notes of pro-PLP SDS faction, Boston, June 30, 1969, p. 8.

133. Then national secretary Mike Spiegel, who opposed SDS participation in the Chicago demonstrations, stated in New Left Notes on Mar. 4, 1968, that it was unrealistic to think such a confrontation could avoid violence, and the actions might play into the hands of the Democratic political leaders.

134. James L. Gallagher, testimony, Oct. 1, 1968, HCUA hearings on disruption of 1968 Democratic Party National Convention, pp. 2233-2256.

135. SDS' position on electoral politics was also expounded in an "Open Letter" written by Carl Oglesby for SDS use in recruiting among supporters of Senator Eugene McCarthy during the Democratic National Convention in August 1968. The letter, originally appearing in New Left Notes, was printed in pamphlet form and introduced as Committee Exhibit No. 9 in HCIS hearings on SDS, pt. 4, pp. 1115-1120.

136.   Election day 1968 was November 5.

137.   New Left Notes, Oct. 18, 1968, p. 2.

138.   Ibid., p. 3.   SDS policy statements with respect to
       high school students and eye-witness testimony re-
       garding SDS'ers' efforts to bring these younger stu-
       dents into the SDS fold have been summarized in a
       special report issued by the House Committee on In-
       ternal Security in 1969 under the title SDS Plans for
       America's High Schools.

139.   New Left Notes, Oct. 18, 1968, p. 2, col. 1.

140.   Guardian, Oct. 26, 1968, p. 3.

141.   HCIS hearings on SDS, pt. 1-A, June 1969, p. 132.

142.   New Left Notes, Sept. 16, 1968, p. 4.

143.   Testimony, HCIS hearings on SDS, pt. 3-B (George
       Washington University), July 23, 1969; Committee
       Exhibit No. 3-A, pt. 3-A of that hearing; The Wash-
       ington Post, Nov. 5, 1968, p. C-1.

144.   Elections, SDS leaflet, undated.

145.   Jody Allen Gorran, Paul R. Sherburne, and Donald T.
       Appell, testimony, HCIS hearings on SDS, pts. 3-A
       and 3-B (George Washington University), July 22 and
       23, 1969; Guardian, Nov. 16, 1968, p. 20.

146.   Guardian, Sept. 28, 1968.

147.   Boston Globe, Sept. 26, 1968.

148.   Guardian, Nov. 16, 1968, p. 20.

149.   Washington Sunday Star, January 19, 1969.

150.   New Left Notes, Dec. 11, 1968, pp. 4, 5; and New
       York Times, May 5, 1969, pp. 1, 30.

151.   Details of the council actions and differences appeared
       in New Left Notes, Jan. 8, 1969, pp. 1-3, 6; Guard-
       ian, Jan. 11, 1969, pp. 4, 5, and Daily World, Dec.
       31, 1968, p. 3, and Jan. 3, 1969, p. 3.

152. New Left Notes, Jan. 8, 1969, p. 3.

153. Ibid.

154. New Left Notes, Dec. 11, 1968, pp. 4, 5. Committee hearings on the activities of the SDS chapter at George Washington University in the Nation's Capital revealed this same split within the local membership. A minority of chapter members advocated provoking a confrontation with police at the time of the Presidential Inaugural. (HCIS hearings on SDS, pt. 3-B, Committee Exhibit No. 20, pp. 956, 957.)

155. New Left Notes, Jan. 15, 1969, pp. 3, 8.

156. A reference to the non-propertied working class--later interpreted to mean industrial workers--which Marx saw as the motive force for a communist revolution, and whose interest orthodox Marxist-Leninist parties always claimed to represent.

157. Guardian, Dec. 14, 1968.

Chapter 5

"WALLS COME TUMBLIN' DOWN": RESISTANCE BECOMES REVOLUTION, 1969

> The revolution is on! No one can sit on
> the fence any longer and think the revolu-
> tion is something in the future. [1]

"Making history" as far as SDS was concerned in the
early months of 1969 involved increasingly militant trouble-
making. It began, for all practical purposes, with a relatively small street action between 12th and 15th Streets N. W.
in Washington, D. C., along the Pennsylvania Avenue Inaugural
parade route on January 20.

When the President's limousine reached that point in
its procession from the U. S. Capitol to the White House, the
new President was greeted with shouted obscenities and a
shower of sticks, stones, and empty drink cans. The perpetrators were some 1,000 supermilitants, including members of SDS, who had been burning small American flags and
shouting their support for the Vietnamese communists while
waiting for the President to appear. Hundreds of the dissidents thereafter rampaged through the crowded downtown section of Washington, pelting motorists with debris, hurling
rocks at policemen, police cars, and store windows, and repeatedly tangling physically with officers of the law. Among
some 100 persons arrested were two persons identified in
subsequent HCIS committee hearings as SDS activists residing
in Ohio and Iowa. [2] Similarly, the months between January
and May were characterized by an upsurge of activism by
youth both on and off campus. These displays were punctu-
ated by acts of disruption and outright violence. This book's
focus on the activities of Students for a Democratic Society
is not intended to imply that one organization deserves credit
for all of the youthful protest activity--violent or non-violent
--occurring in the years under consideration. SDS was most
prominent in major campus disorders, but many disorders

occurred in which SDS members were not present.   The
reader can find sources relating to other radical groups and
the activist milieu of the sixties by referring to the bibliography.

The Attorney General cited as examples of campus
disruptions in which SDS members were involved: the forci-
ble ejection of officials from a Harvard administration building on April 9; occupation of a building at American University on April 23, at George Washington University on April
24, at Columbia University on April 30, at Stanford University on May 1; and the take-over of a meeting room at Northeastern University on May 13. [3]

SDS members were also named as being associated
with some of the terroristic acts sporadically being reported
on and off campus in this period.   Officials of the FBI noted
that Michael Siskind, a Washington University of St. Louis
student and SDS member, pleaded guilty on February 20,
1969, to attempted fire-bombing of an ROTC installation at
the university on December 3, 1968.   The FBI's most wanted
list contained the name of SDS member and ex-student Cam-
eron Bishop, sought after an indictment involving him in the
January 1969 dynamiting of high-power transmission towers
in the Denver, Colorado area. [4]

BUILDING A WORKER-STUDENT ALLIANCE

Another type of SDS off-campus activism in the spring
was illustrated by the appearance of college students on picket lines of striking workers--actions not confined to those
SDS members favoring the Progressive Labor Party line of
building a worker-student alliance.   The new "revolutionary
youth movement" perspective directing increased SDS attention toward non-student groups, particularly where issues of
"racism" could be raised, was promoted when SDS members
from New Jersey colleges and New York City joined with
black workers engaging in a wildcat strike at the Ford plant
in Mahwah, New Jersey, in late April 1969.   Mark Rudd, of
Columbia University fame, and members of the Black Panther
Party were among those manning the picket lines which succeeded in closing the auto assembly plant for two nights.
The SDS aim was to improve the position of black workers
in the plant and union as SDS activists experimented with
ways to reach white and black workers with their revolutionary message. [5]

A similar effort to establish contacts with workers was attempted in April in the Detroit area when SDS members from the University of Michigan and other chapters joined picket lines of white workers who had called a wildcat strike over safety conditions at an auto parts plant. [6]

Although campus protests seemed to reach a crescendo in the late spring months of April and May, some college students had been engaged in highly publicized direct actions since January of 1969. In the first month of the year, for example, SDS members were collaborating with other campus activists in a sit-in at the University of Chicago over the firing of a "Marxist" professor; helped break up a board of trustees meeting at Stanford University (where several months later a sit-in was staged over the same issues) in a protest against counter-insurgency and war-related research; and reportedly engaged in vandalism in a Columbia University placement office when frustrated demonstrators could not locate recruiters scheduled to arrive on campus from the Air Force and Army. [7]

In February, SDS activists along with others were reported involved in small-scale disorders over dismissal of a professor at Michigan State University; in "mobile" picketing which drove away a CIA recruiter from the University of Houston; and by SDS' own admission, driving off a Standard Oil Company recruiter from San Jose State College in California with an aftermath of smashed windows and kicked-in doors. [8]

In March, SDS activists were involved in a physical attack on other students to disrupt and force cancellation of a speaking appearance by the Mayor of San Francisco at Georgetown University in Washington, D.C., and participated in a screaming chair-throwing protest which cut short remarks at the University of Colorado by Dr. S. I. Hayakawa, acting president of San Francisco State College (both incidents in support of black militants at San Francisco State College). In the same month, SDS co-sponsored a mass talk-in, which disrupted efforts of representatives from Chase Manhattan Bank to recruit at Cornell, as a protest against the bank's investments in South Africa. [9]

In April, SDS-led demonstrators were "sitting-in" nonviolently at American University (against police administrator courses and war-related research on campus and for ethnic and other new studies). An SDS-led occupation of a building

at George Washington University registered SDS' objection to
the school's anti-communist Sino-Soviet Institute as well as to
military recruitment and war research. An open admission
policy for black students was also urged by SDS in this occupation which was accompanied by vandalism. Protests against
ROTC and military recruiters were the issues for non-violent
sit-ins led by SDS at Boston University and co-sponsored by
SDS at Fordham University. Opposition to ROTC, defense
research, and law enforcement officers' training served as
the pretext for several mass actions organized by SDS'ers at
Kent State University in Ohio, which led to physical disruption of a university disciplinary proceeding and minor property damage. [10]

EMPHASIS ON ANTI-MILITARISM

During May, ROTC was the target of an SDS-led take-
over of a meeting room at Northeastern University in Boston,
and both ROTC and military recruiting were the complaints
of SDS-led activists who occupied an administration building
at Dartmouth College. The militarism theme was used by
students, including SDS'ers, who sat-in at Johns Hopkins
University. SDS'ers who co-sponsored a sit-in at New York
University preferred to demand abolition of the grading system and open admissions for area high school graduates. [11]
Sit-ins reported in this period were sometimes disruptive
and/or resulted in property damage, but many of them were
reportedly both non-violent and non-disruptive.

More militant actions credited to SDS in the press in
May included: students led by SDS breaking down the door
to a dean's office at Brooklyn College; SDS participation in
a window- and furniture-breaking spree at the University of
Cincinnati; and involvement with others in physical street
fighting with police as a result of demands raised at Seattle
Community College. The latter actions were reportedly taken
in support of various militant black student demands. [12]

During the investigations and hearings conducted during
1969 by the House Committee on Internal Security into Students for a Democratic Society, detailed eye-witness testimony was received on the disruptive type of activity by SDS
chapters at Georgetown, George Washington, and American
Universities in Washington, D.C., and Kent State University
in Ohio. The testimony disclosed a growing militancy in
these local SDS tactics beginning with the early months of

1969, sometimes stimulated by an infusion of new activists
in the local level and the encouragement of disruptive and
even destructive tactics by full-time SDS organizers assigned
to a regional SDS office.

Issues raised early in 1969 by SDS leaflets, rallies,
film shows (actions which sometimes escalated into intimidat-
ing mass marches, sit-ins, disruptions, and even personal
injury and property damage) were shown to fall into the categories of 1) opposition to so-called militarization of the cam-
pus--basically an anti-Vietnam war theme, and 2) support
for various black militants' demands.   Student power demands
tended to occupy the more pacific chapters, whose "educational"-type activity around some popular aspect of the students' relationship to the university, or other "reformist"
type program, was continued in many parts of the country
without attracting the press attention accorded the more militant SDS chapters.

The increased attention to black militants' demands
apparently implemented the December 1968 National Council
decision to support so-called "black liberation" struggles on
the campuses.

The campaign against "militarization" of the univer-
sities--pursued for some years by a number of SDS chapters
--was alleged to be a favorite of campus-oriented activists
in "elite" universities.   This faction--having representatives
at such places as Harvard, Columbia, Princeton, and the
University of Wisconsin--had failed to win the approval of
the December SDS National Council for their program to
"Smash the Military Machine in the Schools."   The program
would have advanced various non-negotiable demands to rid
the campuses of ROTC and war-related research and recruiters.

A regional SDS conference at Princeton on February
3, 1969, endorsed their program, sometimes referred to as
the Columbia Proposal, along with a revised version drafted
by national secretary Mike Klonsky and others.   Later that
month, the SDS national interim committee endorsed the
"principle" of such a campaign without committing itself to
any of the specific proposals.   The Columbia Proposal was
designed for activists willing to move from resisting "imperialism" to combating it. [13]

On campuses where the "anti-militarization" campaign

was inaugurated--with actions around ROTC, military recruiting, war-related research, etc.--it was often called the SDS
spring offensive. It sometimes involved tactics deliberately
escalating in militancy to invite a confrontation with the university administration. Demands were "non-negotiable" demands, and violent tactics were openly sanctioned by many
participants in the "spring offensive. "14

The reasoning of SDS activists supporting this gradual-
ly escalating campus activity--i. e. , the movement from literature distribution and meetings into strikes, picket lines,
noisy non-violent protests and violent disruptions--was explained in HCIS committee testimony as a belief that forceful
tactics were more effective than persuasive tactics in recruiting the youth needed for a broad "grass roots" movement
which would one day seize power over the institutions of
American society. 15

CONCEPT OF "CONFRONTATION" POLITICS

The recruiting value of even those "confrontation"
politics leading to arrests was explained another way by activists in draft resistance writing in SDS' New Left Notes of
February 12, 1969. The authors claimed to have proven the
generalization about New Left politics which holds that in a
confrontation situation which involves arrests, if the organizers of the action are not immediately overwhelmed, there
is a polarization which is valuable in that it brings latent
tensions to the surface and other people are forced by the
action of the radicals to identify with one of the poles. 16

A witness before the committee who had joined an
SDS chapter at the University of Chicago as an informant for
a Government agency testified that SDS'ers and other New
Leftists he knew looked at disruption and destructive actions
not as an end in itself, but as a method of recruitment
through this process of polarization. Polarization, as defined
by the witness, was a movement of people in the country
toward the left and the right, and immobilization of people
in a middle position, which, in his opinion, could only further
disunity in the nation. Youth were to be polarized toward
the left and a willingness to accept the New Left view of
capitalism and "imperialism" by exposing them, through confrontation politics, to the raw taste of violence or quasi-
violence--all of the unpleasant results, in other words, that
stem from a breakdown in or a breakaway from democratic
processes. 17

By their own accounts, most SDS chapters in the New
York City area concentrated primarily on supporting black
student demands at their schools in the spring of 1969, but
were deeply divided over tactics. Some chapters chose to
follow the tactical lead of separate black student groups.
However, when confronted with black militants who talked of
closing down schools by any means necessary, and with tactics varying from mass actions to "terror," SDS'ers were
admittedly at odds over the degree of escalation they were
willing to support. Some wanted to engage in "clandestine
acts." Others were unwilling to proceed beyond picket lines,
marches, rallies, classroom disruptions, and police confrontations. [18]

When the SDS national council met March 27-30, 1969,
at Austin, Texas, the national body had selected the Black
Panther Party as its closest fraternal ally in the black community. A resolution supported the BPP's program for "liberation" of the black colony within the U.S. and pledged to
provide legal defense and educational efforts in the party's
behalf. The SDS council explained that it considered the
BPP in fact to be the vanguard (leader) of their common
struggles against American capitalism and "imperialism."
However, since the resolution alluded to the BPP's "colonial"
struggle against the "mother country," the PLP-WSA faction
objected on grounds that American blacks were not a colony
but members of an economic group--the so-called working
class. In nominating the Panthers for a leadership role in
the revolutionary movement in the United States, SDS observed that the Panthers were also proponents of a revolution in the country as a whole. [19] Another resolution pledged
SDS support to struggles for the right to self-determination
by the entire "Third World" liberation movement within the
U.S., identified as including the black, "Latino," Puerto
Rican, Chinese, and American Indian communities.

The predominantly white SDS relationship toward black
militant organizations was demonstrated by some of the local
chapter activity. When six SDS chapters in New Jersey held
a series of workshops in Newark on February 22, 1969, BPP
members were in attendance. [20] Two days later, SDS and
the Black Student Union teamed up and occupied the office
of the Seattle Community College, demanding that the college
construct a community-controlled branch campus in central
Seattle's ghetto. [21] In March, members of the BPP and SDS
were arrested for disruptions and the burning of literature
belonging to a Naval aviation recruiting team at the University

of Oregon. [22]   A Panther-oriented student organization, called
the Afro-Americans for Black Liberation, formed a coalition
with SDS and others on certain demands of black students at
the University of Houston.   On March 7, 1,500 demonstrators
"practically dismantled University Center" there. [23]   In New
York City Panthers and SDS New York region leaders held a
joint press conference on March 18 to condemn high school
tracking systems and the use of police in secondary schools. [24]

At the meeting in March, in Austin, Texas, SDS severed its "fraternal" ties with the Southern Student Organizing
Committee on the grounds that SSOC had accepted liberal
foundation money and had supported liberal causes. [25]   SDS
also accused SSOC of being "counter-revolutionary." [26] SSOC,
whose original statement of goals and first proposal of organization were written by an SDS drafter of The Port Huron
Statement (presumably Tom Hayden), dissolved itself on June
8, 1969, at its Mt. Beulah, Mississippi meeting. [27]   It had
been associated with SDS since SSOC's founding in 1964.

During the spring the cooperation between SDS, the
Panthers, and other minority groups appeared to increase.
SDS helped raise bail funds and developed a "full-scale program" to defend Panther leader Fred Hampton, who had faced
ten legal charges, and Cha Cha Jimenez of the Young Lords,
a militant group of Puerto Rican youth, who faced eight
charges in Chicago. [28]   The Panthers, together with SDS,
went to the aid of the United Black Brothers of Mahwah, a
black caucus within the United Auto Workers who had led a
wildcat strike at the Mahwah, New Jersey, Ford Motor assembly plant alluded to earlier.   SDS, the Panthers, the
Young Lords, and the Young Patriots (a Chicago-based, white
radical group) formed a coalition which marched, reportedly
3,000 strong, on the East Chicago police station to protest
the slaying of Manuel Ramos on May 4 by an off-duty policeman. [29]

A committee witness formerly active in SDS at the
University of Chicago reported that by the spring of 1969,
some SDS members were fascinated by the gun-carrying
Black Panthers, viewed them as a very effective and fast-
moving organization, and some of the least responsible
SDS'ers even talked of getting their own guns and becoming
"dramatic revolutionaries." [30]

The SDS National Council, at its March meeting, for
the first time unmistakably pledged support to the Vietnamese

communists and the head of the North Vietnamese communist
government, Ho Chi Minh, identified as leaders of the world's
foremost "liberation" struggle (vis-à-vis U. S. imperialism).
"SDS must take the lead in building support for the Vietnamese
people and their revolutionary leadership, " the council declared.   The resolution attacked both the Progressive Labor
Party and Independent Socialist Club for pinning the label of
traitor on "Comrade Ho" and the National Liberation Front
in South Vietnam because the Vietnamese communists had
agreed to engage in peace negotiations with the U. S. Government. 31

     With some 1, 200 youths in attendance, the SDS Na-
tional Council reportedly beat down all attempts by a powerful pro-PLP contingent to push through its own line, while
agreeing to resolutions pointedly critical of the PLP faction's
tactical and foreign policy positions.

     A reaffirmation of the December decision to promote
the building of a broader revolutionary youth movement was
passed with provisions for a summer program to implement
the move off campus.   The resolution, "Hot Town: Summer
in the City, " called upon college students to converge on
cities for a summer of work, revolutionary study, and organizing in communities--especially among community college
students, high school youth, and street youth, although work
places and the armed services were not to be neglected.
The program would help turn college activists into a "cadre"
in addition to recruiting for the SDS' youth movement.   The
resolution expressed belief in the eventual necessity for a
working-class overthrow of the "ruling class" and assumed
that the road to revolution lay in an eventual armed struggle.
For the immediate future, it expressed hope of developing a
cadre for a revolutionary youth movement which would act
as a white mobilized fighting force, capable of giving "effective" support to black "liberation" struggles in the United
States.   The resolution not only called for organizing the
lowest tracked students in high schools, but also for establishing "bases" in community colleges and in the Armed
Forces.

     The low priority of "student power" demands was
demonstrated by a resolution on the schools which described
such demands as a waste of time in view of the schools'
service to the "capitalist" class.   The action carried by only
a three-vote margin, however, and the position was made
subject to review at the next national convention. 32

Georgetown University

One HCIS committee witness testified concerning the committee's hearings on the Georgetown University chapter that that group had no official membership, no roster of members, nor any formality for membership. He stated that to be a member of SDS at Georgetown one had merely to consider himself a member. [33]

Many chapters when initially organizing had sought recognition from their university's administration, while others, such as Georgetown, did not. Georgetown's SDS membership numbered only about fifteen members, and its initial membership resulted from the absorption of former members of Georgetown's chapter of the Student Peace Union (SPU), which had become dormant following the abolition of the parent body. SDS leaders at Georgetown strove to increase membership by setting up a table on registration day in September, containing SDS and anti-Georgetown literature, including a handbook directed at incoming freshmen. [34] SDS propaganda films were also shown in the freshmen dormitories for purposes of predisposing freshmen toward SDS. SDS' major activity for the year was the disruption of Mayor Alioto's planned speech which, in that chapter's view, was worth the risk because, among other gains, three new members had been recruited, it claimed.

Key leaders of this chapter were Emilio Gonzalez, Edward Galloway, Barry Rubin, and Christopher Murray.

Kent State University

Kent State University's SDS chapter evolved from the Kent Committee to End the War in Vietnam, which had decided that it would receive more recognition on campus under the name of SDS. The newly formed SDS chapter submitted an "innocuous" constitution to the student government which provisionally approved SDS' status, thereby providing the group access to the university facilities. Its temporary status continued until its charter was suspended April 8, 1969. [35]

Not unlike the SDS chapter at Georgetown, the Kent State chapter was also small--15 to 24 members out of a school enrollment of 21,000--had no known officers, only "leaders," and no chapter dues.

Kent State's score of SDS members could on occasion, however, muster 150-200 non-members for its major activities on campus. As in the case of the "Alioto incident" at Georgetown, Kent's chapter was able to draw upon assistance from its regional SDS staff located in Cleveland, which was composed of Corky Benedict, Lisa Meisel, Terry Robbins, Bobbi Smith, and Charles Tabasko. The chapter at Kent State, like Georgetown, also received propaganda films produced by Newsreel, a New York-based producer and supplier of New Left films. [36]

During an April 16, 1969, SDS demonstration at Kent State, it was discovered that ten of the fifty-eight persons arrested were not enrolled at the school. Jim Mellen of the REP at Ann Arbor was a guest speaker at a rally which sparked the violence previously mentioned. At subsequent rallies and meetings, regional and national SDS officials also made appearances on campus, including Bernardine Dohrn, the national interorganizational secretary. After the SDS chapter at Kent State was banned on campus, the group continued to use university facilities by the subterfuge of operating under the sponsorship of a local Yippie group. [37] (Georgetown's unofficial SDS chapter operated in a similar manner when it utilized the Student Peace Union chapter's credentials to secure on-campus meeting rooms.)

Leaders of Kent State's chapter were students Howard Emmer, Colin Neiburger, and Edward Erickson, together with Jeffrey Powell, George Gibeaut, and Joyce Cecora, none of whom were students at the university.

George Washington University

George Washington University (GW) granted recognition to an SDS chapter at that institution in April 1966. The chapter, not having a constitution, filed a required certification with the university to the effect that it accepted members without regard to race, religion, national origin, or political persuasion. The certificate was signed by Mike Spiegel, future national interim committee member, then attached to SDS' Washington regional office. The chapter was not officially required to list its officers or membership, but only the names of two persons whom the university could hold responsible for the group's activities.

GW SDS, as with all SDS chapters, permitted--actually

welcomed--non-members to actively participate in its activities. Since chapter dues were not solicited by GW SDS,
funds were acquired by passing a hat at meetings. The group
encouraged its members to acquire the additional national
membership because the assignment of chapter delegates to
the annual convention and to the National Council was based
upon the number of national members who belonged to local
chapters. GW SDS, the largest chapter in the Washington
area, had about 35-50 members (or one percent of the university's undergraduate enrollment), including 15-20 national
members. Its steering committee was formed by both local
and national members. This chapter could attract up to two
hundred non-SDS students to its major activities. HCIS testimony indicated that the GW chapter was generally non-violent
in its methods except when agitated or pushed by non-GW
students or by national or regional directives. The hub of
Washington area SDS activities was the Washington regional
office which was created in September 1967 on the basis of
a $200 loan from the SDS national organization. Its key
leaders were Cathlyn Wilkerson, who gave up the editorship
of New Left Notes to assume the post, Michael Spiegel, and
Jonathan Lerner; all present or former leaders of the national body.

Recruitment techniques of GW SDS were similar to
those employed in other chapters: dorm "raps" (discussions),
Newsreel film showings, literature, and rallies. The Washington outlet for Newsreel was Washington Newsreel, located
at the headquarters of the Washington regional SDS office at
1829 Corcoran Street N.W., Washington, D.C. [38]

A Newsreel documentary film on the student rebellion
at Columbia University April 23, 1968, was among films
shown by the SDS chapter at GWU on the first anniversary
of that uprising. The film, as edited and produced under the
name "The Columbia Revolt," evoked feelings of hostility
among student viewers and was clearly intended to move uncommitted GWU students to similar actions, HCIS committee
hearings revealed. An SDS leader called upon the audience
to join in an SDS-led occupation of one of the GWU buildings
which immediately followed the film showing. [39]

Among the leaders of the SDS take-over of a GWU
building were Nick Greer, student and temporary chairman
of the local SDS chapter, fellow students Chris Folkemer and
David Camp, and non-students Lincoln Pain, William Smiley,
David Phillips, and Cathy Wilkerson.

The American University

The SDS chapter at American University (AU), organized in the fall of 1968, was officially recognized by AU after it had submitted a copy of its constitution, a list of its officers for 1968-69, and an application for recognition. These documents were submitted solely for purposes of acquiring the use of AU's facilities and had no intrinsic value to AU SDS members. [40]

The AU chapter was also loosely organized, having no membership or dues requirements or formal meeting place. Financing was conducted on a contribution basis. Attendance at meetings ranged from 12-15 to a high of 150. The AU chapter used the printing facilities at the Washington regional office or at the university to publish its literature. The AU SDS showed the same Newsreel films that other area colleges used and sponsored. Membership in the AU chapter decreased during the early part of 1969 because of differences of opinion by the membership over the use of violence. A second feature which tended to hold down membership was that the lines of communication between the students and AU's administration were kept open. The administration had also initiated certain changes requested by the students. Another factor which had an adverse effect on recruiting was the resentment created on campus by SDS when, on April 23, 1969, its members occupied the offices of the president of the university after he had been forcibly ejected from the building.

Key leaders and activists of AU's chapter included: Frederic Barsky, Meredith Malmberg, Jack Davis, Garth Sapan, and William Levy.

University of Chicago

The SDS chapter at the University of Chicago (UC) numbered about seventy persons. Attendance at SDS meetings, however, numbered as high as one hundred individuals or, on special occasions, 150. During its January 1969 occupation of UC's administration building, the UC SDS chapter was able to organize about 400 demonstrators. As with many SDS chapters, UC's had no elected officers, and those who conducted its affairs were referred to only as "leaders."

Key chapter leaders and activists were: Howard Machtinger, later a member of the NIC, Daniel Friedlander,

Jane Spielman, Christopher Hobson, David Klafter, Ernst
Dornfield, Jeff Blum, Sally Yogel, and Steve Rothkrug.

The location of UC in the city of Chicago provided that
university's local chapter with the opportunity to draw upon
the services both of regional officers, such as Les Coleman,
and national officials or leaders, such as Bernardine Dohrn,
Mike Klonsky, Mark Rudd, and Tom Hayden.

New Left propaganda movies provided by Newsreel
were part of the regular fare offered by the chapter to non-
SDS students. One movie, which depicted the Columbia University revolt, served as an organizational aid because it
taught, through example, how similar demonstrations should
be conducted.

During a two-week sit-in at UC's administration building SDS provided the participants, many of whom were non-
SDS, with mimeographing services and instructive leaflets.

An insight into how factional problems affected the relationship between the regional and national offices of SDS
was provided during HCIS committee hearings. By the spring
of 1969, testimony showed, the national office of SDS was
ready to dispense with its famed principle of participatory
democracy when it proved to be a handicap in its power struggle with PLP members and sympathizers in the Worker-Student Alliance faction.

A witness testified that the national office had sought
the aid of the Black Panther Party in bringing SDS regional
offices "into line" and under the national office "thumb."
The reason was that regional offices were "too independent"
and therefore fair game for capture by the pro-PLP elements
within SDS.[41]

Regional offices, as well as chapters, were supposedly autonomous units. Constitutionally, regional offices were
"fundamentally responsible" to chapters within a region,
rather than to the national office.[42]

SDS BLOW-UP AT JUNE 1969 CONVENTION

The differing views on tactics and objectives which
had coexisted within the SDS organization in the past degenerated into a civil war when the national convention of SDS
was held at the Chicago Coliseum June 18-22, 1969.

The convention marked the first in a series of irreversible splitoffs of dissenting members into separate and competing organizations or no organization at all. It was the beginning of the rapid decline of SDS from its status as the largest New Left student organization to appear on the American scene since masses of youth discovered the technique of direct action less than a decade before.

At least 1, 500 delegates reportedly attended the national convention. Approximately 600 delegates belonged to the Worker-Student Alliance caucus dominated by members of the Maoist Progressive Labor Party. Although it represented only a minority of the entire national SDS membership, the WSA delegation was acknowledged to be the largest single faction at the convention. Many observers felt that the caucus was in an exceedingly favorable position for a power play.

The advantage enjoyed by the pro-PLP elements was demonstrated early in the proceedings when they succeeded in pushing the passage of two resolutions dealing with procedural matters. Only one such resolution was achieved by anti-PLP forces, led by a majority of the national SDS leadership and referred to as the "national office" crowd or "regulars" for purposes of clarity hereafter.

During the first three days of the convention, pro- and anti-PLP forces contended for the support of uncommitted delegates as well as many delegates belonging to other factions within SDS.

When the convention began, the majority of SDS national leaders, while agreeing to unite to prevent a PLP takeover of the organization, was nevertheless badly split over tactics by which SDS should build a revolutionary youth movement. (Although national leaders remained united during the convention to fight the WSA caucus, their continued differences after the convention resulted in their division into a Revolutionary Youth Movement I faction--also known as the Weathermen--and a Revolutionary Youth Movement II faction.)

Other smaller factions which sent delegates to the SDS national convention included members and supporters of the Independent Socialist Clubs, an SDS Labor Committee from New York, and a Joe Hill caucus from San Francisco. Members of the Communist Party, U. S. A. , and its youth group, the W. E. B. DuBois Clubs of America, also formed

a caucus at the convention. Members of the Trotskyist communist youth group, the Young Socialist Alliance, sent what
it described as "observers. "

In its struggles with the powerful WSA caucus, the
national office group relied heavily upon their allies from the
Black Panther Party, the Young Lords, a militant Puerto
Rican group, and the Brown Berets, a militant Mexican-American organization. Spokesmen for those groups appeared on
the convention podium to attack the WSA caucus.

The radical weekly, the Guardian, expressed the view
that the convention fight against WSA was due not only to the
national office fear of a WSA take-over of the organization.
A second reason, according to the weekly, was a "virtual
ultimatum" to SDS leaders from such groups as the Black
Panthers, who objected to the WSA criticism of "nationalist"
sentiments by racial minorities. [43]

The national office group did not risk a showdown vote
with the WSA forces, however. It chose instead to lead a
walkout of a numerical minority of the delegates late on the
third day of the convention proceedings, June 20. After another day of deliberations in an adjacent meeting room, the
group's spokesmen returned to the convention floor to an-
nounce that they were expelling all members of SDS favoring
the policies of the Progressive Labor Party. Delegates loyal
to the national office majority of "regulars" then gathered at
a church for a separate convention on June 22. The National
officers were elected and a program of action adopted. [44]

The program adopted by this SDS group promised
"mass struggle and militant action" in the summer and fall
of 1969. Increasingly militant demonstrations were to be
staged, calling for withdrawal of American forces from Vietnam. They would reach a climax with a mass demonstration
on the streets of Chicago in the fall, which would also serve
to register SDS support for defendants on trial in that city
on conspiracy charges as a result of rioting at the time of
the 1968 Democratic National Convention. The demonstrations
were also designed to indicate SDS endorsement of the Black
Panther Party and "GI rebellions, " the convention resolution
declared. SDS'ers at this convention session, in addition,
resolved to engage in summer "political" work in the communities and to set up "revolutionary collectives" as part of
their overall objective of building a revolutionary youth movement in America.

Those SDS'ers preferring the policies of the Worker-Student Alliance caucus dominated by the PLP had remained in session in the Chicago Coliseum. On June 22, they also elected a slate of national officers of "SDS" and committed them to a different tactical line.

A resolution dealing with a "tactical program" emphasized the need for SDS'ers on college campuses to establish alliances with "workers" on the campuses, for a struggle against university expansion into neighborhoods where such building programs would have "racist" implications, for campaigns against "racist" courses and institutes at colleges and universities, and for support to "black rebellions." War-related issues were given second billing in the resolutions of this SDS convention. [45]

National officers elected by the "regulars" in session at the church were: Mark Rudd, national secretary; Jeffrey Jones, interorganizational secretary; and William Ayers, education secretary. Its national interim committee was: Howard Machtinger, Chicago; Linda Evans, Detroit; Robert Avakian, San Francisco; Corky Benedict, Cleveland; Barbara Reilly, New York; Noel Ignatin, Chicago; Michael Klonsky, Chicago; and Bernardine Dohrn, Chicago.

The PLP-WSA faction elected a slate of officers with the same titles: John Pennington, a New England regional traveler, as national secretary; Alan Spector, also a New England regional traveler, as education secretary; and Pat Forman of San Francisco State, as interorganizational secretary. Its national interim committee was: Edward Galloway, Georgetown; Michael Golash, Columbia; Fred Gordon, former education secretary; Jared Israel, Harvard-Radcliffe; Leslie Lincoln, University of California (Irvine); Sandy Meyer, University of Illinois (Circle); Becky Reavis, University of Texas; and David Rosoff, Cornell. [46] Alternates Gordon DeMarco, San Francisco State, and James Prickett, San Diego, became regular NIC members at a later date. [47]

The anti-PLP forces seized the national headquarters at 1608 West Madison Street in Chicago--an action which gave it exclusive access to the treasury, membership lists, and printing press. The competing SDS organization growing out of the WSA caucus was forced to set up shop at 173A Massachusetts Avenue in Boston. Both SDS organizations insisted on using the name New Left Notes for their official publications. The national organization in Boston continued

to publish using the name into the summer of 1970.   The
Chicago-based group changed the name of its publication to
FIRE! in November 1969, but it appeared only twice--the
latest and probably last issue appearing under date of January
30, 1970. [48]

        After the SDS group headquartered in Chicago voted to
expel all PLP members, it adopted a kind of loyalty oath to
keep out members who might be inclined to promote Progressive Labor Party politics.   The resolution stated that SDS
members would hereafter be expected to agree to support
domestic "national liberation" struggles by black and Latin
"colonies" (with a right of secession for such groups if they
desired it) and to support abroad the South Vietnamese communist revolutionaries, and the communist governments of
North Vietnam, North Korea, China, Albania, and Cuba.
(PLP'ers had tended to echo Red Chinese criticisms of certain policies of other communist regimes, which in recent
years have included both Cuba and North Vietnam.   The PLP
opposition to "nationalist" objectives of various minority
groups in the U. S. has already been noted.)

        A majority of national offices had been awarded at the
convention of the Chicago-based SDS movement to a group
headed by Mark Rudd, William Ayers, Jeff Jones, and Bernardine Dohrn.   They became known as leaders of the RYM
I or "Weatherman" faction of SDS.   The nickname derived
from the title of a policy paper they submitted to the con-
vention--"You don't need a weatherman to know which way
the wind blows" (a line from a Bob Dylan song).

        A minority of national officers had backed different
tactics for building a revolutionary youth movement.   Their
views were submitted in a paper titled "Revolutionary Youth
Movement II. "   The title thereafter served to designate members of this faction, the most prominent of whom was former
national secretary Mike Klonsky. [49]

        No changes in organizational structure were attempted
at this time which would make any of the positions of the
three major SDS groupings binding on any of the SDS membership.   Some observers noted that, while proposed tactics
might vary, the revolutionary communist orientation of each
of the groups appeared very similar to activists who were
disinterested or even repelled by commitment to a rigid ideology.

The radical Guardian reported that large numbers of
SDS members, including entire chapters on some college
campuses, refused to ally with any of the factions. Such
"independent" positions were taken by the chapters at the University of Wisconsin, and Brooklyn and City Colleges in New
York, as well as by groupings in San Francisco and Stanford,
California, the newspaper maintained. [50]

RELATIONS WITH PANTHERS BECOME STRAINED

The Black Panther Party and other nationalist groups
such as the Young Lords and Brown Berets were extolled in
the newspaper of the Chicago-based SDS following the convention at which they had helped rid the organization of the
Worker-Student Alliance faction. Continued cooperative relations were demonstrated by a rally in Chicago on July 4,
1969, which was co-sponsored by SDS, the Illinois BPP, the
Young Lords, and the Young Patriots. [51]

The SDS relationship with the Black Panther Party became strained, however, as a result of a national conference
called by the Panthers for the purpose of creating a so-called
United Front Against Fascism.

Some 3,000 leftists, predominantly white and representing about forty organizations, allegedly responded to the
BPP call for a conference in Oakland, California, July 18-
21, 1969. Eight of the eleven members of the SDS national
interim committee attended, including the three national secretaries. Groups such as the Communist Party, U.S.A.,
and women's liberation were also represented. The Progressive Labor Party and its sympathizers in the Boston-based
SDS organization were barred, however. The Panthers also
reportedly prevented such left groups as the Independent Socialist Clubs and the Spartacist League from distributing their
literature at the conference. [52]

The Panthers sought support through the conference
for a nation-wide campaign in behalf of decentralizing police
departments and placing police forces under community control. People attending the conference were expected to sign
up to work in United Front Against Fascism committees to
circulate petitions calling for such community control of the
police. [53]

National SDS, dominated by the Weatherman faction,

refused to endorse all aspects of the Panthers' proposed petition campaign.   SDS officials were in agreement with campaigns for community control of the police in "black and
brown communities."   They objected to working for similar
control in white communities, however, on the grounds it
would serve to strengthen "white supremacy."

The Black Panther Party in turn refused an SDS request that the program of a United Front Against Fascism
include support for the SDS demonstration scheduled for the
streets of Chicago in October 1969. [54]

SDS officers reported that other struggles arose during
the United Front Against Fascism conference, involving other
left groups including the CPUSA.   SDS speakers were described as critical of the CPUSA, whose chief theoretician,
Herbert Aptheker, shared the speaker's platform with spokesmen for SDS and other groups.   SDS leaders later declared
they were distressed that the BPP had to run to the CPUSA
for "alliance and material aid."[55]

The Panther-SDS dispute grew more heated following
the conference.   Panther chief of staff David Hilliard declared in an interview that SDS was not so very revolutionary
and that the only white revolutionaries respected by the
Panthers were the Young Patriots.

"We see SDS," said the Panthers' chief of staff, "as
just being another pacification front that's given credit by the
fascist establishment in order to cause confusion in hopes
that this would weaken the support for the Black Panther
Party."[56]

Hilliard denied that the Panthers were aligned with
the CPUSA, which he characterized as an autocracy controlled
by Gus Hall, but conceded that it was "aligned" with certain
factions within the Communist Party.   He specified that those
were the Communists with whom the Panthers had worked on
the UFAF conference and afterwards. [57]

The Boston-based SDS, meanwhile, also contended with
the Chicago-based SDS, sometimes with actual physical violence.   On July 7, 1969, for example, 75 PLP and WSA
members attempted to disrupt a meeting of Weatherman SDS'
New York region at New York University, breaking furniture
and a large plate glass wall, injuring several students in the
process. [58]

WEATHERMAN ACTIVITY--SUMMER OF 1969

The so-called Weatherman faction, which controlled the SDS national organization headquartered in Chicago after the June 1969 convention and included the three national secretaries of SDS, spoke of its goal in global terms: to help achieve the "destruction of US imperialism and the achievement of a classless world: world communism."

Achievement of this goal, the Weatherman position declared, would depend upon white youth organizing themselves into a fighting movement which would operate as part of an international liberation army. A vanguard or leadership role was assigned to revolutionary struggles by "Third World" people such as the Vietnamese communists and by black nationalist revolutionaries within the United States. Ousting of the present U.S. power structure was foreseen only as part of a world struggle, when U.S. military forces had overextended themselves abroad and were being defeated piecemeal. (Some SDS national leaders talked of a future "socialist" society in the U.S. but others referred vaguely to a society which offered "power to the people.")

Defining revolution as a "power struggle" which eventually would involve "armed struggle," the Weathermen declared that a revolutionary movement would become part of a "revolutionary war" when it was powerful enough to defend itself militarily against repression. Eventually, a revolutionary "Marxist-Leninist" party should be formed of cadres operating on a conspiratorial level after the fashion of some Castroite guerrilla movements in Latin America. There was also a need for some kind of revolutionary mass base of persons similar to the Red Guard in communist China, with a "full willingness to participate in the violent and illegal struggle," according to the Weatherman position. [59]

National secretaries Mark Rudd and Bill Ayers, in a television interview in August 1969, described themselves as "communists" who were allied with all the "peoples of the world" struggling against so-called "U.S. imperialism" and who did not think in terms of "loyalty" to any particular communist nation. [60]

A former member of the Weatherman faction explained to the HCIS committee that the group envisioned itself to be part of an international communist movement, although it had no allegiance to other communist movements in the sense of

accepting directives. The Weathermen, according to the
source, disliked Soviet society on grounds that the use of
wage incentives tended to restore competitive, capitalistic
practices. They were most sympathetic to the communist
regimes of Cuba and China where some SDS'ers were in-
trigued by governmental efforts to remold individualistic,
competitive man into a "socialist" man. The Weatherman
cadre organized into "revolutionary collectives," studied the
writings of Marx, Lenin, Mao Tse-tung, Ho Chi Minh, and
Ché Guevara, but were most concerned about training themselves to be full-time revolutionaries and working out a strategy particularly suitable to the conditions in the United States,
according to the same informant who was a member of such
a collective.

The collective was a newly structured grouping devised
by the Weathermen for its full-time organizers or cadres who
would live, study, and plan their organizing efforts together.
In addition to advancing the revolutionary movement by joint
effort, SDS members engaged in mental and physical discipline
in the hope of thereby becoming more effective revolutionaries.
They practiced karate on the theory that the body could be
used as a weapon, and engaged in self-criticism, as well as
receiving criticism from other members of the group, in imi-
tation of what they understood to be part of the Red Chinese
program for creating a new communist or socialist man.

The Weathermen put their tactics into practice in the
summer of 1969.

Testimony received by the HCIS showed that SDS concentrated on organizing high school students and teenage drop-
outs in Columbus and Akron, Ohio, Detroit, and Pittsburgh.
Columbus, Akron, and Detroit served as summer project
headquarters. Other youths in community colleges and in the
armed services were also included in SDS' organizing efforts.
The ultimate recruitment of these youths organized by SDS
was a prime purpose of the summer project, as well as the
development of an experienced cadre from among the organizers who would assist SDS to become a mobilized fighting
force.

SDS'ers were expected to form revolutionary collectives
during the summer and to organize groups trained in karate,
street mobility, and emergency first aid. The police and the
Army were the prospective targets for those who were being
trained by SDS.

In Columbus, about thirty SDS members, living a semi-communal life in three residences, participated. Only about six were from Columbus, however. Funds from temporary jobs and aid from parents supported their activity.

SDS posters in Columbus announced that the object of the summer program there was to develop a cadre of sixteen-year-old communist guerrillas with which to smash the "pig power structure."[61]

SDS members used the lures of free beer and wine and a display of weaponry as organizing measures to entice young teenagers to join them at the Columbus collectives for more discussion on their program. The general thrust of the SDS "pitch" to teenagers was that they should provoke the police and create confrontations which in turn would develop sympathy for their cause.

Youths in a lower income neighborhood in Columbus were told by the SDS organizers that the poor should take money from the rich so that all would be equal. To accomplish this, the prospective SDS recruits should "knock off the police and burn down the stores and stuff like that, so that they can get the money."[62]

While SDS perpetrated acts of vandalism in Columbus and expended considerable efforts to organize youth, an HCIS committee witness testified that SDS' summer program failed as a recruitment measure. For example, by mid-August, SDS members found themselves engaged in fist fights with youths from lower-income families who believed that SDS' middle-income members didn't understand the problems of the poor.

SDS organizers had talked about getting and using guns and running around the streets, particularly at their proposed "national action" in Chicago in the fall. Some Columbus youths who had lived and run in the streets as youngsters believed that this was just "romantic" talk.

The SDS'ers in Columbus had access to a mimeograph machine which was the property of a church. Money for mimeograph paper was raised locally because the national office provided none. The HCIS hearing record revealed, moreover, that money always went to SDS' Chicago headquarters,[63] rather than to its field workers.

During July 1969, SDS carried its summer program into Garfield High School in Akron, Ohio, and invited the students who were taking summer courses to go outside with them for talks. Leaflets, which equated the role of teachers with that of the police, were distributed in the classrooms. Recruitment at this high school was also a failure because student interest ranged from disinterest to active antagonism toward SDS. SDS organizers in Akron, as in Columbus, included members from other parts of Ohio and from other states. Also, as in Columbus, three houses, or so-called collectives, were rented for the purpose of providing SDS members with living quarters and temporary local headquarters.

In preparation for its summer program in Detroit, SDS rented a number of dwellings in the Motor City. Orientation meetings were conducted by William Ayers, national education secretary, on the weekend of May 31-June 1. SDS organizers studiously prepared themselves by reviewing the income level and ethnic background of the inhabitants in various sections of the city, as well as the situation (i. e., agitation potential) in local high schools, and in the labor sector. Organizers were also advised of what procedure to follow if arrested.

On May 30 and 31, at a rock festival at the State fairgrounds near Detroit, mimeographed leaflets were circulated to high school youths, inviting them to get acquainted with SDS over the summer months. As in the other summer programs in urban areas, SDS placed emphasis on recruiting youths to attend its forthcoming, so-called "national action" in Chicago, in October. Of equal importance, SDS wished to build up a permanent Detroit SDS organization. SDS members made appearances at the Henry Ford Community College, at rock concerts, drive-ins, and a suburban beach. Working youths, high school students, "freaks, " and "greasers" represented the types of persons SDS sought to enlist in its activities.

The Motor City SDS members met with the same unsatisfactory response from the students at Macomb County Community College in Warren, Michigan, as their SDS colleagues had received in Ohio. Ten young women disrupted an exam on July 31 at the college by making speeches, sprinkled with obscenities, on the subjects of women's liberation, the war in Vietnam, and black "oppression" in America. One committee witness said that the antics of these

women would more likely drive students further away from
SDS' views.

Vandalism in the form of slogans painted on walls and
walkways was employed against five Detroit high schools, followed up by the distribution of propaganda leaflets.   These
high schools were also invaded by SDS activists who chanted
slogans and handed out literature.   Violence broke out at one
high school when fifteen non-student demonstrators attacked
two teachers, one a man and the other a woman.

SDS literature invited students to join SDS' revolutionary youth movement and to join the fight on the side of the
communists in Vietnam and the so-called liberation fighters
in the United States. [64]

An organizing technique used in Detroit by SDS included a street action to prepare demonstrators for the proposed "national action, " which would include street fighting
in Chicago.   The focal point of this street action was Detroit's Wayne State University, which SDS charged was "everyone's enemy" because of its war research and racism.
SDS leaflets suggested that travelers to Chicago bring helmets, goggles, bail money, and "boots for running and kick-
ing. "[65]

On September 3, 1969, following plans formulated at
a Midwest Regional SDS Conference in Cleveland, August 29-
31, SDS moved into Pittsburgh with two dozen demonstrators,
only two of whom were Pennsylvanians.   Participants came
from Illinois, Michigan, New York, Ohio, New Jersey, and
Colorado.   As in many SDS summer actions elsewhere, wom-
en of what the Weathermen called their "red army" were in
the vanguard.   Twenty young women commandeered the facilities, including the mimeograph machine, of the American
Friends Service Committee (AFSC) in Pittsburgh to produce
propaganda leaflets for high school actions which began on
September 4.   Protests from six AFSC staffers were ignored
by the SDS women who threatened them with violence.

At noon on September 4, about fifty young females invaded the South Hills High School in Pittsburgh, distributed
leaflets, and disrupted classes.   Twenty to twenty-five young
women ran through the hallways chanting slogans.   Some reportedly lifted their blouses and T-shirts to display bare
breasts.   Twenty-six demonstrators were placed under arrest.   They were subsequently found guilty of disorderly

conduct and fined. SDS leaflets urged students to go to Chicago and participate in the National Action planned by the "Weatherman"-controlled national organization.

HCIS committee witnesses said that SDS tactics in Pittsburgh were ineffective as a recruiting technique. The SDS "women's militia" had even alienated local members of SDS, including members of the University of Pittsburgh chapter, by their expressions of contempt for the work of UP SDS. 66

All the above-mentioned summer action programs were, in effect, preparatory training courses for SDS' mass National Action planned for Chicago, October 8-11, 1969. Arrangements for the National Action were made at a meeting held in Cleveland, August 29-31, 1969. Mark Rudd, SDS' chief executive, predicted that the Chicago action would bring "thousands and thousands" of young people to Chicago to fight the Government and the police. 67 Capitalizing on youth's restlessness and dissatisfactions, SDS intended to bring youngsters to Chicago for further training as part of a fighting revolutionary youth movement. The Chicago action would mark the opening of a "second front" (i.e., for the Vietcong). It would bring the Vietnam War to America.

THE WEATHERMAN'S "NATIONAL ACTION" IN CHICAGO

From October 9-11, 1969, the SDS Weatherman-controlled national organization and its supporters engaged in repeated violent confrontations with the Chicago police.

A week prior to the "national action," Washington, D.C. police stopped a vehicle occupied by several members of SDS. In the auto were ten three-foot lengths of quarter-inch chain, ten steel helmets, and twelve gas masks. HCIS committee investigation revealed that one of the occupants of the vehicle and three other youths--all Weathermen from Baltimore, Maryland--had recently purchased nearly $300 worth of similar materials from a Washington, D.C. firm. All were subsequently arrested for mob action during the Weathermen's National Action in Chicago.

The SDS national office had sent out notices to its members offering medical and legal aid for those who came to tear apart "pig city. "68 Potential demonstrators were

advised to take first-aid training and to become familiar with
"street" medicine. SDS suggested that as much bail money
as possible be brought to Chicago. Lawyers would also be
on call. Militant wall posters, prepared and distributed for
posting around Chicago, stated that SDS'ers had "to actively
fight." SDS was bringing "the war home" and "Amerika"
would be "the final front."[69]

In an instructive article in New Left Notes in September, SDS expounded on the virtues of street fighting by "affinity groups." An affinity group, as defined by SDS, was a
group of people who had some reason for "hanging together."[70]
It was composed of youths who trusted each other, went
around or attended school together. The advantage of these
small-group operations was not merely that of street mobility,
but also in a "tight scene" (i.e., a fight) with the police it
would prove advantageous. Moreover, since these groups
were expected to return home and conduct their own local
actions, based upon their October experience in Chicago, it
would prove helpful if the members of such units knew each
other before taking part in the National Action.[71]

SDS also arranged for "Movement centers" where
National Action participants could eat, sleep, plan, and organize their "affinity" groups.

Competitively, Revolutionary Youth Movement II (RYM
II), a faction within the national organization which differed
ideologically and operationally with Weatherman or RYM I,
planned separate demonstrations at the same time in Chicago.

During the four-day action, SDS founder Tom Hayden
addressed the demonstrators, as did SDS leader Bernardine
Dohrn. Many demonstrators were equipped with white helmets and heavy sticks, to some of which were attached Vietcong flags. Some demonstrators had six-inch lengths of
one-inch or half-inch pipe. Four SDS'ers were arrested
and charged with possession of Molotov cocktails.

Violence reached a climax on the final day of the
SDS National Action. Hundreds of demonstrators marching
in downtown Chicago suddenly went on a rampage. Rocks,
railroad flares, and lengths of chain were pulled from beneath the garments of demonstrators and used to break windows of stores and autos along the parade route. Some
demonstrators charged headlong into police officers, more
than fifty of whom were injured before the rioting was

quelled. An assistant corporation counsel for the city of
Chicago was completely paralyzed from the neck down for
weeks after he was assaulted by one of the demonstrators. [72]

The hearings disclosed that only 600 youths, instead
of the predicted "tens of thousands," made an appearance in
Chicago. The police made 283 arrests, of which 83 were
females. Of those arrested, 108 were students. The participants came from 25 states, the District of Columbia, and
Canada, revealing the mobility of some SDS activists. [73]

RYM II, in contrast to the destructive mob actions of
Weatherman SDS'ers, conducted a non-violent, orderly demonstration. RYM II rallies were aimed to enlist support
from "exploited" workers at the International Harvester Trac-
tor Works and at the Cook County Hospital.

An HCIS committee investigator testified that while
RYM II did not reject the Weathermen's position on armed
revolutionary struggle in America, it believed that this struggle should wait until the revolutionary forces and the "masses"
were prepared for it.

The National Action, to some observers, signaled a
striking application of the turn by an SDS faction from "resistance" and "provocation" tactics to the tactics of premedi-
tated physical attacks or "combat." The new tactics were
in keeping with the Weathermen's repeated proclamations at
this time that "the revolution is on" in the United States. [74]

The last public meeting held by the Weathermen after
what observers labeled as the Chicago "fiasco" was a National Council meeting at Flint, Michigan, December 26-31,
1969. Dubbed the "war council" by the Weathermen, its 400
participants were not all supporters of the "fighting in the
streets" line. A number of radicals reported being turned
off by Weatherman discussions of violence for the sake of
violence, which included expressions of delight by a national
officer over a then recent mass murder carried out by a
group of hippie cultists in California. [75]

Weatherman leaders expressed their preference at the
war council for operating a small paramilitary organization
which could carry out urban guerrilla warfare, the Director
of the FBI has revealed. They envisioned an underground
movement, using tactics such as those employed by Arab
terrorists, according to Mr. Hoover, and stressed the

absolute necessity for killing police.   Weathermen also called
for self-instruction in the use of guns and bombs. 76

HCIS committee investigation disclosed that publications
available at the war council included a manual on the pur-
chase, handling, and firing of various types of guns.   The
manual was titled Firearms and Self-Defense, a Handbook for
Radicals, Revolutionaries and Easy Riders, published in December 1969 by an International Liberation School, Berkeley,
California.

The tone of the council meeting was carried out in the
decorations as well.   From the ceiling of the meeting hall
hung a six-and-one-half-foot cardboard replica of a machine
gun.

Following the October street violence in Chicago a
former Weatherman stated that many members left SDS--
sending membership well below the 300-400 estimated to be
in the faction at the time of the National Action.   Former
SDS chapters which did not agree with the Weatherman off-
campus line were simply not recognized by Weathermen as
belonging to SDS, the committee was informed.   There was
little to appeal to a college youth in the Weathermen's position that youths should quit school to join a movement of
revolutionary cadres and that all schools should be shut down.
Some chapters publicly changed their name or dissolved in
an effort to disassociate themselves from Weatherman violence.

An ex-Weatherman accurately predicted that remaining
Weatherman activists would operate underground in 1970.

REVOLUTIONARY YOUTH MOVEMENT II

The faction of the Chicago-based SDS, headed by Mike
Klonsky and dubbed Revolutionary Youth Movement II, operated
as an "internal" faction from shortly before the June 1969
national SDS convention until November of the same year.

The position paper of RYM II submitted to the June
convention showed that its backers had agreed to support the
idea of an eventual armed struggle in the U.S. for communist goals.   It supported creation of a revolutionary youth
movement which would work toward such goals, but differed
from the Weathermen in urging that SDS tactics be aimed at

winning masses of supporters. Workers, young and old,
and members of minority groups could become allies if SDS
worked to support the needs of such groups and did not engage in self-isolating super-militant acts, RYM II claimed.

Eventual violent revolution in the United States was
foreseen and expressed in near-orthodox Marxist terms.
RYM II declared, for example, that the U.S. "ruling class"
must be deposed by the "proletariat" in a "violent civil war, "
following which a "dictatorship of the proletariat" would be
established. The role of the revolutionary youth movement
was to "seed" a larger movement and help to create the
"revolutionary cadre" needed to develop a "communist" party
to lead the revolution. This future "communist" or "Marxist-
Leninist" party would be "guided by the science of the proletariat, the teachings of Marx, Engels, Lenin, Stalin, and
Mao. " SDS members were to "take seriously the job of
helping to build the communist party" and begin by studying
"revolutionary principles of organization as Lenin, Mao, and
others have written about them, " and by "taking communist
ideology to the mass of the people. "[77]

The Weatherman program for street fighting in Chicago in October 1969 was opposed by the RYM II faction, which,
as previously noted, sponsored separate and independent rallies, unmarred by violence, in other sections of the city on
the same days. RYM II collaborated in the demonstrations
with local organizations of the Black Panthers and Young
Lords and expressed itself as concerned about various community problems around which those other organizations had
been campaigning. Disagreement with the Weathermen's
tactics--which RYM II described as alienating rather than
winning friends for a revolutionary youth movement in Amer-
ica--culminated in the physical separation of the faction at
a national conference at Emory University in Atlanta, Georgia,
November 28-30, 1969.

According to reports in the underground press, the
result of the conference was a new, independent organization
known as the Revolutionary Youth Movement. Completely
dominated by women, RYM rejected being defined as any
kind of "Marxist-Leninist organization" and refused to make
"socialism" one of its goals. The orientation of the new
group would stress support of an "anti-imperialist" and black
liberation struggle in the U.S., albeit in solidarity with communists in North and South Vietnam, Cuba, and Red China.[78]

SDS (THE PRO-PLP ORGANIZATION
BASED IN BOSTON)

The SDS organization which operated from a Boston headquarters had been formed by the SDS Worker-Student Alliance caucus which was under the control of the Progressive Labor Party. [79]

The PLP itself had been organized in January 1962 by persons expelled from the Communist Party, U.S.A. PLP advertised itself as a truly revolutionary Marxist-Leninist or communist organization seeking to bring about a revolution in the United States. It was frankly sympathetic to strategies enunciated by the Red Chinese communists. It spoke of eventual violent revolution in the U.S. in traditional Marxist-Leninist terminology. PLP portrayed revolutionary violence as an act of self-defense required by the unwillingness of the ruling class to relinquish power peacefully. [80]

As previously indicated, SDS'ers sympathetic to the PLP approach held that revolution in the United States could not be achieved without relying on assistance from the industrial working class. The "working class" orientation of PLP was reflected in the Boston-based SDS program of building "worker-student alliances" on and off the college campus.

The publications of this SDS organization also backed a program of direct actions on campus against "militarization" of the university, in other words, actions against ROTC, war-related university research, and military recruiting.

In the summer of 1969, members of SDS were engaged in a "work-in" in private industry or helping to man picket lines in trade union disputes (to bring the "workers" the SDS revolutionary message while establishing a rapport between college students and the working man). In the fall of 1969, the SDS organization urged its college student members to take part-time jobs on campus so that this flirtation between student and worker could continue throughout the year.

In Washington, D.C., for example, SDS members and supporters had joined picket lines formed by truck drivers and warehousemen striking against the Curtis Brothers Furniture Company in June 1969. SDS'ers usually outnumbered the strikers who were represented by Warehousemen's Local 639 of the Teamsters Union.

As in its summer projects elsewhere, SDS misread
the issue and the feeling of the workers whom they were trying to aid. SDS members injected a racial issue into the
furniture company strike, over the objections of the union
business agent. SDS participants were students from Washington area universities and included an SDS national officer.
Some arrested demonstrators were equipped with nun-chakus,
weapons made from two sticks joined together by a thong and
used in the Far East.

A committee witness testified that neither the union
nor management approved of SDS' "assistance." A union
representative stated that negotiation had been hampered by
the students. Striking employees also were annoyed by the
SDS'ers who, while including elements from the Chicago
Weatherman faction of SDS, were predominantly adherents of
the Boston-based SDS. Ed Galloway, a member of the Boston
NIC and a former leader of the Georgetown University disruptions in the spring of 1969, was one of the pickets.

While the Boston-based SDS deplored the Weatherman
street fighting in Chicago, it was quick to explain in press
releases and in its publications that it was not less militant
or less violent. The organization was only concerned that
violence be correctly directed. Weatherman violence alienated
workers, the SDS in Boston argued. Its own model of student
militancy was the long and violent strike that plagued San
Francisco State College in the academic year 1968-69. That
action, according to SDS of Boston, involved thousands of
students in the longest student strike in history, and had
raised an issue of racism, which the faction advocated should
be a basis for agitation whenever possible.

The official publication of this SDS group took credit
for disruptive actions at various universities in the fall of
1969 by students agitating on behalf of improved wages and
working conditions for university employees. For example,
it claimed that stimulus from one of its chapters led to fighting between students and police in a campus demonstration
of General Electric Company strikers. (The demonstrators
also demanded wage increases for campus workers.)

One of the largest anti-Vietnam war demonstrations
ever held took place on November 15, 1969, in Washington,
D.C. Boston-based SDS members planned to participate in
this Mobe-initiated acitivity which, as a Mobe press release
stated, would conform to "the legal and nonviolent discipline"

established by the anti-war coalition. [81] Assurances from Weatherman SDS that its participation would be nonviolent were given to Mobe leaders. New Mobe, possibly the largest anti-war coalition of organizations in the United States, was made up of scores of organizations, including all varieties of communists, plus radical, New Left, and pacifist groups. DCA, CPUSA, SMC, SWP and its youth arm, the YSA, RYM II, and WSP were among those listed on Mobe's steering committee, the body responsible for all of the Mobe's demonstrations. [82]

Boston SDS stated that it would participate in Mobe's rally in Washington, D. C., but that it would march under its own slogans. It was critical of the three major groups behind the demonstration--Mobe, SMC, and the Vietnam Moratorium Committee--because it believed that the rally's sponsors were building an "alliance" in the wrong direction, that is, with businessmen, liberal politicians, and university administrations. The correct alliance, it claimed, would include students and workers who would fight against the above-mentioned liberal elements with whom Mobe was affiliating. [83]

Boston SDS, during the Washington rally, would not only promote its own views, but would put on a separate demonstration at the U. S. Department of Labor to express support for some 150,000 striking General Electric workers. [84]

INTERNATIONAL OPERATIONS

On the international front in 1969, SDS elements, despite the splintering of the organization at home, continued to maintain relationships with communists abroad.

During the summer of 1969, an SDS delegation visited Cuba for meetings with representatives of the National Liberation Front of South Vietnam. The SDS delegation included Bernardine Dohrn, member of the national interim committee of the SDS headquartered in Chicago, and Kathy Boudin of the organization's National Action staff. Members of this SDS delegation reported in the radical press that they had spent two out of five weeks in Cuba meeting with the Vietcong. The Vietnamese delegation also included representatives from North Vietnam. [85]

It was indicated that the Vietnamese delegation had specified in advance the type of Americans they wanted to meet with--hardcore New Left organizers--who, as it turned out, were mainly from the SDS. The Vietnamese communists were concerned over the lull in anti-Vietnam war activity in the United States, and the purpose of the meeting called by the Vietnamese communists was to prod American radicals into motion against American involvement in Vietnam. The SDS delegation agreed to do everything it could to speed up what it described as the inevitable defeat of the American forces in Vietnam. The SDS delegation consented to plan militant actions which it hoped would build another war front within the United States and provide material aid to the Vietcong. The Vietnamese communists' advice on the best type of recruit that the SDS should get for this activity was given by Huynh Van Ba, leader of the Vietcong delegation, who told the SDS delegation to look for the person who fights hardest against the police and pick that one. Ba cautioned that the one who uses the best rhetoric is not necessarily the one who fights best.

In the summer of 1969, SDS was a major force behind recruitment of a Venceremos Brigade composed of Americans who, in two groups, would be sent to Cuba to help harvest its 1970 sugar crop. An SDS resolution which appeared in the June 18, 1969 issue of New Left Notes explained the purpose of the brigade as follows:

> A brigade of 300 Americans (called the Venceremos brigade) is being organized to go down to Cuba and cut cane for the 1970 harvest. The brigade will be divided into two sections ... Members of the brigade will be recruited from activists in the revolutionary movement in this country: blacks, Latinos, white working class youth, students and dropout GI's.
>   Political purposes of the brigade:
>   1. To politically, morally and materially support Cuba in the critical sugar harvest of 1970 with its goal of 10 million tons.
>   2. To educate people about imperialism and about the international revolution against imperialism. This will be accomplished through a well-developed education and propaganda program. The program will aim at developing an understanding of U.S. imperialism, not only in its most blatant militaristic aspects (as in Vietnam) but also its

role in distorting and impeding economic development throughout the Third World.

To gain a practical understanding of the
creative application of communist principles on a
day-to-day basis. The New Left in the advanced
capitalist countries has, in the last decade, clearly
defined itself within the tradition of socialist and   .
communist struggle begun a century ago. The
American mass media and educational system have
made the word communism into anathema: this
experience will help us to develop ways of combat-
ting anti-communism.

New Left Notes, in its issue of July 8, 1969, contained
an announcement that applications were available from the
SDS national office to persons willing to serve in a Cuban
sugarcane-cutting brigade. This was coupled with the appeal
that everyone should apply. Applicants were told to expect
two months of hard physical labor if accepted into a 300-man
force of Americans who would actively and materially support
the Cuban revolution by working in the Cuban sugarcane harvest. [86]

Julie Nichamin and Karin Ashley were the SDS representatives on the Venceremos Brigade's organizing committee.
Nichamin was in charge of processing applications for the
brigade. [87]

In December 1969, a brigade of 250 Americans arrived in Cuba to assist in the sugarcane harvest. The only
organization within the brigade seemed to be a Weatherman
SDS group of about 25. The other Americans apparently
joined the brigade as individuals. [88]

The second group of sugarcane harvesters, which left
the United States in February 1970, involved between 600 and
750 youths, according to varying estimates in the press. [89]

Despite much propaganda about what brigade members
would accomplish in helping Castro harvest a ten-million-ton
crop, subsequent publicity indicated that the American youths
contributed little, but could not be held responsible for what
turned out to be a critical failure. Cuba's total sugar crop
fell short of the goal by more than one million tons, forcing
Castro to fire several top officials in his regime. What the
members of the Venceremos did not understand or appreciate
was the fact that Castro's eighteen-month campaign to exceed

the pre-Castro record--a seven-and-a-quarter-million-ton harvest completed in only four months--may have severely crippled Cuba's sugar-producing potential for years to come.

NOTES

1. SDS mass paper, The Fire Next Time, September 1969 (HCIS hearings on SDS, pt. 6-B, p. 2131), which also said: "We must be willing to lay down our lives if necessary, for we will win by any means necessary."

2. The Washington Post, Jan. 20, 21, 1969; New Left Notes, Jan. 22, 1969, p. 3; and HCIS hearings on SDS, pts. 2 and 7-A.

3. Attorney General John N. Mitchell, testimony, May 20, 1969, Special House Subcommittee on Education.

4. J. Edgar Hoover, testimony before House Subcommittee on Appropriations on the 1970 FBI appropriation.

5. The Washington Post, April 29, 1969, p. A-10, and May 4, 1969, pp. A-1, 6.

6. The Movement, June 1969, pp. 12, 13, 21.

7. Gerald Wayne Kirk, testimony, HCIS hearings on SDS, pt. 5, August 6, 7, 1969; New Left Notes, April 29, 1969, p. 6; Guardian, February 1, 1969, p. 2.

8. New Left Notes, February 28, 1969, p. 1; Guardian, March 8, 1969, p. 10; New Left Notes, March 13, 1969, p. 7.

9. HCIS hearings on SDS, pts. 1-A and 1-B (Georgetown University); New York Times, March 7, 1969, p. 18; New Left Notes, March 13, 1969, p. 7.

10. HCIS hearings on SDS, pt. 4 (The American University) and pts. 3-A and 3-B (George Washington University); Baltimore Sun, April 15, 1969; New York Times, April 16, 1969; HCIS hearings on SDS, pt. 2 (Kent State University).

11. New York Times, May 14, 1969; The Washington Post, May 8, 1969; New York Times, May 6, 1969.

12. New York Times, May 3, 1969; Washington Evening Star, May 21, 1969; New Left Notes, May 30, 1969, p. 5.

13. Both the original Columbia Proposal and the revised draft were reproduced as Committee Exhibit No. 16 in HCIS hearings on SDS, pt. 2, pp. 612-619. See also discussion of the proposals in New Left Notes, January 15, 1969, pp. 3, 8, and February 12, 1969, p. 9.

14. HCIS hearings on SDS, pts. 1-A, 1-B, and 2.

15. See, for example, testimony of Thomas M. Sneeringer, HCIS hearings on SDS, pt. 1-B, June 5, 1969.

16. New Left Notes, February 12, 1969, p. 11.

17. Kirk, testimony, HCIS hearings on SDS, pt. 5, August 7, 1969, p. 1691.

18. The Movement, June 1969, p. 9.

19. New Left Notes, April 4, 1969. New Left Notes on February 28, 1969, had printed a lengthy interview with James Forman of SNCC, in which Forman insisted that blacks, as the most "oppressed" portion of the U.S. population, had to give direction to revolutionary struggles in order to protect those things for which they were fighting, and it was absolutely essential that whites be prepared to accept black leadership. Forman also urged support for the Black Panther Party and "other para-military groups."

20. Newark, N.J., Star-Ledger, February 23, 1969.

21. New Left Notes, March 7, 1969, p. 1.

22. Guardian, March 8, 1969, p. 10.

23. New Left Notes, March 20, 1969, p. 6.

24. Guardian, April 5, 1969, p. 10.

25. New Left Notes, April 4, 1969, p. 3.

26. Christian Science Monitor, June 2, 1969.

27. Guardian, June 28, 1969, pp. 10, 11.

28. New Left Notes, April 10, 1969, p. 3.

29. Guardian, May 10, 1969, p. 7.

30. Kirk, testimony, HCIS hearings on SDS, pt. 5, p. 1691, and summary of Kirk's testimony in HCIS Annual Report for the Year 1969.

31. New Left Notes, April 4, 1969, p. 7.

32. Ibid., pp. 6, 8.

33. HCIS hearings on SDS, pt. 1-B, p. 346.

34. HCIS hearings on SDS, pt. 1-A.

35. HCIS hearings on SDS, pt. 2.

36. Ibid.

37. Ibid.

38. HCIS hearings on SDS, pt. 3-A.

39. The film, "The Columbia Revolt," was viewed by HCIS and a transcription of the sound track was made part of the hearing record as Committee Exhibit No. 16 to HCIS hearings on SDS, pt. 3-A.

40. HCIS hearings on SDS, pt. 4.

41. Kirk, testimony, HCIS hearings on SDS, pt. 5, p. 1689.

42. SDS constitution, originally printed in New Left Notes, June 10, 1968, and reproduced as Committee Exhibit No. 42 in HCIS hearings on SDS, pt. 6-B, pp. 2107-2110.

43. Guardian, June 28, 1969, pp. 1, 3, 6, 11. Events at the convention are described in testimony of Herbert Romerstein, HCIS hearings on SDS, pt. 5, August 7, 1969, pp. 1711, 1712; in issues of New Left Notes summarized in Committee Exhibit No. 43, HCIS hearings on SDS, pt. 6-B, pp. 2111-2117 and 2133-2135. Internal differences are also discussed in FRED, "the

socialist press service, " vol. 1, No. 23, July 21, 1969, pp. 22-27; Young Socialist, July-August, 1969, p. 23; The Militant, July 4, 1969, p. 6; Guardian, July 26, 1969, p. 7; Daily World, June 24, 1969, p. 11; and The Washington Post, June 22 and 23, 1969.

44. Factions attending the convention session at the church reportedly included RYM I, RYM II, members of the International Socialist Clubs, the Bay Area Revolutionary Union, and the Joe Hill caucus. The Communist Party newspaper, the Daily World, previously referred to, announced that the CPUSA and W. E. B. DuBois Clubs caucus attended the final convention session of the SDS "regulars, " but issued a statement to the assemblage criticizing some of the major policies of the SDS leadership.

45. HCIS hearings on SDS, pt. 6-B, Committee Exhibit No. 43, pp. 2111, 2112, and 2133, 2134.

46. HCIS hearings on SDS, pt. 5.

47. New Left Notes, Boston, September 20, 1969, p. 2.

48. HCIS hearings on SDS, pt. 6-B. Committee Exhibit No. 43, and pt. 7-B, Committee Exhibit No. 44.

49. HCIS hearings on SDS, pt. 5, Committee Exhibit No. 14; pt. 6-B, Committee Exhibit No. 43; and Herbert Romerstein testimony, pt. 7-B, December 17, 1969, p. 2465.

50. Guardian, July 19, 1969, p. 4.

51. New Left Notes (Chicago), July 8, 1969, p. 1.

52. Guardian, June 21, 1969, p. 3; July 26, 1969, p. 3; and August 16, 1969, p. 4; New Left Notes (Chicago), July 24, 1969, pp. 1-3.

53. Guardian, August 16, 1969, pp. 4, 14.

54. New Left Notes (Chicago), July 24, 1969, pp. 1-3.

55. Ibid.

56. Guardian, August 16, 1969, p. 14.

57. Ibid.

58. New Left Notes (Chicago), July 8, 1969, p. 3.

59. Weatherman position paper, "You don't need a weather-
     man to know which way the wind blows," New Left
     Notes (Chicago), June 18, 1969, pp. 3-8.

60. Interview, August 30, 1969, Station WJW-TV, Columbus,
     Ohio, the transcript of which was entered as Commit-
     tee Exhibit 45 in HCIS hearings on SDS, pt. 6-B.

61. HCIS hearings on SDS, pt. 6-A.

62. HCIS hearings on SDS, pt. 6-A, p. 1756.

63. Ibid.

64. HCIS hearings on SDS, pt. 6-B.

65. Ibid.

66. Ibid.

67. HCIS Annual Report for 1969, p. 104.

68. HCIS hearings on SDS, pt. 7-B.

69. HCIS hearings on SDS, pt. 7-B, Committee Exhibit No.
     37.

70. New Left Notes, No. 30, September 20, 1969, p. 7.

71. Ibid.

72. HCIS hearings on SDS, pt. 7-B.

73. HCIS Annual Report for 1969.

74. Ibid. and HCIS hearings on SDS, pt. 6-B, p. 213. The
     Weathermen's publication announced it would apply its
     National Action strategy in an appearance on the
     streets of Washington, D. C., in the period around
     November 15, 1969, when mass anti-war demonstra-
     tions brought a quarter of a million persons to the
     city. SDS militants were among the various groups
     represented in a rally on November 14 by 3, 000

persons which ended with an attempted march on the
South Vietnamese Embassy. It was broken up by
police using tear gas, but not before acts of vandalism
were committed. SDS'ers were also among the more
militant demonstrators who surrounded the Justice Department building on November 15, where windows
were broken and paint thrown on the building before
tear gas was used to halt the disorder. (Source: J.
Edgar Hoover, March 5, 1970, testimony before House
Appropriations Subcommittee.)

75. Liberation News Service, January 3, 1970, pp. 20 ff.

76. J. Edgar Hoover, report on FBI operations during the
     fiscal year 1970, released by the Department of Jus-
     tice, July 14, 1970.

77. HCIS hearings on SDS, pt. 6-B, p. 2115.

78. The Great Speckled Bird, December 8, 1969.

79. Herbert Romerstein, testimony, HCIS hearings on SDS,
     pt. 5, p. 1712.

80. House Committee on Un-American Activities, Annual
     Report for the Year 1963, summary of statements of
     Progressive Labor Movement, later known as Pro-
     gressive Labor Party, pp. 13-18.

81. HCIS hearings on SDS, pt. 7-B, Committee Exhibit No.
     44, summarizing various issues of New Left Notes
     published in Boston, pp. 2605-2612.

82. Press release, New Mobilization Committee to End the
     War in Vietnam, November 10, 1969, p. 1.

83. Press office list of steering committee members, New
     Mobilization Committee, November 1969.

84. New Left Notes (Boston), November 1 and 13, 1969,
     summarized in Committee Exhibit No. 44, HCIS hear-
     ings on SDS, pt. 7-B, pp. 2606, 2609, 2610.

85. New Left Notes (Chicago), September 12, 1969, p. 3;
     Guardian, August 30, 1969, p. 6; Guardian, Septem-
     ber 13, 1969, p. 12; Workers World, August 27,
     1969, p. 4; and Daily World, August 20, 1969, p. 9.

86. Romerstein, testimony, HCIS hearings on SDS, pt. 5,
     p. 1716, and pt. 7-A, p. 2309; also summaries of
     New Left Notes (Chicago), June 18 and July 8, 1969,
     in Committee Exhibit No. 14, pt. 5 of hearings and
     Committee Exhibit No. 43 in 6-B of hearings.

87. The Militant, September 12, 1969, and Miami News,
     August 9, 1969.

88. Guardian, December 20, 1969.

89. Washington Evening Star, February 24, 1970, p. A-2,
     and The Washington Post, February 9, 1970, p. A-3.

Chapter 6

VANDALS IN THE BOMB FACTORY:
END OF THE ROAD TO ANARCHY, 1970

> We are behind enemy lines. We are the
> sons and daughters of the enemy.... We
> have to force the disintegration of society,
> creating strategic armed chaos where
> there is now pig order. [1]

Following the Weathermen's rioting on Chicago streets
in October 1969, the weekly chronicler of New Left activity
in the United States, the Guardian, declared that "SDS is
dead. "

"All over the country, " it observed, "SDS chapters
are announcing disaffiliation from the parent body. Most of
the grass-roots chapters in SDS refuse to align with any of
the factions. If they do not proclaim independence publicly
or abandon the name, they are quietly severing relations with
the national office. "[2]

Press accounts of local chapter activity tended to con-
firm the Guardian report. The SDS chapter at Cornell University, for example, was handicapped by a split into four
competing factions. The chapter at Vanderbilt University
voted to disaffiliate from the Chicago national office and
change its name. A new name was also the response of the
SDS chapter at the University of Pittsburgh in order to dis-
avow the so-called anarchists in control of the national organization.

The Weathermen were reported in the underground
press to have had the support of only about 300 cadre members of SDS at the June 1969 national SDS convention. [3] A
former Weatherman has estimated that defections after the
Chicago rioting sent the strength of the faction well below
the 300 mark by the end of the year. In the opinion of many
other radical youth, the militant, centralized Weatherman

cadre was using tactics which would simply "wipe out" revolutionaries or win them long terms in jail. The Chicago street
action in October 1969 was viewed by many as a suicidal
"death trip. "[4]

Speeches by Weatherman leader and new national secretary Mark Rudd after the convention extolled the virtues of
violence against "pigs, " whom he identified as including not
only the police but also bureaucrats, soldiers, and all members of the Establishment.[5] Rudd talked of his faction's efforts to build a white fighting force for a people's war against
"imperialism" which had already begun. He was vague about
what alternative a revolution would offer the American people.
In a television interview in Ohio in the late summer he considered his organization dedicated to "power to the people. "[6]

In a speech at the University of Rhode Island in September, he told students it was not possible to discuss spe-
cifics on what would happen after a revolution because the
results would vary in different countries. The immediate
concern, to Rudd, was the political and military defeat of the
present power structure, after which the outlines of a new
society would become clear.[7]

The last issue of the Weatherman's national publication, FIRE!, issued under date of January 30, 1970, declared
in reference to its December national council meeting: "Over
the holidays we plotted war on America. " The Chicago street
fighting in October was praised in FIRE! as the "best organized white street action" ever to "hit" this country.

The SDS paper noted that the resulting arrests and injuries meant new forms of fighting had to be developed--pos-
sibly launched by collectives being built around the country.
The Weathermen were "building an army, a centralized military organization, " and its "military strategy" would be based
on the political objective of "the disintegration of society" by
"creating strategic armed chaos. " In the process of creating
the army, the publication declared, the Weathermen were
mindful of the need to mold themselves into "self-conscious,
self-reliant communist revolutionaries. " Their position was
based on the optimistic belief that "youth" will make and
keep the revolution throughout America and the entire world. [8]

The Weathermen were described by some of their own
members as romantics fancying themselves to be urban guerrillas and trying to apply the tactics of Ché Guevara's rural

guerrillas in underdeveloped third world nations to a highly
industrialized, democratic society. [9]

COMMITMENT TO ACTION AHEAD OF IDEOLOGY

The distinctiveness of New Left organizations such as
SDS, in an earlier period, had been alleged by sympathetic
adult observers to rest in 1) their commitment to action before being committed to any program or ideology (i. e., without planned results), [10] and 2) an anti-bureaucratic, anti-cen-
tralist outlook expressed by the term participatory democracy. [11]

A Guardian columnist noted that by late 1969 the
Weathermen were innovative in imagining that white youths
could organize themselves as revolutionaries to move on their
own, rather than serving as a catalyst or organizer for other
persons (workers, etc.). For that reason, however, the
writer observed, the Weathermen were not very good "orthodox" Marxist-Leninists. [12]

An unsympathetic historian declared that New Leftists
had departed from their initial "populist" faith in the need
for individual participation in decision-making processes (participatory democracy). After people failed to follow the student lead, the critic said, the radicals became apologists for
"putschist" action by a small student elite, which, with the
help of guerrilla-type violence, would impose its will on the
recalcitrant majority of the American people. These New
Leftists were told that "in principle" at least they were emu-
lating the political tactics of V. I. Lenin, who led a minority
in seizing power in Russia for the good of the workers even
if the latter did not appreciate the efforts. [13]

As previously noted, the Revolutionary Youth Movement II faction which existed within the Chicago-based SDS
organization after the June 1969 convention actually accepted
the orthodox Marxist-Leninist goal of a revolution to establish a "dictatorship of the proletariat" in the U.S.A. (the
same goal which guided Lenin and his Bolsheviks more than
half a century earlier). The Boston-based SDS was under
the influence of the "Marxist-Leninist" Progressive Labor
Party which also had a dictatorship of the proletariat as its
goal. [14]

The reasons for the break-up and subsequent decline
of SDS have been discussed by many observers.

A former community organizer for SDS in the mid-
sixties--speaking from a continued New Left orientation--com-
mented that by January 1969 the New Left student movement
was already turning toward revolutionary rhetoric, militant
or romantic ideologies, factionalism resembling that of the
old left of the 1930's in America, and "desperation and militancy."

The student movement, including SDS, the organizer
complained, was "becoming more dogmatic, factionalized ...
less tolerant of organizers who wish to experiment in ways
that deviate from the untested assumptions of the factions."[15]
The reason, according to this former organizer in the ghettos,
was that the New Left had become "frustrated" because no
revolutionary "movement," no "mass" radical organization had
emerged.   The norm, he said, was individual, local efforts
and incidents, and unconnected rebellions on high school and
college campuses.   The New Left, this SDS'er concluded, had
proved it was no political threat, but merely a "cultural phenomenon."[16]

IMITATING STREET GANGS

The Guardian, in a post mortem with particular reference to the Weathermen, said that SDS'ers, motivated by
guilt and hate of white America, had wrongly attached themselves to black militants and artificially transposed to America the "exemplary acts" of Ché Guevara's rural guerrillas.
SDS'ers, the Guardian complained, were unwilling to work in
white communities in a long, slow, and difficult organizing
process that was necessary in view of the unreceptive attitude
of the majority of the American population.[17]

An analysis by the self-styled radical Liberation News
Service on November 22, 1969, declared that the Weathermen's talk of creating a white fighting force to ally with
black revolutionaries was a strategy for "fighting" in a tough
gang style.   They were imitating street gangs, motorcycle
gangs, and to some extent the Black Panther Party.   The result was to alienate SDS from students and working people
and to destroy the largest New Left organization in the U.S.
The reasons for this turn, according to LNS, included: 1)
students' frustration over the knowledge they were powerless
to make a revolution alone; 2) "the movement on campuses
has lost some steam"; 3) "the politicization of the working
class" was a slow process; 4) anxiety to appear more radical

than others, which moved SDS'ers constantly to the left; 5)
adulation of "Third World" revolutionaries and, in particular,
Fidel Castro's suicidal assault on the Moncada Barracks in
Cuba six years before his revolution was successful; 6) the
inherent impatience of the young which led them to grasp at
the straws of "instant revolution" as "instant revolutionaries. "

One SDS member credited developments in domestic
black nationalist movements with the move of SDS from participatory democracy to a revolutionary Marxist outlook.
SDS, he wrote, "has consistently supported the political viewpoints and actions of the most militant segments of the black
movement and has consciously shaped its own analysis and
program in response to those elements as they have evolved
during the sixties from Malcolm X to S. N. C. C. to the Black
Panther Party. "   Therefore, in the opinion of this SDS member the "evolution in S. D. S. theory from a vaguely defined
populism to a revolutionary interpretation of Marxism has
been spurred at each point by the increasing radicalization of
the black liberation movement. "[18]

The New Left magazine, Leviathan, for October-November 1969, deplored the fact that SDS was riddled by factional controversy and infighting, and that differences had
hardened into rigid and dogmatic positions.   The reasons lay
in the decision of SDS leaders to transform SDS from a cam-
pus-based student organization to a revolutionary youth movement, the magazine's editors declared.

As long as SDS was a student movement in elite colleges and universities, its strategy "evolved easily and naturally out of its practice. "   Moving off campus to include
high school, working, and street youth called for "conscious"
efforts to define a new strategy and forms of struggle.   This
opened the way for contention by those attracted to differing
methods and outlooks. [19]

The radical Guardian was pleased to find that the SDS
move toward a revolutionary youth movement was accompanied
by the growth of Marxist-Leninist politics in the organization.
The paper protested the dogmatic stand of SDS leaders, however, which led some to talk approvingly of Stalin and the
need for a dictatorship of the proletariat and a vanguard
(Leninist) party.   Such talk, the Guardian noted, was the
property of small groups at national SDS meetings who--even
if they developed a communist ideology--might find no SDS
membership left to put it into practice because of "the
growing gulf between leadership and membership. "[20]

Articles in the socialist quarterly, New Politics, of
October 1969, charged that in less than a decade SDS had
abandoned belief in electoral processes, distrust of the dog-
mas of old left organizations such as the Communist Party
and Socialist Party, and hope for reform of the present U.S.
"system." It had instead adopted a rhetoric and style worthy
of Stalin as it shifted loyalty "from one to the other of the
two class systems struggling for the world." The weakness
in SDS which led to this transformation, in the opinion of New
Politics articles, was SDS' lack of a consistent political program, which meant that it reacted to events pragmatically. [21]

MESSAGE FROM CPUSA

The view of the Communist Party, U.S.A., was illustrated by the following message to the Weathermen appearing
in a column in the December 27, 1969, edition of the official
party newspaper, the Daily World: "To Students for a Democratic Society and its Weathermen: May you outgrow nihil-
ism, astrology, anarchy and other diversionary ideas to take
the front-line place with the workers to which your youth,
energy and devotion entitle you."

The Trotskyist Socialist Workers Party suggested that
lack of a "clear revolutionary program" was SDS' failing,
once it decided to build a "revolutionary" youth movement. [22]

Rhetorical violence covered an emptiness among the
radicals caused by lack of coherent or realizable goals, a
conservative magazine also observed. Marxism was available
to answer a demand for content in the New Left, to fill the
"ideological vacuum." [23]

A Marxist ideology was introduced to the SDS national
leadership chiefly through the instrument of the Progressive
Labor Party, whose youth members had been openly working
within SDS since early 1966, according to analyses in both
new and old left publications. The analyses contended that
Marxist-Leninist "politics" were originally adopted by many
SDS leaders simply as a method of fighting against, or in an
effort to debate with, persons promoting the PLP line within
the organization. [24]

A former SDS member at the University of Washington
campus also expounded in October 1969, on the impact of the
PLP:

"PLP introduced Marxist terminology to SDS and, for the first time, raised the issue of the working class as the agent of social change in the U. S., " the former SDS'er said. "The leadership of SDS came to adopt the rhetoric of PLP, but continued to differ on the question of the role of the working class in changing American society," according to an account in the University of Washington Daily of October 2, 1969.

The New Left monthly, The Movement, noted that SDS activists had long been mistrustful of the presence within SDS of a strongly disciplined cadre affiliated with the Progressive Labor Party. The Movement said that PLP members within SDS nevertheless deserved some credit for pushing the SDS toward support of the Vietcong and for a lessening of hostility to the orthodox Marxist view that "working class" allies are needed by any group preparing for revolution. The Movement pointed out that in the course of endless debates within SDS over PLP politics--particularly in the months leading up to the 1969 SDS convention--SDS leaders made the mistake of adopting the same dogmatic attitude as the PLP they fought.[25]

Factions within SDS were not the only reasons SDS "disintegrated" after the expulsion of PLP elements in June 1969, according to another analysis. The New York staff of Leviathan, many of whose members had been active in SDS on national or local levels, declared that SDS activists were guilty of false self-confidence based on illusions. As a result, SDS engaged in unrealistic and isolating actions which left them frustrated and impotent, according to this analysis which was written in the form of a self-criticism on New Year's Day, 1970.

The New Yorkers explained that SDS members were under the illusion that they were immune from any serious reprisal by the American power structure and that they could make a revolution "without anything very serious ever happening to us. "

Such notions were attributed to the fact that SDS'ers enjoyed a privileged status as students at elite colleges and universities where they were allowed to demonstrate, sit-in, and even seize buildings without severe reprisals. The sympathies of other students, aroused by police confrontations, also encouraged SDS'ers in their feeling of immunity, as they continued to ride the crest of a continuous upsurge of antiwar feeling and black militancy, both on and off campus, the article declared.

The New York youths felt that a temporary lull in the anti-war movement following the start of the Paris peace talks[26] and the "repression or cooptation" of militant black leadership on most college campuses made it increasingly difficult for SDS to move large numbers of students into militant actions around its own politics and demands. The great mass of students who joined in earlier anti-war struggles also "did not join us in the transition to anti-imperialist, pro-communist politics," the writers asserted. SDS'ers accordingly grew more and more isolated. The move off campus to build a revolutionary youth movement was attributed in part to this SDS isolation and to the suspension or expulsion of SDS chapter members by college authorities.

Frustration and a feeling of impotence, brought on by this isolation, led the Weathermen to accept permanent isolation by operating as a small cadre organization, the New Yorkers said. The Revolutionary Youth Movement II faction, for the same reasons, adopted an "Old Left" line and tried to win allies while engaging in less militant forms of struggle.

The solution suggested by the writers for Leviathan was to quit trying to make a revolution in the U.S. and simply make it more "costly" for the U.S. "ruling class" to continue the Vietnam war. The group proposed engaging in a "systematic, coherent, explicit way" in what were formerly isolated, local attacks on "imperialist institutions." "Attacks on ROTC offices and draft boards, attempts to force our way onto an army base, mysterious bombings and acts of sabotage" were cited as examples of tactics used in the past in isolated and localized instances. In the future, the New Yorkers wrote:

> What we need to do is first to publicly identify a whole series of institutions and targets--ROTC, military research centers, draft boards and recruiting stations, army bases, factories and offices of corporations engaged in war and war-related production--which form an integral part of the war machine; and second, to make it as clear and as public as we possibly can that we are going to be attacking all those institutions and targets as part of a coherent, systematic national (or more precisely, international) strategy to drive the U.S. out of Vietnam. [27]

The radical Liberation News Service claimed that by the time of the December 1969 national or "war" council of the Weatherman-run SDS, even the Weather Bureau (Weatherman leadership) had undergone an internal split over this issue of terrorist tactics. According to LNS, one faction wanted to continue organizing "street" youth and another faction was for "terrorist action" exclusively. [28]

The December 1969 "war" council signaled the end of above-ground Weatherman operations, Liberation News Service reported. Sometime over the weekend of February 7 and 8, 1970, even the SDS national headquarters in Chicago was quietly vacated. [29] Law enforcement authorities remarked on the virtual disappearance of Weatherman leaders from public view around this time.

That terrorism was on the agenda for at least a section of the Weatherman underground operation was dramatically and tragically demonstrated on March 6, 1970. A series of explosions and a fire destroyed a Greenwich Village townhouse in New York City on that date. Authorities uncovered three bodies and a basement workshop which had contained dynamite, blasting caps, timing mechanisms, and homemade fragmentation bombs. A police official said that persons in the townhouse were putting together the component parts of a bomb and obviously something went wrong.

Two bodies in condition to be identified were those of Diana Oughton, a regional organizer for SDS in Michigan during the 1968-69 academic year who was active in the Weatherman faction the following summer, and Ted Gold, SDS leader at Columbia University in 1968 and reputed member of an SDS faction known as "the Mad Dogs" late in 1969. [30] Several months later, a message from the Weatherman underground identified the third body as that of Terry Robbins, an SDS member from Kent State University in Ohio, who was also active in the Weatherman faction. [31]

Observed fleeing from the townhouse after the explosion was Cathlyn Wilkerson, another member of the Weatherman clique, whose father owned the townhouse. Miss Wilkerson had at one time been a coordinator of regional activities for SDS in Washington, D.C.

A Justice Department investigation into this explosion and other aspects of underground Weatherman activity resulted in a Federal grand jury indictment of 13 Weathermen on charges of conspiring to bomb and kill. [32]

The indictment, brought in Detroit on July 23, 1970, alleged that the conspiracy began to take shape during the Weatherman "war" council in Flint, Michigan, in December 1969 and that further plans were made at a Weatherman meeting in Cleveland, Ohio, on February 4. Mark Rudd reportedly stated at the February session that Weathermen were going underground and would bomb police and military installations and carry out assassinations.

To direct their underground bombing operation, according to the indictment, the Weathermen and co-conspirators "would organize a 'central committee,'" the members of which would be assigned to Berkeley, Chicago, Detroit, and New York City.

Bearing out information that was obtained by HCIS investigators, the grand jury reported that this "central committee" would be in command of "clandestine and underground 'focals,' consisting of three or four persons" who would engage in the bombing of police and other civic, business, and educational buildings throughout the country. [33]

Members of the Weatherman "focals," it was further charged, would use false identities and communicate through coded messages as they traveled about the country, obtaining firearms and explosives and using them to bomb buildings.

Several of the indicted Weathermen were alleged to have been making dynamite bombs on the day of the aforementioned townhouse explosion in New York City in March. The grand jury also maintained that a number of the defendants had rented an apartment in February on the North Side of Chicago where local police uncovered a bomb factory the following month.

Specific purchases of explosives and meetings by the defendants were also described in a total of 21 "overt acts" which the grand jury cited as evidence of a bombing and killing conspiracy by the 13 Weathermen. Named in the indictment were: Mark W. Rudd and William C. Ayers, two of the three national SDS secretaries, Bernardine R. Dohrn, Kathy Boudin, Linda Sue Evans, Cathlyn P. Wilkerson, Dianne Donghi, Russell T. Neufeld, Jane Spielman, Ronald D. Fliegelman, Larry D. Grathwohl, Naomi E. Jaffe, and Robert G. Burlingham. [34]

DECLARATION OF WAR

The grand jury in Detroit also took note of a highly publicized "Declaration of a State of War" which was sent to various communications media and purported to be a message from "the Weatherman underground" composed by Bernardine Dohrn on May 21, 1970. [35]

- "Revolutionary violence is the only way," according to this declaration. "We will never live peaceably under this system." The Weatherman message described the faction's tactics as an adaptation of "the classic guerrilla strategy of the Vietcong and the urban guerrilla strategy of the Tupamaros [in Uruguay] to our own situation here in the most technically advanced country in the world."

After identifying the third body in the rubble of the Greenwich Village townhouse as Terry Robbins, the "Declaration of a State of War" maintained that the Weatherman underground still could count on "several hundred members" who "move freely in and out of every city and youth scene in this country." The communication described the underground as an "invisible" one, combining "guns and grass":

> We fight in many ways. Dope is one of our weapons. The laws against marijuana mean that millions of us are outlaws long before we actually split. Guns and grass are united in the youth underground.
> Freaks are revolutionaries and revolutionaries are freaks. If you want to find us, this is where we are. In every tribe, commune, dormitory, farmhouse, barracks and townhouse where kids are making love, smoking dope and loading guns--fugitives from Amerikan justice are free to go.

The Weatherman declaration concluded with a promise to attack within the next 14 days "a symbol or institution" of American justice. The attack would celebrate the example of Eldridge Cleaver, H. Rap Brown, and "all black revolutionaries who first inspired us by their fight behind enemy lines for the liberation of their people."

Coincidentally or not, on the night of June 9, 1970, a dynamite time bomb exploded in a men's room of the New York City police headquarters. Doors and windows were smashed and eight persons slightly injured. On the following

day, the Associated Press received a hand-printed message
signed "Weatherman," which claimed credit for the bombing
because "the pigs in this country are our enemies."36

Public messages also emanated from the Weatherman
underground in honor of the 17th anniversary of the beginning
of revolutionary activity by Fidel Castro (July 26).

Before dawn on July 27, 1970, a phone call to a New
York City newspaper from a Weatherman announced that the
faction had just bombed the Bank of America in that city for
reasons including the honoring of the Cuban revolution. A
pipe bomb had indeed exploded outside the Wall Street office
of the bank, shattering glass entrance doors. Letters signed
"Weatherman Underground" with a Detroit postmark were
sent to newspapers in New York and San Francisco on July
25, 1970, declaring that the Cuban revolution was being celebrated by Weatherman attacks on "American imperialism"
with "rocks, riots and bombs."37

The fate of SDS following its commitment to a revolutionary program appears to justify the distrust of student
revolutionaries expressed by the very authorities revered by
some of these students--Karl Marx and V. I. Lenin.

Observing the revolutionary student movement in mid-
19th century czarist Russia, Marx and his collaborator,
Friedrich Engels, noted that the movement from its incep-
tion was inclined toward terrorist action, was attracted to
an anarchist's or nihilist's creed of destruction and tended
toward irrationality and irresponsibility, and wanted to put
socialist ideas into immediate application.38

Lenin was initially enthusiastic about student movements, which had been the most active revolutionary force
in Russia up to the time of the unsuccessful revolution
against the czar in 1905. He found no use for them, however, in building a disciplined revolutionary force for a "socialist" revolution in Russia in 1917. His grounds included
a belief that students lacked the proper psychology and were
intrinsically incapable of the necessary discipline and single-
minded political commitment required of a professional revo-
lutionary.39

Complaints of SDS activists that Vietnam war-related
issues were less evocative of student protest in 1969 seemed
to be confirmed by the results of a formal study and analy-

sis of campus protest movements by a private research corporation.

The study, covering 292 major protests on 232 college campuses in the period from January to June of 1969, was completed and released to the public in January 1970. It disclosed the degree to which various issues were involved: 49 per cent of the protests concerned concessions demanded by black students; 44 per cent involved demands for more student power by black or white students; 22 per cent dealt with war-related issues such as ROTC, military recruiting, military research, and the war itself. SDS and other groups with radical views were reported active in less than half of the white student protests and in 28 per cent of all protests. While most protests were non-violent, there was disruption in interfering with normal use of university facilities in 26 per cent of the protests, injuries in 22 per cent, and property damage in 19 per cent. A total of 3,652 students were arrested in the disorders. [40]

DEMONSTRATIONS INCREASE IN 1970

The school year 1969-70 saw a sharp increase in protest demonstrations on college campuses. The rate of protest was at least as high as in preceding springs, even before a great upsurge in demonstrations following the extension of the American military effort from South Vietnam to Cambodian soil on April 30, 1970, and the death of four Kent State University students during a protest on May 4, 1970.

A total of 1,785 demonstrations was recorded by the close of the school year, FBI Director Hoover announced. Sit-ins and building seizures numbered 313; ROTC installations were attacked in 281 instances; 73 protests involved military recruiting on campus; and 101 actions opposed Government research or corporate recruiting. In addition, campuses were plagued by 246 instances of arson or attempted arson and 14 bombings. As a result of disruptions, eight individuals died, 462 were injured, and damages exceed $9,500,000, the FBI chief reported. [41]

Studies and analysis of student and youth activism-- non-violent and otherwise--have been undertaken from the approaches of the psychiatrist, psychologist, sociologist, economist, and political scientist. Being analyzed for their impacts and possible effect on campus unrest were everything from parental training, the mass media, and American emphasis on technology and science, to the Chinese communists' chaotic "cultural revolution" of the late 1960s.

An educator expressed the opinion that protests were going to be a "fact of life" on American college campuses for many years to come and that educators were going to have to learn to live with them. [42]

However, during the summer of 1970 there was increasing evidence that many students, faculty members, and college and university administrators were showing growing concern for the future of the entire system of higher education. Some indicated they were determined to restore order and purpose to the campus environment when the new school year opened in the fall.

Large numbers of students participated in 1970 election campaigns throughout the Nation, showing a preference for working "within the system" instead of against it. At George Washington University and other schools, groups of students filed damage suits against school administrations for having closed classes during the spring "student strikes" organized by campus radicals. Many other students indicated they had been "turned off" by the constant harassment, repeated interruption of their studies, interference with classes and examinations, and other disruptions caused by radicals.

There was certainly reason to hope, in the summer of 1970, that the pendulum was swinging away from the extremism and militancy that swept across so many of the nation's campuses in recent years.

NOTES

1. SDS publication, FIRE! Jan. 30, 1970.

2. Guardian, Oct. 18, 1969, p. 10.

3. "SDS: Heavy Weather Ahead," Los Angeles Free Press, Oct. 31, 1969, p. 2, reprinted from Dock of the Bay.

4. Guardian, Dec. 6, 1969, p. 11.

5. New York Times, Sept. 26, 1969, p. C-49.

6. "Power to the people" is the slogan of the Black Panther Party. All three national secretaries in the Weatherman-run SDS appeared at the television interview in Cleveland, Ohio, Aug. 30, 1969. Secretary Ayers described the alternative SDS worked for as a "socialist state." Both Ayers and Rudd described themselves as "communists" or "revolutionary communists" in a sense which did not involve loyalty to some power such as the U.S.S.R. or Red China, but solidarity with "people" of the world who called themselves "Communists" and were fighting against "imperialism." They said the foreign policy of a "fascist"-type government in the United States was "imperialist." (Transcript of TV interview entered into record of HCIS hearings on SDS, pt. 6-B, as Committee Exhibit No. 45.)

7. Providence, R.I., Bulletin, Sept. 24, 1969. (Note: This position resembles the Castroite strategy outlined by Regis Debray which stressed concentrating on revolution and leaving alternatives to existing systems to be worked out later. A view of the third world as the crucial and decisive arena of struggle for defeat of U.S. "imperialism" is offered by the Chinese communists, and in that sense all major SDS factions were "Maoist" oriented. Weathermen have additionally been charged with strong inclinations toward anarchism.)

8. FIRE!, Jan. 30, 1970, p. 3.

9. See, for example, account of former SDS member Bernard Donanberg, HCIS hearings on SDS, pt. 6-A, Committee Exhibit No. 18.

10. Staughton Lynd in The New Left: A Documentary History, ed. Massimo Teodori.

11. Teodori, op. cit.

12. Guardian, Dec. 6, 1969, p. 11.

13. Feuer, The Conflict of Generations, pp. 410, 411.

14. The Progressive Labor Party monthly, Challenge, of March 1970, p. 19, described a national council session of the Boston-based SDS held in Los Angeles early in February 1970 at which a PLP student organizer discussed a strategy for building "a revolutionary

movement to smash the bosses' state and set up the
dictatorship of the proletariat. "

15. Rothstein in The New Left, a Collection of Essays, p.
     287; also pp. 272, 273.

16. Ibid.

17. Guardian, Apr. 4, 1970, p. 9.

18. Kazin in American Scholar, Autumn 1969, p. 650.

19. Leviathan, October-November 1969, p. 3.

20. Guardian, July 5, 1969, and reprinted Jan. 3, 1970,
     p. 9. RYM II approved of both Stalin and the de-
     sirability of the dictatorship of the proletariat in the
     United States in its position paper presented to the
     June 1969 SDS national convention.

21. New Politics, October 1969, pp. 45-57.

22. The Militant, Feb. 28, 1969, p. 12.

23. National Review, Feb. 27, 1969, p. 191.

24. New Politics, October 1969; The Movement, July 1969,
     p. 6; Socialist Revolution, vol. 1, No. 1, January-
     February 1970, pp. 129-143.

25. The Movement, July 1969, p. 6.

26. Preliminary peace talks in Paris got underway May 10,
     1968.

27. Leviathan, February 1970, pp. 4-11.

28. Liberation News Service, Apr. 4, 1970, pp. 22, 23.

29. Chicago Tribune, Feb. 10, 1970, p. 4.

30. LIFE, Mar. 27, 1970; Liberation News Service, Mar.
     18, 1970, p. 33; New York Times, Mar. 11, 1970,
     p. C-37; Chicago Tribune, Apr. 12, 1970, p. 11;
     Liberation News Service, Apr. 4, 1970, p. 22.

31. See p. 148.

32. New York Times, July 24, 1970, p. C-35, and The
     Washington Post, July 24, 1970, pp. A-1, A-3.

33. The origin of the "focals" team concept is derived from
     use of the Spanish word "foco" which means to focus
     or direct attention upon a given object. In the con-
     text that it is used by modern revolutionaries, research
     by Latin American experts suggests the terminology
     was used by the late Ché Guevara when, on Apr. 16,
     1967, he sent a message to the communist Triconti-
     nental Congress meeting in Havana urging future em-
     phasis or, as he put it, "foco" on the destruction of
     the United States. Ché declared that "none of us will
     be safe" until U. S. power is irreparably crippled. In
     the handbook on guerrilla warfare, prepared, with
     Ché's help, by French reporter Regis Debray, it was
     recommended that "the guerrilla focos, when they
     first begin their activity, are to be located in regions
     of highly dispersed and relatively sparse population."
     Tactics described by Debray's book were applied in
     the opening of a "new Vietnam" in Bolivia--an adven-
     ture that ultimately resulted in Ché's death and De-
     bray's capture and imprisonment as a member of
     Ché's band.

34. The first five named were among 12 Weathermen who
     had been indicted by a Federal grand jury in Chicago
     on Apr. 2, 1970, on charges of conspiring to cross
     State lines to incite a riot in Chicago. The indict-
     ment grew out of the violence attending the SDS Na-
     tional Action, Oct. 8-11, 1969. Others accused of
     conspiracy to riot in Chicago--but not named in the
     bombing conspiracy--were: national interorganizational
     secretary Jeff Jones, Judy Clark, Terry Robbins,
     John Jacobs, Howard Machtinger, Michael Spiegel,
     and Lawrence Weiss.
            All but one of the 12 (Linda Evans) were still
     eluding an FBI manhunt as of Aug. 1, 1970. Five of
     the thirteen indicted for bombing conspiracy had been
     apprehended.
            A number of the defendants, it might be noted,
     were also sought by Chicago authorities on a variety
     of local charges growing out of the National Action
     (chiefly mob action and assault). A local grand jury
     on Dec. 1, 1969, had indicted 29 participants in the
     Weatherman street fighting in October, and on De-
     cember 19 the same jury indicted 35 demonstrators.

(Chicago Tribune, Dec. 20, 1969, p. 3, The Washington Post, Apr. 3, 1970, pp. A-1, A-11, and July 26, 1970, p. A-5.)

35. Declaration summarized in New York Times, May 25, 1970, p. C-37, and printed in full in the Quicksilver Times, Washington, D.C., June 9-19, 1970, p. 11.

36. The Washington Post, June 11, 1970, p. A-22.

37. The Washington Post, July 28, 1970, p. A-3, and July 29, 1970, p. A-3.

38. Feuer, The Conflict of Generations, pp. 162, 163.

39. Ibid., pp. 47, 48.

40. New York Times, Jan. 14, 1970, p. C-13.

41. Hoover, FBI release on operations during fiscal year 1970.

42. The Washington Post, Apr. 12, 1970, pp. 1, 6.

Chapter 7

FROM RAGS TO RICHES--ROUND TRIP:
ANATOMY OF A REVOLUTIONARY MOVEMENT

> ... Today's youth clearly sees that some
> things have fallen into decay. But what
> it doesn't see is that you can't build an
> enormous mass of knowledge in a single
> generation. The danger is that many of
> them want to tear down everything and
> start again from zero because they are
> under the illusion that the equivalent of
> it all can be rebuilt. We can restart at
> zero, but in that case ... we will go
> back about 200,000 years ... [1]

Despite all the propaganda, screaming protest, violent demonstrations, and upheaval, it is still difficult for many Americans to comprehend the phenomenon of the SDS in the decade of its existence. What Dr. Konrad Lorenz says in the quotation at the beginning of this chapter points up the danger in the activities of the Weatherman faction of SDS, and it is a credit to the young people of the United States that the destructive doctrines of the Bernardine Dohrns found acceptance among only a minuscule portion of the student population.

So what may be concluded about SDS? This volume has shown:

1) In just ten years, SDS moved from peaceful protest to civil disobedience and finally to acts of revolutionary violence. From working to improve the system, SDS evolved into an organization seeking to destroy the system. At its zenith, SDS chose to identify with the communist governments of North Vietnam, North Korea, China, and Cuba and viewed itself as the nucleus of a revolutionary youth movement dedicated to violent overthrow of the present form of government

in the U. S. and the goal of a "classless world: world communism. "

2) Many individual leaders of SDS who have publicly
characterized themselves as "communists" or "Marxist-Leninists" influenced the direction and operation of SDS, and
various communist organizations or parties, in fact, infiltrated SDS. These organizations included the pro-Peking
Progressive Labor Party, the Trotskyite Socialist Workers
Party, and the Moscow-controlled Communist Party, U. S. A.
These organizations, together with members of their youth
groups and affiliates, exercised varying degrees of influence.
The Progressive Labor Party representatives in SDS were
the largest single delegation in attendance at the final SDS
national convention in June 1969, when the organization was
splintered by factionalism which reflected the rivalries among
the diverse organizations and individuals vying for the control or leadership of SDS. While the Communist Party,
U. S. A. infiltrated SDS, provided speakers and limited financial assistance, the committee did not find that this single
party dominated or controlled SDS.

3) It was primarily student opposition to the war in
Vietnam which provided the issue around which SDS--a relatively obscure student protest group--could rally dissenters
in growing numbers to demand that the United States withdraw from Vietnam; that the universities and colleges end
defense-related research; that the universities refuse to cooperate with the Selective Service System; that the universities
publicly disclose details of all contracts with the U. S. Government; that military and other Government recruiters not
be allowed on the campus; that firms engaged in defense-related research or manufacturing be barred from campus recruiting; and that the Reserve Officers Training Corps be
abolished.

The Vietnam war gave the SDS its most potent and
persuasive issues and appeals because the war has had direct
personal effect on male students of draft age. The existing
draft laws appear to have contributed to disruptions on campuses insofar as some young people went to college to "hide
from the draft" rather than to obtain an education. In addition to students not academically motivated, others may have
developed a guilt complex because they felt "safe" while others their own age were fighting in Vietnam. They became
easy prey for SDS militants who radicalized them and thus
helped them rationalize their draft avoidance actions.

4)   The potential of the SDS for creating campus disorders has been demonstrated to be far out of proportion to
its size.   A relatively small number of SDS activists was
able, in a very short time and against the will of the great
majority of the student body, to disrupt some aspect of the
educational process on many of the nation's campuses.   While
accurate statistics are not available, it is believed that less
than two per cent of all college students engaged actively in
any disorders causing physical injury or property damage.
However, some of the actions of SDS militants struck a suf-
ficiently responsive chord to enlist the sympathy of many less
militant students and to neutralize the campus "silent majority." For example, in one of the cases investigated in the
spring of 1969, the 15 to 20 estimated hard-core SDS activists at Kent State University, even when supplemented by
some 150 to 200 sympathizers, appeared insignificant when
compared with a total student enrollment of 21, 000.   This
SDS minority nevertheless succeeded in provoking four disturbances on the campus and forced the Kent State University
administration to divert many man-hours and funds to the
task of combating SDS efforts to disrupt the functioning of the
university.   (It was with profound shock that the nation received the news May 4, 1970, of the fatal shooting of four
Kent State students during another campus demonstration.)

A small band of SDS members in a large student population was also successful in creating a campus disorder at
Georgetown University where there were approximately 20
SDS members in a student body of over 3, 000.   In addition,
the SDS chapter at George Washington University, which had
a hard-core membership of about 20, mustered 150 out of a
total of 13, 500 students to a radicalizing movie film presentation which immediately preceded the seizure of the university
building housing the Sino-Soviet Institute.

Efforts of local SDS activists were often bolstered by
appearances on campus of non-students from nearby communities, functionaries from SDS regional and national offices,
and itinerant radicals from other parts of the country.

5)   By words and deeds many SDS chapters showed
their utter contempt for university reform efforts and the
orderly process of negotiated settlement of grievances.   SDS
members, making demands for university reforms, exhibited
an incredible lack of sincerity of motive with regard to the
issues about which they complained.

A favorite SDS tactic was the creation of a series of escalating conflicts between students and the university administration for the purpose of "radicalizing" students in an effort to persuade them to identify with the Vietnamese or Cuban communists as part of a revolutionary movement to smash American "imperialism." The issues raised by SDS chapters, such as the draft and ROTC, were intended primarily to service this revolutionary objective. In many cases, university agreement with SDS demands would not have brought peace to the campus. SDS leaders committed to the destruction, not the reform, of the university system were prepared to escalate their demands beyond reason in the hope of triggering a physical confrontation which would polarize and radicalize other youth. Although the forms of protest activity utilized by SDS varied, the technique of seizing and holding academic buildings captured SDS' imagination as the best device for dramatizing their essentially non-negotiable demands.

6) SDS activists exerted a disproportionate impact on the university campus as a result of militant speech fests in dormitories and at campus rallies, as well as through the showing of propaganda films and the energetic use of mimeograph machines. At American University, the SDS chapter printed inflammatory literature on a printing press which belonged to the university and which was available to any campus organization.

7) SDS' strength lay primarily in its ability to "politicalize" a large segment of students, either on the force of a specific issue or because of a university's response, such as calling in outside police. SDS also had the advantage of picking the issue on which it planned to seek a confrontation. SDS tactics were based upon a formula of confrontation in the hope that the administration would overreact. This was expected to make SDS an underdog worthy of sympathy and support from the student body.

8) Testimony by college administrators pointed to the efficacy of the availability of police assistance and court injunctive processes in ending campus disorders and suggested that universities be allowed to attack the problem of campus disorders caused by SDS militants without additional Federal legislation to the same end. For example, at George Washington University the temporary restraining order obtained from the U.S. District Court was effective in causing SDS members to leave a campus building they had occupied.

9)   SDS leaders traveled extensively to communist countries and the SDS exhibited a rapport with radical organizations and individuals in foreign countries.

10)   Speeches and literature of the SDS Weatherman summer organizers during 1969 displayed an obsession with violence, possibly as part of their romantic fantasy that they were following in the footsteps of Ché Guevara. The sporadic 1969 summer raids on high schools and colleges by these SDS activists appeared to alienate rather than attract other young people.

11)   Application of the "worker-student alliance" strategy by the faction of SDS influenced by the Progressive Labor Party, illustrated by its intervention in a labor dispute in the Washington, D.C., area, produced no evidence that this approach was successful in attracting mass support to the SDS banner.

12)   The Weatherman SDS faction in its October 1969 National Action in Chicago showed that it had chosen physical violence as its way of building a revolutionary youth movement in the United States. The costly failure of the "Bring the War Home" confrontation "turned off" many of the potential student followers of the organization.

13)   Vast changes in curricula and scholastic procedures plus wider student participation in administrative decisions seriously blunted support for the radical demands of the SDS. For example, the existence of open channels of communication between students, faculty, and administrators of American University and university decisions to give students a voice in university planning were reported to be responsible for the failure of the SDS chapter at that university to bring about disruptions.

SDS PROSCRIBES FREEDOM OF OTHERS

A particularly troubling aspect of SDS tactics was the willingness to use the most violent and obnoxious means to reach SDS goals, such as the seizure of university buildings, disruption of classes, holding administrators hostage, and the silencing of those who disagreed with SDS objectives. Such tactics are anathema to the principles of academic freedom which undergird the entire educational system. They can in no way be justified as a means of obtaining rights allegedly

denied or in protest of inequities unremedied. The violent
disruption of the university is, of itself, an infringement of
the rights of professors to teach and of students to learn,
free from harassment and interference.

The United States Supreme Court has flatly rejected
the argument that people who want to protest have a constitutional right to do so whenever and however they please. In
February of 1969, the Supreme Court (Tinker v. Des Moines,
Iowa Independent Community School District, 393 U. S. 503,
1969) ruled that the right of students to engage in peaceful
protests does not include a right to disrupt the educational
process. Thus, it is clear that students do not enjoy any
special privileges to interfere with the rights of other students or, as the Supreme Court ruled: "... conduct by the
student in class or out of it ... is ... not immunized by
the constitutional guarantee of freedom of speech."

Freedom of dissent is vital to the maintenance of a
democratic republic and is essential to the general welfare.
Condemnation of the SDS and its protagonists is not to be interpreted as readiness to curb critics of social, political,
or economic aspects of American society. But the right to
be a student carries other fundamental rights than the right
to dissent. Among these rights which must also be protected
are the right to use classrooms and research facilities free
from occupation by demonstrators, the right to use libraries
free from seizure by militants, and the right to study in an
atmosphere of reason and civility. The academic enterprise
is a fragile structure that can only be maintained through
genuine tolerance and free speech and a belief in free inquiry. When one group asserts that it has a monopoly on
these civil rights, the eventual result is likely to be repression and reprisals. Consequently, freedom in the academy
cannot be absolute; it must be relative. One can pursue
one's own ideas and activities within the university only in a
non-violent, uncoercive way. Violence and force, even if
only psychological, displace reason rapidly. At the point at
which reason is intimidated, the university ceases to exist.

SUMMING UP

The Students for a Democratic Society has ceased to
be a viable national organization. Some of its splintered
factions live on--the most notorious as fugitives in anarchy,
underground and seemingly beyond the point of no-return.

The bulk of its one-time adherents have found new homes.
Many have been absorbed by ten years of maturing and experience into the established channels of our national life.
Others are engaged in developing new organizations of protest,
resistance, and radicalism, or swelling the ranks of campus
groups seeking to fill the vacuum caused by the demise of the
nationwide SDS organizational structure.

In 1960, an embryonic organization of students reached
out to channel the exploding idealism of young white America's
concern for civil rights into an effective instrument for cor-
recting some of the inequities and inadequacies of this most
affluent and fundamentally free society.   Their dreams, at
times, outstripped their capacity to be effectual.   They
yielded to the temptation to abandon ideological restrictions
on membership and opened their doors to radical extremists.
As the ranks swelled, both the direction and objectives of
SDS changed radically--from dissent on behalf of reform to
open resistance, and finally to revolutionary violence and
virtual anarchy.

Events--the assassination of a President and his
brother and the added slaying of a national civil rights leader,
plus two other symbols disturbing to America, ghetto rioting
and the growing magnitude of the war in Vietnam--provided
ample crises for rallying growing numbers of students in
search of excitement and a role in making history.   But the
penetration of SDS by extremists of the Left coupled with an
organizational growth carelessly handled, over-zealous leaders
who enjoyed more response from rhetoric than from reason,
and the constant tug-of-war over the "town" or "gown" (street
or campus) approach SDS should take, provided more than
enough ingredients for its eventual eruption and disintegration.

The story of SDS makes one aware that youthful ide-
alism--so vital to the progress of any society--is effective
only when it is taken in balance, in relationship to all other
elements in the body politic.   As long as SDS resisted penetration by extremists and undemocratic ideologies, as long
as it was self-disciplined and dedicated to the peaceful pursuit
of sincere social concerns, as long as it encouraged orderly
dissent, it held the potential for making a useful contribution
to American life.   Instead, it lowered barriers to participation by extreme elements of the Left, compromised its initial
self-restraint, and came to view itself as a galvanizing organization for demonstrations escalating in militancy.   It
adopted protest for protest's sake, rhetoric for rabble-

rousing's sake, and, ultimately, confrontation for the sake of polarization. Above all, SDS failed to develop and advocate programs and solutions to the social ills. Its idealism was dissipated in ad hoc responses to crises. The Students for a Democratic Society became a misnomer. Its strident cries became wild and often incoherent, and its credibility dwindled in the eyes of its adherents and those it sought to enlist. What the Students for a Democratic Society promised at the end was the destruction of democratic society.

Merely because the organization of SDS is now virtually a thing of the past does not mean that the problems raised by the rapid proliferation of campus unrest through the decade of the 1960s are apt to fade. They may become more critical as newer organizations take shape and emerge as the new voices of radicalism among American students. These voices will undoubtedly emerge as the United States encounters new crises, especially when the system itself seems to be at fault.

If the American people apply the lessons learned from the SDS experience intelligently, great progress can be made in balancing idealism and realism in a free society that wants to "build, not burn," as SDS once urged. But if the legacy of SDS is to be an even more virulent manifestation of student radicalism, the awful warning of longshoreman-turned-philosopher, Eric Hoffer, is likely to become a reality in American life. He once wrote, with respect to campus violence, "When freedom destroys order, the yearning for order will destroy freedom." Indeed, this is what nearly happened. The people, afraid of the SDS brand of radicalism, turned in 1968 during crisis to a right-wing politician named Richard Nixon who, with a large group of anti-democratic associates, attempted systematically to destroy the freedom he promised to protect. The real lesson to be re-learned and re-affirmed is that extremism from whatever source cannot be tolerated and that the rights of the individual citizen must be preserved as the most supremely important expression of a democratic society--rights to be protected against abuse by even the leader of the State.

NOTE

1. Dr. Konrad Lorenz, physiologist, in an article entitled "A Talk with Konrad Lorenz," written by Frederic de Towarnicki in New York Times Magazine, July 5, 1970.

IV

THE LITERATURE OF THE STUDENTS
FOR A DEMOCRATIC SOCIETY

This section, consisting of 40 selected items from a collection of almost 2, 000, presents a representative cross-section of materials by and about SDS. Most items are mimeographed ones produced by SDS chapters but there are a few important items originating with government agencies. Any scholar who wishes to use the entire SDS collection the editor has compiled, should contact Dr. Paul Kraus, Director of Libraries, Illinois State University, Normal, Illinois 61761. The "SDS Collection" is housed in the "Special Collections."

1. SDS: AN INTRODUCTION

The Emergence of the New Left

In the spring of 1968, thousands of students in New York's Columbia University erected barricades and battled police following a successful four-week strike against University complicity in the Vietnam War and racist expansion programs in nearby Harlem. At the same time, hundreds of thousands of French workers and students--after seizing factories, schools, and streets--nearly toppled the DeGaulle government. Significantly, the mass revolt grew out of student protests against the policies of the first French "multiversity" at Nanterre. In West Germany student strikes and demonstrations involving thousands were directed against the Government's passage of "emergency laws" giving near-dictatorial powers to itself. In Japan, Italy, and the Scandinavian countries, similar actions have been occurring as well.

The identifiable thread running through these internationally dramatic events is an assortment of radical student organizations. These groups make up the core of what has come to be known as the New Left. Although they have only been visible to the general public for the past two or three years, most of these organizations first formed in the late 1950s and early 1960s. Generally, they are made up of students and unaffiliated young people within those advanced capitalist countries with highly developed technological societies.

The post-World War II rapid transformation of these economies had a similar effect on their systems of higher education--the growth of the "knowledge factories" or multiversities. With the dominant social themes of this period being affluence, consumption, and adjustment, the young men and women were expressing their cultural oppression and personal alienation with growing intensity. Out of apathy and the gray flannel suit emerged James Dean, Marlon Brando, and the Angry Young Man--the Beat Generation. Also, following the Hungarian Revolt crushed by the Soviets in 1956, hundreds of young intellectuals left the European and US Communist Parties in disgust over the crimes of Stalin.

All this, to be sure, was only an undercurrent, a minor key. In the mainstream was the Cold War, Joe McCarthy, the silent generation filing into heavily-mortgaged Ozzie and Harriet suburbia, the prototypes of Carl Oglesby's man of those times--slim-waisted, swivel-hipped, bullet-headed make-out artists. While many young activists of today may find these images rather alien, this is where the history of the New Left begins. These were the conditions giving birth to our present movement.

The Growth of SDS

The central force of the New Left in the United States has been Students for a Democratic Society or SDS. We are a young, rapidly growing movement; only sixty-odd people attended our founding convention at Port Huron, Michigan in 1961. Even by early 1965, SDS had fewer than twenty-five hundred members with chapters on less than forty campuses. However, with its April 17th, 1965 March on Washington to End the War in Vietnam, SDS grew in national prominence. Presently, there are over forty thousand national and local SDS activists in more than three hundred chapters in universities across the country.

In the early years, SDS was a coalition of liberals and radicals, working from a multi-issue perspective on the questions of peace and disarmament, civil rights, poverty, and university reform. We supported reform Democratic electoral campaigns, and in 1964 even put out a button saying "Part of the Way with LBJ."

Our bitter yet powerful experience with American politics in the 1960s has moved us considerably away from our original Left-liberal stance. Today SDS is a mass radical and anti-imperialist student movement. The critique we are developing of American corporate capitalism has brought us to advocate the necessity of an activist and revolutionary politics for the New Left.

Where Do We Stand?

On Vietnam and US Foreign Policy

SDS completely opposes the US Government's immoral, illegal, and genocidal war against the people of Vietnam.

We insist on the immediate withdrawal of all US personnel
from that country.   Moreover, we see the US policy in Vietnam as part of a global strategy for containing revolutionary
change in the "Third World" nations of Asia, Africa, and
Latin America.   Rather than the result of an essentially good
government's mistaken decisions, we see the world-wide exploitation and oppression of those insurgent peoples as the
logical conclusion of the giant US corporations' expanding and
necessary search for higher profits and strategic resources.
That system is most properly named imperialism, and we
stand by and support all those who struggle against its on-
slaught.   They are our brothers and sisters, not our enemies.

On the Draft and the Military

        SDS demands the abolition of the Selective Service
System.   We see the Draft as racist and anti-democratic,
procuring manpower for aggressive wars abroad.   Moreover,
through the "deferment" system, the primary coercive function of the Draft is "channeling" the lives of millions of young
people outside the Military into lifelong vocations deemed
"essential" by corporate military elites rather than freely
chosen by themselves.   We urge and will organize all young
men to wage a collective struggle in resistance to the Draft
by refusing to serve in the Military.   We also seek to break
the barriers placed between us and our brothers in uniform.
When forced by threat of imprisonment or exile, some of us
will organize within the Armed Forces, advocating desertion
and other forms of resistance to US foreign policy.

On the Black Liberation Movement

        SDS has long and actively supported the struggle of
black Americans for freedom and self-determination.   Racism
and exploitation confront black people as a group, together as
a people.   From this given condition of their daily lives,
black people must act as a group in establishing their common
identity, and in planning a strategy to challenge their oppression.   We do not simply "tolerate" the growth of black consciousness, we encourage it.   Criticizing "black power" as
"racism in reverse" is as mistaken as denouncing the American Revolution of 1776 as "colonialism in reverse."   In addition to confronting all aspects of institutionalized racism in
American life, we strongly believe that the strongest support
we can afford the black movement comes from our efforts to

engage exploited whites in the struggles and values of radical politics.

On Labor and the Struggles of Working People

From its beginnings, SDS has recognized the crucial role that the working class has to fulfill in any movement for radical social change. More recently, we have rejected the false notion that most Americans are "middle-class." Considering professional, service, white-color, and university-trained technical workers as a "class" separate from blue-collar industrial workers serves only to confuse and divide millions of workers and students and prevent them from realizing the corporate capitalist source of their exploitation and their common interest in uniting against its oppression. To further the unity and radical consciousness of the working class as a whole we support the rank-and-file insurgencies of working people against their employers, the Government, and corrupt union leadership. Our concern is not only the improvement of wages and working conditions for our brothers and sisters in the shops, but for a transformation of all labor issues growing out of alienation and lack of control into a movement against the capitalist system itself.

On the Student Revolt

SDS views the multiversity as a knowledge factory, a kind of service station producing skilled manpower and intelligence for integration with the marketable needs of the major corporate, government, and military institutions. Neither the content of the educational process, nor the ends to which our learning and resources are directed, further the fulfillment of humane social needs. Rather, the "knowledge commodity" (ourselves and the results of our work) is shaped to further the production of waste, social oppression, and military destruction. The recognition of this process has been the driving force in our work to transform student "alienation" into a radical force reaching out and uniting with constituencies beyond the campus in struggles against oppressive university administrations.

From Moral Outrage to Radical Vision

The New Left has not been noted for the completeness

or coherence of its analysis or strategy for change. Within
the ranks of SDS exists a variety of political positions: socialists, anarchists, communists, and humanist liberals.
Nonetheless, the interplay of these ideas with a common commitment to action has produced a rich and powerful shared
political experience emerging from an on-going struggle. We
have looked primarily to that experience as the source and
test of political truth, rather than to this or that dogmatic
catechism. While not shunning analytical work, we have always seen this focus as a basis of our strength and authenticity.

      Whatever the degree of the New Left's diversity, how-
ever, we have always asserted a common clarity in our
values. Within our vision, all authentically revolutionary
movements are seen as first, last, and always movements
for human freedom, whatever form their demands may take
in a given historic period. The New Left radical consciousness began with the perception of a gap between the actual
reality of our daily lives and the accessible potentiality for
human fulfillment already in existence. This tension--the
contradiction between what is and what can be--first futilely
sought its resolution in a quest for personal salvation.

      When the interests of the dominant social order denied
the realization of that potential, we discovered our powerlessness, our unfreedom. Moreover, the social character of our
oppression revealed the need of a collective struggle for liberation. We discovered our deepest personal hopes and desires were the widely-held aspirations of many. That dis-
covery has led to our affirmation of a common humanity with
all of the oppressed.

      At present, the contradiction between the brutal and
dehumanized reality of advanced corporate capitalism and the
liberating potential of its technology and productive organization has never been greater. Planned obsolescence and waste
production increase in the midst of growing scarcity. Frag-
mented job specialization and meaningless toil expand; while
cybernation and automation contain the possibility of total job
integration, the abolition of alienated labor, and the vast expansion of free and creative activity. From this viewpoint,
all the world's people have never been more oppressed. At
this moment of history, on the other hand, the potential of
the struggle for human fulfillment has never been greater.
The New Left will be at the center of that struggle. Our
humanity is at stake. Join us.

(Distributed during March and April, 1969 at Cornell and Yale Universities.   Collected by the compiler June 11, 1969.)

2. THE PORT HURON STATEMENT

Introduction: Agenda for a Generation

We are people of this generation, bred in at least modest comfort, housed now in universities, looking uncomfortably to the world we inherit.

When we were kids the United States was the wealthiest and strongest country in the world; the only one with the atom bomb, the least scarred by modern war, an initiator of the United Nations that we thought would distribute Western influence throughout the world. Freedom and equality for each individual, government of, by, and for the people--these American values we found good, principles by which we could live as men. Many of us began maturing in complacency.

As we grew, however, our comfort was penetrated by events too troubling to dismiss. First, the permeating and victimizing fact of human degradation, symbolized by the Southern struggle against racial bigotry, compelled most of us from silence to activism. Second, the enclosing fact of the Cold War, symbolized by the presence of the Bomb, brought awareness that we ourselves, and our friends, and millions of abstract "others" we knew more directly because of our common peril, might die at any time. We might deliberately ignore, or avoid, or fail to feel all other human problems, but not these two, for these were too immediate and crushing in their impact, too challenging in the demand that we as individuals take the responsibility for encounter and resolution.

While these and other problems either directly oppressed us or rankled our consciences and became our own, subjective concerns, we began to see complicated and disturbing paradoxes in our surrounding America. The declaration "all men are created equal ..." rang hollow before the facts of Negro life in the South and the big cities of the North. The proclaimed peaceful intentions of the United States contradicted its economic and military investments in the Cold War status quo.

We witnessed, and continue to witness, other para-

216

doxes. With nuclear energy whole cities can easily be pow-
ered, yet the dominant nation-states seem more likely to unleash destruction greater than that incurred in all wars of
human history. Although our own technology is destroying
old and creating new forms of social organization, men still
tolerate meaningless work and idleness. While two-thirds of
mankind suffers undernourishment, our own upper classes
revel amidst superfluous abundance. Although world population is expected to double in forty years, the nations still
tolerate anarchy as a major principle of international conduct
and uncontrolled exploitation governs the sapping of the earth's
physical resources. Although mankind desperately needs revolutionary leadership, America rests in national stalemate,
its goals ambiguous and tradition-bound instead of informed
and clear, its democratic system apathetic and manipulated
rather than "of, by, and for the people."

Not only did tarnish appear on our image of American
virtue, not only did disillusion occur when the hypocrisy of
American ideals was discovered, but we began to sense that
what we had originally seen as the American Golden Age was
actually the decline of an era. The worldwide outbreak of
revolution against colonialism and imperialism, the entrench-
ment of totalitarian states, the menace of war, overpopulation,
international disorder, supertechnology--these trends were
testing the tenacity of our own commitment to democracy and
freedom and our abilities to visualize their application to a
world in upheaval.

Our work is guided by the sense that we may be the
last generation in the experiment with living. But we are a
minority--the vast majority of our people regard the temporary equilibriums of our society and world as eternally-func-
tional parts. In this is perhaps the outstanding paradox: we
ourselves are imbued with urgency, yet the message of our
society is that there is no viable alternative to the present.
Beneath the reassuring tones of the politicians, beneath the
common opinion that America will "muddle through," beneath
the stagnation of those who have closed their minds to the
future, is the pervading feeling that there simply are no alternatives, that our times have witnessed the exhaustion not
only of Utopias, but of any new departures as well. Feeling
the press of complexity upon the emptiness of life, people
are fearful of the thought that at any moment things might
thrust out of control. They fear change itself, since change
might smash whatever invisible framework seems to hold
back chaos for them now. For most Americans, all crusades

are suspect, threatening.   The fact that each individual sees
apathy in his fellows perpetuates the common reluctance to
organize for change.   The dominant institutions are complex
enough to blunt the minds of their potential critics, and en-
trenched enough to swiftly dissipate or entirely repel the
energies of protest and reform, thus limiting human expect-
ancies.   Then, too, we are a materially improved society,
and by our own improvements we seem to have weakened the
case for further change.

Some would have us believe that Americans feel con-
tentment amidst prosperity--but might it not better be called
a glaze above deeply-felt anxieties about their role in the
new world?   And if these anxieties produce a developed indifference to human affairs, do they not as well produce a
yearning to believe there is an alternative to the present,
that something can be done to change circumstances in the
school, the workplaces, the bureaucracies, the government?
It is to this latter yearning, at once the spark and engine of
change, that we direct our present appeal.   The search for
truly democratic alternatives to the present, and a commitment to social experimentation with them, is a worthy and
fulfilling human enterprise, one which moves us and, we
hope, others today.   On such a basis do we offer this document of our convictions and analysis: as an effort in understanding and changing the conditions of humanity in the late
twentieth century, an effort rooted in the ancient, still unful-
filled conception of man attaining determining influence over
his circumstances of life.

(Collected from the SDS at the University of Virginia at
Charlottesville on March 15, 1970.)

3. THIS IS TO CERTIFY THE MEMBERSHIP OF

. . . .
Signature

in the Students for a Democratic Society.
The SDS is an education and social action
organization dedicated to increasing democracy in all phases of our common life. It
seeks to promote the active participation
of young people in the formation of a movement to build a society free from poverty,
ignorance, war, exploitation and the inhumanity of man to man.

. . . . Secretary, SDS

Students for a Democratic Society
1608 West Madison Street
Chicago, Illinois 60612

STUDENTS FOR A DEMOCRATIC SOCIETY

is an association of young people of the left. It seeks to
create a sustained community of educational and political concern; one bringing together liberals and radicals, activists
and scholars, students and faculty. It maintains a vision of
a democratic society, where at all levels the people have
control of the decisions which affect them and the resources
on which they are dependent. It seeks a relevance through
the continual focus on realities and on the programs necessary to effect change at the most basic levels of economic,
political, and social organization. It feels the urgency to
put forth a radical, democratic program whose methods embody the democratic vision.

Preamble, SDS Constitution

(Collected at the University of Chicago, November 14, 1969.)

219

4. DEAR McCARTHY SUPPORTERS:
    An Open Letter

> The following "open letter" was written
> just prior to the 1968 Democratic Conven-
> tion; it was addressed to those young Mc-
> Carthy supporters who came to Chicago
> for the Convention. Although it is thus
> unable to foresee later developments, it
> is nonetheless a clear exposition of SDS's
> position on electoral politics at the pres-
> idential level.

We recognize in you many of our own aspirations.
We think you should recognize in us the best possibility of
their attainment.

So this open letter is in part a plea and in part a
polemic. Its single theme and main assumption are that each
one of you is a hundred times more important than those people whose cause you have given your capacities for concern,
hope, and work. Because we believe this, you give us hope.
Because you do not, you make us angry.

We're writing this just before Convention time, on the
threshold of what we in SDS think will be the bureaucratic
assassination of your fondest and most foolish political dreams.
We know that many of you are wrestling right now with the
question of coming or not coming to Chicago for the showdown ... or the farce. And we read that the busses are being filled as rapidly as they are chartered.

The decision to come must not have been easy. Had
you paid attention to the old pros on your man's campaign
team and stayed home, you'd never have been able to shake
the doubt that you surrendered something important without
putting up a fight. But on the other hand, the post-primary
spectacle of Humphrey's inner-sanctum power must have made
many of you too cynical to think that anything you could do--
anything that ordinary people could ever do--would keep the
Machine from choosing the man who had chosen it. And in
this case, the potentially bloody business of facing off against

Daley's primed and beefed-up cops would look like a rather
freaky piece of idleness.

Our idea in SDS is that you should have stayed home.
Not because Chicago seems scary, but because back home
is where we think your most important political work awaits
your skills and commitments.   Our idea is that this Convention will amount to a macabre Roman circus best enjoyed
from the greatest distance.   Not just because we think Humphrey's already bagged it, but also because we wouldn't be in
the least surprised, at the critical moment, to find your man
holding up the winner's hand.   Even more than that, it's because we think that the miracle you're praying for, a Mc-
Carthy nomination, wouldn't begin to make nearly the difference for yourselves, the nation, and the world which you believe it would.

We know, of course, that you've heard it all before
from SDS, that ratpack of cranky, never-satisfied, know-it-
all, self-righteous novice revolutionaries, those super-radi-
cals who yelled and yelled about the wolf at the door and then,
when at last a man showed up with a willing disposition and
a rifle in his hands, complained that his rifle's bore was too
small and its sight too untrue for the job, and that the problem wasn't really the wolf anyway, or even the door that
could be threatened by the wolf, but rather the house itself
in its entirety.   "A wolf's at the door and you nuts want to
start tearing down the house to build a new one--which you
don't even have plans for.   Smart!"

Who knows?   Maybe your man will somehow pull it
off and beat Nixon.   And stop this war--these wars, rather,
a key feature of our country's current and abiding distress
being that Vietnam is everywhere.   We share your hope that
the joke is going to be on us.

And if your man loses, but loses close?   We can
anticipate the bitterness with which some of you may accuse
us of having laid back in the crisis.   "We had a chance.
Another pair of hands might have saved the game."   This so-
called New Left which said in the early 1930s: 'After Hitler,
us.'   "Once again," you may say, "the world will have to pay
the price of this all-too-unblemished political morality."

Since we won't be able to answer you then--if indeed
things do unfold that way--we want to answer you now.

HOW WE GOT WHERE WE ARE

In the beginning, back in the heroic period of the civil-rights struggles--say from 1964 through 1970--our assumptions were barely "radical" at all. Black people should be free. Nothing extreme about that. It's the cardinal promise of the country's official morality. The Movement's demands could not have been simpler: "Live up to these promises, America." And we assumed that somewhere in its mysterious heart, America really wanted to do that. And that it could.

You know the end of that particular story. Heartbreak and terror.

At best, change went sideways: more laws, more criminals. As often as not, change went backward: more phoniness, more despair.

Being as curious as anybody else, we wondered why nothing our liberal government did ever worked the way our liberal politicians said it would. Why did the Welfare programs only seem to make poverty more humiliating? Why did all these civil-rights laws leave the black man's desperation unrelieved? Why did the shadow of progressivism only consolidate the substance of reaction?

And why did nearly everybody agree that peace was war?

Why were the conventional peacenik marches, orderly to the fault of a yawn, increasingly assaulted in Los Angeles, Chicago, and New York by unprovoked police?

Why did the press always cover it up?

The growing numbers of public figures who belatedly discovered that the War in Vietnam was a dangerous mistake --why did they continue to support the persistent repetition of the Congo, Guatemala, Bolivia?

Maybe the problem was deeper than we had supposed?

So we studied things again: racism, poverty, the War. We found that our search for convincing explanations drove us to look harder at this American past of ours and to probe more skeptically these democratic institutions which, we had been told, were to facilitate needed change, not obstruct or deny it.

A pattern appeared: the pattern of the International Communist Conspiracy and our valorous national effort to defeat it in behalf of democracy, Shakespeare, miniskirts, Caltex, and so on. Everywhere in the world our Cold War leaders looked they saw conspiracies, agitation, subversion, and insurrection. We followed their trembling fingers, their furious gaze, and ourselves took a long hard look at this nightmare. How could we not? Not only our lives but the powers of increase of the motherland herself were alleged to have been placed in jeopardy by all these colored devils. What did we see?

In the first place, hunger everywhere. In the second, despair everywhere. Then indignity and humiliation. Then dozens and dozens of two-bit dictatorships which our freedom fighters found peculiarly tolerable. And finally we saw--everywhere--the Yankee businessman, attache case in hand, at home it seemed in any of these "Free World" countries from Vorster's South Africa to Stroessner's Paraguay, from Papa Doc Duvalier's Haiti to post-bloodbath Indonesia, up and about, making a buck--a very pretty one, judging from all corporation reports--while for some mysterious reason the economics of all these lucky "host countries" kept lagging farther and farther behind. And behind this ubiquitous businessman, this traveling universal, we saw the smiling face of your AID field rep. Or was he CIA? And behind even him, trying to blend in with the native faces, trying to escape attention in the shadows of certain jungles, the Fort Bragg graduate, the jaunty cutthroat of the Special Forces, country-x team.

Vietnam was no "mistake"--not until the Vietnamese made it one.

Nor was racism, really, until Watts, or perhaps not even until the killing of King forced them to see that the loving patience for which King stood had long since been killed beneath King's feet--by their own inaction.

What has been their response?

There sits the Kerner Commission report on everybody's bookshelves, a best-seller. Damned from the mouths of its own "responsible" elite, white America, befuddled and

uptight enough as it was, is now asked to understand that the
main problem here is white racism but that the main solution
is the creation of two million new jobs in the next three
years.   So how will black jobs stop white racism? Won't
black preferentialism in fact intensify it?   And for that matter how are two million new jobs going to be created when an
array of domestic and international pressures on the economy
will force unemployment above 5% by the end of the year?
And if the problem really is white racism, why is it that the
police of all major and most minor American cities--exactly
the forces which constitute the most immediate and virulent
aspect of white racism--are being allowed to arm themselves
for a counter-insurgency effort worthy of Vietnam?

        More important: Why does this Commission, which
in other respects seems able to see realities, fail totally to
grasp the situation's leading and most obvious features, namely, that white racism's sting is a result of black powerlessness before it, that white racism's only lasting anodyne is
therefore black power, and that the core of any realistic
program must consequently be black control of black communities, black police responsible to black people, black health
facilities, black housing control, black schools teaching what
is relevant to black children, black control of the black community's financial base.

        But this lapse is not really so mysterious at all.   If
black people began to govern black communities, maybe white
people would begin to get the idea.   If that happened, who
could predict the fate of the system of centralized top-down
control to which all of us are tied in all our institutions?
If America began in earnest to practice the democratic act,
those who now govern might not be governing much longer.
The interest systems which now dictate our social priorities
might no longer dictate them.   The social and economic regulations which now pre-determine the general cast of American lives might be shortly abandoned--and with them, the
miniature elite whose special interests these regulations now
serve.

        The Movement's collective experience over this decade
drove it irresistably to a conclusion which none of us were
happy to accept:

        Americans are not a self-governing people, and we
never have been.

AND SO, EUGENE MCCARTHY

Is McCarthy the pay-off of these years of protest?
Does he represent the partial fruition of our efforts to build
a movement for changing America?

Or is he only another attempt to emasculate that protest?

Is he what the Movement has been working for?   Or
against?

How in fact are we to define McCarthy so that we can
at least be sure that we're talking about the same thing?

Perhaps by his record?   Surely you're tired by now
of listening to the dreary list of his illiberal votes: his as-
sent to the witch-hunt politics of the '50s (as late as 1959 he
voted for the Student Loyalty Oath Bill), his vacillation on
civil rights (in 1961 he voted against withholding Federal aid
from segregated schools), his occasional anti-Labor stands
(against extension of minimum-wage coverage in 1960, against
the rail workers in 1963), and maybe most galling of all, the
tardiness of his opposition to the War (he voted for every war
appropriation bill, for the Tonkin Gulf resolution, and against
the 1966 amendment which would have exempted non-volunteer-
ing draftees from service in Vietnam).   He has consistently
opposed the admission of China to the UN, and clings to the
view that there is nothing structurally wrong with our foreign
policy: "We still have the fleet," he said last November,
"we still have Japan, we still have a position in South Korea,
we have built up a strong base in Thailand...." And in
April, asked if we needed to take a new approach to international affairs, he answered "No. We do in Vietnam, in
Southeast Asia. But not in Korea, not in Japan, not in India,
not the North Atlantic Treaty Organization."

But you have heard this.

You are doubtless a little worried about the suggestion
of hypocrisy in his dissent. He sought to provide an alternative, he said when he announced his candidacy last November,
to those who "become cynical and make threats of support
for third parties or fourth parties or other irregular political
movements." As if so explicit a subordination of content to
form were anything but the essence of cynicism.

You have often been informed, moreover, that his chances of victory are galactically remote. You knew this, after all, from the start.

So add it up.

His record: to be charitable, call it ambiguous.

His present policies: to give the benefit of the doubt, say that they do not quite hit the nail on the head.

His real power: to be optimistic, assume that it is still in the process of formation.

What is the sum?

MCCARTHY-IN-PRACTICE

A definition of McCarthy-in-practice: the probably unproductive compromise of policies which are ambiguous, if not dubious, to begin with.

Which is merely one way of putting what most of you already claim to know.

Then why do you continue to support him?

We think there are reasons. One has to do with an illusion. Another with a reality. And another with a failure of nerve.

You visualize McCarthy as a man in the process of change. You imply that he should no more be judged by what he used to be than, for example, SDS itself.

In a time like this, that is no ground for fantasy. Above all, we need clarity now, not subtle evocations of mood. And in the measure that McCarthy has been clear, his case against the War remains explicitly a traditional case for anti-Communist containment.

It was only his dedication to the containment policy which led him to challenge the Administration in the first place. He saw the truth to which political vanity had blinded Johnson, namely, that it was not possible to impose upon the Vietnamese a government of French colonial officers, and that the desperate attempt to do so was creating the gravest crisis

of the Cold War period: it was cracking the Atlantic Alliance.
Not alone in this awareness, he was also not the first to
voice it. We do not say that his decision to oppose Johnson
openly was easy. Within its own framework, it was perhaps
even courageous. But this courage is that of the timid among
the craven, the diffident among the abject, the whisperer
among the silent. There are other standards of courage in
a world which remembers Ché Guevara, meets again, every
day the ordinary Vietnamese peasant, and knows Fanny Lou
Hamer. Compared to what we need, in any case, his dis-
tinction is a small excursion from an abysmal norm.

We think you project onto the future McCarthy the
virtues which you know he must come to possess. The current moral and physical turmoil certainly seems to beg for
heroes. McCarthy is honest. He has candor and integrity
and intelligence enough to distinguish victory from defeat.
With a desperation which we can easily understand, you treat
him as if he were already the man he has not yet even promised to become. This is illusionment.

The Reality: It is just that Left politics in America
is hard. There is not much room for movement in that direction. Not much is possible. Play to secure the marginal
victory and avoid the central defeat.

So it comes down to the famous hand in hand.

If it does nothing else, the McCarthy campaign represents itself implicitly as the Leftmost ideological position at
which political realism still endures. Above all, you have
told us, this is no time for utopia, romance, or extremist
provocations. The very power of the case the New Left made
for stopping the War, in fact, is a conclusive argument for
an expedient politics. So McCarthy won't join the Vietcong.
At least he'll bring off the capitulation without totally freak-
ing everybody out.

Don't demand socialism tomorrow. Demand, instead,
that capitalism, starting today, begin creating for itself a
more human heart.

Don't demand for tomorrow that real democracy establish itself in our society.

Demand, instead, that the old elites at once start be-
having better.

Very tempting, this realism of ideals, and we ourselves will cheerfully confess a preference for effectiveness
over uselessness.

But this practicality--with respect to exactly what
policies does it commend itself to us?   How desirable in
themselves are these policies?   And how exclusively are they
the property of McCarthy?

McCarthy has already persuaded us that his overriding
objective is the defense of the same American Empire which
we find flatly unsupportable.   That he should see the cessa-
tion of large-scale military action against Vietnam as the
pre-condition of revamped containment/imperialism--we find
this not at all hard to understand.   This is also why the big
corporations have turned against the war.   They, too, want
to find new security for those key positions in Europe and
Latin America which the Vietnam "diversion" has left exposed.
They, too, are passionately concerned about the international
equilibrium of the dollar, and they understand that a sharp
de-escalation of the War is a basic current requirement for
the health of the North Atlantic economic system.

McCarthy (and Rockefeller), among all the candidates,
possibly understood this best, maybe even first.   That may
be commendable.   The point, however, is that in one way or
another the futility of the War has become clear even to
Nixon.   Any President must contrive to abandon the War.
The Vietnamese have so decreed.

McCarthy's campaign is important.   It is one manifestation of the breakdown of the political coalitions put together in the 1930s.   At least indirectly, it expresses the
emergence of a newly politicized and activist "grass roots"
constituency, that of the post-war generations.   It imperfectly
embodies the new spirit of participant democracy.

But practicality?   Realism?   Granted the sincerity of
his occasional New Left flourishes, McCarthy's "practicality"
amounts in the end to the adulteration of the necessary critique of the War, the obscuring of its sources in the system
of American expansionism.   It amounts to a moderating of
already timid proposals which therefore lose whatever character they might have had: better negotiations maybe, inviting the NLF into a coalition whose other elements are precisely the forces the NLF has been struggling to expel and
which have precious little constituency other than the US
State Department, and on all other problems of foreign policy

the retention and even reinforcing of the Truman-to-Johnson containment line.

No question: Such a policy is "practical," "possible," and "realistic." We've had it for years.

And we haven't even raised yet the most obvious question: Since so many of you argue that we New Leftists should have compromised a bit for the sake of this "realistic alternative," we wonder why so few of you have argued that McCarthy can win?

The Failure of Nerve: Almost every young supporter of McCarthy we talk with is well to the Left of his champion. Many express the same dissatisfactions with his policies that we have expressed. Almost nobody thinks there is more than a 100-to-1 chance of his winning. The bird in the hand which was supposed to justify all sorts of tactical compromises turns out on inspection to be only a possible bird in the hand.

Then why all the excitement about "really making a difference?"

We have to say this bluntly:

We think you are afraid of your own politics, and that you are employing the McCarthy campaign as a means of making your dissent look respectable and "legitimate."

Fear of honest thought and its political imperatives; of effecting a clean break with the powerful institutions which have squandered so many lives; of abandoning the security of the system whose outrages you attack; of becoming your own "base of legitimacy": Is McCarthy a reprieve?

So What Do We Want You To Do?

Above all, to understand your own importance.

Not to borrow others' causes for fear of the difficulty of your own.

To grasp the fact that the authenticity which you find in McCarthy is there only because you have put it there; that his special virtues are merely small versions of your common possibilities.

Honesty? Yes.   You are more honest.

Rebelliousness?   Yes.   Your rebellion is better, even
if it has not yet discovered its proper gait and idiom.   You
dance better.   You write better poems.

The only really interesting practicality of his campaign, in fact, is that it has your support.   He needs you.
The institutions which have mis-educated, mis-employed,
mis-ruled your lives need you.

You don't need them.

This battle, after all, is one that we have begun: the
young ones began it, not the old ones.   Only the young ones
will be loyal to it.   The old ones remember too many defeats
and erroneous victories.   It is our generation's fight.   For
obvious reasons, its imagery condenses around Vietnam, the
American ghettos, the inflicted poverty of the Third World.
But its underlying content goes beyond them.

We think that the present stakes are immense.   What
we think is happening, in all this confusing and frightening
disorder, is the unfolding of a new stage of human history,
the writing by a new generation of a new human agenda--old
in its essential hopes, new in the possibility of their realization.

A birth is trying to take place.   Certain high-class
killers in league with certain clowns are trying to hold the
baby back, while a few political priests suggest politely that
the birth of a little finger might be permissible.   In behalf
of everything old, used up, and dying--in other words, in
behalf of their own privilege--they fight against everything
new.   So many undertakers in the delivery room.

The point is not to make deals with them there, but
to get them out.

"That cannot happen. "

Perhaps that is true.   But since it must happen, it
will, and whether it can or not makes no difference.

Like most of us, you are mostly of the middle and
upper-middle classes.   We have not been hungry, cold, or
afraid.   We have grown up with the Cold War, which made

anxiety an ordinary state, and the Machine, a presence in
our lives at once abstract and immediate, and which made
habit of miracle.

Our task is first to clarify the main issues of the
world we must live in.

Revolutionary communism?   That is the primary form
taken on by the struggles of the forcibly dispossessed to re-
possess themselves of their identity and destiny.   American
power has no business opposing those struggles.   Americans
indeed must learn to rejoice in the human bravery that brings
them into being.   For when those who are now oppressed
are not oppressed, then the masters will also be liberated
from their permanently desperate vigils.

The militant nationalism of American blacks?   Far
from being a threat to us, this anger enriches us and we
welcome it.   There is no man, no law, no government that
can substitute for this creative movement of the people.

The defense of property rights?   Americans have already been de-propertied by the very system whose demand
for property worship is most feverish.   Our task is not to
lament this event but to move forward through it.   We do
not deny that once upon a time property rights constituted the
base of the development of social wealth.   Men paid a high
price in suffering for the political guarantee of these rights
to a privileged elite.   There is no longer the remotest need
for either that suffering, that guarantee, or that elite.   Current and future wealth is wholly socialized in every respect
but that of ownership.   The completion of its socialization
is the only way to avoid the on-coming international war of
race and class and to restore the chance of national sanity.

Our parallel task is to create the political means by
which we can pursue our objectives.

This requires, above all, that we face a simple fact:
Political institutions designed to perpetuate a system of power will never become instruments for the transformation of
that system.

If you want to stop not only the Vietnam war but the
system that begot it, if you want not merely to blur the
edges of racism but to change the system that needed slaves
in the first place and could "emancipate" them only into

ghettoes in the second, if you want not merely to make deals
with irrationality but to liberate reason for the conquest of
joy, then you will have to go outside the system for the preparation of your means.   You will have to go inside yourself
first to rediscover the feeling of your own possible freedom,
and from there to the feeling of the possible freedom of
others.

Pride and communion.

That's what the Movement is about.   That's what we
think you should be about.

STUDENTS FOR A DEMOCRATIC SOCIETY
Washington Regional Office
3 Thomas Circle, NW
Washington, DC
20005
202/332-1387

(Received from the Students For A Democratic Society, 3
Thomas Circle, N.W., Washington, D.C. on September 3,
1968.)

5. REPORT ON HUMBOLDT PARK
NATIONAL GUARD ARMORY

The SDS surveyed the Chicago area prior
to the 1968 Democratic National Convention. This surveillance report on the
Humboldt Park National Guard Armory
and the following document on the Chicago
Avenue Armory substantiate the kind of
advance work the SDSers did. The numbers herein refer to numbers on rough
maps not reproduced in this book.

Address: southeast corner of Kedzie and North Ave.

Talked to guard on duty, said there would probably be little
action here, although 4,000 could be pulled if needed, most
riot duty went from South Side and Chicago Ave. armories,
had only 3 or 4 men in armory on weekends, monthly drills.

There were steel bars on all ground floor windows.

Neighborhood mostly white and Puerto Rican lower
middle class, park is haven for winos. Many young kids in
neighborhood, private homes, wooden houses.

The park on the south and eastern sides forms a
natural place to gather or regroup people. North Ave has
heavy traffic with a narrow concrete divider down the middle.
The blocks to the north all have alleys running down the middle serving garages behind houses.

There are 8 minor entrances, a row of five on the
west side that look like a row of troops could come out of,
and three big doors on the north where trucks and tanks
could drive out.

Peaceful picketing could be kept to the north and west
sides of the building, as few as 100 persons would look OK.
An attempt to block exits would call for at least 750 cadre
and would only be symbolic anyway.

Starting at NW corner and proceeding clockwise

233

entrances are: 1. basement level garage-sized doors with
ramp up, facing west; 2. small door for a single person
facing N; 3. garage-sized double doors facing N, also slightly above street level, ramp to street; 4. same as 2; 5.
same as 1, facing E (1-5 all symmetrically centered on N
side of armory); 6. double person-sized doors, up ramp
from street, facing E; 7. same as 6; 8. slightly larger,
around corner, facing S; 9. 3 large doors big enough for
motorcycle, about 3 ft above ground level face S but enclosed
by fence, hard to maneuver out of; 10. same as 2, next to
9; 11. double doors to offices, up about 5 steps from street,
facing W; 12-16. large double doors, each recessed into
wall of building, big enough for motorcycles with sidecars,
but not cars to drive through, all face W; 17. same as 11.
In addition, there are three low, climbable wooden gates at
entrances to ramps to doors 1 and 5 (18 and 19) on the street
level and to the fenced enclosure of doors 9 & 10, facing W
(20).

In addition there is a basement door on the east side
with two doors, one of which is blocked by scrap metal, the
other may still open. Maybe a surprise entrance/exit, down
a flight of steps from ground level.

It would seem impossible to get in or out through
windows.

There is a gas pump at the bottom of slight ramp
down from east side raised platform.

There is a pond with bushes, etc., in the park about
200 yds SE of armory, can't be seen from ground floor or
armory but from roof.

Element of surprise after dark more likely.

(Distributed by the University of Chicago SDS on August 9,
1968. Collected from the Regenstein Library, University of
Chicago, on April 17, 1973.)

6. REPORT ON CHICAGO AVE. ARMORY

Address: W end of block E of Seneca Ave., N of Chicago, S of Pearson

Noticed sign at top of main stairs inside; "Demcon Briefings 3rd Fl." E end of building is offices on 2nd and 3rd floors, maybe 1st, too. W end is large parking lot 2nd floor--would be indoor parade ground, motor pool probably below that--door 5 had ramps leading up and down, large enough for tanks.

Immediate neighborhood: upper class N parks E and W, Restaurant, campus S, hospitals further S, business further W, Lake further E. Chicago campus of Northwestern Univ to immediate SE.

Seems like easily demonstrated around or even blocked.

Doors: starting NW corner and clockwise 1. Large double doors up a few steps probably for offices, facing N; 2. same as 1; 3. large doors center of E side, face E, up a few steps, lead to flight of steps to offices, about 10 feet wide; 4. three single person doors, street level or a few steps up; 5. street level large double doors big enough for tanks; 6. large aluminum door, slide up, big enough for tanks; 7. set of 4 small doors, face W; 8. same as 7. large windows below ground level, in wells, along N wall, indicate lower level, probably S side is ramps to these two levels.

North side Pearson St. 2 way street E of Seneca, one way E W of Seneca. Michigan Avenue very wide & busy. Parking lot on N side of Pearson between Mich. & Seneca, vacant lot with 2 large billboards on W end of same block. Church on SW corner of Mich and Delaware, big construction on block between Mich and Seneca and Dela. & Chestnut. High rise wealthy apartments due N. Blind alleys--parking lots off DeWitt Pl between Chestnut and Pearson, one blind alley, one thru alley to E off Dewitt between Chestnut and Dela., also stairs down to basement level shopping center, hallway leading to elevator in a hotel-escape route?

Construction work NE of armory 4 trailers on S side

of Pearson, N side, some open area, piles of sand, concrete bags, wooden horses, cement blocks, lumber, timbers, iron pipes, iron U's for setting concrete, rocks. Also a truck, and entrance to underground parking lot.

Broad sidewalk runs along E side of armory with concrete stumps at each end to keep cars, not motorcycles out. E of that a low chain link fence, then a cinder track, fenced with iron spike 4 ft fence, hard to climb, but 8 ft gaps. Tennis courts fenced in, then baseball field, facing SE. Driveway for park vehicles runs between Pearson and Chicago, then playground and park admin. buildings, then Lake Shore Drive, a natural military hwy, better than Mich. Tunnel for pedestrians at SE corner of this n block crosses under to lake, which is concrete slabs. Park area about 3/4 mile south. Local lanes are: W of Express, easy to walk across, too. Only one low guardrail to hop across, but much traffic. Campus has two alleys running N-S with lockable fence in middle--possible escape, regroup--points, large lawn on NE corner of that block, also.

Small parking lot E off Fairbanks, possible escape routes. Superior one way East, Huron W, S of Superior and E of Fairbanks are parking lots for hospital, S of Huron is VA research hosp., N is private hosp. Block SW of Huron & Fairbanks is private parking lot, block north of that is 3 story city parking lot.

The block due S of armory has alley in line with door # 6, goes through to Superior, also branches W and through to Mich. ? Hosp on SE corner of that block with fire alarm out front.

Very wide sidewalk S side of Chicago, with overhang building, with a large area just W of armory where fountain not fully installed, good for regrouping, hidden by awning for Carriage House, S of Armory. W of armory is small park, bordered by 4 ft chain link fence, easily climbed, two exits S, one N, large exit W around small first aid garage/office, which has parking lot with exit N on Pearson, wide grass strip S to Chicago, stone wall to W separates from waterworks offices. Good place to gather and march from.

750 could easily block all doors symbolically, also possible provocation: detour Lake Shore Drive traffic into immediate neighborhood with wooden horses, etc., then stop cars with other wooden horses, then saturate with people,

then let air out of tires of more and more cars until tanks, etc. in armory can't get out.   A few cars sacrificed for most direct blocking of garage doors.   Aluminum door could be bent out of operation.   Could NWU form a sanctuary? Source of cadre?

Lots of fire hydrants for further confusion, first aid for gas attacks.   Construction site(s) would provide barricade materials.   Apartment houses and hotels provide many blind alleys, which connect, for possible escape through confusion.

(Distributed by the University of Chicago SDS on August 9, 1968.   Collected from the Regenstein Library, University of Chicago, on April 17, 1973.)

7.   CONVENTION NOTES

published by the March 23rd
first issue   February 17, 1968
CONVENTION COMMITTEE
Room 315   407 South Dearborn   Chicago   60606
Phone 939-2666
MINUTES: FEBRUARY 11 MEETING
SUMMARY:

On February 11, an ad hoc committee of 34 people
(names attached) met in Chicago to discuss a method for making decisions about a possible challenge to the Democratic
National Convention.

The meeting was co-chaired by Carlos Russell from
New York and Rennie Davis from Chicago.

The agenda included:
Morning: General discussion of alternative perspectives and programs for the Convention
Afternoon (early):   Black and white workshops to
develop a democratic method for making
decisions about possible actions and programs related to the Convention
Afternoon (late):   Report from the two workshops.
Establishment of an interim committee.
Adoption of a structure proposal.

The decisions, stated briefly, were:

(1)   to establish an interim committee of the following
people: Carolyn Black, Earl Durham, Corky Gonzoles, Lincoln Lynch, Carlos Russell, Rennie Davis, Dave Dellinger,
Bob Greenblatt, Tom Hayden, Sue Munacker

(2)   to call and plan for a representative movement
conference on March 24-25 in the mid-West.   The conference

238

participation should include representation from all major
black liberation and anti-war organizations with attention given
to the breadth constituency base, and interest of the people
receiving invitations

(3) to prepare people attacking this conference to
make political decisions. Working papers outlining four alternative strategies should be encouraged to discuss the various proposals prior to March 23-24.

(4) to develop an agenda for the March conference
which can allow decision-making on a general strategy for
the Democratic Convention and establish machinery for developing and carrying out that strategy.

MEETING MINUTES:

(Apologies for omission or misrepresentation, if any)

Dave Dellinger: Reported on the background to this Chicago
planned meeting. In December, the National Mobilization to
End the War in Vietnam discussed the Democratic Convention
as a possible target for a major movement convergence. The
Mobilization decided to initiate a broad conference of movement representatives to consider possible actions at the Chicago Convention. To plan this conference, the officers of
the National Mobilization called a meeting in New York to
discuss the feasibility of such a conference. The planning
session in New York (Jan. 27) had virtually no representation
from black organizations. The New York meeting established
an interim committee to prepare for a second planning meeting in Chicago that would seek to be more representative of
the movements. The interim committee included Rennie
Davis, Dave Dellinger, Tom Hayden, Carlos Russell, Cora
Weiss. February 11 was set as the date for a second planning meeting.

The meeting today is meant to be open ended. We may decide that we would not want to work together. We should
not consider ourselves bound by earlier meetings.

Carlos Russell: Proposed agenda for the meeting. Morning:
Discussion of alternative strategic perspectives on the Democratic Convention. Afternoon (early): black and white workshops to develop a democratic method for choosing a strategy. Afternoon (late): Discussion of any structure proposals.

The agenda has been discussed informally by groups that met last night. Is there additional discussion or suggestion?

Sidney Peck: I didn't know that people were going to meet last night and could have been present. We have had problems in the last two meetings with communication and must correct this if we are to work well together.

Carlos: Suggest that Rennie Davis and I report on informal meetings last night.

Rennie Davis: Last night, I reported that I thought the major movement position on the Democratic Convention could be reduced to four paragraphs and that the movement should be given an opportunity to decide one of these four views.

(1) DISRUPTION

One view, popular in the press, holds that the movement should prevent the Convention from assemblying. The Democratic Party is totally illegitimate and should be destroyed. The movement should do everything possible to disrupt its deliberations in August.

(2) ELECTORAL ALTERNATIVES

A second view says that the movement must offer a concrete political alternative to a Johnson-Nixon race. We should call for the creation of a third party and/or project. Presidential candidate who runs against racism and imperialism. Perhaps in August we should hold a counter-convention to nominate our own slate.

(3) STAY HOME

A third view forsees any demonstration playing into Johnson's hands. Johnson wants violence and is setting up the movement for a giant "bust" in which the movement will lose support from average Americans. The best thing is to stay home or organize demonstrations in every city except Chicago.

(4) DISCIPLINED COORDINATED DEMONSTRATION

A fourth view argues that thousands of people will come to Chicago whatever we do. We should take advantage of this time to dramatize to the world the millions of Americans who feel unrepresented by a Johnson-Nixon "choice." This

view emphasizes local organizing and education about the
Democratic Party to prepare the country for August, and
organization against disruption and violence in Chicago.

Art Waskow has sent us a memo which suggests some specific ideas for the #4 approach.   Art would emphasize local
organizing this summer which helped the country to focus on
the illegitimacy of the Democratic Party and its unwillingness
to act creatively on the crisis of our cities, racism, and the
war.   Perhaps Democratic Peoples Assemblies could meet
locally which would take up these issues.   People could then
come to Chicago demanding that the Convention focus on the
crisis and take up the major problems in an "open forum."
On the first day, the demand would be that the Convention
focus on the crisis of the cities.   Demonstrations could be
organized at welfare offices, police stations, schools and
urban renewal offices to dramatize this demand.   On the
second day, actions would dramatize the war and foreign
policy by focusing on draft boards, induction centers and
corporate war manufacturers.   The last day might center on
the unrepresentativeness of the Democratic Party as an institution, which cannot claim to represent the interest of
ordinary Americans because of its control by business, military and political interests tied to the Democratic gravy
train.   Art has developed his scheme in several pages and I
suggest that you read this memo.

Carlos: I will report on the black caucus meeting last night.
Not everyone expecting to attend the meeting today was able
to come.   FDP, for example, had an emergency executive
committee meeting today in Mississippi and expressed regrets
they could not have someone here.   George Wiley will be
arriving later today.   Dave Dellinger has reported that John
Wilson is expected.

Radical whites today are basically occupied with anti-war
activity.   Blacks are focusing on black liberation.   Any participation of blacks in a parallel strategy with whites at the
Convention will be based on a dual theme of racism and
imperialism.   Any preparation for the Convention would see
blacks organizing around black liberation locally and whites
reaching out to their own communities around the issue of
war and imperialism.   The #3 position, advocated by some,
is a cop out.

We believe a parallel structure of anti-war and black liberation organizations around a Convention challenge is possible.

But on questions of common policy, the two leadership groups would meet together and function together.

Unless there are questions about the reports, I suggest we get right into the general discussion on perspectives.

Lincoln Lynch: We want a confrontation? What forms will this confrontation take? What contingencies are we planning for hippies, yippies and so on? I could go on but these are some of the questions.

Corky Gonzoles: I am wondering what relation the Mexican-American community will have to any possible structure. I must remind the blacks, who sometimes overlook us, about the oppression of their brown brothers and sisters. If the structure were divided into black and white, where would the browns fit?

Sid Lens: At the Pentagon in October, we said we could no longer operate within the system. Now we must find ways to convince Americans outside the movement to join us outside the system. It will not serve our purpose to disrupt the Convention. We must expose it. Americans must learn that the chairman of the Democratic Party is also the President of Con Edison, hardly a position for a man who is expected to care about the poor.

Tom Hayden: As organization develops to challenge the Democratic Party, it must project a non-violent, legal face. We cannot call for violence, although violence is a major method of change in this society. We cannot mobilize thousands to fight a war at the Convention. Wars may be fought locally. A national mobilization is another matter. It must be legal and have a particular kind of political meaning. It must be designed to reach out to new people. New people will come to the Convention not because of America's racist and imperialist policies but because the party doesn't represent anyone. Our major emphasis should be on the unrepresentative nature of the Democratic party.

Fred Halstead: We should have a demonstration in Chicago whether or not it is allowed by the city. We should definitely go ahead with an action. But it would be a mistake to develop a national organization as the real purpose behind such an action. Once we agree on the action, we need a loose coordinating group to bring people to Chicago, and nothing more.

Sid Peck: Our previous national actions had limited objectives. Now there are signs that our objectives will be too
broad. We cannot move too fast or beyond the meager base
that we have. We do not yet have a base against imperialism,
for example. And we should not make a mechanical division
between imperialism and racism either. The two issues affect all Americans.

Sue Munacker: It is not premature to discuss the issue of
imperialism. Many people--more than we realize--are ready
to consider that perspective and with them, we should talk
about the war in those terms. Those who are not at that
level, we should reach in other ways, without dismissing the
broader perspective in our work.

It seems ludicrous to discuss what should happen on specific
days in Chicago. We should be focusing on what people do
now. Is the action of the summer going to fit into the time-
tables of our different organizations? Do different groups,
such as draft resistance, prefer many local actions rather
than one national action? We should be talking about how we
will organize between now and the spring.

Jim Rollins: I oppose, at this time, a demonstration in
Chicago, because we can't come out with anything that gives
us power. We should continue to work locally.

Stewart Meacham: We should develop a paper of demands, a
program or document on war, racism and self-determination.
The document, should have radical content but be expressed
in a moderate tone with emphasis on reason and moral arguments. It should deemphasize ideological terms.

Dave Welsh: I have talked to radicals inside and outside
the Peace and Freedom Party and all are opposed to any
petitioning of the Democratic Party. Are we for reforming
the Democratic Party or building a mass movement? If we
petition the Democrats it will only serve the interests of the
dump-Johnson campaign. We should say fuck the Democratic
Party. Also, we should focus on actions against the police,
as an illegitimate use of state power.

Bob Greenblatt: I like the idea of a "people's convention."
Since we should be discussing in August what happens in the
fall, perhaps after the funeral march on the Democratic Convention, we should march back to our own convention to decide on next steps for the movement.

Dave Dellinger: We are confusing the discussion of local organizing and spring and summer activity with what will happen in August. We need to be more precise about what could happen in Chicago. Certainly, there has to be many levels in which people can participate. While the Pentagon action moved the consciousness of the nation and of the participants, there was not enough preparation and follow through. We should begin now to expose the Democratic Party. We must expose the electoral illusion. Discussions and working papers should raise the Chicago action in a broader perspective.

Lucy Montgomery: I want to agree with much of what's been said. I only want to say that I don't believe anyone can control what will happen in Chicago. I like the idea of the people's assembly.

Charlene Mitchell: Why are we "opposed" to the war and "concerns" about racism? Whites have to begin to oppose racism. Blacks, each time they mention racism, must refer to the Mexicans and Puerto Ricans.

Fred Halstead: Radicals should never petition the Democratic Party, unless we are petitioning to abolish capitalism. We must explain the need to break with the Democratic Party. I believe it is possible for the movement to set a tone for the Chicago action and I believe the movement should. Finally, I agree with the idea of a document which would have radical content but moderate tone.

Dagmar Wilson: At some point, we've got to stop street walking and go to war. But I don't want to go to war over nothing. It's not that I'm copping out, but it's too soon for war. I'm not sure about this event. I feel we need to do more than back away at a dying system. We need, somehow, to construct an alternative.

Corky Gonzoles: In our movement and demonstrations, we must distinguish between those who have something to lose and those who do not. We must support those who will put their bodies on the line. And we must find a way to get economic support to these people, before OEO and the Ford foundation buy them off.

WORKSHOP REPORTS:

Afternoon: Nearly all afternoon was spent in black and

white workshops considering ways that the issues raised by
the four alternative strategic perspectives might be discussed
and voted on in a representative movement gathering.   The
summary report of those two workshops follows:

Carlos Russell: These were the decisions of the black workshops: (1) we agreed on the idea of a dual movement conference to consider and vote on the different perspectives;
(2) We will circulate a position paper on the issues in the
next several days to all black people who attended the Black
Power Conference in Newark and the NCNP Convention and
to members of the Puerto Rican and Mexican American communities; (3) we established an administrative group to carry
out the details of preparing for the conference.   The group
is Caroline Black, Corky Gonzoles, Lincoln Lynch and Carlos
Russell; (4) final decision about the general strategy, the relationship between blacks and whites and the black leadership
for any coalition would be decided at the convention.   The
convention would operate somewhat like the planning meeting
today.   There would be some joint sessions, but most of the
work would take place in separate workshops; (5) The four
people on the administrative committee would function only to
prepare for the movement conference.   Any permanent structure would come out of the conference itself.

Tom Hayden: These were the decisions of the anti-war workshop: (1) We should call and prepare for a large movement
conference.   The conference would be invitational and include
three types of representation: from constituency organizations, from coalition or area-wide groupings, from individuals expressing strong interest; (2) The convention would be
asked to consider the four perspectives and to establish machinery for developing and carrying out the adopted perspective;   (3) An interim committee would (a) develop an invitational list in consultation with the broadest spectrum of movement leadership; (b) contact people to write working papers
on the various positions and ideas circulating about the Democratic Convention; (c) organize pre-conference meetings to
discuss the various perspectives, through organizational or
regional contacts; (d) take general responsibility for the administration and management of the conference; (4) The suggested date for the conference is March 23-24; (5) The interim committee would consist of 14 people.

The discussion which followed attempted to resolve diver-
gences in the two proposals.   The principal item dealt with
the size of the two interim committees.

It was argued that the committees did not have to be politically representative if a smaller, administrative committee
would follow the guidelines developed by this planning meeting.   The final decision was to add Earl Durham to the black
interim committee and to cut back the white committee to the
following people: Rennie Davis, Dave Dellinger, Bob Greenblatt, Tom Hayden, to work as staff for the conference preparation.

Participants:

Kendra Alexander, NCNP,
   black caucus
Carolyn Black, National Du-
   Bois
Greg Calvert, SDS
Dovie Coleman, WRDA
Tom Cornell, FOR
William Darden, WSO
Rennie Davis, CRR
Dave Dellinger, Natl Mob
Don Duncan, Ramparts
Earl Durham, BCCC
Corky Gonzoles, Crusade for
   Justice
Bob Greenblatt, Natl Mob
Vernon Grizzard, Boston Re-
   sistance
Fred Halstead, SWP
Don Hammerquist, CP
Jim Hawley, Peace and Free-
   dom
Tom Hayden
Frank Joyce, People Against
   Racism
Sid Lens, Natl Mob

Obed Lopez, LADO
Lincoln Lynch, URF
Stewart Meacham, AFSC
Charlene Mitchell, black cau-
   cus
Lucy Montgomery, Women's
   Coalition
Sue Munaker, Radical Wom-
   en
Sid Peck, Ohio Peace Ac-
   tion
James Rollins, black cau-
   cus
Fred Rosen, NY Resist-
   ance
Paul Rupert, CADRE, Re-
   sistance
Jack Spiegel, Chicago Peace
   Council
David Welsh, Peace and Free-
   dom
George Wiley, NWRO
Dagmar Wilson, WSP
Leni Zeiger, Berkeley cam-
   pus

organizations listed for identification only.

(Distributed by the Students for a Democratic Society, February 17, 1968. Collected in the Special Collections, Regenstein Library, University of Chicago, August 22, 1972.)

8. SUGGESTIONS FOR LEGAL SELF-DEFENSE IN CHICAGO

1. <u>Preventive measures:</u> Chicago pigs have at their command a wide assortment of criminal laws that can be used to extend your stay here forcibly. Some important points: Disorderly conduct and mob action offenses are defined broadly enough to encompass most innocent conduct. There is no legal right to resist even an unlawful arrest or search in Illinois. Vehicle stops for alleged traffic violations are often accompanied by thorough searches of passengers and car (watch the officer searching the car for a plant of contraband.) If you are cited for a traffic offense and you have no Illinois driver's license, you must post $25 cash or a valid bond card to stay out of jail pending the trial of your case. If you are in the presence of any male under the age of 17 or any female under the age of 18 years old and either of you are engaged in any so-called illegal activity, you may be busted for contributing to the delinquency of a minor. If you yourself are under the age of 17 and in any public street, highway, building or place after 11:30 P. M. on Friday and Saturday or after 10:30 P. M. on other days, you may be convicted of a curfew violation unless you are accompanied by a parent, legal guardian, or some "responsible" adult approved by them.

The law also prohibits having any alcoholic liquor in any vehicle unless it is in its original unbroken package.

In Chicago, the best defense is, therefore, to avoid non-strategic confrontations with the pigs.

2. <u>What you must say:</u> If you are stopped by a pig, Illinois law permits him to require that you state your name, address and an explanation for your conduct if he has some grounds to be suspicious. The law also permits the pig to search you for weapons if he suspects some danger. Of course drivers must show their license. SAY NOTHING MORE. If you think you can talk a pig out of a charge, you don't know Chicago. Whatever can be said in your defense should be said with the advice of a lawyer in open court. You have a constitutional right to be silent, so don't give the enemy his ammunition.

3. **If you are busted:** You have a legal right to make a reasonable number of phone calls but you will often be required to have your own set of dimes.

If your requests to use the telephone are denied, mentally note the name and number of every pig who denies the request.   Lawyers, available anytime of day or night, may be reached by calling the following law clerks of the PEOPLE'S LAW OFFICE:
    Seva Dubuar, Flint Taylor or Kalman Resnick: 782-8908
    Charles Linn: 955-2607

4. **Once you are in the custody of the pigs, do not talk to anyone.** Pigs or other prisoners (a few of whom are cops) --no matter what they promise or threaten, you have a constitutional right to remain silent, give your name, address and age--and nothing more!

5. **If the pigs try to question you, or if they try to put you in a line-up,** demand that they first allow you to contact your lawyer.   You have a constitutional right to have present a lawyer of your choice during any questioning or line-up.   Ask for a chance to call a lawyer whenever you are questioned or asked to participate in a line-up.   Refuse to answer questions or to participate in a line-up or to be identified (but do not resist physically), unless they will wait until your lawyer arrives.

6. **Remember every word you say may hurt a brother or sister.**   The only thing you need to say is, "I do not wish to answer any questions."   Even if your lawyer is present you should refuse to answer all questions, --otherwise, you may harm yourself, the struggle and the people.   No defendant was ever hurt by keeping his mouth shut.   You know you are innocent, but the pigs know you are a dissident-- so they will do everything possible to keep you off the streets.

7. **Bail.**   Your bail will probably be higher than most others.   Ten percent of the amount set will be sufficient security to get you out, and bail sometimes is lowered after a hearing by the court.   The fact that you live out of the state will, however, militate against their setting a low bail.   A lawyer can advise you of biographical facts that will support motions to reduce bail.   You should have in mind the names, addresses and phone numbers of persons who can be contacted for bail money.

8. If the pigs beat you, threaten you or promise anything to you, remember each pig's name, the time and place.

9. If the pigs put you in a line-up without your lawyer being present, say nothing, but concentrate on everything that happens, and the people involved. Memorize how many other people there were in the line-up, the appearances of these people, their height, weight, etc.--in comparison to you. Memorize what was said and who said it during the line-up proceedings. Remember what was done and by whom. Also remember the time and place of the line-up and what the people listening to the line-up proceedings (such as pigs) said or did.

10. If you have time to prepare for your arrest leave all your personal belongings that you do not want the pigs to have with a friend. Make sure there is no contraband on you. Give your lawyer a call and have him go with you when you turn yourself in. Bring this instruction sheet, a supply of dimes (for phone calls), a supply of cigarettes, and reading material. If you do not have time to prepare for your arrest, be cool; remember that the pigs are looking for an excuse to shoot you.

(Distributed by SDS at the University of Chicago and the University of Illinois at Chicago Circle, July 15, 16, and 17, 1968. Collected September 4, 1968.)

9. YOUR "RIGHTS" UNDER THE LAW

The "Catch 22" to this whole discussion is that you are required under law to obey the orders of a cop even if those orders are unlawful. The other point to keep in mind is that your rights under the law are basically irrelevant and that the decisions of the powers that be will be based on political and not legal analysis.

You have a right to peacefully picket or leaflet or speak on any sidewalk so long as you do not block the sidewalk or cause it to be blocked, without any permit. The exception to this is picketing on a sidewalk in front of a private residence, which is prohibited.

Police can regulate traffic pretty much as they see fit. That means they can stop you at intersections and keep you out of the street.

You have a right to speak and leaflet on publicly owned property, public parks and plazas, for example.

A recent Supreme Court decision holds that you have a right to leaflet even on private property if it is used for public access (for example, the parking lots of large shopping centers). Don't push on this one; its limits are narrow and poorly defined.

Bus and train stations in Chicago are private property.

If you enter a building or other property and are asked to leave by the owner or his duly authorized agent, you must do so or you are guilty of trespass. This is true even of publicly owned buildings.

Under the new stop-and-frisk law, a cop can stop you, ask for your identification and frisk you if he feels that you "might" have a deadly weapon.

To a cop, a protestor is always guilty of disorderly conduct, no matter what he is doing. The city ordinance on this is very vague and is probably unconstitutional.

Remember: The law, the courts and the cops are there to serve someone's interest--but that someone isn't you.

Misc.

Out of state drivers licenses cannot be used for bond in traffic arrests. You will need a bond card or $25 cash if you get picked up on a traffic violation.

If you have any questions, call the Chicago Legal Defense Committee at 641-1470-1-2. But DON'T TIE UP THEIR LINES IF THERE HAVE BEEN MANY ARRESTS. Unless, of course, you are one of those arrested or you have bond money for someone in jail.

August 25, 1968

IF YOU ARE ARRESTED

1. Remain organized.

2. Have the phone number of the Chicago Legal Defense Committee (CLDC), 641-1470, 1471, 1472, and the Friends of Chicago Legal Defense (FCLD), 243-2672, 2673, with you at all times.

3. Get the name (or badge number) of the cop who ACTUALLY arrests you. This is very important since they will later assign an "arresting officer" who you never saw before and who will testify as to your guilt.

4. Don't talk to the cops. Don't give them any statement of any kind. You should give them your correct name and address.

5. Try and get names of witnesses and note the presence and identity of any photographers who might have gotten a picture of the events surrounding the arrest.

6. As soon as possible, learn the names of all people arrested with you and determine whether or not they have bond resources. If they have outside contacts who can raise bond money, find out how to get in touch with those contacts.

7. As soon as anyone in the group arrested can make a

phone call, they should call the CLDC at 641-1470, 1, 2. Give the CLDC: 1.) The names of all persons arrested, 2.) the bond resources of those persons, 3.) tell them what jail or detention center you are at and the charges against you. If you can't get through to CLDC, call FCLD at 243, 2672, 3.

8.   When you get into court, demand that you be repre-
     sented by a CLDC lawyer. If, for manpower shortage,
     a CLDC attorney is not in your court, the Bar Asso-
     ciation volunteer is better than nothing--unless they
     are clearly messing over our people.

9.   Make sure your lawyer knows your personal history
     (background is important in setting bond amounts) be-
     fore your bond hearing.

10. Ask your lawyer to make a demand for immediate trial
     and to ask for copies of all charges.

11. After you are out on bond, come to the CLDC office at
     127 North Dearborn, room 637. Bring with you: 1.)
     a bond receipt, 2.) the time and place of your bond
     hearing, 3.) copies of charges, 4.) a description
     of events (in triplicate). The description of events
     should include: 1.) Your name, address, and phone,
     2.) a narrative of all events surrounding the arrest
     (political rhetoric excluded), 3.) identification of
     police, witnesses, photos or photographers, medical
     data (if any), 4.) name of your attorney, and, 5.)
     statements of anyone who has knowledge of your case.

12. Under law, your rights in jail are: 1.) a right to
     make one phone call, 2.) a right to have bail speedi-
     ly set, 3.) a right to consult an attorney of your
     choice, and 4.) a right to remain silent.

REMAIN ORGANIZED

IMPORTANT NOTE: AS SOON AS YOU ARRIVE IN THE
CITY, FILL OUT AN ARREST FORM AT ANY OF THE OR-
GANIZED HOUSING FACILITIES, MOVEMENT CENTERS,
OR OTHER MOVEMENT PLACES. THEN RETURN THEM!!!
WE MUST HAVE THESE FORMS TO GET YOU OUT OF

JAIL IF IT COMES TO THAT.

The best place to pick up arrest forms is at the housing center.

547 S. Clark

(Distributed in Chicago on August 25, 1968. Collected September 14, 1969 in the Special Collections of Regenstein Library, University of Chicago.)

10. NATIONAL LAWYERS GUILD

5 Beekman Street
New York, N.Y.   10038
(212) 227-1078

PRESIDENT
Victor Rabinowitz
New York

EXECUTIVE SECRETARY
Kenneth Cloke

ADMINISTRATIVE SECRETARY
Joan Levenson

VICE PRESIDENTS
Hon. George B. Crockett, Jr.
Detroit

Osmond K. Fraenkel
New York

John T. McTernan
Los Angeles

Stanley Faulkner
New York

Benjamin Smith
New Orleans

Herman Wright
Houston

Max Dean
Flint

Ann Fagan Ginger
Berkeley

Father Robert F. Drinan, S. J.
Boston

SECRETARY
Herman E. Gerringer
New York

TREASURER
David Scribner
New York

ADVISORY BOARD
John M. Coe
Pensacola

Earl B. Dickerson
Chicago

Benjamin Dreyfus
San Francisco

Hon. Robert W. Kenny
Los Angeles

Malcolm Sharp
Chicago

Thomas I. Emerson
New Haven

Ernest Goodman
Detroit

January 19, 1968

Dear Friend:

A meeting will be held at the office of the National
Lawyers Guild, 5 Beekman St., Room 610 at 7:30 on Friday,
January 26th to discuss the establishment of a nationwide legal defense apparatus to deal with the projected legal problems arising out of the political protest planned for the Democratic National Convention to be held in Chicago this summer.

The meeting will be attended by the planners of the
political protest and by the lawyers and law students nationally who wish to be of some help in sorting out the complex
legal problems posed by the possibilities of injunctive suits
to stop the convention proceedings, mass arrests, civil disobedience, coordinated nationwide protest, civil suits for
police brutality, and numerous other legal problems we must
begin to face now.   We will prepare forms, affidavits, research memoranda, and a handbook on mass arrests.   We
desperately need your help, ideas, criticisms and suggestions.

Please attend the meeting, but if you are unable, send
us your name and address and any written suggestions you
may have, and we will forward information to you.

Sincerely,

Ken Cloke
Executive Secretary

KC:ak

(Received from The National Lawyers Guild on January 28,
1968.)

11.   MEDICAL HELP IN CHICAGO

Medical Committee for Human Rights and the Student Health
Organization have been asked to provide medical presence by
a number of organizations whose members plan to be visiting
Chicago from August 26-30, 1968.

In response to these requests, MCHR and SHO have set up an
apparatus for medical presence to become effective Saturday,
August 24th and to continue through Friday, August 30th.
This apparatus will include medical alert phone lines, mobile
first aid teams, stationary first aid centers, private physicians' back-up offices, other general information about medical care resources in Chicago and housing for out-of-town
medical volunteers.

There will be three levels of service.   The first will be first
aid centers which will be equipped with personnel and supplies
to render first aid if required.   The second will be mobile
first aid teams which will be dispatched to the sites of activities as indicated.   These will be supplied with first aid equipment.   The third will include physicians whose services will
be available in their offices as necessary.

The mobile first aid team will bear the primary responsibility
for service at the site of activity.   This service will include
giving information about health or medical care if requested;
render first aid, if necessary; act as a calming influence, if
possible, should panic situations arise; make referrals to
first aid centers or doctor's offices or emergency rooms as
indicated and transport, if possible, sick or injured persons
away from the site of activity and to a source of medical
care.   Wherever possible patients should be removed from a
site of activity to another source of care.   Vans identified
with red crosses will be at the sites of activity.

The first aid center will be more fully equipped and will care
for persons, or refer them if indicated, to other sources of
care.   However, physicians are requested to bring their bags
supplied for emergency care.   (If you have a scissors and
flashlight, please label it with your name and bring it with
you.)   The first aid center will also be the point of dispatch
for mobile teams so that all mobile teams will be asked to
report to a center and will be assigned from there with their

256

entire team. They will report back to the center (by phone
or in person) at the end of their assignment.

All medical volunteers are requested to maintain a neutral
posture relative to any activities at the site. Medical volunteers will wear arm-bands with the red cross on white coats
or uniforms at all times that they are on duty at a site of
activity. Medical volunteers wishing to participate in the activity at the site are requested to remove their white coats
and arm-bands and act as individuals. No volunteer should
participate in the activity at a site if he is actively on duty
as a member of a medical aid team. Any volunteer who
does not feel it is possible to submit to this discipline is
asked not to serve on a medical team.

Medical volunteers wearing the arm-band with the red cross
have some assurances of safe conduct from the police. It
is hoped that the medical symbol on the arm-band will be
recognized as a neutral, medical insignia and will be treated
as such. If, despite the neutrality of medical personnel and
present assurances of safety, any of the medical care personnel are detained or arrested, legal counsel will be available.

(Distributed by SDS August 25, 1968. Collected June 18,
1972 at the University of Chicago Special Collections.)

12. RADICAL EDUCATION PROJECT

The Radical Education Project (REP) was initiated by the Students for a Democratic Society in June 1966 "as an intellectual center for the New Left Movement in America."[1] Recent literature of the organization further defines its role as "providing our activist Movement with a research, education and publication arm--an 'internal education' institution of our own."[2]

The REP was originally very closely tied to SDS, even to the point of having a nine-member advisory committee chosen by the parent organization.[3] By the summer of 1968, it was reported that the group had become "independent" of SDS.[4] Recent REP literature, however, indicates continuing cooperation between the two groups, both in the distribution of propaganda (including films by the Newsreel) and in the organizing of "movement schools" to "provide intensive weekend seminars for SDS chapter people on specific topics."[5]

Regarding membership restrictions, the group states: "REP is non-exclusionist. We reject the rhetoric of anticommunism and the myth of human affairs as a morality play between the forces of good and evil, capitalist freedom and communist slavery."[6] The sponsor list, reflecting this nonexclusion principle, includes identified members of the Communist Party such as Victor Perlo and Philip S. Foner, along with prominent New Left figures such as Staughton Lynd and Herbert Marcuse.[7] Another sponsor is David Dellinger, who is alleged to have "described himself as a Communist, although not of the Soviet variety."[8]

The REP has been active in several conferences. In April 1967, REP and SDS cosponsored a conference on "Perspectives for Radical Change" organized by the Michigan State chapter of SDS.[9] Also in April 1967 was a "Conference on U.S. and China" held in New York City under the auspices of REP and SDS.[10] Other conferences either organized or participated in to a significant degree by REP include the first "Radicals in the Professions" conference (July 1967), a conference on the "University and the Military" (November 1967), and the "New University Conference" (March 1968).[11]

Literature distributed by the Radical Education Project

258

includes "over 80 articles" and "a number of movement jour-
nals and newspapers."[12]   Other items include the "Movement
Speakers Guide,"[13] study guides, and pamphlets on such topics as imperialism, the third world, China, and the "Black
Colony" written by such people, organizations, and publications as Anna Louise Strong, Ché Guevara, Carl Oglesby,
New Left Notes, the North American Congress on Latin America (NACLA), SNCC, and the Communist newsweekly Guardian.[14]   The REP also regularly distributes such publications
as The Movement, Radical America, and the Black Panther.[15]
The official REP newsletter is Something Else, formerly
called Radicals in the Professions.[16]

NOTES

1.   Brochure, "Radical Education Project," circulated Feb-
     ruary 1969; REP letter circulated April, 1967.

2.   REP letter circulated April 1969.

3.   Brochure, "The Radical Education Project: An Intro-
     duction and an Invitation," circulated April 1967, p. 6.

4.   New World Review, Summer 1968, p. 32.

5.   REP letter, Nov. 21, 1968; REP letter, February 1969.

6.   Brochure, "The Radical Education Project: An Intro-
     duction and an Invitation," circulated April 1967, p. 3.

7.   Brochure, "Radical Education Project," circulated Feb-
     ruary 1969.

8.   Ibid.; also 1969 FBI Appropriation, p. 54.

9.   Michigan State News, Apr. 20, 1967, n. p.

10. Village Voice, Apr. 20, 1967, p. 16.

11. Brochure, "Radical Education Project," circulated Feb-
     ruary 1969.

12. Ibid.

13. Ibid.

14. "REP Literature List," April 1969.

15.   Ibid.

16.   Ibid.; also REP letter, February 1969.

(Staff Study, Committee on Internal Security, House of Representatives, Ninety-First Congress, First Session, mimeographed, 1969.   Received by the compiler June 19, 1970.)

13. STUDENTS FOR A DEMOCRATIC SOCIETY

The increasingly crucial role played by violence and revolutionary Marxism-Leninism in the ideology and operations of Students for a Democratic Society was emphasized in official statements by FBI Director J. Edgar Hoover.

Referring to the New Left generally, the Director stated:

> Never before in our history has there been such a strong revolutionary Marxist movement of young people so eager to tear down established authority. While it is the immediate goal of the New Left to gain complete control of our educational system, it is apparent that it hopes to lead a revolution ultimately designed to overthrow our system of government. [1]

TERROR ON THE CAMPUS

Mr. Hoover pointed out that during the preceding 12 months, "sit-in, seizure of campus facilities, destruction of university property, and the use of organized terror and violence disrupted more than 225 campuses" around the nation [2] and that, during the last academic year, there was more than $3,000,000 in damage to American colleges and universities. [3] During this same period, there were some 1,000 arrests in connection with violent demonstrations, along with uncounted injuries and at least two deaths as a result of campus riots. [4]

In addition, Director Hoover reported that fire bombs, other explosives, rifles, and shotguns "became familiar weapons in these so-called demonstrations" and that there were some 61 cases of arson or bombings on college campuses. [5]

Referring specifically to Students for a Democratic Society, Hoover asserted that "SDS remains at the core of the New Left" and was the instigator of much of this campus unrest. [6]

As an illustration of the typical FBI investigation as
a result of SDS activities, he cited the case of SDS member
Michael Sherrod Siskind, "who attempted to set off a fire
bomb at a Reserve Officers' Training Corps installation at
Washington University, St. Louis, Missouri, on December 3,
1968. Siskind pleaded guilty after being charged with sabotage and received a five-year prison term. "[7]

MARXIST-LENINIST IDEOLOGY

Of the growth of revolutionary Marxist-Leninist thinking in SDS, Mr. Hoover had this to say:

> Some time ago it abandoned the concept of 'partici-
> patory democracy' which it had championed in years
> past and eagerly embraced the principles of Marx-
> ism-Leninism, even to the extent of publicly an-
> nouncing its new goal of revolution. In so doing,
> it became the primary target for 'old left' takeover,
> and today we see old-line communists of every
> stripe seeking to seize and capitalize on the revo-
> lutionary zeal of the SDS. The Communist Party,
> USA (pro-Moscow), the Progressive Labor Party
> (pro-Peking), and the Socialist Workers Party (pro-
> Trotskyite) are all looking forward to a bright fu-
> ture in the SDS, provided they are able to gain
> control. [8]

In this connection, Mr. Hoover cited the attempt by
Progressive Labor to seize control of SDS at the June 1969
convention in Chicago, an attempt which resulted in a split
between the national office and Progressive Labor factions,
each of which now claims to be the real SDS. Each faction
now has its own national officers "and will in the future attempt to lead students with opposing brands of Marxism-
Leninism. "[9]

REVOLUTIONARY OBJECTIVE

The Director pointed out that, despite the split in
Chicago, the "feuding factions did not for a moment lose
sight of their joint objective, " which he described as the destruction of American "Imperialism" and the "achievement
of a classless society through international communism. "[10]
He further emphasized the importance of the young in this

design, an importance which he ascribed to the SDS belief
that the young have a lesser stake in society and are therefore more receptive to new ideas and more capable of moving
in a revolutionary direction. [11]

NEED FOR POSITIVE ACTION

Looking to the future, Mr. Hoover predicted that "unless college and university authorities take positive action to
control campus violence," it will continue and that "opposing
forces, each claiming to represent the true SDS, will clash
on campuses throughout the country for controlling power."[12]

The FBI Director warned:

> Those who rally to the support of the New Left and
> participate in activities championed by SDS do so
> under no illusion. The issues are now clear. Time
> and the internal wranglings of the organization have
> brought one basic and important truth to the surface.
> The youthful idealism of 'participatory democracy,'
> so frequently espoused by SDS while striving for
> student approval, has been cast aside. The Marx-
> ist dogma is in full command. SDS now calls for
> outright revolution. [13]

MEMBERSHIP

In regard to membership, Mr. Hoover noted that the
SDS has an estimated 250 chapters and claims some 40,000
members, but in actuality it has been able to influence the
thinking and actions of many additional thousands of students. [14]

CONTINUING THREAT

In pointing out the continuing threat the SDS poses to
our internal security, the FBI Director emphasized that "The
SDS openly espouses the overthrow of our institutions of free
society (called the 'Establishment') through violent revolutionary action."[15]

NOTES

1. Department of Justice release, July 15, 1969, p. 1.

2. Ibid., p. 2.

3. Ibid.; see also FBI Law Enforcement Bulletin, September 1969, p. 1.

4. FBI Law Enforcement Bulletin, September 1969, p. 1.

5. Department of Justice release, July 15, 1969, p. 2.

6. Ibid.

7. Ibid., p. 3.

8. Ibid., p. 2.

9. Ibid., p. 3; see also FBI Annual Report for Fiscal Year 1969, p. 21.

10. FBI Law Enforcement Bulletin, September 1969, p. 1.

11. Ibid.

12. Ibid.

13. Ibid.

14. FBI Annual Report for the Fiscal Year 1969, p. 21.

15. Ibid.

(Committee Staff Study, Committee On Internal Security, House of Representatives, Ninety-First Congress, First Session, transcript of hearings, pp. 2140-2141)

14. LET THE VOICE OF THE PEOPLE BE HEARD

On July 4, 1776, the rich people in the 13 colonies declared their independence from Great Britain and thereafter proceeded in the name of freedom and democracy to bring misery to three-quarters of the world.

During your picnic, take time to remember that this land was paid for with the blood of the red man (Ohio--that's an Indian name, but there ain't no more Indians in Ohio).

Remember the millions of blacks whose slave labor laid the foundations for America's ruling class's wealth and continues to do so today. Ask yourself if they're free yet, or better yet, ask a black.

Hey woman, when you're celebrating Independence Day, ask yourself if you're free. Free from being treated like a servant or a whore? As long as you remain that delicate little doll who is a slave to society and fashion, you're not a person--you're a thing.

Hey worker, how can you be free when you have no control over the only thing you have to live by--your labor. You know your boss is screwing you. And what about your union? It's not the one your fathers fought for when they were massacred in the nation's mines and factories.

When the fireworks explode, think about the fireworks in Vietnam and then think of whose side you're on. Are you with Rockefeller, Nixon, Johnson, and Kennedy who are fighting for big business and riches for a select few or are you with the NLF/Vietnamese people who are fighting for their independence and the GI's who don't want to die so the rich can get richer.

The wealthy Americans had their revolution in 1776 but now, in 1969, the poor people of the world are having theirs. Guatemala, Santo Domingo, Cuba, China, Vietnam, the Ryuku Islands, Angola, the black colony in the United States--all these people are saying: "No, WE WILL NO LONGER BE RULED BY THE RICH." All power to the people. Dig it--you don't make a million a year. All you do is work and die for the ones who do. The revolution has

come.   You are one of the people.   Which side are you
on?

ALL POWER TO THE PEOPLE
FREE HUEY
FREE ALL POLITICAL PRISONERS
LONG LIVE THE VICTORY OF THE PEOPLE'S WAR

(Distributed by SDS at Ohio State University, Columbus, Ohio,
October 2, 1969.   Collected October 14, 1969.)

15. PRESS RELEASE

Students for a Democratic Society
1608 West Madison
July 31, 1969   Chicago, Illinois
(312) 666-3874

PRESS RELEASE   PRESS RELEASE   PRESS RELEASE

It has been almost a year since we were last in Chi-
cago--at the Democratic Convention. Almost a year since
thousands of young people crowded around this state, confronting tear gas and the brutality of Daley's pigs. Chicago
last summer was the site of the death of the Democratic
party. It was the site of the exposure of the hypocrisy and
lies that candy-coat this imperialist system. It was the
site of the emergence of a young, militant movement committed to fighting for an end to the Vietnam war, and an end
to the imperialist system that made the war inevitable. And,
Chicago last summer--with the use of open state violence--
showed people all over the world that when imperialism's
velvet glove is removed nothing but a mailed fist remains.

ON OCTOBER 11, 1969, SDS IS CALLING FOR TENS
OF THOUSANDS OF PEOPLE TO RETURN TO CHICAGO TO
MOUNT A MASSIVE OFFENSIVE AGAINST THE WAR IN
VIETNAM, IN SUPPORT OF THE BLACK LIBERATION
STRUGGLE, AND AGAINST THE INCREASING POLITICAL
REPRESSION THAT HAS PARTICULARLY MENACED BLACK
AND BROWN COMMUNITIES. We intend to return to Chicago
precisely because it has come to symbolize what a government held together by force is all about. And we intend to
return with masses of young people from the high schools,
community colleges and the streets with workers from the
factories and with GI's. All are people who are screwed
by the imperialist system. The same system that is attempting genocide in Vietnam and in the black and brown communities at home.

We will go back to Chicago to show the rulers of this
country and the people of the whole world that we will not
be turned around by terror tactics and fascist repression.
We will make it absolutely clear that the only way to deal

with the terror and repression that this government hands
down daily is to fight back.   And we will show workers and
working class youth the possibilities for change that exist
when we ally with the struggles of the oppressed peoples of
the whole world--the National Liberation Front, the Black
Liberation Struggle, the guerillas in Guatemala.

On October 11, we will not simply demand that the
rulers of this country bring the troops home.   This time we
raise a new battle cry: BRING THE WAR HOME.   We do
not want troops to be withdrawn from one place and then de-
ployed to another.   We do not see that withdrawing the 82nd
Airborne from Vietnam to be used in the black community of
Detroit is much of an advancement.   Rather, we want a total
defeat for the world-wide system of imperialism: We declare
our will to fight until there are no occupation troops left--
either in Vietnam, any other foreign countries, the black and
brown communities and the schools.   And, we declare our
intention to aid in the building of another front--the final
front--in the worldwide struggle against imperialism.

We also demand: FREE ALL POLITICAL PRISONERS,
especially leaders of the Black Liberation Struggle like Huey
P. Newton, Ahmed Evene, Martin Sostre and Fred Hampton.
INDEPENDENCE FOR PUERTO RICO, and an end to the imperialist exploitation of the Puerto Rican nation.   AN END
TO THE SURTAX, a tax paid out of the pockets of the working people in this country to kill workers in Vietnam.

And, we express total support to the National Liberation Front and the Provisional Revolutionary Government of
South Vietnam.   To the BLACK LIBERATION STRUGGLE in
America.   To the Conspiracy 8, who led the struggle in
Chicago last year.   And to GI's who have struggled for their
basic civil rights, and have rebelled against tyranny and class
oppression within the Army--from Ft. Hood to Doc To.

On October 11, we will hold a massive march around
these demands.   SDS will request parade permits for this
march.   But we know all too well the wrath of the Chicago
pigs.   And we affirm the right of all people to self-defense
against violent attacks by the police.

This movement will not be confined only to Chicago
and October 11.   On Sept. 14-18, the International Industri-
alists Conference, called by the Stanford Research Institute,
a leading brain center for counter-insurgency, anti-people
research, will be the focus of major demonstrations on the

West Coast. At the same time, the Japanese World Trade
Fair will be taking place, also in San Francisco and will be
addressed by President Nixon. In 1970, the U. S. -Japanese
Security Treaty and Independence for Okinawa will be the
central focus for major demonstrations by our revolutionary
comrades in Japanese Zengakuren. We will join them in our
common struggle against U. S. imperialism, fighting from
within the guts of the monster.

SDS has also called for major regional, local, city-
wide actions around the same demands and slogans as the
October 11 National Action in Chicago. The November 8
movement, beginning approximately one year after the election of Richard Nixon, will provide the opportunity for the
American people, in their home communities, to fight against
the war: that fight, that struggle against the U. S. ruling
class, will continue until all U. S. troops are withdrawn from
Vietnam and the Provisional Revolutionary Government of
South Vietnam is in Saigon.

At this point in history, the oppressed people of the
Third World are leading the attack against Yankee imperialist
aggression. The Vietnamese are resisting and fighting back.
Black and Brown people within the United States are resisting
and fighting back. On October 11, tens of thousands of working class youth will come to Chicago to join in that fight and
to bring the war home.

(Distributed by SDS in Chicago, Illinois on July 31, 1969.
Collected September 12, 1969.)

16. SDS, NATIONAL OFFICE

This is addressed to anyone who's coming to Chicago to tear apart pig city Oct. 8-11. Most of the information has to do with how regions are going to operate in Chicago. There's a reason for that--regional organization is the key to discipline during the action and individuals should look towards the leadership of their region for direction:

THINGS TO KNOW AND DO:

1. All regions (and unattached individuals) should call 641-7133 upon arriving in Chicago. This will be the central communication number which will handle questions in where your region's movement center is located, how to get there, what other phone numbers you need to know, etc. Don't talk too long--the lines are going to be tied up enough already.

2. People (especially regional collectives) should bring plenty of food with them. Concentrated juices, bread, spaghetti, canned goods, peanut butter, jelly, paper cups and plates, plastic knives, forks and spoons, large pots--all should be brought with you to Chicago.

3. Everyone in the regions, particularly in collectives, should already have received first-aid training from medics in your area. Also, everyone (without exception) should have read Medical Cadre and should be familiar with the street medicine suggestions outlined in the last issue of New Left Notes. The suggestion that many people in regions wear "first-aid belts" should be taken seriously--it was put forth seriously.

4. People in each region should have set up bail funds before they get to Chicago. These funds will be supplemented immediately upon arrival at the movement centers by collecting money from everyone there for bail. Everyone should bring lots of bread--most of it should go to the bail fund. Finally, upon arrival at the movement centers, every person should fill out cards with names of bail contacts back home who can be hit for quick bread. All bread will be turned over to the central bail fund.

5.   Each region, city and chapter will be assigned to one of the three Core Areas.   Those not listed below should call 641-7133 upon arriving in Chicago for their assignments.

In Evanston under the leadership of the Michigan collectives will be Wisconsin, Michigan, Niagra, and New England.   These groups should report to Garret Theological Seminary at 2121 Sheriden Road, in Evanston for their assignments.

In Lincoln Park, led by the Chicago collective, will be Illinois, Indiana, Colorado, the Pacific North West, Washington, D. C., and the South.   These groups should report to St. Luke's Lutheran Church at 1500 W. Belmont.

In Hyde Park the Ohio collective will provide the leadership for people from New York and Pennsylvania.   They should report to University Disciples Church at 5655 S. University.

6.   All regions will be responsible for maintenance, security, cooking and communication in their respective movement centers.   Teams should be assigned, especially for security, immediately upon reaching Chicago.

7.   A legal center has been set up with lawyers on call throughout the whole action--available for bail reduction hearings, court appearances, etc.   The number for people to call if they get busted or know someone who's been busted is 922-6578.   We'll take it from there.

8.   Medical centers are being set up throughout the city, as well as ambulance service and teams of street medics.   A medical assistance number will be given to everyone at the movement center.

POWER TO THE PEOPLE

Robby Roth
Russ Newfeld

National Action Staff

SDS, 1608 West Madison, Chicago, Illinois 60612
phone (312) 666-3874

(Distributed by SDS at the University of Illinois at Chicago
Circle, October 3, 1969. Collected on the same date.)

17. ABOLISH ROTC

Professor Greene's Letter to
East Campus Academic Forum

Dear Editor:

I have talked to a number of faculty members about abolishing ROTC. Very often they raise two objections: first that such an action would be a violation of academic freedom; second, that it would create a hardship for those students who desire ROTC training. I hope I can generate some discussion by replying to these objections.

Not every act of speech is just that. Words are the means by which we perform all sorts of actions. Thus we use words to vote, make promises, and issue commands. Therefore, even if we concede, as I am not sure we should, that no speech should be suppressed because of the wickedness of the ideas expressed, we must acknowledge that suppression may be permissible and even necessary if the speech is a part of a morally objectionable action. My objection to the continuance of the ROTC is based upon this principle, and upon the fact that ROTC lectures are not simply acts of speech but parts of an action, the training of military officers, which is as much a part of waging war as the manufacture of bombs and napalm.

I do not want to defend the idea that all wars are immoral, or that all military training at universities is immoral. I object to Georgetown's ROTC program because it is directly related to the war in Vietnam, which I believe is very immoral. I realize, of course, that many, perhaps most of the faculty believe that we are following a wise policy in Vietnam, or at worst, are making a political but not a moral mistake. This is not the place to argue the merits of our Vietnam policy. My point is that the continuance of the ROTC program is not morally neutral; it presupposes that either the administration sees no connection between the ROTC and Vietnam, which is unlikely, or that it approves of the war, which is a strong possibility, or that it believes that although the war is wrong, abolishing the ROTC would have either no effect or a bad effect on our Vietnam policy.

273

While I regret the inconvenience the abolishment of the ROTC might cause some of our students, I think we ought to balance this inconvenience against the inconveniences born by the people of Vietnam, and the poor in this country, black and white, who are sent to Vietnam in disproportionate numbers because of the injustices of the Selective Service System. When I first came here four years ago, an administrator told a meeting of the faculty that he had sent letters to students who had been suspended for academic failure the previous spring inviting them to return to school in the fall because the war was heating up in Vietnam and he did not want to see them drafted. This occurred at a time when the morality of draft deferments for good students was being questioned throughout the country. Georgetown protected its own, but only at the expense of others. The army was not ten or twenty men short that fall. Those letters only make sure that the men who risked and perhaps lost their lives were poor, instead of rich, black instead of white. I am ashamed to say that though I felt then as I do now, I said nothing. But as I recall that meeting, neither did anyone else.

I am interested in communicating to Father Quain the extent of faculty dissatisfaction with the ROTC. I would appreciate it if you would answer the questions below or in some other way express your opinion. My office number is 106 Loyola. Will you teach class on military day to protest against the ROTC? Should ROTC be abolished? Should ROTC be denied academic credit?

Professor James Greene
Philosophy Department

ABOLISH ROTC

The case for abolishing ROTC at Georgetown rests not on the fact that it maintains low academic standards or similar concepts which would make of the university an "ivory tower" but because the policies and interests served by ROTC are essentially wrong.

ROTC AND U.S. FOREIGN POLICY

The goals and processes of U.S. foreign policy are most obvious today in Vietnam. Here an American military presence is needed to continue, indeed to increase the ex-

ploitation of the Vietnamese people by U. S. corporate interests. U. S. corporations have long recognized the importance
of Southeast Asia and its potential for making profits under
the "free enterprise" system and U. S. statesmen are no less
well aware of this. In the words of the former Ambassador
to Vietnam, Henry Cabot Lodge, "Vietnam does not exist in
a vacuum - from it large storehouses of wealth and population can be influenced and undermined. " Senator Gale McGee
(D-Wy.) has formulated U. S. intentions even more clearly,
"That empire in Southeast Asia is the last major resource
outside of the control of any of the major powers of the
globe. I believe that the conditions of the Vietnamese people,
and the direction in which their future may be going are at
this point secondary, not primary. " Thus the main antagonism in Vietnam is clearly defined: It is between U. S. corporate interests and those of the Vietnamese people. U. S. involvement in Vietnam is not a recent phenomena [sic]. The
policy pursued today has its roots in the policy of President
Kennedy and before him Presidents Eisenhower and Truman.
After defeating Japanese imperialism in Southeast Asia, the
United States financed the French colonialist attempt to maintain control over Vietnam. When the French were defeated
the U. S. government installed the Diem dictatorship and
aided its attempts to undo any reforms gained by the Viet-
Minh for the people. But U. S. involvement during this period
was not primarily military but political and economic. Since
1965 however the massive infusion of U. S. troops has made
this an "American War. " What is important to realize is
that it is not U. S. involvement in the war in Vietnam that
is new but the strength and unity of the Vietnamese people
in fighting back against U. S. domination.

There is no doubt that in the present phase of the
war the United States has committed spectacular moral
crimes against the people of Vietnam. Since the suspension
of bombing over North Vietnam, American bombing raids
have not decreased but have been concentrated on civilian
areas under the control of the National Liberation Front
(NLF). According to the Senate Judiciary Committee report
on "civilian casualty and refugee problems in South Vietnam":
"The majority of refugees interviewed claimed they were
either deposited in camps by the Americans or fled to camps
in fear of American airplanes and artillery. " Unable to win
people away from the NLF by social programs, the U. S.
Government has used massive and spectacular violence to
drive peasants from NLF controlled areas. But these ex-
traordinary acts of aggression should not be allowed to obscure the more subtle violence imposed by the landlords
and their allies, the American corporations.

This domination meant poverty for most of the Vietnamese people and drove them to revolt. 6, 300 landlords (2% of the population) owned 45% of the land and forced the peasants to pay 50 to 60% of their crops in rent alone (i. e. not counting taxes). But these are not unique or even unusual conditions for they exist in many other countries in Latin America, Asia and Africa. It is this less overt violence-- the violence of age-long oppression backed up by American political and economic guidance and, if necessary, military aid--which has plunged much of the Third world into revolt against the landlords and against American corporate interests.

It is to maintain this subtle violence that the U. S. has set up military dictatorships in Guatemala, Greece, Thailand, etc. and has sent 1, 175, 000 of its troops abroad (over 500, 000 in Vietnam). Thus in many countries besides Vietnam, the U. S. keeps in power governments which keep their own people in poverty while granting generous concessions to U. S. corporations in return for military protection--from the people. In Guatemala 2% of the people own 80% of the land and over 50% of the people suffer from malnutrition   By 1967 the U. S. had stationed over one-thousand military personnel there and supplied napalm to the government to fight the guerrillas. In Greece, where the U. S. has supported right-wing political factions since World War II, the present junta came to power by invoking a NATO contingency plan which was intended to "save Greece from Communism. " In Thailand there are already over 40, 000 U. S. troops attempting to suppress a peasant rebellion similar to that of Vietnam.

It should be obvious by now that the U. S. policy in Vietnam is harmoniously integrated into the larger pattern of the American government's interests and goals around the world. Vietnam is anything but an exception; the policies pursued there are isolated neither in time nor in space. They are the same policies pursued all over the Third World since the end of World War II. It would be a grievous error to think that American policy in Vietnam is a misguided or even immoral but isolated case and that because of it America's leaders (economic and political) are slowly becoming enlightened; it is rather exactly the opposite.

The central role of the American Military is to implement a policy of securing world-wide markets for American investments and trade. This aim means installing and supporting reactionary governments and suppressing popular revolts. The case for abolishing ROTC rests on evidence that

ROTC is essential to the smooth functioning of the American military in its pursuit of these goals in Vietnam and elsewhere.

First of all, ROTC is the main source of officers. The function of ROTC is well known and there is no argument on this point. It has best been summed up by GU ROTC Cadet Col. John Hoffman: 'The object of the military science program is to train military officers. This is its sole purpose and goal. It is the reason the program was instituted.' And the ROTC program admirably fulfills this function; according to the N. Y. Times (Jan. 5 '69) ROTC supplies 50% of the Army officers, 35% of the Navy and 30% of the Air Force. Even more important is the fact that in the Army, ROTC provides 65% of the first lieutenants and 85% of the second lieutenants.

Secondly, there is no present alternative to ROTC. This would mean that a successful attack on the ROTC program would have the desired result of crippling the present imperialist policies of the U. S. government. Even with a considerable effort to expand OCS and West Point, the immediate result of the abolition of ROTC would be to dry up the supply of officers for the military. Thus to abolish ROTC would make it more difficult to continue the Vietnam War or initiate similar wars.

Thus an attack on ROTC is an attack on the imperialist policy of the U. S. government. While we oppose the present policy of the armed forces of the U. S., this does not mean that we oppose the military per se. We feel that the university should refuse to cooperate with the military as long as they pursue the present policy of opposing popular revolutions. The Vietnam war is just the latest and most flagrant example of these policies.

On the other hand, while abolishing ROTC on every campus in the U. S. would cripple the present foreign policy of the U. S., it would not impair the defense capacity of this country. In other words while it is possible to see the rulers of this country withdrawing from Vietnam and avoiding other Vietnams, it is impossible that they would abolish the Army.

Finally, an attack on ROTC is not an attack on

students in the ROTC program. We believe that ROTC ma-
nipulates students into signing up by appealing to their immediate needs--money to help at school, fear of the draft, etc.
We feel that many ROTC students are in a position to see--
and actually do see--the illegitimacy of the military as an
instrument of U.S. foreign policy, and that many of them
thus can be won to our position.

We demand an end to U.S. imperialism in the form
of political, economic and military exploitation abroad....
We demand an end to ROTC on the Georgetown campus.

THE NATURE OF THE UNIVERSITY AND
THE FIGHT AGAINST ROTC

Opposition to the demand to abolish ROTC at Georgetown stems primarily from two different sources: from those
who realize that Georgetown is not an apolitical institution
but who support the present policies of the government and
Georgetown's role in the formation and implementation of
these policies, and from those who believe that the University is or should be politically neutral.   Understanding both
these positions and the ensuing alliance between their proponents will help to clarify the case for abolishing ROTC.

Many of the men who control Georgetown University
and determine its policies (e.g. the Board of Regents, the
Trustees, the Administration and some of the prominent faculty)
actively support America's current economic structure and the
policies which spring from it.   Thus, to give just one example, it
is in the interest of O. Roy Chalk of the Board of Regents to support American policy of suppressing a popular revolution in order
to protect the profits he makes in Guatemala.

These men realize that Georgetown is not and cannot
be apolitical.   They know that Georgetown functions to incul-
cate the dominant American values and ideology and to recruit trained experts in keeping with the needs of the existing social order--needs as seen by corporation executives
and government leaders.   The Board of Regents, the Trustees, the Administration and their allies in the faculty correctly perceive that the fight against ROTC is a direct attack on the policies they seek to protect.   Moreover, they
realize that this attack on the policies can be broadened to
include other issues at Georgetown.   Thus they fear the related fight against Georgetown's involvement with the Inter-

national Police Academy and the 352nd Civil Affairs Group
of the army reserves.   They fear opposition to Georgetown's
connections with Operations and Policies Research and the
Center for Strategic and International Studies and resulting
ties with the CIA.   They fear the possible student support
of Georgetown employees in their struggle to win a union and
gain decent wages.   They are afraid - for in all these areas
they have vested interests in preserving the present political
alignment of Georgetown University.

A campaign to abolish ROTC would be a frontal attack
on policies that the Trustees and Administration would prefer
to keep hidden behind a facade of university "neutrality. "
If the present political committment of the University were
ever effectively revealed (as we are attempting to do), then
those who hold the ideal of the apolitical university might oppose its existing policies.   At the present, however, the belief that the university is and ought to be devoted solely to
the pursuit of "knowledge" and "truth" provides allies for
those seeking to protect the present policies of the university.
Thus, many who uphold the ideal of the "apolitical" university see the campaign to abolish ROTC as an effort to make
Georgetown take a political stand.

In reality, Georgetown is anything but apolitical or
"neutral" and therefore opposition to abolishing ROTC is a
defense of the reactionary status quo.   It is this liberal
ideology which encourages students and faculty to conceive
of themselves as privileged beings above the conflicts of the
world with a "right" to be "neutral" and "apolitical. "   However, the conflicts continue and the "neutrals" are implicitly
allied with the dominant powers, who make the University
serve their own vested interests.

Moreover, the ideal of neutrality itself is both misleading and undesirable.   We recognize the current political
alignment of the university and seek a realignment of the
university with the interests of the people of America and
the world.   In this regard there can be no neutrality.   This
is because universities live in an economic world with limited
resources.   Decisions must be made about who is to be hired
and fired, what research is to be done, what training will be
done and who will get the funds necessary to train and research.   These decisions are political decisions.   At present
they are made by external institutions, both governmental
and private, who control funding.   They are made by men
who were trained in universities under similar control.
That these men follow reactionary models is obvious.   It is

in this light that Georgetown's claim to public service must
be evaluated.   Today Georgetown serves the interests of the
corporations and government; neutrality must be seen for
what it is--assent to the current political alignment.

The effect of this de facto alliance of the Administration and Trustees and those who advocate an apolitical university is an attempt to restrict the scope of the ROTC question to academic issues and to resist student efforts to broad-
en discussion on the question to include the substantive political issues.

The Academic Argument for ROTC

The attempt to change the academic status of ROTC,
as opposed to abolishing it, is an attempt to convert opposition to ROTC based on the policies it serves, into opposition based on its inferior academic standards.   At any rate
the truth--that ROTC implements oppression of people all
over the world--is turned into the feeble and misleading plea
that ROTC does not really belong in high academic circles.

"Civil Liberties" Arguments for ROTC

The two major civil libertarian arguments have been
used to block the abolition of ROTC on political grounds.
The first asserts that students have a "right" to have ROTC
training.   Basically this argument affirms the "right" of
students to participate in the oppression of people at home
and abroad.   The function of the U.S. Military has been to
implement an imperialist foreign policy by aiding in the suppression of popular revolutionary movements and securing
world-wide markets for American investments and trade.   It
is this, the function of the US Military and thus of ROTC,
which denies students the "right" to participate in it.   Moreover, this argument presupposes the "right" of the Army to
establish ROTC at American universities in either curricular
or extra-curricular form.   This "right" most certainly does
not exist if ROTC is used by the Army for the same ends
that it now serves.   (It should be observed that this reasoning would not lead to the abolition of a "club" that simply
studied American counter-revolutionary tactics--only institutions which involved contractual relations with the Army to
turn out officers to implement these policies.)

The second civil liberties argument is one which

warns against setting precedents for throwing organizations
off campus for political reasons.   This argument falsely as-
sumes that the politics and function of the organization concerned are never relevant to its acceptability on campus.
(It is interesting to note that this argument is usually presented as a veiled warning with the example of SDS in mind.
The warning is inappropriate for their is no analogy between
ROTC and SDS; ROTC, as we argued in the previous article,
is instrumental in the pursuit of American imperialist policy;
SDS opposes this policy.)

It may be clear that despite the current alliance between those who actively favor present University policies
and some of those who uphold the ideal of university neutrality, the correct application of the ideology of the apolitical
university would lead to an alliance with those who seek abolition of ROTC, but, hopefully, it may be just as clear that
this ideal of neutrality is itself highly questionable.   Most of
those who seek to fight current University practices do not
seek neutrality but a realignment of the University with the
interests of the people of America and the world, not with
their rulers and oppressors.   Today, Georgetown University
serves the interests of a small minority of men controlling
the corporations and government, not the interests of the
people at large.   Concerning this central question, the question of alignment with corporations and rulers--or with the
people, there can really be no neutrality.

Who does Georgetown serve ?

Who should Georgetown serve ?

Who does ROTC really serve ?

WE DEMAND

1)   ROTC--all branches--be abolished immediately
(being prohibited from using any part of our university).
Those receiving financial aid through ROTC be given equal
scholarships by the university.

2)   Our university immediately sever all relations
with:
   A)   the International Police Academy
   B)   the Center for Strategic and International
         Studies

C) the Army's 352nd Civil Affairs Reserve 'A' Unit

3) University Departments and individual faculty members immediately sever all ties with the Department of Defense, State Dept's Bureau of Intelligence and Research, CIA, and other groups which serve the U.S. Military.

4) In order to ensure the above, full disclosure of the university budget.

(Distributed by SDS on the Georgetown University campus on May 9, 1969. Collected by the compiler January 11, 1970.)

18. NOT WITH MY LIFE YOU DON'T!!!
A Georgetown Student Handbook

Life At Georgetown ...
An Introduction

Students have begun to play a very important role in
changing American society. We are no longer accused of
apathy--now, if anything, we are accused of being overzeal-
ous, too honest. Students have become fully committed to
and deeply involved in the realization of their ideals. Throughout the country universities are the scene of exciting free
thought and seriously challenging committment [sic]. There is
a revolution going on here in America, a revolution of values,
of politics, of lives. The universities have become a center
for this challenge to the establishment, and students are the
force behind it. We have tried, with this handbook, to describe a part of that revolution and its content.

But, before we begin, perhaps it would be wise to consider the reality of Georgetown today. Are our four years
at Georgetown liberating ones for us? Do we learn to free
our thoughts and our lives from a system we can't accept?
Is the Georgetown student really a part of this revolution that
is sweeping American campuses? Unfortunately, the answer
seems to be no. We have been standing on the sidelines
imitating, but not really joining in. Georgetown is more
characterized by the freshmen who tell you that they would
commit themselves, but they are afraid of jeoporodizing [sic]
their careers, and by upperclassmen who constantly preach
moderation and cooperation with the Administration, or, finally, those recent graduates who see the main achievement of
their four years in their ability to handle themselves in society. These are the real Georgetown students--not really a
part of the new, and yet too young to fit in with the old generation.

Georgetown's backwardness would be easy to explain
if the impetus needed to bring something of the spirit of the
true university to campus had to come from the faculty or
the Administration. But, at other universities, the impetus
has been coming from the students, and it is to ourselves
that we must look for an explanation of GU apathy.

Perhaps the explanation can be found in the background
of our rather homogenous [sic] student body.   We are mostly
of middle class Catholic origins; many of our parents have
only recently made it, and in fact we, and our professional
ambitions, are often the final stage in a process of social acceptance.   Neither has our strict Catholic upbringing helped
to foster any creative escapes from this process.   Perhaps,
we simply have farther to go than our Jewish brothers from
New York City who lead the organization of such a movement
oriented school as Wisconsin.   It is easy to understand that
students whose training and background inspire them to "make
it," are not about to challenge the system in which they put
their hopes.   And then, too, the environment of Georgetown
must have some effect.   Located in Washington, one of the
centers of established power, the fashionable Georgetown,
home of those who have succeeded in the system, and in a
university that caters to and trains students for careers in
the system, with all this can one really expect too much?

What then is the reality of the present Georgetown
and its students?   If things continue as they are, the University won't really challenge you enough to break from your
past.   And, even if you do manage to see through what is
happening at Georgetown, and you don't get out, you'll probably end up shutting yourself off from reality in some alternative world like drugs.   Or, perhaps you'll join GUCAP and
try to do "something."   But, in the Georgetown environment
you'll probably never have a chance to understand exactly
what you oppose, let alone come close to changing it.

That is our Georgetown, a university that seems to
work best in training for cocktail party conversations, or
the very difficult skill of being socially acceptable in the fast
moving American jet set.   A university whose greatest intellectual achievement seems to be reached in turning its best
students into profound cynics.   A place where the latest
fashions and the psychedelic culture of our movement are
very prevalent, but it is clear that it is more form than content.   Georgetown has a way of automatically co-opting anything sincere, of insuring that nothing will disturb its highly
varnished and empty shell.

This handbook must, therefore, be a challenge to
those who somehow survive.   We must try to build an alternative to the present Georgetown.   We must work together
at overcoming the past and present forces that channel into
leading less human lives.   We must build ourselves so that
we can transform Georgetown from a tool of our corupted

[sic] society into something more of a force that can free the
rest of trapped America.   Until then the Georgetown experience will not liberate, but only help to enslave unknowing
students in lives they will never be satisfied with.

Accept this handbook as an invitation to join us!

UNIVERSITY SOCIETY

At Georgetown, as at universities everywhere, involvement of the university in society has been the ever-growing
trend.   One finds programs for financeers: the Savings and
Loan Forum and the Forum on Investment Banking; conferences on foreign affairs: CONTAC; research programs:
Project Themis, the Center for Population Research, the Institute of World Polity, the Center for Strategic Studies; urban
programs: the New Careers Program and GUCAP; and finally military training in the form of ROTC.   With all this it
is impossible to make a case for Georgetown's noninvolvement
in American and, indeed, World society.   As Academic Vice
President Fitzgerald put it, "Georgetown is responding to the
new intellectual currents and to the social forces that sur-
round it. "   Yes Thomas, you said it!

The prime function of Georgetown University is the
training of men and women in the skills necessary for the
efficient functioning of the system.   The 1969 Undergraduate
Entrance Bulletin tells it like it is: College graduates "serve
as educators, public servants, and statesmen; they work in
business, law, medicine, and research. "   Again, "Graduates
of the School (of Foreign Service) have been much sought after
in almost all areas of business and professional activity. "
Again, "the managerial class is large and growing rapidly.
The demand of men with professional, college-level training
in business administration is constantly increasing as a result of the growing complexity of the American economy and
the accelerating impact of technology on the methods of management. "   And finally, "Various branches of the federal
government need linguists to work on strategically important
languages. "

Without this continuing source of manpower provided
by the universities, the system of corporate power would
crumble.   Thus, it is obvious why the university ignores the
irrationality and inhumanity of the existing system--the university is so deeply connected to, and implicated in, the

status quo.   The university serves as the finishing process
of socialization.   After having been instilled with the false
values necessary for the perpetuation of an inhuman system,
we young people are being trained to run and service that
system.

The interrelatedness of the university with society
makes it impossible for a woman or man to think critically
or make critical judgments concerning him or herself and
their society.   The University is, as Cardinal Newman is
quoted in the Bulletin, "the place in which the intellect may
safely range and speculate. "   Please note the word "safely. "
The "safely" defined limits are those which don't confront the
reality of corporate capitalism, of imperialism, of oppression
America and the Third World, of distortion and repression
of human values, and the manipulation of men and women for
profit.

The interrelatedness of the university with society is
demonstrated by the men who rule Georgetown, the 15 directors.   That 9 are priests (of these, 8 Jesuits) would lead one
to think they would be detached from the inhuman values of
capitalism; rather, they seem to have accommodated themselves to the status quo.   The corporate interests are well
represented: Assistant Secretary of Defense Enthoven; oil-
man-financeer Lauinger; manufacturer-financeer Reiss; manu-
facturer-financeer-liberal Salomon; publisher Sweeterman;
professional educator Walton.

The programs and projects that Georgetown participates
in and initiates are shaped by the prevailing forces of corporate capitalism.   Many examples can be cited: the Center for
Strategic Studies serves the interests of the military and, in
turn, the huge military-industrial complex.   The Center for
Population Research serves the State Department's interests
by talking about "overpopulation" in "underdeveloped" countries
without mentioning the cause--capitalistic exploitation.   The
Physics Department serves the Department of Defense's interests for transoceanic communication (Project Themis), a
part of the military's increasingly more sophisticated system
of social coercion and human destruction.   The manpower
needs of the Army and Air Force are well served by the
ROTC programs.   The system's need to squelch urban insur-
rections is served by the 352 Civic Affairs Reserve unit (and
"Civic Affairs" means preparing for pacification and counter-
insurgency operations in the Middle East.)   And the pacification of Afro-Americans is served by the Center for Metropolitan Studies, GUCAP, and the College Orientation Program.

All of this takes on prophetic meaning when one real-
izes that the social crisis of our time is rooted in the nature
of capitalism--a system that can't solve its own problems.
It is rooted in the very nature of capitalist production, where
production for profit rather than use is the moving factor,
and men are regarded as objects to be used and manipulated.
The result is an economic and social system, with the universities playing their crucial part, which grinds up human beings in the degrading, corrupting, stultifying mill of vast
corporate empires; which warps and cripples people through
continuous exposure during upbringing and education to the
output, the propaganda, and the sales efforts of business.
Become aware! The institution you have now entered is central to the existence of that system.

THE CENTRAL INTELLIGENCE AGENCY

Personnel Representative will be on campus
15 & 16 November
to recruit undergraduate and graduate candidates
for employment.

Please consult the Director of your Placement Service for information concerning career opportunities and to schedule an appointment for interview.

POWER
and
powerlessness

The Student Body participates directly at Georgetown in admission, discipline, academic, social,
and athletic policy. In addition, students play an
important role in formulating all policy relating to
student life through the S. A. P. A. C. --(Quoted from
the Student Body President's welcoming letter
to freshmen, September, 1968)

Student Power. What is it? Do the students at
Georgetown have it?

Perhaps student power has been most simply defined
in the model bill of student rights developed by the American
Association of University Professors and the National Student

Association. It says that students have the right to a "tangible say" in the decision making processes of a university. In other words, students should have the power not only to say what they think on academic and non-academic matters, but also, they should have significant positions on policy making boards, so as to have a chance to effect the ideas on these matters that they hold.

Does this, or anything like it, exist at Georgetown? The Student Body Presidents' letter quoted above certainly gives you the idea that it does. But, in truth, an analysis of decision making processes at Georgetown shows just how little the student body has to say on just about any policy decisions. For example:

Academic decisions are those concerning hiring and firing of faculty, curriculum, admissions, standards, budget allowances, etc. In short, everything that will effect how you are educated in the next four years. AT NO POINT in the final academic decision making process do the students have representation, or even an effective voice in the selection of the men who will make these decisions. You have no say at all in how or who will attempt to shape your thoughts and opinions in the next four years.

At the top of the Georgetown University power structure is the Board of Directors. Self-appointed, this crucial body has no student or lay faculty representation. Nevertheless, it is here that all final, binding policy decisions are made. It is here where all final appeals of a serious nature are decided. Among the powers of the Board is the appointment of the President of the University, an office which has traditionally been given to a Jesuit. The president carries out the policies approved by the Board, and has wide authority to make policy decisions, and interpret the Board's directives. He, along with his vice-presidents, makes the key decisions which most immediately effect the students' lives. Again, as with the Board, students have no guaranteed voice in the selection of the president or the vice-presidents, though they may, depending on the whim of the Board, be "consulted."

For the student, the most important man in the power structure's chain of command, and, in fact, the man who runs the University, is the Academic Vice-President (most recently Fr. McGrath and Fr. Fitzgerald). He is the man the Board depends on to make all decisions regarding course,

faculty, and standards.   In turn, one of the most important
bodies he consults is the Budget Committee, which is knowledgeable on all monies received and dispensed by the University.   Once again, there is no student representation on this
body.   In fact the data of the Budget Committee are among
the best kept of Georgetown's secrets.   It is just about impossible for you, as a Georgetown student or any of the
Georgetown student governments to find out anything about
your University's financial status--and the fact that your tuition money is wrapped up in that status doesn't make a bit
of difference.   Thus, when the annual increase in tuition and
room and board is announced, students can talk, petition,
pass resolutions, and demonstrate all they want.   It makes
no difference.   In the end they remain ignorant of the University's financial position, and why the increase was deemed
necessary.

    Each school in the University (Foreign Service, Col-
lege, etc.) has separate committees to handle matters per-
taining only to its affairs.   The most powerful of these are
the Executive Faculty Committees.   These usually have a
total of 15 members, and a maximum of **THREE** students out
of the 15.   The other 12 members are appointed by the Deans
of the Schools and the President of the University, the latter
with the advice and consent of the Faculty Senate.   Thus, the
students, who make up a clear majority of the University
community, are in a distinct minority on these committees--
a minority so small that one doubts that this represents, in
fact, a "tangible say."

    Equally crucial to the students' academic life are the
Standards Committees, composed entirely of faculty members,
with students having no say in their selection.   These men
decide, among other things, what QPI students must have to
graduate, to avoid probationary status, etc.   In July of this
year a former Georgetown student had to deal with the Foreign
Service Standards Committee.   He was a junior last year, on
probation.   He passed all of his courses during the Spring
semester and then signed for, and paid for summer school
courses.   After several weeks he received a letter from the
Dean, acting at the behest of the Standards Committee, telling
him that he was dismissed from Georgetown, and that he
would not be readmitted.   He lost the money he had spent
on summer school, and, he was unable to find an appeals
method opened to him.

    It should be clear by now, that the important decision

making apparatus of Georgetown is entirely controlled by the
Jesuit Administration, with not only the students, but, to a
large extent, the faculty, cut out and ignored. The Administration has had the 20th century intrude on its tidy little 19th
century fiefdom several times in the past four years. As a
result of the pressures that have arisen two bodies have been
established which provide a veneer of student and faculty
power. The faculty now has a Faculty Senate, which serves
mainly as an advisory body, not a policy-making body. The
students now have a similar group impressively titled the
Student Affairs Policy Advisory Committee. Even on this
committee, out of 13 members, only FIVE are students.
These five are appointed by the undergraduate student governments. There are also five faculty members (appointed by
the Faculty Senate and the Council of Deans) and three administrators (the Vice-President for Student Development, the
Dean of Men and the Dean of Women).

     Thus, in all the major academic decision making ma-
chinery of the University there are only five students, who
act solely in an advisory capacity. This isn't a "tangible
say, " it's not even an "important role. " It is just part of
the game the Jesuit Administration is playing to placate students.

     Let us now consider the non-academic decisions.
These are the regulations concerning dress, hours, dorm
and classroom behavior, and the like, which are contained
in the G-Book.

     The mood and intention of the G-Book is reflected in
the following quote:

          ... regulations are necessary for developing individ-
          ual self-discipline and preserving common good.
          It is your responsibility to know and observe these
          standards.

Obey, because it is good for you and the society if you do.
Don't worry about how these regulations were decided upon.
Don't worry about their reasonableness or their rightness.
Don't worry about changing them. Don't even bother thinking
about them. Just learn them, and obey.

     In this same spirit, the G-Book on one page says:
"The Student Press is free of censorship and advance approval

of copy. " and on the very next page says: "The advisor has
the right to see all copy in advance and advise as he sees
fit.   If he judges the copy to be libelous he has the right to
cause the copy to be deleted from the publication. "

No censorship?   Bull!

The Board of Directors of the University and the President have the final decisions in all non-academic matters,
just as they do in academic matters.   The student then is
excluded from all say, much less "tangible say, " except at
the whim of the top Administrators.   So, according to a recent decision of President Campbell, the decision to call in
the Metropolitan Police in case of student protests lies with
the University Administration--"Student Council Presidents,
if available, MAY BE CONSULTED. "

The Student Personnel Office (SPO) is primarily responsible for promulgating and enforcing the G-Book regulations.   In both of these functions students and faculty have
advisory roles, and, in some cases, may make decisions.
However, all such decisions are subject to review and/or
revision by the SPO administrators, the President, and the
Board of Directors.   The year before last a Jesuit, Fr.
Zeits, was head of the SPO.   He was relatively popular with
the students, he was also removed from his position by the
Jesuit Administration--officially he resigned.   Students protested, petitioned, passed resolutions, etc.   All to no avail.
Fr. Zeits left.

All cases of "serious discipline problems" or appeals
of decisions of the Dean of Men in discipline are handled by
the University Discipline Board.   This board is composed of
four faculty members (one from each school chosen by the
Deans with the President's approval), five students (the Yard
and Walsh Area Presidents and their appointees), an SPO
administrator (who is secretary of the Board), and the Dean
of Men (who is chairman of the Board and votes only in case
of a tie).   Any student going before the Board is potentially
faced with a five man faculty-administration coalition, with
an administrator having the tie-breaking vote.   In the case
of an appeal of a decision of the Dean of Men, if there is a
tie vote, it is the Dean of Men himself who casts the deciding vote.   Besides this, all proceedings of this Board are
kept entirely secret.

Why can't the students handle discipline problems

themselves? Why is the Board so heavily weighted in favor
of the faculty and Administration? Why secret proceedings?

To further enhance the pro-Administration bias of this
Board, any appeals of its decisions are taken to a board
called both the Review Board and the Appeals Board, which
is composed of the Academic Vice-President, the Dean of the
involved student's school, and one other Dean chosen by the
other two men. No students. No student voice in selection.
It is a loaded game no matter how you look at it.

Every year the University collects more than $600,
000 in student activity fees. Of this, $450,000 is distributed
by the Administration, with no student say, and not even an
accounting of it to the students. The remaining $150,000 is,
in theory, appropriated by a six-member student board. In
practice however, the power of those six students is severely
limited by the Vice-President for Student Development and his
associates. Thus, even student money for student affairs is,
in fact, allocated by the Administration.

Throughout all of this you might have wondered if
there was a student government at Georgetown. Well, in
fact, there is not one student government, but three separate
undergraduate student governments--one for the East Campus,
one for the College, and one for the Nursing School. For
the most part, these governments concern themselves with
running dances and passing largely ineffectual resolutions.
Their record, in-so-far as concrete achievement of power
in significant University decision making, is miserable.

Not only do these governments not further student
power, but the very fact that there are three governments
impedes progress in this field. Last year, during the annual student-administration tuition battle Fr. Fitzgerald,
Academic Vice-President of the University didn't show up at
a student meeting he was scheduled to appear at to discuss
the tuition increase. He also refused to appear at a Walsh
Area Council meeting (the more "liberal," anti-Fitzgerald
group), but did appear at a College Council meeting (the
more "conservative," pro-Fitzgerald group) to defend his
policies. This is typical of the Administration's ploy of playing one student group against the other, and thus thwart effective student action.

Student Power? There is no such thing at Georgetown. It is Jesuit Power. It is Administration Power. And

it is going to stay like that until enough students and faculty members get disgusted enough with the present course of the University and with the Administration's abuse of power. When, and only when, the students and faculty say to the Administration, "Your role is to serve us, and only us, and to serve us as we direct you to serve us"--that's when there will be student power. And more importantly, that's when the University will be returned to its proper position vis-a-vis the student and the society-at-large. For, student power is not an end in itself, it is a proper means toward achieving the end of a truly liberal education. An education which produces creative, critical, intelligent, moral people, not just another batch of IBM numbers.

FUNCTIONAL EDUCATION:

The University As
Corporate Boot Camp

We have seen the intricate part the university plays in society and how it thus becomes an accomplice in perpetrating the status quo. We have seen that this role is maintained at Georgetown particularly by a monopolizing of power and the disenfranchisement of the student's rights. Now we must ask what it means for us as individuals and what this system is really trying to mold us into.

As a student entering Georgetown University, you have high expectations. You anticipate membership in an academic community where, under sustained stimulation, your creative and critical intellect will develop. You anticipate a total living experience which will foster full growth and maturation as a human being. Unfortunately, the experience of Georgetown students can be of but slight encouragement for you. Your anticipations may be realized but your Georgetown environment will be, at best, inhibitive. Here is a candid description of what you have to look forward to academically.

"OBJECTIVITY" & "FREEDOM"
IN THE ACADEMIC COMMUNITY

"Objectivity" is a prime requisite for the development of a truly critical intellect. This nebulous quality is perhaps the one most celebrated and most professed in the academic community. The phrase "academic freedom" occurs fre-

quently as the guardian of "objective inquiry" by professors.
In fact, even approximations of academic objectivity are rare
in American universities.

Since the late 1940's Americans have generally accepted a bi-polar view of the world in which a bloc of communist nations has striven constantly to expand at the expense
of the non-communist "free world" whose chief bulwark has
been the United States. American society, according to this
view, has been engaged in a life-and-death defensive struggle
against a world conspiracy. American support for dictatorial
regimes in Greece, Formosa, South Korea, Guatemala, South
Vietnam, and elsewhere has been justified in terms of this
need for protection against communism. During the late
1940's and early 1950's there was near-hysterical concern
over the threat of communism in the U. S. itself, a concern
that is sometimes reflected even today, as a charge of communist influence in Negro ghetto uprisings. (Communists
have about as much to do with these revolts as Black People
had to do with the Russian Revolution of 1917.) For purposes
of this discussion, however, the important thing about the
Cold War mythology is that for the last two decades it has
exerted a profound influence on American scholarship.

Most academicians, who after all are part of their society, have shared the American belief in a black-and-white
struggle between communist aggressors and American de-
fenders; rather than trying to achieve an attitude of critical
detachment, they have enlisted in this supposed struggle. As
a result, American scholarship during this period has been
virtually useless in providing meaningful analysis of either America itself or of the rest of the world. An economy propped
up by huge military expenditures (conservatives are right in
claiming that World War II, not the New Deal, took us out
of the Great Depression) has been discussed in economics
texts as though it were perfectly normal and not at all un-
healthy. The existence of urban slums was virtually ignored
by scholars until the mid 1960's, when it was discovered as
a "problem" to be alleviated, rather than as a standing indictment of the American economic and social system. The
dramatic worldwide expansion of American business in the
post-war period, aided and protected by the Government, has
been ignored by scholars who cannot admit that America seeks
to dominate other countries. Historians have reported that
the American past has been singularly free of conflict (true,
up to a point, though Civil War was the bloodiest conflict in
history up to that time, and although labor-management strug-

gles have been more violent here than Europe), and many of
them have gone on to say how fortunate we are to have had
a "consensus" on major problems.   In a similar vein, soci-
ologists and psychologists have reported that the lower classes
are made up of intolerant, narrow minded child-beaters who
presumably could not be trusted with political power but must
be regarded as a potential menace to the stability of society.

Furthermore, as described in the first part of this
pamphlet, the university has become deeply compromised by
research and other activities which serve the governmental-
industrial-military complex.   Faculty members who are involved in and dependent upon such activities are ill suited to
foster "objective" (read, "impartial") critical intellect in their
students.

The phrases "objectivity" and "academic freedom"
have been abused to the point that they are now mutated concepts which distort reality and screen activities which, while
performed under university auspices, contradict any reasonable concept of freedom.

Freedom is never an absolute concept; whether in society at large or the university, it is always relative.   The
words "academic freedom" do not in any way justify or ex-
onerate or compensate for activities which directly or indirectly assist in the domination, exploitation, and oppression
of peoples anywhere in the world.   The credo of Georgetown
University reads, "We believe that academic freedom should
not be used as a pretext to advocate systems which destroy
all freedoms. "   We would amend this to state, "We believe
that academic freedom should not be used as a pretext to
serve systems which destroy all freedom. "

THE FACULTY

The faculty of the university are, by-and-large, the
highly refined products of the University.   They are hired
in accordance with criteria which are remote to the needs
of students (who have no part whatsoever in hiring).   In decisions on the subsequent retention or dismissal of the faculty, the student has no role.   The development and maintenance of meaningful educational relationships with undergraduates are necessarily low on the list of priorities to which a
professor adheres if he is to maintain (or advance) his position.   Only the exceptional professor becomes involved with

undergraduates and this is almost always at the students'
initiative.

THE CLASSES

The lecture class is the predominant mode of student-
faculty contact. (This type of class is ideally suited to the
Jesuit maxim that "The student is an empty vessel. ") Passive receptivity is the rule in lecture classes. Individual expression is difficult and infrequent; true debate is impossible
and non-existent.

The student is evaluated by the test-grade system which
is painfully familiar to high school students. One soon real-
izes that "getting by" is quite simple. One need only develop
a facility in adopting to demands (or idiosyncrasies) of the
particular professor (or graduate student "grader"). It is
possible to get by comfortably, with above average grades,
by exercising no critical intellect and by exercising just
enough creativity to develop methods for passing tests.

The student quickly learns that examinations are not
the place for independent, critical, creative thought. Re-
warding grades go to the student who follows the given norms
and those grades will be his permanent record of academic
"achievement" and his guarantee of future security.

CURRICULA AND COURSE CONTENT

As noted above, a university which is so deeply implicated in the existing political-economic-social structure can
hardly provide an objective environment for critical and creative intellectual development. The University's prime role
comes to be the transmission of a pre-determined set of values. Indeed, this seems a concise and accurate statement
of the mission of Jesuit educators. In short, the University,
and Georgetown is a good example, seeks to provide personnel with safely built-in value systems for a status quo society.

The constellation of "disciplines" from which the university draws its curricula militates against true objectivity.
Disciplines are abstract, arbitrary delineations with no coun-
terparts in reality. To the degree that an economist deals
exclusively with that abstraction "economy" (or the political
scientist with "government") he misrepresents the continuum

which is reality.   To the degree that he deals with reality, he betrays his abstract discipline.

The professional schools at Georgetown, because of their inter-disciplinary approach, partially correct this "falsification by discipline." However, the curricula of these schools hold a great danger for the student.   The inter-disciplinary approach in these schools is designed to provide trained professionals to fill existing roles in society.   WHAT THIS MEANS IS THAT WERE THE SCHOOLS TO DEVELOP IN THEIR STUDENTS AN OPEN, OBJECTIVE, PERSPECTIVE WHICH CRITICIZED OR DENIED THE PROFESSIONS OR PROFESSIONAL STRUCTURES (GOVERNMENTAL SERVICE, INTERNATIONAL BUSINESS STRUCTURES, ETC.) THE SCHOOLS WOULD BE DENYING THE PURPOSE FOR THEIR OWN EXISTENCE.   The professional schools (as well as the College in a slightly more subtle way) have a vested interest in preventing the student from fully developing his creative and critical powers.   The faculty and administration's commitment to the "institutional life" of Georgetown University (a deceptively deadly type of animation) sustains and perpetuates the existing system.

As Georgetown University is a microcosm of the contradictions which beset American education, so is its location, Washington, D.C. a microcosm of the contradictions which are endemic to America.   The seat of national government, focal point for national and international interests is also the home of a majority black population which is oppressed in a sprawling ghetto.   Yet probably the only intimate contact you, a Georgetown student, will have with a black person is when the maid in your dorm rolls you out of bed to change your sheets.   Georgetown University and the Georgetown "community" at large seems blissfully ignorant of what exists on the other side of Rock Creek and by-and-large the student will be influenced only by the dominant, unfortunately normal, cultural system which, in its turn, will serve to reinforce his training as a future member of the system.

RIGHTS????

It should be quite clear from the previous sections that your rights as a student at Georgetown are very limited. By way of an introduction, it might be good to outline briefly the basis of the power which controls us.   Actually there seems to be three sources for this power which the Administration wields:

(1)   The first source is their strictly legal rights as owners of the University property.   Students have challenged this thoroughly American practice by placing the human values of community and democracy above property.

(2)   The second source rests with the Administration's threat of discipline and, ultimately, dismissal.   This develops from the average student's fear of jeopardizing his career by getting an indelible mark on his record.

(3)   The third source is the myth of the Georgetown community.   The Administration arranges things so that they control while giving the illusion that their control is nothing but community self-discipline.

Events seem to be weakening the last two sources of power, inevitably forcing the Administration to rely on its ownership of the University for control.   The struggle at Columbia is a perfect example of this.

CAMPUS DISCIPLINE

It is hard to see how anyone has any significant rights under the campus discipline system.   Such rights would necessarily mean that students have some say in deciding what the disciplinary regulations are.   The fact is that regulations are dictated.   Students have no say.

Leaving that aside, under the present system you are granted the following privileges:

(1)   you may appeal any acts of discipline taken by your prefect or house master to the Dean of Men.

(2)   in a serious matter, you may appeal any action taken by the Dean of Men to the University Discipline Board.

(3)   you may appeal a decision of the Discipline Board to a special body composed of the Academic Vice-President, the Dean of your school, and a second Dean chosen by the other two members.

In appearing before the Discipline Board you have a right to submit oral and written arguments, call witnesses either of character or of fact, and cross-examine accusing witnesses (at the discretion of the Board).   The same procedures apply to the review board made up of the Academic V-P and the two Deans.

In working reality the discipline apparatus of the

University has some serious flaws which tend to limit your
ability to get a fair hearing. On all levels discipline personnel take the simultaneous role of prosecutor and judge. This
has led to some very unfair proceedings, all protected by the
blanket of closed meetings. As the issues of student rights
become clearer and the decisions of the discipline apparatus
begin to become more obviously administration decisions, the
significance of these flaws will become more important.

Remember, you always have the right to tell your fellow students about what is happening to you. Until things
change, the protection of student solidarity will probably be
your only and certainly your most effective right.

CAMPUS POLICE

The University security force does not normally concern itself with enforcing University regulations other than
those affecting the safety of the campus. Generally the
"watchdogs of the Administration" are dormitory personnel,
not the security force.

While generally well disposed towards students, the
security force remains solely at the disposal of the Administration. In a confrontation between students and the Administration, the security force will not be on our side.

The security police are unarmed and cannot generally
make arrests. In fact, only 3 officers of the force have
been commissioned by the D. C. government as official police.
Legally, they are simply a private group, whose authority
rests in enforcing the property rights of the University. If
a situation arises that requires forceful police action, the
Seventh Precinct will be called immediately for assistance.
The fact that the security forces wear uniforms gives them
no more power than any other agents of the Administrators.

MUST YOU SURRENDER YOUR ID CARD?

The G Book gives the following as an example of un-
acceptable conduct: "the failure to produce proper identification or supply one's correct name when asked to do so by a
prefect or other University official. " This rule is usually
interpreted in the form of a command to surrender your
Georgetown ID. Security police have been instructed to ask

for proof of student status, and if none is produced, to then consider the individual as an outsider, i.e. trespasser. This ingenious regulation puts the student in the dilemma of either turning himself in, or refusing and risking double punishment in the case that he is identified at a later date. There is, however, beyond the campus discipline system, no legal basis for such a request, and there are occasions when turning yourself in would not be very smart.

YOUR RIGHT TO PROTEST

With the continuing movement toward student liberation across the country, University officials have armed themselves with a plan of reaction to counter any similar outbursts of freedom at Georgetown. Out of a series of top level meetings came, on May 28, 1968, an official "Policy on Unlawful Protest." From this we learn that:

> Georgetown deplores unlawful protest. Any protest or demonstration which seriously impedes the normal and orderly functioning of the University is unlawful. Should this occur, it is the responsibility of the University to act to remedy this situation.

The University further defines an obstruction as covered by the above to mean:

> Any serious or complete impeding of a University activity is a form of protest, unlawful by its very nature, and not to be tolerated.

In effect the administration has provided itself with a definition of legal protest that precludes any effective action by students. Even if a majority of the students oppose something, they have no right to do anything but bring the matter to their elders. Any action they take on their decision would necessarily obstruct the University activity to which they are opposed; automatically their act becomes "unlawful by its very nature." This is a flagrant demonstration of the kind of respect that the administration has for student rights.

If a confrontation does come, the 7th Precinct Police will be called and the students arrested for either unlawful assembly or trespass. True student rights will come only from determined and concerted actions by students.

THE USE OF MARIJUANA

On June 5, 1968 president Campell promulgated "A drug policy for Georgetown University. " Unsurprisingly the document reveals that our administration considers the use of marijuana to be a sign of an unbalanced student in need of psychiatric care; and that moreover such a student is irredeemable and does not belong in a university. Georgetown's rules on marijuana use "shall be enforced and are applicable regardless of the status of the violation in the civil courts. "

The rules state that:

1. The provision of or merchandising of drugs including marijuana will ordinarily result in expulsion.

2. The penalties envoked for possession, consumption, or sharing of marijuana, or misconduct resulting therefrom, may range from rehabilitative consultation up to and including suspension, depending on the seriousness and extent of the offense.

Past experience demonstrates how few rights students have when it comes to these matters. The administration not only accepts the civil law but actively goes out of its way to enforce it. The University seems to be trying to weed out marijuana users before they have a chance to besmirch the cherished reputation of "the Georgetown Gentleman. " Last year the Dean of Men threatened to implicate certain innocent students if they did not report to him on the use of marijuana at Georgetown. This method of investigation led to the dismissal of at least one student. This prosecution is but a symptom of the close connection between GU and the American society that demands conformity as the price of survival and success.

THE DRAFT

American society is no different from GU when it comes to "rights. " In fact, our University is but a microcosm, a training ground for participation in that larger society where "rights" are more numerous but just as vacuous. The Georgetown Students for a Democratic Society are opposed to American wars of economic and political expansion (such as in Viet Nam) and to the suppression of Black Americans. We don't think that young people should be forced to defend the interests of American business anywhere. Consequently, we know all the ways to stay out of the army. Several of our members are experienced draft counselors. If you have any questions about your rights under the law you should contact us as soon as possible. Particularly if you hope to gain recognition as a conscientious objector, or if you are a freshman and plan to marry soon, contact us immediately.

In general, as an undergraduate, the Military Selective Service Act of 1967 provides as follows: Section 6. (h) (1) ..."the President shall ... provide for the deferment ... of persons satisfactorily pursuing a full time course of instruction at a college, university, or similar institution of learning and who requests such deferment. A deferment granted to any person under authority of the preceding sentence shall continue until such person completes the requirements for his Baccalaureate degree, fails to pursue satisfactorily a full time course of instruction, or attains the twenty-fourth anniversary of the date of his birth, which ever first occurs..."

In essence this guarantees you a deferment for the number of years it takes to complete an established undergraduate program. "Satisfactorily pursuing" means that you are making proportional progress toward your degree each year e.g. in a four year program, you must complete twenty-five per cent each year. You have from October until October to fulfill this obligation (which means that you can make up courses in summer school).

You also have other very important rights under the Selective Service Law, only a few of which are:

(1) You may appeal any classification made by your local board.
(2) You have a right to exemption from military "service" as a conscientious objector.
(3) You may transfer your physical to where you are residing (e.g. to Washington).

THE MOVEMENT

sds is a difficult and complex thing to describe: it

is as much a form of on-going experience as an organization.
In a sense, sds undergoes a perpetual identity crisis.   Because of its strong anti-elitist and decentralist strains, sds
is as diverse as its 300 college chapters and its 40,000 members.   Thus perhaps the best approach to the difficult problem of description is a history of the development of sds.

sds found its origins in the civil rights struggles of
the early 1960's.   Composed largely of middle-class, white,
college students, sds sought, simply enough, freedom for
black people.   We asked only that America live up to her
cardinal promise of freedom for all men.   We assumed America could and would fulfill that promise.

When America faltered, we began to ask "Why?"

Why were benevolent, liberal governments unable to realize
     even their professed goals?
Why did the celebrated "civil rights laws" of the 60's leave
     the black man's desperation unrelieved?
Why were people, at home and abroad, condemned to lives
     of poverty, disease, and starvation, while we enjoyed
     an overabundance of wealth and material comfort?
     (Afterall wasn't there a War on Poverty?   a Foreign
     Aid program?)
Why was America fighting an undeclared war on the Asian main-
     land?
And finally, why were our efforts to seek answers and to
     demonstrate our concern scorned and suppressed by
     American "leaders"?

We studied things again: racism, poverty, the war.
We found that our search for convincing explanations drove
us to introspection, to a more critical look at the American
past and to more skeptical probes of the "democratic institutions" (which we had been told were to facilitate needed
change, not obstruct or deny it.)

A pattern appeared: the pattern of the International
Communist Conspiracy and our valorous national effort to defeat it in behalf of democracy, Mustangs, John Wayne, and
miniskirts.   Everywhere our Cold War leaders looked, they
saw conspiracies, agitation, subversion and insurrection.

What did we see?

In the first place, hunger everywhere.   Then indignity

and humiliation.   Supporting these conditions we found dozens
of petty dictatorships; governments which our crusaders for
freedom found peculiarly and comfortably tolerable.   Then,
curiously, we saw everywhere the familiar American businessman, attache case in hand, at home it seemed in any of these
countries from Vorster's South Africa to Stroessner's Paraguay, and from Papa Doc Duvalier's Haiti to post-Sukarno
Indonesia, up and about, making a buck, while for some reason the economies of these "host" countries lagged farther
and farther behind.   And behind this traveling universal...?
The smiling face of your A. I. D. field representative (or was
he C. I. A. ?)   And behind him...?   Trying to blend in with
the native faces, lurking in the shadows of certain jungles,
the Fort Bragg graduate, the jaunty cut-throat of the Special
Forces' country-x team.

        And at home...?   First, we saw black people trapped
in a cycle of racist oppression.   But soon it became clear
that racism was a major symptom of a more fundamental
malaise.   Poverty disregards race ... poverty destroys lives
in Appalachia as well as the Delta, in the barrios as well
as on the reservation.   Then, not expectedly we saw the
ubiquitous American businessman, this time with a domestic
complement of public and private servants, of lawyers and
law enforcers.   His corporations perpetuated exploitation
with a cycle of superfluous and waste production, planned obsolescence, and consumer indoctrination.

        And finally, we saw in the ranks of the complicit
business, military, and government, alumni of our own Universities, the end products of the "educational" process we
were being subjected to...

        We saw these things not because we wanted to; we
were not obsessed with repudiating the institutions which
would have been our legacy.   We saw these things because
we seek the truth about the world in which we live and because these things are an inescapable part of the reality of
that world.

        Thus far, sds would seem to be a largely negative
reaction.   This is far from an accurate description, for the
sds critique of America grows out of a strong desire for
truth and from a deep and abiding faith in man, in the human
potential for creative cooperation, for love.   Moreover, sds
stands fundamentally and unequivocally committed to the
principle that people must have control over (and thus responsibility for) their own lives.

This student handbook expresses the attitudes of the members of Georgetown sds.

If you have questions, or if you have reservations about our position, feel free at any time to contact us: we look forward to seeing you.

If you find yourself in substantial agreement, <u>JOIN US.</u>

(Distributed September 11-16, 1968 on Georgetown University campus, Washington, D. C. by Georgetown SDS. Collected by the compiler September 15, 1968.)

19. RACIST STRIKE-BREAKER
PLANS TO SPEAK AT GU

THE FIGHT AGAINST RACISM AT
SAN FRANCISCO STATE COLLEGE

No previous American university struggle has been as
long, violent and bitter as the strike being waged at San
Francisco State College. Led by the Black Student Union
and the Third World Liberation Front (composed of Latin
American, Mexican, Phillippino and Chinese students), the
vast majority of students at SF State have been on strike
since November 6th to press for implementation of 15 demands which have been developed over the course of two
years. These demands speak directly to the survival of the
non-white student in the university and attempt to relate education directly to the community. From the very beginning
the policy of the administration, Board of Trustees and hack
politicians like Governor Reagan and Mayor Alioto was to
crush the strike by almost any means they could feasibly use.
They had to do this because these demands have sharply attacked their power.

First of all, the BSU and TWLF demand the rehiring
of George Murray, instructor and Minister of Education of
the Black Panther Party. Murray was suspended because he
spoke to the necessity of Third World people arming to defend themselves and called upon black students to bring guns
to school to defend themselves against the frequent police attacks. This demand relates directly to the black community
where the police are a daily menace. The second political
point of the demands is for the immediate creation of Black
and Ethnic Studies Departments with the power of hiring,
firing and determining course content to be in the hands of
the Third World people. Thus they demand that Third World
people of the community have the power to determine their
own education: learning the nature of their oppression, who
is responsible for it and what can be done to change these
conditions. The third set of demands put forth by the Third
World students hits at the very heart of the issues involved
in the SF State strike and most clearly exposes the racist
and class nature of the whole educational system. The BSU
and TWLF demand the admission of all minority students who

306

apply, regardless of "qualifications." While at first this
demand might seem impossible and senseless, it addresses
itself to the solid core of the black community and its needs.
San Francisco's primary and high schools, where the vast
majority of Third World people receive their education, are
rotten--so rotten that the college in their community (SF
State) considers them "unqualified." Thus only ten percent
of the SF State student body is Third World, far below the
proportion of minority people in city elementary and secondary schools--and even this small percentage is declining.

The strike call of the Black Student Union and the
Third World Liberation Front was answered by white students
who formed a supportive strike committee. The major position accepted was that the main issue of the struggle was
racism. The main role of white students was seen to be
struggling against and confronting the racist ideology which
had been pounded into students' heads, and building further
support among students.

In response to these demands which affirm self-determination for the Black and Third World communities of
San Francisco, the men who control California have called
upon their puppets--Reagan, Hayakawa, Alioto--to crush the
strike at any cost. After failing to bribe and buy off the
students, Alioto and the administration sent in the cops--
up to 650 at a time with 1000 in reserve. The students
fought against the power of those who run California and the
police they use to enforce their racist policies. The highest
point of the struggle came on December 3rd (Bloody Tuesday) when students battled 650 cops for 2 hours with numerous casualties on both sides. After this point the strike
grew to encompass over 80% of the students and eventually
a supportive strike by teachers. Against this background
Alioto has vowed to keep the campus open and has tried to
enforce his promise by using police relentlessly to break
the strike.

MAYOR OF SAN FRANCISCO/BANKER/LAND OWNER/
LIBERAL/RACIST-ALIOTO

Alioto is a very revealing example of the politicians
that America breeds. As a Kennedy liberal, he is a favorite
of the Democratic Party (of California) and a probable candidate for governor. And at the same time that he talks the
liberal line about change in America, he sends his cops to

repress those who want to do somthing real about change by
fighting racism.   A contradiction for liberalism?   It's a bitter pill for those who really believe that liberal politics offer
a viable solution to America's problems.

Alioto and his liberal fellow-travelers have their primary allegiance to the business interests that exercise power
in our country--not to America's people and their needs.
His past could tell us that: he made his fortune from the
lands of Japanese-Americans stolen while the owners were
in the infamous "detention camps" of World War II.   He
headed the Rice Growers Association and used his capital to
found a bank and a real estate company.

In the time of crisis, when rhetoric is not enough,
when people are demanding real change, Alioto will always
turn up on the side of the business and financial interests.
Liberal politicians are puppets of the powers that put them
in office--the rhetoric of America's liberal politicians has
always been meaningless.   Their effect has always been co-
option of the real desire for change.   The struggle at S F
State has revealed Alioto's real interests and, similarly,
as the people begin to demand more real change, the true
colors of all of America's politicians will be exposed.

WHAT IS TO BE DONE?

There can be only one response to Alioto's appearance at Georgetown.   We must actively participate in the
struggle against racism that our brothers at San Francisco
State are waging.   We must make it clear that we won't be
bought off with liberal talk that does nothing--we will fight
racism, the institutions and system it perpetuates, and the
few people who profit from it.

We must fight the racism of Georgetown University
itself.   Our reponse to Alioto must show our seriousness
and determination to win the fight against racism.

RALLY AT JOHN CARROLL STATUE
THURSDAY 7PM

(Flier distributed March 13, 1969 by SDS at Georgetown University on the occasion of San Francisco Mayor Alioto's appearance on campus)

20. WHY WE DID IT,
WHY IT HAD TO BE DONE

> There's something more dangerous about
> attacking the pigs of the power structure
> verbally than there is in walking into the
> Bank of America with a gun and attacking
> it forthrightly. Bankers hate armed rob-
> bery, but someone who stands up and di-
> rectly challenges their racist system, that
> drives them crazy. I don't know if there
> are any bankers in the audience tonight
> but I hope there are ... And I hope par-
> ticularly that there's one here from the
> Bank of America. I heard today that
> Brother Cesar Chavez (leader of Mexi-
> can-American migrant workers in the
> grape strike) has declared war on the
> Bank of America. The Bank of Ameri-
> ca is Alioto's Bank. --Eldridge Cleaver

Life and Death in Mayor Alioto's America

Mayor Alioto: who is he, what is he:

Alioto is a very revealing example of the politicians
that America breeds. As a Kennedy liberal, he is a favorite of the Democratic party (of California) and a probable
candidate for governor. And at the same time that he talks
the liberal line about change in America, he sends his cops
to repress those who do something real about change by
fighting racism. A contradiction for liberalism? It's a
bitter pill for those who really believe that liberal politics
offer a viable solution to America's problems.

Alioto and his liberal fellow-travelers have their
primary allegiance to the business interests that exercise
power in our country, not to America's people and their
needs. His past could tell us that: he made his fortune
from the lands of Japanese-Americans stolen while the owners were in the infamous "detention camps" during World

309

War II. He headed the Rice Growers Association and used
his capital to found a bank and a real estate company.

In time of crisis, when rhetoric is not enough, Alioto
will always turn up on the side of the business and financial
interests. For example, he has close connections with the
Bank of America which has opposed the migrant workers attempt to organize through the grape strike. Liberal politicians are puppets of the powers that put them in office, the
rhetoric of America's liberal politicians has always been
meaningless. Their effect has always been co-option of the
real desire for change. The struggle at San Francisco State
and the general political repression in the city of San Francisco has revealed Alioto's real interests and similarly, as
the people begin to demand real change, the true colors of
all of America's politicians will be exposed.

San Francisco State--Period of Rational Discussion

October 28, 1968--George Murray, instructor, an-
nounces student strike for Nov. 6 over several issues re-
volving around institutional racism at the university. He expresses the view that Blacks should arm themselves against
racist violence. October 31--Chancellor Dumke issues order
to suspend Murray. President Smith and faculty agree that
the firing is a violation of due process. Reinstatement of
Murray becomes one of strikers' demands. Tuesday Nov.
12--Faculty asks for resignation of Dumke. Alioto's Tactical
Squad sent on campus and Black students are attacked and
photographed at AFROTC headquarters on campus, twenty-
two are eventually arrested. Nov. 13--cops on campus attack Nesbitt Crutchfield, a leader of the Black Students Union
for no apparent reason according to witnesses, beating him
senseless, and then charge him with assaulting a police officer. Faculty votes to close campus and meet in continuous
session until rational solutions are found. Trustees meet in
L. A. and Reagan demands campus reopen. Faculty member
claims trustees don't give a damn about education. Black
trustee Edward O. Lee asks other trustees not to act until
they have a chance to hear more about campus problems.
Trustees vote to forcefully reopen the campus immediately;
Faculty refuses to go back to work. In a few days, Smith
resigns and S. I. Hayakawa is appointed president. Hayakawa liberally uses Alioto's Tactical Squad to break the strike
of students and faculty and suspends all official student expression by a court order freezing all funds for student body
use.

Political Suppression in San Francisco

      Political repression in San Francisco focuses around
the Black community and especially attempts to organize a
political base within the ghetto. George Murray, Black
Panther Minister of Information and a teacher at San Francisco State, was framed on a sentence of violating parole in
allegedly carrying a concealed weapon and received six
months. The car the weapon was found in wasn't Murray's
and the police have been unable to prove that he had ever
seen or possessed the gun but he sits in jail because he en-
dangers Alioto and his friends who have economic interests
in maintaining the ghetto status quo. Black Student Union
leaders Jack Alexis and Jerry Bernards were also arrested
on the same charge and for the same reasons in spite of the
fact that the Black Panther Party specifically forbids its
members carrying weapons concealed or in cars. Terry
Cannon, a leading movement activist in the San Francisco
area, got 3 months (brought down from 6 months demanded
by Alioto's SF city prosecutor) for saying an obscenity. In
the face of the actions of the American corporate structure
calling any collection of letters a "profanity" is absurd.

      Eldridge Cleaver had his parole revoked because he
journeyed to NY to exercise his "right to free speech" on
the David Susskind Show. He has fled SF to avoid becoming
another of Alioto's political prisoners. On January 16, 1968
at 3:30 AM, SF police without an arrest or search warrant
kicked in the door of his apartment, drew their guns, and
proceeded to ransack the place. Finding nothing incriminat-
ing they left.

      There is no formal recognition of political prisoners
in San Francisco or America in general but a practical recognition is arising. People opposing the power structure
are given harsher sentences for simple misdemeanors which
are often trumped up anyway. Now appearing are attempts
to convict organizers for felony charges on "conspiracy to
commit a misdemeanor." Alioto is really into all this. He
made the SF Tactical Squad (especially selected for size and
brutality) the gruesome instrument it has proven itself to be
at SF State. Alioto's mayoralty has seen frame-ups, terror
raids, extreme sentences, and political repression including
repression of the right to strike and the daily repression of
the ghetto population.

- - - - - - - - - -

1. Nature of free speech--Free speech must be rationally
evaluated in the context of the existing society. Effective
speech is not free. It is limited to certain people and certain viewpoints. Free speech often costs money in the sense
of getting elected to political office or buying time or owning
a newspaper. Mayor Alioto and the millionaires who run
corporations and our governments have that access to newspapers, tv-radio time, and the public ear, but the people
they oppress: the blacks in our ghettos, the students at San
Francisco State, the Vietnamese people do not have "free"
speech. Thus, Alioto may come here and rationalize to you
his use of repression. He has power, he is respected.

        Using the state apparatus to "legally" repress political
activity is as real as directly denying people free speech.
What then is the meaning of following the "rules" when the
Aliotos of this society use official power to "legally" violate
these very same rules. Respecting the rights of the ruler
when the ruler does not respect the rights of the ruled is
effectively granting him an indefinite lease on the power to
perpetrate repression. To allow this situation is moral bank-
ruptcy of the highest order. In such a context, free speech
is a distorted concept. The morally inviolate right of free
speech occurs only in a meaningful environment of justice.
That environment does not exist in San Francisco, nor at
Georgetown University, nor in America.

        You may have noticed that in the many newspaper and
tv-radio presentations on the "Battle of Healy" that no SDS
people were quoted or consulted. The papers used their
"free speech" to present their side. How could we ever
reach as many people as the Post or NBC news to counter-
act their inaccuracies? The Publisher of the Post is a director of Georgetown, and the paper has connections with
the new dean of the law center. They are not objective,
they have interests in common with Alioto and racism and
the continuation of the Vietnam War, and the Georgetown administration.

2. Why not a debate--Ultimately, words don't fight racism
and repression. We have seen this with the Kerner Commission report and the hypocrisy of GU hosting a review of
it last week. We saw it with the Poor Peoples' campaign
and the hypocrisy of GU hosting a concert on their behalf
(see section below on Georgetown tradition). People have
had dialogue around the Vietnam War for years and it still
continues. People have been discussing poverty even longer

and it's getting worse, not better.   There must be a time
for talking to stop and meaningful action to begin.   Mayor
Alioto would have us debate forever while he and the powers
he represents use physical force to support their interests
and run around the country trying to rationalize it.   One
doesn't dialogue about oppression.   The way to fight such
things is to effectively deny the oppressors their "right" to
oppress and this means attacking their "freedom" to rationalize such actions under the guise of free speech.

3.   Students Rights--One student said on television that the
majority of students had sympathized with or supported SDS
but that the action against Alioto had turned them off.   In the
past, whites have said that ghetto riots turned them off to
civil rights and people supposedly against the Vietnam War
say that actions intended to end that war (not to talk about it)
turned them off.   After years of oppression and a worsening
situation, they still want actions to be aimed at pleasing
them.   However, tactics are created by reality, not whim.
We are not risking expulsion and hospitalization because it's
fun but because it's necessary.   Liberals are willing to ap-
plaud Abernathy but they are unwilling to put their bodies on
the line, unwilling to realize the consequences of their analysis of America, unwilling to have their "rights" inconvenienced
in the slightest way.   They say that killing and repression
and racism at home and abroad are OK but they are no excuse for militant action, these policies are no excuse for
stopping their perpetrators from speaking.

        Those who put their slightest "rights" above the end-
ing of the oppression of black people in America (who consider observation of their rights as being more important
than say, acting against racism at Georgetown), are generally those who are unwilling to do anything at all to defeat
these things.   We would ask those who were "turned off"
what they had done, how they had ever sympathized?   People
can no longer gear their lives to the belief that those tactics
defined as "illegal" (precisely because they have a chance of
working) are not worth the inconvenience of the apathetic and
self-righteous.   Rights are, necessarily, relative and that
ending racism at Georgetown has a higher priority than preserving Georgetown's "traditions" which embody and institu-
tionalize racism.

4.   The Question of Violence--The fight against oppressive
institutions and the people who run them and profit from them
is defined by that oppression.   Violence is too often thought

to be the monopoly of the State. It is perfectly moral and
legal for Mayor Alioto to use violence and try to break an
anti-racism strike at SF State. It is perfectly moral and
legal for cops to repress people rebelling in the face of poverty. It is perfectly moral and legal for people with state
power to use massive violence to forward their economic interests through imperialist wars. But when those who put
their bodies, their futures, when they put everything on the
line to strike a blow against those things in the person of
that great liberal hero Joe Alioto then all of a sudden violence
loses its glory and becomes an immoral cancer not in the
"Tradition of Georgetown University." The time when the oppressors have a monopoly on violence is over. It took a long
time for the movement to come to this realization. We have
debated for a long time while we watched the "respected"
members of our society continue to do exactly what they
pleased. That time is over.

We still talk, we talk to build an educational base, to
explain--in the case of GU to try to explain how things operate in the US but at some point the talk must end. Alioto
and his friends have defined the battle and now they must accept consequences.

Georgetown Traditions--Mr. Hurson, amidst much applause,
told of his pride in Georgetown traditions. One must ask
what the GU traditions are? One is segregation, to put it
specifically, institutionalized racism. Only about 30 of 4000
students are black and one has to rely on the charity of the
faculty and student body for a few more scholarships (a conscious soothing maneuver?). Another great GU tradition is
underpaying non-academic employees. GU, after the Federal
Government, is the largest employer in DC. The cafeteria
workers, maids, police, janitors of GU are paid very poorly
even after years of service. Last year, an attempt was
made to help the workers organize a union, but the Administration used every means of harassment and intimidation to
prevent this organization and prevent the exercise of free
speech by the workers. Our racist yearbook was most em-
barrassing to the purveyors of GU tradition. Furthermore,
a petition in favor of voluntary tuition increases for scholarship and support of the Poor People's Campaign could not
obtain signatures half as easily as one opposed to the Campaign (which is now so warmly received). The College Yard
(led by Hurson) was the only student council which would not
support the Campaign and Father Hurson helped co-opt an
attempt by students to get GU to offer unused facilities to the

campaign and the Administration (led by our beloved FR.
Fitzgerald) stalled and refused to meet with the students until a sit-in occurred and GU never did help the Campaign.

   In addition, there are GU's "International Free Speech"
endeavors like the International Police Academy, Center for
Strategic Studies, 352 Reserve Unit, and ROTC which trains
for violent repression and not for protecting the free speech
of the Vietnamese. Georgetown's Administration in its self-
righteous, morally-oriented attacks is rather disgusting. Perhaps they owe an apology to us rather than vice-versa.

```
        R              WORDS NEVER
F       A              STOPPED RACISM--
I       C
G       I              ONLY ACTION WILL
H       S
T       M
```

(Distributed by SDS on March 12, 1969 at Georgetown University, Washington, D.C.   Collected November 22, 1970.)

21. DARE TO STRUGGLE, DARE TO WIN

Georgetown Action

Everyone knows the fact: Alioto was not able to speak at Georgetown. Tactically, it was not very difficult. We had seventy people with a clear objective, and we had, despite forewarning, an opposition that was surprised and un-prepared. In terms of the objective gained, and more, in terms of the collective experience that we went through and the support we gave to the struggle at S. F. State, we had a very successful evening.

However, on what I believe is the critical criteria, the outcome may not be as clear. Did the action help to build the revolutionary student movement at Georgetown? First, a little discussion on actions in general. It seems as though the function of an action changes according to the level of consciousness of a constituency. From the beginning ac-tions are educative. They are the practice partner to theory and must always be an integral part of the politics of our organization. Actions taken in a constituency with a very low level of revolutionary consciousness are used primarily as an educative tool to express politics. In a more highly developed constituency, actions do the same, plus organize people into attacks on the system. The final end in the scheme is the act that is the revolution. Each successive stage is characterized by a larger number of people involved.

At the opposite end of the scale from revolution is the situation in which an action taken by a revolutionary van-guard has no support in the constituency and produces only alienation. That kind of action would be called adventurism. Some people have claimed that the action at Georgetown was just that: adventuristic and destructive to the movement rather than educative and constructive.

To see if this is true or not, we will have to begin with a little history. By the start of this semester the Georgetown chapter had adopted a plan for a spring offensive. It was to be focussed on a series of anti-imperialistic de-mands:

1. abolish ROTC

316

2.   sever all relations with the International Police
      Academy, the Center for Strategic Studies, and
      the 352nd Civil Affairs unit of the Army

3.   University departments and faculty sever all ties
      with the Defense Dept., State Dept., CIA and
      military money.

4.   full disclosure of the university budget to ensure
      the above

We planned to begin this program with a long and
comprehensive educational program, hopefully culminating in
enough support for an effective action around the demands before the semester ended.   These plans were concretized and
carried out by several means: the chapter published and distributed two issues of a newspaper that contained the results
of our research on Georgetown, we sponsored a Cuba week,
did extensive freshman dorm work with both our newspapers
and the Black Panther film.   Simultaneously the chapter issued several leaflets dealing with specific campus issues and
made an attempt to directly challenge the liberal leadership
for the energies of those students looking for change.   All
of this seemed to be making some impact.   Students began
to give us a certain amount of respect for our research and
competency.   One student was quoted after the Alioto affair
as saying that he thought that before Thursday a majority of
the students were sympathetic to S.D.S.   This we doubt, but
it is true that among many students, in particular the Freshmen, we were slowly, but clearly gaining ground.

The decision to take the action around Alioto was, at
one and the same time, an integral part of, and a break from
this spring program.   The decision flowed out of our spring
program because we felt that action on our theory was an integral part of the revolutionary politics that we wanted to express.   We went on the assumption that capitalism and its
inhumanity produce dissatisfactions, and that the best way to
build a student movement is to openly lay out the only politics that can ultimately deal with the problems people have.
Up until Alioto, we were getting a lot of liberal support for
our debating ability, but we could provide students no meaningful solution until we introduced the concept of struggle
into our politics.   It was clear to us that an action was
called for.   We also expected the action to provoke a lot of
interest in our program among the students, specifically because we felt such an action around correct politics injects

some reality into the life of students whose lives are forcibly
isolated and deliberately irrelevant.

However, the Alioto action did, in some ways, interrupt our spring program. We had not done any of our educational work around racism--instead our focus had been on
imperialism. Before the action the chapter had prepared and
distributed a leaflet on Alioto--that was the total operation.
The question before the chapter, then, was whether we had
enough consciousness to make the action non-adventuristic.
We knew that it would have been harder to take an action
around ROTC, but that it was possible. For manpower reasons the chapter decided on Alioto, and took the risk that
the base laid by the chapter for anti-imperialistic politics
would carry over onto racism, and make the action constructive. The risk was taken and it appears now that we were
right. The campus was polarized, not between us and the
other students, but on a much broader level between progressive and reactionary students. In dorm work that immediately followed the action, we found that although we had a
lot of explaining to do about Alioto and S. F. State, the progressive students had not been alienated. It was indicative
that on Thursday immediately following the disruption large
groups of students stayed afterwards and for hours engaged
SDSers in heated and not always bad debates. And although
it is too early to tell, it also seems that about three new
people have joined the chapter as a result of the action.

In general, since the event, the Georgetown chapter
policy has been to remain as much as possible on the offensive. The demonstration was our politics--defense and
hedging are not. We stayed after the disruption and rapped
with people, we prepared a leaflet and continued our dorm
work. Those who have been selected out by the administration for discipline will demand an open hearing which we
will then publicize and turn into a political trial and platform
for our views. We will have a special issue of our paper
on racism ready in time for our trials. Our confidence has
prompted the school paper editor to remark that "members
of the SDS were anything but apologetic. In fact, an SDS
flyer distributed Monday attacked the administration and said,
'perhaps they owe an apology to us, rather than vice versa.'"

We are also beginning to try to deal with our failure
to communicate with the Black Student Alliance. We have
been invited to a BSA meeting Monday night, and a new organization, a Third World Liberation Front, is being formed

to attempt to bring some radical politics to minority groups at Georgetown.

After the trials next week, we have decided to immediately refocus on ROTC and anti-imperialism, organizing Abolish ROTC committees all over campus, and perhaps take another action to show that we plan to continue the struggle.

In conclusion, then, the Georgetown action must be seen as a necessary part of the expression of our revolutionary politics. People must be shown that we not only understand America but we are prepared to change it. That is why action, open resistance that can win, must be part and parcel of our politics. If we have laid a base for understanding of our views then we need not fear alienating people by such actions. Our views and our sense of struggle are the only solution to the oppression of America. We need to communicate that to our brothers; the reality of everyday life under capitalism will bring people around to the struggle with us. Capitalism can't stop its oppression abroad and at home; it can't give our brothers the meaning that their lives need and can't find in America's educational institutions of alienation. The progressive students at Georgetown, and there are many of them, should never be alienated from the struggle against capitalism. If we can remember that they are our brothers, we have only to dare to struggle, and dare to win--and they will join us.

(Distributed by SDS on Georgetown University campus, April 14, 1969. Collected by the compiler, August 17, 1971.)

22. VIEW FROM THE OUTSIDE

April 14, 1969

THEY HAVE A CHOICE BE-
TWEEN WHETHER THEY WILL
BE A FRIEND OF LYNDON
BAINES JOHNSON OR A FRIEND
OF FIDEL CASTRO.   A FRIEND
OF ROBERT KENNEDY OR A
FRIEND OF HO CHI MINH. AND
THESE ARE DIRECT OPPOSITES.
A FRIEND OF MINE OR A
FRIEND OF JOHNSON'S.   AFTER
THEY MAKE THIS CHOICE
THEN THE WHITE REVOLU-
TIONARIES HAVE A DUTY AND
A RESPONSIBILITY TO ACT.
   --Huey P. Newton

contribution: ten cents

BOB DYLAN ON WHITE SKIN PRIVILEGE

Bullet from the back of a bush
took Medgar Evers' blood,
a finger fired a trigger to his name,
a handle hid out in the dark,
he hand-held the spark,
two eyes took the aim,
behind a man's brain,
but he can't be blamed,
He's only a pawn in their game.

The south politician
preaches to the poor white man
you got more than the blacks, don't complain.
You're better than them,
you've been born with white skin, they explain.
And the negro's name,
is used, it is plain
for the politician's gain

320

As he rises to fame,
but the poor white remains,
on the caboose of the train,
but he can't be blamed,
He's only a pawn in their game.

The deputy sheriff, the soldiers, the governors
get paid,
and the marshals and cops get the same.
But the poor white man's used
in the hands of them all, like a tool.
He's taught in his schools,
from the start by the rule,
to protect his white skin,
to keep up his hate,
so he never thinks straight,
about the shape that he's in,
but he can't be blamed,
He's only a pawn in their game.

From the poverty shacks he looks from the cracks
to the tracks,
and the hoofbeats pound in his brain,
And he's taught how to walk in a pack,
to shoot in the back,
with his fist in a clinch,
to hang and to lynch,
to hide 'neath a hood,
to kill with no pain,
like a dog on a chain,
he ain't got no name,
but he can't be blamed,
He's only a pawn in their game.

Today Medgar Evers was buried from the bullet
he caught,
they lowered him down as a king,
but when the shadowy sun,
sets on the one
that fired the gun,
he'll see by his grave,
on the stone that remains,
carved next to his name,
his epitaph plain,
Only a pawn in their game.

RACISM AT GEORGETOWN

Georgetown is an institutionally racist university in four ways: its treatment of its largely black, non-academic work force; the composition of its faculty and student body; the content of its courses and curriculum; and its relationship with the D.C. black community.

WORKERS

When attempts were made last year to unionize the non-academic workers, the University blocked and broke an agreement with Local 63 of the Firemen and Oilers Union. Their actions included intimidation of workers and anti-union campaigning. On January 30 of last year, Father Collins, vice-president of the physical plant, informed workers that a "company union" had been established to "look after the interests of the workers." This "union" was organized by supervisory personnel along with Fr. Collins and has done nothing to help the workers or improve their conditions and is for all practical purposes non-existent.

There are strong reasons why Georgetown opposes better conditions for its employees. Workers are paid barely enough to keep them above the poverty level with wages in the housekeeping department starting at $1.52 an hour. Compared with this, the federal government estimates that for a family of four a "moderate" standard of living in D.C. requires over $9500 and the median income of the families of GU students is $25,000 a year. Yet GU workers, many with large families, start at $3160 a year.

Hospitalization and insurance for employees are also poor policies. These policies would pay about $200 for pregnancy expenses while a decent amount of care would require $800.

Seniority does not guarantee job security, promotion, or decent wages. Employees working five, ten, fifteen years often receive less than $2.00 an hour to support their families. There are sharply defined wage ceilings in each department and transfer between departments is almost impossible.

The University has developed two efficient strategies for keeping the workers down. First, the employees are divided into a social hierarchy with different uniforms and "privileges." The housekeeping department is considered to be at the bottom of the artificial caste system. While the department is all black it has a white supervisor heading it. "Lucky" housekeeping workers, in the GU Hospital, may get promotions to the transporter department where they get 5¢ an hour raise. "High-ranking" ward clerks and medical records personnel get a little over $2.00 an hour. In the central sterile supply sector, one of the biggest departments, a white supervisor runs an almost completely black group. These examples are typical: the University attempts to replace decent wages with "social status" and to divide the workers. This leads to infighting rather than to a strong sense of unity.

Another University tactic is giving some workers new uniforms and telling them that they are now "supervisors." They are given pads of paper and told to report other workers for the slightest infractions. Hiring and firing is totally arbitrary. Workers who are absent from work must bring a written note from a doctor and may be fired even if their excuse is valid.

There are other disadvantages for workers at Georgetown. They cannot live near the University because of lack of money and lack of integrated housing. They must travel long distances, making 2 or 3 bus transfers, and often leaving their homes at 6 a.m. Since there are no child care facilities for them (and many of Georgetown's employees are working mothers) they must leave their children at home or with relatives or even bring them to work.

It is important to remember that most of these workers are black (or Spanish-speaking) and that they are forced to live in D.C.'s slums. While their labor constructed the University and maintains it, they will never be able to send their children there. They are faceless to Georgetown's affluent student body and they are the people directly suffering from American racism. Racism is not an isolated phenomenon far off in Mississippi; it is right here at home in D.C. and in Georgetown.

FACULTY AND STUDENT BODY

Nearly 160 years of Georgetown history passed before the first black American was admitted and only about five

years since the first black scholarship student. This long
history of direct racism is something that is still present
through "tradition," attitude, and atmosphere. It is also
present through hiring practices--there are no black American faculty members; and admissions practices--there are
less than 30 black students in the University out of 4100 students.

Since the Spring of 1967, the Administration has turned
down at least 5 scholarship plans for black students. Last
year, a petition was signed by more than 700 students pro-
posing a $45 tuition raise per student to provide for 490
small money grants, 12 full scholarships for black DC residents a year for four years, and pay raises for 450 non-
academic workers. While the Nursing School and East Campus Student Councils voted to endorse the plan (and the Yard
voted against it) nothing was ever done to implement the
proposal--the Administration refused to consider it.

Two major excuses have been utilized by the University and its apologists. First, they claim that they do not
have sufficient funds even though the past few years have
seen large tuition raises with little or no increase in services or educational quality. The point should be made that
if there are not sufficient funds, then sufficient funds should
be found or workable plans should be proposed which would
raise those funds. The fact is that the Administration has
had opportunities and alternative plans offered in the past and
could even admit students without any substantial cost (com-
muting students who could be fitted into existing class sched-
ules)--if they wanted to, but apparently they don't and people
should realize that financial excuses are just a facade. The
second excuse is that black students really don't want to
come to Georgetown. This is understandable as a product
of (rather than a cause for) our school's well-known racism.

"Georgetown's Negro students when not carrying
books... (or) wearing Georgetown jackets are most often
taken to be part and parcel of the Physical Plant. (Hoya,
1/11/68)." Ironically, the same issue of the Hoya also
contained a racist article ridiculing "Pebbles" and they were
outdone by last year's yearbook which had more racial slurs.
Obviously, individual black students are not made to feel
over-welcome.

COURSE AND CURRICULUM

Georgetown has an obvious lack of black or other ethnic studies courses or departments, but it is the more subtle racism that is more dangerous. Georgetown does not address itself to the needs of the black community of Washington; its courses do not teach the history of black or working class people but instead teach concepts opposed and detrimental to those people's needs. It isolates, physically and intellectually, the white students from the realities of American life. It is an instrument for preserving prejudices and misunderstandings.

The courses and curriculum at Georgetown University serve the interests of the American corporations engaged in oppressing and exploiting black and white working people, specifically in the perpetuation of the myth of "middle class America." The uncritical accepting of this lie blinds students to the life they will face after graduation.

COMMUNITY RELATIONS

The Georgetown University Hospital is not known for its good relationship with the Washington community. There are few black nurses and only 2 black doctors (as of last year) associated with the Hospital. The white medical personnel, many of whom are Georgetown graduates, exhibit many racist and paternalistic sentiments. Doctors call black people by their first names while addressing white patients as "Mr" and "Miss." One doctor refuses to even come in physical contact with black patients: he is a Georgetown graduate.

With only 2 black doctors associated with the GU Hospital (and considering that most black D.C. residents have black doctors), it is virtually impossible for black people to get into the Hospital, unless they can pay the fees ... and very, very few can.

The GU Hospital had a tacit working agreement with George Washington and Children's Hospitals to keep medical students and interns from Howard University out of Children's --which gives the best pediatric training in the city. Georgetown students, on the other hand, got their training at Children's and Georgetown Hospitals. The agreement was broken last year only with pressure from Howard plus the threat from radical GUCAP members to make it public and pull out their project.

There is the case last year of the Poor Peoples' Campaign requesting unused space from Georgetown and other area universities, for the Poor Peoples' Free University. After a long series of refusals, meetings, and finally a sit-in, the Administration refused all of the GUCAP and PPC requests.

There is the position on the Board of Regents of D.C.'s leading racist, O. Roy Chalk, who owns slum properties, is implicated in Latin American exploitation, and owns D.C. Transit with which he milks local residents.

Georgetown's concern with the black community is manifested in the statistics: in a city where 71% of the people are black, less than 1% of Georgetown's students are black.

The Administration's fear of reprisals on the University during last April's rebellion demonstrates their knowledge of their position in the community.

ADMINISTRATION REACTION

The Administration's reaction to Georgetown's racism is typical of institutions which try to preserve themselves from radical transformation. Their major action (?) has not been in identifying the sources of racism, but has been in the field of public relations. They have publicized the presidency of Father Healy, built up GUCAP to six times its real-life size, publicized small-scale scholarship drives by faculty and GUCAP, and sponsored Abernathy and the Kerner Report symposium.

There have been a few scholarships--very few. There has also been a strong attempt to attack, bait and destroy SDS, instead of the racism of Georgetown. There was also a "Policy on Unlawful Student Protest" formulated in direct response to the Poor Peoples' Campaign.

The reality of Georgetown's racism is indisputable. There is the lily-whiteness of the undergraduate, graduate and medical schools; the lily-whiteness of the indifference of black people's role in history and other areas; the isolation of students from the reality of the ghetto.

How much longer will it go on?   As long as people
are not willing to put their bodies where their mouths are!

Remember Brother Malcolm

born May 19, 1925.   Assassinated Feb. 21, 1965.

(Distributed by SDS at Georgetown University, April 14, 1969.
Collected by the compiler May 29, 1972.)

23. INTERNATIONAL POLICE TRAIN
     AT GEORGETOWN

A STUDY OF "PUBLIC SAFETY"
AS PUBLIC REPRESSION

The International Police Academy is located in the
D. C. Transit Building, directly across the street from the
Walsh Building. In its day-to-day operations, the IPA pro-
vides an example of the reality of American foreign policy
as contrasted with the view taught in the Foreign Service
School.

The IPA is the key activity of the "Public Safety" division of the Agency for International Development (AID)
which is the main agency charged with the spending of American foreign aid money! The "Public Safety" Division is assisted by police groups and representatives of the Department
of Defense, State, Justice, and Treasury. According to
David Bell, former AID director, "the Public Safety and Military Assistance Programs have mutually supporting objectives of counter-insurgency."

Furthermore, according to General Bernardo Leyva
(head of the National Police of Colombia), "Solidarity of
police forces around the world, and especially in the Americas, is necessary if they are to promote that social peace,
that personal security and tranquility, that internal peace of
nations which constitute the goal and the task of police."
To fulfill this role, the Public Safety Division has three basic activities: (1) the training of police forces through the
IPA, (2) the supply of American "advisors" to train police
forces at home, (3) the supply of police equipment to various
countries. The IPA, founded in 1962, replaced the Inter-
American Police Academy which moved from Panama to
Georgetown. The Division is budgeted at about 16 million
dollars a year.

From this budget, $220,000 a year is appropriated
to pay rent to O. Roy Chalk for the use of the building.
The facilities include a rifle range, two auditoriums, a gym,
a photo lab, a 5,000 book library, class rooms and a weapons vault. Every three months the IPA graduates about 130

policemen from two courses which run from 13 to 17 weeks.
Students come from 46 countries (60% from Latin America)
and so far about 2,500 have gone through the training program.   The International Association of Police Chiefs, a predominantly U.S. organization, has a contract from AID to
help administer the program which also has close ties to the
U.S. Army and the FBI.

Much of the Academy's instruction takes place in the
Police Operations Control Center:

> ... a green and gray room with four rows of
> banked seats, overlooked by a glass-enclosed con-
> trol booth and projection room.   At the front of
> the POCC is a magnetic game board on which has
> been constructed the map of a mythical city, Rio
> Bravos, capital of the republic of San Martin.   Stu-
> dents elect officers who sit at a long V-shaped desk
> in front of the board.   Each has a phone and ac-
> cess to a teletype machine.   From the control
> booth, faculty field commanders alert the students
> to a communist-inspired riot at the city's univer-
> sity, or to a bombing attempt by communist sub-
> versives from the hostile neighboring country,
> Maoland.   The students deploy their forces on the
> board and plan strategies, much as they would from
> a real police control center. --(New Republic, Feb-
> ruary 11, 1967)

One favorite game features a specially-made movie
"The First Line of Defense" which shows how the police
forces of San Martin, a "democratic" Latin American country where the people support the police and government,
fight against "communist subversives" and striking factory
workers with flying wedges, tear gas, and fire hoses.   At
the end of the film the police are talking to a group of smiling children: "A new day dawns over the city of Rio Bravos
... the day is calm, the people of the town are peaceful.
Yet somewhere, in this town and a thousand other towns,
somebody is planning to destroy the security of the people.
But such plans are not likely to succeed as long as the civil
police, the first line of defense of the rights of citizens, enjoy the confidence of the people and have confidence in their
own ability to enforce the law."

Georgetown is connected to the IPA indirectly through
O. Roy Chalk and the use of the D.C. Transit Building for

University office space. The school is directly connected
through an AID contract for language training which was worth
$411,000 last year. The contract provides that the school,
through the American Language Institute (part of the School
of Languages and Linguistics), agrees to train IPA students
and any other students whom AID chooses. Students at the
IPA use Georgetown language laboratories and other facilities.
This training facilitates liaison operations with English-speak-
ing Green Berets and AID advisors when they return to their
native countries.

Superficially, the IPA's activities might be defended
in the rhetoric of the "Free World" and "democracy" as used
above. However, any realistic analysis of the actions of the
Academy would decimate such arguments. To put it bluntly,
the IPA trains Latin American police forces how to more efficiently repress their people and to better protect their native dictators (and thus the profits of U.S. corporations).
Advisors and equipment from AID are used to put down popular revolts and strikes and to maintain the fascist status
quo in under-developed nations.

Behind the rhetoric, behind the niceties, behind the
liberal facade (Bobby Kennedy was a key supporter of the
IPA and gave a graduation speech there), behind the AID and
the Alliance for Progress slogans are the sharp realities.
The United States is training minor league gestapos and
Georgetown is helping. Now, extensions of the IPA philosophy
can be seen on the home front. Ironically, the D.C. Police
used IPA facilities in putting down last April's riots.

According to David Bell, "The popularity of the heads
of state in all the countries that we are working with I am
sure varies. It is obviously not our purpose or intent to assist a head of state who is repressive." Why is this "obviously" not our purpose? The question based on the repressive reality must be: can a nation which resorts to such
tactics and is dependent on such actions be democratic? Do
the starving Latin American peasants feel that their rights
are the same as those of the wealthy? Do they feel protected
and secure because of the police of their police states? The
rationale of the IPA is a farce, a murderous farce.

It is ironic that John Hannah, former president of
Michigan State University, is now head of AID for the Nixon
Administration. Michigan State started out by training police
for the Diem dictatorship and rendering other aid. Appar-

ently, the aim of our foreign policy and that of our university system has not changed.   Under-development of poor nations has become an aim, not an enemy, control and repression march with it.   The word often applied to such activities is "imperialism."

CASE STUDY OF EFFICIENT REPRESSION

The theory is laid down here in Georgetown--right across the street from GU's School of Foreign Service--in the "Public Safety" Building where the Government trains international foreign police under the supervision of the "Agency for International Development."   But the foreign police don't learn the theory for theory's sake--that is not how one becomes "internationally developed."   They go home with all our US education in their beneficent minds and apply the nightsticks and gun that much better.   They go home to the Dominican Republic, for example, where we really need them--now that the US marines have come back home.

According to the IPA Review of October, 1967, the police of the Dominican Republic "had become infamous during the years of dictatorship, as they were used as a tool of repression and their obvious lack of professionalism did little to enhance their image in the public eye."   (pg 2). The answer to this problem according to the same Review was that "surgery was necessary in order to begin to open the many fine intellects in the National Police to new ideas and creative thinking."   So they took the old cops with "fine intellects" and gave them "surgery" in the form of three seminars run by "four National Police Officers" (supposedly fine intellects who didn't need surgery) and four AID "public safety advisors."   The way they changed the "repressive" cops into nonrepressive ones was through courses in "police financing," "the history of the Dominican national budget," and the "Building and maintaining of the National Police image as a public servant."   In other words, the effort was made to adopt tactics more subtle and efficient rather than to materially change the "repressive" nature of the police.

Mr. Covey T. Oliver, Asst. Secretary of State, talking to the same sort of "fine intellects" in 1967 told them what the US feels the foreign police they train should do. "At his best a policeman isolates problems before they can develop and nips them in the bud."   In the same address,

332 Vandals in the Bomb Factory

referring to the population explosion he continues, "These
new citizens--predominantly young people--will clamor for
education, jobs, homes, land, food and other basic human
needs. If social justice cannot be provided crises will occur.
It is our job ... to help avoid serious potential upheavals. "
The meaning is clear, obviously the police can't provide
"basic human needs" and that the "crisis" does repeatedly occur around the world points to the fact that the indigenous
governments can't supply them either. So the whole process
must revert back to an increasing emphasis on IPA "students"
because the interests of the US must be maintained whether
"education, jobs, homes, land, food, etc." are provided or
not. In fact they can't be provided because, significantly
enough, most capital gains are drained from the Dominican
Republic and the rest of the third world to the US because
the US controls the key segments of the economies of these
countries. So, by Mr. Oliver's own definition, the crisis
must come and it must be nipped in the bud. This is what
AID means in the final analysis: nipping the physical demands for "basic human needs" in the bud.

For this the US taxpayer lays out millions of dollars
per year. Millions to teach a cop better methods to destroy
the physical yearnings for goals which are heard time and
time again in the rhetoric of US politicians, but which are in
violent contradiction to the profit-oriented policies of US business interests in the lands of the foreign police themselves.
Thus, under the sloganism of anti-communism the US people
are duped into supplying money, facilities, and personnel to
perpetrate a more efficient repression contrary to their own
interests. Georgetown University is directly complicit in
this process. We in the GU SDS do not wish GU to sever
ties with IPA to preserve an ivory tower purity, but to exert
a pressure that will eventually destroy IPA and similar agencies as well as the profit-oriented men and institutions whose
interests IPA "students" serve and maintain. It is time the
students of Georgetown recognized the situation the IPA represents and acted on the knowledge of what this means to the
peoples of the world--poverty, starvation, repression and
death.

(Distributed by SDS at Georgetown University on February 10,
1969. Collected January 17, 1971.)

24. NOTES FROM MAGGIE'S FARM

OHIO REGIONAL SDS   MARCH 1969

Notes from Maggie's Farm is a regional newsletter of Ohio sds. It is published monthly--or thereabouts--in Cleveland, Ohio. All unsigned articles are the responsibility of the regional staff, and the editors: Enid Zuckerman, Sharon Cliffel, and Jim Powrie.

Regional staff: Corky Benedict, Lisa Meisel, Terry Robbins, Bobbi Smith, and Charlie Tabasko.

Regional Offices: 1643 Belmar, Cleveland 44118 (216-421-3015); and $1706\frac{1}{2}$ Summit Street, Columbus (614-294-3975).

This is the first issue of NOTES FROM MAGGIE'S FARM. We hope to publish monthly--if we get bread to put it out, and articles from you to print.

* * *

Since the Regional, the staff has been going through a lot of changes. We've been trying collectively to consolidate our politics and sharpen our theoretical understanding of American capitalism. The New Left has been agnostic and "anti-theoretical" for many years, and the importance of theory--as well as the experience of other revolutionaries--has only become clear in the last six months or so:

The power of the ruling class is irrevocably in conflict with the needs and potential of the people, and, as revolutionaries, we are going to have to develop a coherent politics, program and strategy to deal with seizing that power and building socialism. The production of the Organizer's Manual around the militarism demands, we hope, was an initial attempt collectively to lay out the kind of politics that will make our movement relevant to America.

Organizing around the military proposal has been varied--some schools are planning extensive campaigns around ROTC, police training institutes and war research. Other

333

schools are still looking for ways to get off the ground.
Dealing with racism and working with black groups continues
to be a serious problem, though the OSU people may have
something going around the trials of 34 blacks indicted for
seizing the ad. building last spring.   Their trial is April 6.

*   *   *

The regional conference is coming up: April 18, 19
and 20 at Oberlin.   It should deal with some real key stuff:
Repression (Bernadine Dohrn from the N.O. and Kathy Boudin
from New York will speak); summer program; and an evalua-
tion of chapter organizing this year--with particular emphasis
on high schools and community colleges.   Plan to be there.

And be sure to start sending articles to us soon.
We'd like to come out again in April.

Fight for socialism!

-- the staff.

VIETNAM WILL WIN

A national liberation movement is built upon the unify-
ing of all elements in the colonized nation against the imperialist power.   The battle is waged in both political and
military forms and is aimed at making it impossible for the
imperialist power to hold on in the colony.   That strategy is
aimed at the final destruction of world imperialism--Lin
Piao's statement on the rising of the "rural" areas of the
world--the third world--against the "urban" areas--the U.S.
and Europe--is the definitive statement of this strategy.   The
Lin Piao thesis should be discussed throughout the movement
because any revolutionary strategy in the U.S. will have to
weigh the relative importance of third world movements in
destroying imperialism.   But it is important to remember
that in any specific national liberation struggle, the goal of
the colonized people is to wrest control of their country from
the oppressor nation.

The unity of all elements in the country is essential
to this effort.   In the Program of the NLF released in September 1967 this principle is clearly stated: "The South
Vietnam National Front for Liberation constantly stands for
uniting all social strata and classes, all nationalities, all

political parties, all organizations, all religious communities,
all patriotic personalities, all individuals and all patriotic
and progressive forces, irrespective of political tendencies,
in order to struggle together against the U.S. imperialists
and their lackeys, wrest back our sacred national rights, and
build up the country."

By 1965, the NLF claimed control of 80% of the territory of South Vietnam and 2/3 of the population: after Tet,
the Front added to its areas much of the contested areas
around the large cities and along major highways.

These liberated zones exist not as sanctuaries against
U.S. troop movements or particularly B-52 bombings, but as
areas in which the organizational force that commands the
people's loyalty is the NLF.   Guerrilla warfare, as we all
know, requires the support of the population, and the Front's
military effectiveness is built of practical necessity on political effectiveness.

The major change in the war, then, over the last
three years, cannot be described just in military terms.
The central element is rather the Front's increasingly effective unification of various class and social elements which
has made the Front more and more effective as a military
and political force.

NLF & THE PEACE TALKS

At the same time, the U.S. has lost any trace of political support in the South and has been forced to resort
more and more to a strictly military operation.   The pacification programs, aimed at providing the Saigon puppet regime with political control in the countryside on the basis of
massive U.S. military might, has been destroyed and the
Saigon regime's support in the cities is continually undermined by Front political activity.   In the last six months,
the U.S. has abandoned all major ground offensives as too
costly and now relies solely on bombers that can drop more
explosive power on South Vietnam in a day than the Hiroshima
bomb dropped on that city.

The inability of U.S. imperialism to produce with its
military might any trace of political support among the people has forced the U.S. to go to the negotiating table.   It is
clear that their goal at the table is to internationalize the

conflict as at the Geneva accords, so that "great Powers"
(read Soviet Union) can force the Front to accept some kind
of redivision of Vietnam and a military withdrawal by the
NLF. The seeming ridiculous question of the shape of the
conference table points to the U.S. strategy of denying the
Front any kind of independent political status in the South
after the war.

But if this is the U.S. aim, then why is the Front
willing to talk? First, it should be clear to all that the NLF
is at least as aware of imperialism's designs as the sagest
revolutionary in the States. The talks must be seen as an
extension of the Front's struggle on both political and military
fronts in South Vietnam: they are the means by which the
Front plans to consummate the victory it has achieved in the
South.

Let us look at the conditions which have shaped the
Front's strategy in Vietnam. The world communist movement is severely divided and because of that, the Vietnamese
have not had the assistance of "two, three, many Vietnams."
If a coordinated attack had put pressure on the U.S. military
resources in Europe (Berlin), Latin America, and Africa,
then at some point U.S. military strategists would have been
forced to withdraw from Vietnam.

But given the state of the Communist world movement,
the NLF could not completely force an end to U.S. military
operations even if they succeeded in destroying every base
in South Vietnam: the U.S. could still fly in bombers from
Thailand, Guam, Okinawa and the Seventh fleet.

The Vietnamese should not be told that for ideological
reasons they cannot consolidate their triumph in the South
until people's war destroys all of imperialism's outposts in
Asia and the Pacific. From the NLF point of view, the talks
are the machinery by which the U.S. can extricate itself from
a losing proposition and the NLF establish a political structure in the South that follows their program. That program
calls for a "government of national union" in which all the
elements now involved in the struggle to drive out the U.S.
would participate.

All the cards at the negotiating table are not in U.S.
hands. The capital outflow for the war is affecting monetary
stability and is allowing the crisis in the urban centers to
become more and more aggravated. Clearly the imperialists

would stick it through if they could see the pay-off--a stable colony ready to be raped--in the future. But the Front has denied them that possibility and is continuing to force the political disintegration of the Saigon regime while the talks struggle to get underway.

Furthermore, the U.S. has to submit to the humiliation of the talks going on while assaults on the cities continue in the South. Withdrawing from the talks would severely affect public opinion around the world--many capitalist nations look to a U.S. withdrawal anxiously because of pressure from mounting left forces and their fears about economic stability.

The question arises: Even if the U.S. withdraws, can we be sure that the revolutionary anti-imperialist elements in the Front would be able to direct the course of the new regime?

The answer lies in the dynamic of the national liberation struggle. An alliance shaped in struggle against an imperialist power has to meet criteria that will allow the alliance to continue to build as the battle intensifies. Thus, landlords cannot enter the Front just because they see the Front is stronger in the area than Saigon; they must submit to a reduction in their rents and use their rewards to support materially the armed forces of the NLF. In other words, class elements enter the Front not around their particular class interests but as a part of mounting anti-imperialist struggle.

Once the U.S. has been forced to withdraw, then the full fury of class struggle that underlies the building of a national alliance can be unleashed. Within a government of national union, the power of the peasantry and the workers will have to be faced by all other class elements; either they will submit to the will of the people who have fought this bitter anti-imperialist struggle for years, or, to use the language of the Front describing the fate of the Saigon puppets, they will be "severely punished."

There is, for example, no contradiction between the Front's program calling for an "independent, democratic, peaceful, neutral and prosperous South Vietnam" and the call for active support of "the national liberation movement of the peoples of Asia, Africa and Latin America against imperialism and old and new colonialism" as well as the American anti-war forces and "black people in the United States." If your own struggle has defined the scope and character of the

enemy in terms of imperialism, then it is clear that keeping
your freedom means helping others involved in struggle
against the same enemy.

This does not guarantee the victory of the Vietnamese
revolution; if logic alone prevailed, capitalism would have
been crushed long ago.   But the ability of the Vietnamese
Communists to bring together a front capable of waging a
battle on the level we see in Vietnam attests to their understanding of the way in which social elements move.   The
Front has come to the talks because it sees the possibility
of completing their victory through the talks; but maintaining
the military and political offensive in the South, they must
at some point force the U. S. to withdraw.

Our duty is to force imperialism's hand as soon as
possible by showing that their costs are rising here as well
everyday the war continues.   It is only then, when our rulers
are convinced that they are losing more than they can ever
regain, that they will beat a retreat from Vietnam.

(This article was excerpted from the N. Y. Regional Newsletter, #2, January 10, 1969.   Steve Halliwell works with
the NYU chapter of sds.)

THE NLF IS GONNA WIN!

SUMMER PROGRAM

By Mark Real

As campus organizing broadens and intensifies at
Kent, it is important that further strategy develop for a
youth (in contrast to an exclusively student) movement in the
Akron-Kent area.   The first section of the December NC
resolution "Toward a Revolutionary Youth Movement" articu-
lates some of the basic analysis of such a position.

This paper will hopefully serve to stimulate suggestions as to ways in which Summer 1969 could be a time to
begin such a movement.

Akron, a culturally depleted industrial city blighted
by the paternal control of four huge rubber companies has

economic and political importance apparent by any strategic
criteria. As many SDS members as possible should be encouraged to participate in programs which would reach out to
young people in the area and at the same time provide intensive training for organizers. Supplemented by a proposed
series of "organizers schools" to be conducted on a regional
basis, we would hopefully develop a deepened class consciousness and begin to see our political commitments on a life
basis.

The following suggests broad areas in which people
can work: both the theoretical and practical basis needs improvement, and people should be thinking particularly about
more clearly defining 1. how organizers can be trained and
cadres built; 2. how we can best pursue the broadening of
the movement and building of class consciousness this summer. In any event, these sketches:

1. WORK-IN

People who have to take jobs (or those who don't need
to but want the experience and who could share their earn-
ings) should be encouraged to go in teams to the rubber plants
and large industries, others to small shops, hospitals and
department stores where union organizing is going on. Educational sessions for the participants are critical. Living in
North Hill, a working class area, should be considered.

2. COFFEE HOUSE

A cultural-political way of providing summer visibility.
Hopefully a way to attract young people, especially high
school students in the North Hill area of Akron.

3. HIGH SCHOOL ORGANIZING

Train organizers and form cadres at each school
from Ohio Union of High School Students contacts. Establish
communications between schools and staff for fall follow-up.

4. AREA-WIDE NEWSPAPER

This could be an important organizing tool, supple-

mented by wall posters, etc. These people could also staff
a movement office communications center.

5. KENT STATE CAMPUS

Dormitory and Classroom organizing would continue.
Last summer, literature tables and film programs attracted
new people. Plans for an intensive counter orientation program in the Fall, student handbook, etc. could be developed.

6. AKRON UNIVERSITY

As little organizing is going on here, organizers must
be trained and a cadre formed. Trustees research and intensive orientation work should begin.

7. RADICAL RESEARCH CENTER

To perform relevant research and train organizers in
the skills and use of research. Local ties to imperialism
(rubber companies and banks) and racism (Board of Education, Urban Renewal) should be uncovered, and attacked as
a city-wide mobilization target.

8. RADICAL ARTS PROJECT

Combination guerilla theater--rock band group could
extend agit-prop organizing to locations where young people
gather. With proper leadership it could be a way to involve
and immerse new people in radicalizing, liberating kinds of
experience.

(Thoughts about the summer are being kicked around
quite extensively since this article was written, and a major
part of the Regional Conference at Oberlin April 18-20 will
deal with summer program--Ed.)

ACTION AT OBERLIN

There's Something

Happening Here .....

Thursday, February 20th there was noise on the Oberlin campus. It was loud, disruptive noise--and just possibly it was also the noise of the birth of the revolutionary movement at Oberlin.

For many years Oberlin has been "isolated. " Set in a small town that is totally dependent on (and, therefore, exploited by) the college, Oberlin has been a perfect tool for the ruling class: building on and reinforcing the elitism of the well-intentioned, well-to-do, training the professionals who rationalize orders and smilingly, "liberally" engage in genocide. The class nature of the college and the very subtle oppression of students explains where the student body is at:

They are passive.

They are bored.

They are "liberal. "

About a month ago an sds group formed--mostly in response to an upcoming demonstration against Marine recruiters. For the past several years, the local Resistance has been staging (often militant) non-violent demonstrations against military recruiters. Their perspective has been very appealing to the alienated sons and daughters of the ruling class: liberal guilt, non-violence, non-obstructionism, and rational discourse.

Sds, on the other hand, seemed to be formed out of a political (and personal) need to get away from moralistic mind fucking--the cult of Oberlin. The sds people set up three programs prior to the recruiter action--dealing with imperialism (the NLF and Cuba) and racism (the movie, "Black Panther"). Grafitti began appearing on various buildings stating "Work, Study, Get Ahead, Kill, " and "The NLF Will Win. " Some unknown radical threw a brick through the window of the recruiting office, and "Vietnam Will Win" posters were placed on trees around the campus.

The tactics planned by the Resistance for the Thursday demonstration sounded like something out of civil rights lunch counter days. A "non-coercive" sit-in was planned that would force both recruiters and students to walk over the protesters in order to have an interview--"to bear moral witness" against military recruiting.

Sds realized that no sit in would jolt the Oberlin

liberal.   He is too used to them; they are too much a part
of Oberlin's heroic past.   Optimally, sds' position was to
block the recruiter altogether.   But, given the strength of
the Resistance, and sds' newness, significantly influencing the
sit-in tactics seemed impossible.   So, sds needed a tactic
that would provide mobility, help build revolutionary consciousness and build for larger actions in the future.

On Thursday, an NLF flag flew in the campus square.
Fifty-nine people were participating in the Resistance sit-in,
starting at 8:30 am.   About 100 people were also in the building, either in a "support" sit-in or looking on.   Sds people
arrived at about 9:30, and, while the sit-in was going on,
showed two films: "Hanoi-13," a Cuban film about Vietnam,
and a Newsreel film about street fighting in San Francisco
called "Haight. "

At 10:00 am the Dean of the College told the people
sitting in that they were being coercive.   They all submitted
their names to the administration ("we're not ashamed of
what we're doing") and continued to sit-in.   A little past
11:00 the recruiter left, and was followed off the campus by
the Resistance protestors.   Sds called a rally for 1:30.

The major point of the rally was to indicate that we
had to go beyond, both tactically and politically, the timid
attack on the recruiter.   We had to deal with the administration (the lackeys) and the trustees (the bosses).

Between 200 and 300 people came to the rally.
Jeremy Pikser of Oberlin sds and Howie Emmer of Kent
rapped about imperialism, and the university's role in per-
petuating imperialism, racism and class oppression.   Someone from the audience got up and talked very personally
about how Oberlin was destroying her, and people were ready.
When an sds guy said we should go into the administration
building, people went.

A minor confrontation with President Carr occurred
inside the building.   Carr was real up tight (he thought that
"Work, Study, Get Ahead, Kill" was an sds plan to kill him),
and people booed him or laughed at him.   People left the
building soon after and held another rally outside, vowing
that this was only the beginning of the university's troubles.

Perhaps it was.   It is not clear yet just how important the action was, or, in fact, if sds can be successful

at Oberlin at all.   Maybe bourgeois ideology and class privilege run too deep.   But now, as never before, there are
kids at Oberlin with a political ideology and a commitment to
move on it who are ready to find out.

HIGH SCHOOL USA

By Juan Gonzalez - Columbia SDS

Benjamin Franklin High School, on 116 Street in East
Harlem, has a population of approximately 3,000 students,
92% Black and Puerto Ricans.   As of this year, according
to the Board of Education statistics, 100 are enrolled in the
vocational program, 670 in the academic (college preparatory)
program, and 2,286 in the general program.   The graduating
class of June 1967 comprises 20 graduates of academic cur-
riculums, 50 graduates of the vocational curriculum, and 130
graduates of the general curriculum.   Of the 763 students
who entered in September 1964, 29.8% of the original class
received diplomas, of which 1.8% were academic.   Drop-
outs, transfers, or unaccounted for students number 60.2%
of the class.

The situation of Ben Franklin is duplicated more or
less throughout the majority of New York City public high
schools.   Black, Puerto Rican, and white working class kids
are systematically prepared for semi-skilled jobs and for
America's military in high schools occupied daily by from 4
to 15 New York City police.   In Washington, D.C., for instance, recent studies report that 80% of all public school
graduates are in the army within two years.

Black students have been in the forefront of these
rebellions, just like Black University students.   They are
the worst victims of the high schools.   Over 50% of all
Black and Puerto Rican students in New York City drop out.
Only 20% of those who graduate from academic high schools
go to college.   Meanwhile, in Vocational High Schools, where
60% of the students are Black and Puerto Rican, and where
the possibility of jobs awaiting graduates in the vocation they
are trained for is slight, no one goes to college.   Black
high school graduates have a higher unemployment rate than
white drop-outs, and those Black graduates who find work
average lower pay per week than white drop-outs, according
to the Bureau of Labor Statistics.

For the average Black and Puerto Rican high school student, then, the schools are prisons, part of the same elementary school system that determined his functional illiteracy in the first or second grade, part of the same system that assures the dilapidated housing, the unavailability of decent jobs, and the police and court system ready and eager to strike at him if he begins to protest. What has not been as apparent as the Racism of the schools however is the class nature of the educational system. The high schools prepare white working-class kids for similar semi-skilled jobs, prepare them for impressment into the working class army, paid twelve cents an hour to kill and be killed in other countries to protect the empires of Standard Oil, General Motors, Englehard Industries.

According to a 1961 study by Patricia Sexton, 5000 of the nation's 26,500 high schools produce 82% of all college bound students. The overwhelming percentage of Black and Brown students in non-college tracks in high schools are matched by large numbers of white working class kids in the same tracks. In one mid-west city, Sexton found 25% of the students whose family income was below 7,000 dollars were in the college preparatory courses, whereas 79% of those with incomes over $9,000 were being groomed for college. Radicals were not aware of the deep felt resentment of the white working class kids against the schools until Dec. 1968, when they joined with Blacks and Puerto Ricans in the high school student strike--thousands of students walking out, leaving the middle class radicals and liberals in the building worrying about their grades and catch-up studies.

SDS has begun to realize that it can develop into a revolutionary socialist movement only if it fights with and in the interests of Black and white working class people. At present, the best and most organic way to develop that orientation is to ally with the inherently revolutionary fights emerging among young working people.

The movement now makes perhaps the most revolutionary demand yet: open admission to colleges of all Black, Puerto Rican and white working class students who wish to attend, with autonomous Black and Latin studies departments.

This demand strikes at the very foundation of an elite university like Columbia. It calls for a reappropriation of the wealth and resources of this university and a redirection of its function so that it serves the needs of the working

class and not the needs of the corporate class for war research and production of managerial personnel for corporations.   This demand will mean the ending of special privileges
enjoyed by many people who both work and study at the present Columbia University.

       Socialists must destroy these privileges and fight that
oppression.   In the long run, the general well-being of society will be raised at the expense of the immediate class
privileges of a few.

(Collected November 24, 1972 in the Special Collections of
the Cleveland State University library, Cleveland, Ohio. This
flyer was distributed by SDS during March, 1969 on the university and college campuses of Ohio.)

25. THE WAR IS ON AT KENT STATE

THE WAR AT KENT STATE

Terry Robbins & Lisa Meisel
Ohio regional staff

> Historically, all reactionary forces on the verge
> of extinction invariably conduct a last desperate
> struggle against the revolutionary forces, and some
> revolutionary forces are apt to be deluded for a
> time by this phenomenon of outward strength but
> inner weakness, failing to grasp the essential fact
> that the enemy is nearing extinction while they
> themselves are approaching victory.
>
> --Chairman Mao Tse-Tung

The war is on at Kent State University. Two weeks
of intense struggle have seen SDS lead several major actions,
rallies, marches, and raise the political consciousness of
thousands on the campus, while the pig-thug Administration
has responded with swift and heavy repression. To date,
seven people have been charged with inciting to riot (felony),
four with malicious destruction of property (felony), and over
fifty more arrested on various other charges and suspended
from school. Bail for those arrested has already exceeded
$120,000.

Specifically, this was in response to the positing of
four demands by SDS to the administration:

1. Abolish ROTC

> Today, reliance upon colleges and universities for
> officers is greater than ever. For example, the
> 1968 graduating classes contained over 11,000 new-
> ly commissioned officers, who, as they enter the
> ranks of the active army, will fill 85% of the re-
> quired annual input needed to provide the junior
> leaders for today's troop units. The armed forces
> simply cannot function without an officer corps
> composed largely of college graduates.

346

--U.S. Army Instructor's Group
ROTC, Harvard University

We are opposed to ROTC for 3 reasons:

1) It provides the leadership for an army engaged in protecting imperialism by suppressing popular movements at
home and abroad.

2) ROTC is a "privilege"--available primarily only to those
who can go to college. It strengthens the view that ordinary people in America are unworthy to guide the nation's destiny. "... Who is prepared to trust their sons
--let alone the nation's destiny--to the leadership of high
school boys and college drop-outs?..."--U.S. Army In-
structors' Group.

3) Actually, that privilege is really a delusion, and ROTC
people are themselves oppressed. ROTC can only be
seen as an alternative to an even worse reality--the
draft; and also, second lieutenants (75% of whom are
from ROTC) are being killed at an incredibly high rate
in Vietnam. Just as many college kids are being chan-
nelled into managerial slots in civilian life (teachers, social workers, etc.)--and turning off to those slots with
great rapidity--so ROTC is the army's middle man, serving the generals and the privates.

It is argued that ROTC should be maintained because
it is a "basic civil liberty" of the students to join any organization they choose. This is a serious distortion of the issue
because of what ROTC does. Because of its role in oppressing the peoples of the Third World, the only "right" that
ROTC and the Army have is the right to conquest. And that
is no right at all.

2. End Project Themis Grant to
the Liquid Crystals Institute

There are only two institutes in the U.S. developed
solely to study liquid crystals--Kent State has one of them.
This year the Liquid Crystals Institute received a research
grant from Project Themis to develop "liquid crystal detectors." ("Army Research and Development Magazine"--July/
August 1968 issue). In the last year Project Themis has
funded 43 new counter-insurgency research programs in 24

states. "The Project's objective is twofold--to create new
centers of scientific excellence responsive to Department of
Defense solutions to problems in the future; and to achieve a
wider geographical distribution of defense research funds,
giving preference to institutions that receive little or no
D.O.D. support of science."

Kent State is part of Project Themis' spidery web of
institutions which are currently developing sophisticated weaponry to be used against people's struggles for their freedom.
Liquid crystals are extremely sensitive to heat, and are used
in devices to detect campfires in jungle areas and in some
cases to detect body heat at long range. (The "sniffer" is
currently used in Vietnam and a similar device was used in
Bolivia to find and kill Ché Guevara). The tremendous strategic importance of "liquid crystal detectors" can be seen by
the fact that every country in Latin America, Southeast Asia
and many in Africa, guerilla warfare is being waged by people's movements struggling against U.S. imperialism. A
parallel struggle has begun and will continue on Kent's cam-
pus--the development of Liquid Crystals for Project Themis
must be stopped.

3.   Abolish the Law Enforcement School

4.   Abolish the Northeast Ohio Crime Lab

The members of the ruling class are the only real
criminals in this society. Corporate financiers reap tremendous profits at the expense of the poverty-stricken unemployed, the tax-ridden worker and the mortgaged middle class.
Law enforcement defends the American status quo and therefore protects the interests of the ruling class. Black people,
the most oppressed, witness overt police violence daily.

Blacks are colonized. They are oppressed not only
as part of the working class but as a people. Huey Newton,
jailed Minister of Defense for the Black Panther Party, describes the role of police as an occupying military force in
the black colony: "The pig can't be in the colony to protect
our property, because we own no property." Pig violence
in the black colony does not result only from the sadism of
individual policemen. Just as in Vietnam military violence
in the black colony is intended to protect the business interests of monopoly capitalism.

The Law Enforcement School and the Northeast Ohio
Crime Lab serve two different functions in protecting ruling
class imperialism and racism against the black colony.   The
Law Enforcement School trains students for police careers.
It was the Law Enforcement School which invited the racist
Oakland pigs to recruit at Kent this past fall.   The North-
east Ohio Crime Lab serves all of the police forces in north-
east Ohio with identification and lab processing techniques.
So doing they play an important role in evidence gathering
procedures.

The struggle began on April 8, when SDS held a rally
and marched through classrooms to the Administration building in a support of the four demands.   The demands were
presented to "stop this University's ability to serve imperialism and racism, to challenge fundamentally some of the ways
Kent State serves the ruling class."

The rally brought out about 400 people, and about 200
went on the march.   A fight ensued at the Administration
building between SDS and some pigs who were blocking the
way.   Kids' reaction to the fight was generally favorable.
The Administration's reaction was not.

Waiting for dark, the University did four things: (1)
they suspended SDS' charter as a recognized campus organization; (2) they suspended six people: Ric Erickson, George
Gibeaut, Colin Nieberger, Jeff Powell, Rebel Flanagan and
Curt Resnick; (3) they pressed charges against five of the
six--Ric, Howie, George, Colin and Jeff--on assault and
battery; and (4) they sought and received a court injunction
keeping the same five people off the campus until May 1.

The six people suspended were singled out by the Administration as "SDS leaders."   Before two weeks were out
they would all be in and out of jail four times, each time
on an escalated charge.   The organizational ban against SDS
meant that we could not use University facilities for any
reason.

Violating the organizational ban as much as possible,
we held several rallies and dorm raps in the next few days.
We stressed the political nature of the Administration's actions, reaffirmed our four demands and our determination
to fight, and added a fifth demand: open and collective hearings for all those suspended.

Like it had done with the other four demands, the

University ignored our demand for open and collective hearings, and set Wednesday, April 16, as the trial date for Colin Nieberger. We resolved to open it up.

A rally scheduled just before the hearing drew about 2,000 people. Most were friendly, but a sizeable right-wing fraternity contingent was also there, heckling. Jim Mellen of REP--an 'outside agitator' down for the week--addressed the crowd, and responded to the hecklers by saying:

"I know that there are some pigs out there who still think we should occupy Vietnam. And there are some pigs out there who still think we should go into the ghettos and push people around. Well, what we're telling you is that you can't do it anymore: We're no longer asking you to come and help us make a revolution. We're telling you that the revolution has begun, and the only choice you have to make is which side you're on. And we're also telling you that if you get in the way of that revolution, it's going to run right over you!"

About ten minutes later, it did.

After the rally, we marched--about 700 strong--to the Music and Speech Building, where Colin's trial was to take place. We found all the doors chained shut, pigs at every door, and a contingent of angry, right-wing jocks blocking our entrance through the main door. We fought: for about half an hour, SDS fought the jocks to a near stand off, and had them pleading that if only we'd go away, they'd go away, too. Instead, we went to another entrance, where the chains were already broken, and surged in.

We found the doors to the third floor chained shut and protected from the inside by several pigs. Chanting "open it up or shut it down," about 150 SDS people broke through the doors and the pigs, and rushed to the hearing room.

The hearings, of course, were cancelled the minute we got there. We had been fighting almost continually for an hour. We decided to split.

But the University had something else in mind. As we were leaving the building, we were stopped by State Highway Patrolmen, city pigs, university pigs and plainclothesmen. We were detained for 4-1/2 hours while the University figured out what to do with us.

Crowds began gathering outside. We spoke to them
through bullhorns, talking up the demands, why we had busted
up the hearing, and how the lackeys of the ruling class had
us locked up in the building. Before it was all over, over
90 of our people escaped; but 58 were arrested, charged with
trespassing, and arraigned at $1,000 bail each.

Among those arrested were the six students who had
been suspended out of our first action. They were on cam-
pus--under University escort--to testify at Colin's trial.
Nonetheless, they, too, were charged with "trespassing," and
five were charged with contempt of court in violation of the
injunction prohibiting them from being on campus.

Two days later, on April 18, they were all charged
with inciting to riot.

Since the action and the busts, several things have
happened:

--a liberal, civil liberties coalition has grown up to
alternately defend SDS' "rights" and viciously red-bait us;

--The Ohio Regional Conference--150 people from 12
chapters across the state--scheduled to meet last weekend
at Oberlin, met instead at Kent. Kids from chapters all over
the state spent the weekend rapping in dorms, and held a
rally on the campus Sunday night;

--On Monday, April 21, one person was arrested and
three others sought for malicious destruction of property
(felony: $5000 bail). Ric, Howie, George, Jeff and Colin
were found guilty of contempt of court, sentenced to 10 days
in jail and fined $200 each (it is on appeal). And bail for
the six charged with incitement to riot was set at $4000 each.

The situation at this point in the struggle is very
mixed. On the one hand, the repression has clearly hurt
us: over sixty of our people have been banned from the campus, at least 11 face heavy charges, with total bail exceeding
$120,000, and the Administration has succeeded to some ex-
tent in scaring a lot of people and obfuscating our original
demands, allowing the civil liberties whiz-kids to spring up.

On the other hand, SDS has made several key advances:
We have fought, and fought hard, making it clear that we are
serious and tough. We have constantly stressed the primacy

of four demands, maintaining that political repression is only
an extension of the people's oppression, never getting hung
up in civil libertarian or pro-student privilege defenses of
our actions. We have demonstrated tactical flexibility, using
confrontations, rallies, dorm raps, wallposters, etc.--all
geared to increasing the possibility or reality of struggle in
a given tactical situation. And we have clearly raised the
political consciousness of almost the entire campus, winning
over many new people, and making it possible to win over
many more in the future.

And, of course, the struggle is not over. New leadership for the chapter is emerging with great rapidity. We're
working on more elaborate explanations of the demands, getting back into the dorms, hitting back at the organizational
suspension and raising money for the legal defenses.

But, most important of all, through struggle, we have
made it absolutely clear that the war being waged in Vietnam,
in Guatemala, in the black colony in America, will be fought
as well at Kent State University.

(One final note: We haven't even started paying court
costs or lawyers fees, yet. Contributions are urgently
needed, and can be sent to: Kent SDS Legal Defense Fund,
c/o Candy Erickson, 217 North Depeyster, Kent, Ohio 44240)

(Distributed by SDS at Kent State University, Kent, Ohio on
April 28, 1969. Collected by the compiler June 21, 1969.)

26. THE PEOPLE'S FIGHT IS OUR FIGHT

People are fighting for their freedom. The Vietnamese, under constant fire from B52's, grow increasingly resolute in their struggle to win their right of self-determination with each new horror committed against them by U.S. imperialism. The Black Panther Party, in the face of killings and frame-ups committed against them by the courts and the cops, carry on the leading battle for black liberation in the colony at home.

But as Vietnamese and black people continue to struggle, the level of ruling class genocide becomes more and more severe and the threat of total annihilation a real possibility.

The just demands of the peoples of the world for self-determination and human freedom must be chosen above the global profit-making machine of the American ruling class. People must make one choice or the other in their own lives. The two are irreconcilable.

The just demands of the people of the world for self-determination and human freedom must be fought for and met. The gigantic profit-making machine of the American ruling class must be put to a grinding halt because the two are irreconcilable.

All American universities serve the needs of the ruling class. At Kent the final and highest ruling bodies are the Trustees and the Regents. They are the only ones with real power and they are members of the ruling class (see Who Rules Kent? by Kent SDS). There are three basic ways in which American universities serve the imperialist and racist needs of the ruling class: The production of manpower and research for racist and imperialist war-making and the perpetuation of ideological justifications (telling lies) in order to get away with racist and imperialist exploitation (anti-communism, for example).

At Kent, several weapons are produced for racist and imperialist war:

353

ROTCs on campuses across the nation supply the army with 85% of its 2nd lieutenants, 65% of its 1st lieutenants and half of its officers on active duty. ROTC supplies the leadership for the imperialist American army which puts down just rebellions of poor people in the Third World who are liberating themselves from imperialist exploitation, i. e. Vietnam, Guatemala, Dominican Republic, Cuba, etc.

Liquid Crystals Institute is a Defense Department funded part of Project Themis, the Army's massive counterinsurgency program. Liquid crystals are used in a heat sensing device which is used to detect jungle hideouts of guerrilla bands. It was this device which the US used to find and kill Ché Guevara in the jungle of Bolivia.

The Law Enforcement School has the same function as ROTC. Just as ROTC enforces the martial law of imperialism in the Third world so does the Law Enforcement School produce cops who enforce military law in the black colony at home. Cops are used as a white occupation army to protect the property of the super-markets, slum landlords, etc. who exploit black people. Racism and imperialism go hand in hand (who cares what happens to the "gooks, " "spic" and "niggers"-dig it?).

Northeastern Ohio Crime Lab has the same function domestically as the Liquid Crystals Institute has abroad. It develops sophisticated weaponry and techniques of counterinsurgency to be used against the people--particularly blacks.

The ruling class uses Kent State University to kill and contain the people who are exploited by the ruling class imperialists and racists! The people's struggle has been brought home to Kent.

ABOLISH: ROTC, LIQUID CRYSTALS, LAW ENFORCEMENT SCHOOL, NE OHIO CRIME LAB! JOIN US kent sds   JOIN US kent sds

(Distributed by SDS April 8, 1969 on the Kent State University campus. Collected by the compiler in the Kent State library Special Collections March 22, 1973.)

27. COLUMBUS BLACKS REBEL,
     REPRESSION HITS SDS

REBELLION HAS HIT THE COLUMBUS,
OHIO PIG POWER STRUCTURE

During 3 days of war against the avaricious white business men and the pigs that protect the pig power structure,
white owned stores were fire bombed, pigs were sniped at,
and pigs thrown out of the black community. Over 1,000 National Guardsmen had to be called in to put down the people.
Total damage to capitalist property in 3 nights was estimated
at half a million dollars. Over 400 black people are now in
jail on arson, looting, burglary, grand larceny and curfew
violations. And, to top it off, instead of charging the ruling
class that runs this country for its crimes against the Black
Colony, the Man has leveled the stone racist charge that
SDS is responsible for the riot. Black people don't need us
to show them who the enemy is--and they don't need us to
tell them when to fight! 4 SDS people have been arrested
and 5 more are being sought on charges of "inciting to riot."
Bail has been set for $25,000 per person and the arraign-
ment has not been set until 6 weeks from now.

COLUMBUS IS A PIG TOWN

Tensions within the black community have been steadi-
ly mounting for some time. Two years ago, pigs cordoned
off the entire east side on the basis of a rumor that Black
Militants were about to enter the city to stir up trouble.
Last spring, 34 black students at Ohio State University were
arrested following the occupation of the University's Administration Building and charged with conspiracy, kidnapping, etc.
Charges totalling 300 years in all. Two black doctors were
severely beaten by local pigs, and then convicted of resisting
arrest and assaulting the pigs. Several high schools were
closed down this year due to black rebellions in the high
schools. Most notable was West High where 80 black brothers and sisters were arrested after the school's pig principal
refused to allow ceremonies honoring Malcolm X. Forty
whites were involved in the demonstration but were not arrested.

355

During this period of constant simmering unrest, the
Black Panther Party was formed in Columbus. This let the
racist businessmen and their pigs know that the black community was preparing to fight back. In April the pigs attempted to scare off the Panthers with a cowardly nighttime
gunfire attack on the Panther office. Needless to say, it
failed, and the Panthers have continued to operate and prepare for attacks to come.

A CITY WIDE REVOLUTIONARY YOUTH MOVEMENT

Organizing among the white working class and working
class youth began only recently. Some work has been done
around a community house the last couple of years, and, this
year, an SDS chapter functioned at Ohio State.

This summer, a group of 25 people from the Ohio
SDS regional program moved into 3 working class neighborhoods throughout the city. People have gotten together mostly with high school and gang kids, on the beaches, in the
streets, the bars and pool halls. Some are working in factories. Our aim--to develop cadre; 16 year old communist
"guerillas, " to build a city wide revolutionary youth movement to smash the pig power structure. In the last week
several SDS people were arrested for busting up some classes
at a local high school, and the project was beginning to get
into mass agitational and organizing work around the national
action. Then came the rebellion. On July 21, a white,
fucking, sissy businessman in the black community murdered
a black man.

VAMPING THE PIGS

Starting around 7 PM roving bands of black youth--
between 40 and 70 strong--started smashing white-owned
store fronts and stopping traffic. Nightfall came, and the
number of black people increased--groups constantly multiply-
ing and dividing until several well disciplined fighting units
existed. By 10 PM the young people had successfully run
the pigs out of the community. Sniper fire broke loose and
a good friend of the mayor was offed, trying to play piglet
during the rebellion. The situation for pigs and piglets raged
out of control, and the mayor was forced to call in the national guard. Firemen refused to enter the black community
unless "escorted" by ten pig cars. The cars were not

available--and the pigs not willing--so the fires continued to
burn. More than half a dozen fires were out of control by
11 o'clock.

At the same time, the National Guard replaced the
pigs, black Vietnam veterans replaced the roving bands of
black youth. The vets made the guard look as inexperienced
as they actually were; snipers would move from building to
building, and as soon as the Guard thought they had a sniper
spotted, he would appear on the other side of town firebomb-
ing a supermarket. These tactics continued throughout the
night, and by early morning, an estimated $300,000 damage
to white-owned property had been done. Ninety percent of
all firebombings and lootings had taken place against racist,
avaricious businessmen. White-owned stores and businesses
were well-known and marked out before the night that most
of them were hit.

Tuesday, during the day, the black community was
cool, but everyone knew that things would jump off again that
night. RIGHT ON! About 11 o'clock, black youths filled
Franklin Park, chanting, singing, lighting fires, and establishing a "liberated zone." Pigs moved in from all direc-
tions, but people managed to escape the park. However,
the pigs were also everywhere in the streets, hotels, and
bars. Almost everywhere that people ran turned into a pig
trap. About 100 young kids were arrested for curfew violations, bail set at $1000 each. Later that night, the charges
were changed on at least 30 people to arson, grand larceny,
looting and rioting. Fires were set throughout the night, but
the struggle began to die down.

Wednesday night, black people decided that since the
pigs were in their community, they would go to other sections of the city. Firebombs were reported almost everywhere except in the black community. Heavy damage was
done.

PIGS HIT SDS

Also on Wednesday night, the shit started hitting SDS.
Earlier in the day people were out leafletting about the rebellion in working class neighborhoods. They were leafletting
on foot since holes had been drilled in the radiators of their
cars the morning before. That night pigs raided one of the
houses on a warrant for "illegal possession of firearms."

Three SDS people were arrested at that time as suspicious persons.   Once in jail that charge was changed to "inciting to riot. "   One other person was picked up and five more are being sought on the same charges.   All nine had been leaf-letting Wednesday afternoon.   Seven others have been arrested as "suspicious persons. "   (That's right.   Columbus may be the last place left--or the first place yet--to have a law against being "suspicious. ")

In addition to the arrests, the pig mayor, the pig Chief of Pigs, and the Pig Adjutant General of the Guard all made statements accusing SDS of being responsible for the riot; "outside agitators, peddling communist propaganda. " People have been flooded with anti-SDS shit from the pig press.   The radios carry the names of the 5 SDS people still being looked for every hour.   And the mayor has stated that, since we are "known revolutionaries, " he will personally try to press charges against all of us for sedition and treason.

Our response has been to say "Roll the repression on. "   One of the most important things we have learned about the black liberation struggle--and its rebellions--is that the only way to fight repression is to smash the system that creates it.   And, in this particular situation, the pigs have shown their blatant racism by alleging that a bunch of white kids--and not the fascist power structure of Columbus--are responsible for the anger, frustration and rebellion of the black community.   The white gang kids we've been rapping with have generally dug this; they're hip to the fact that black people don't need whites to show them how to fight.   And they were also somewhat impressed and scared by the heavy repression against us, and our insistence on staying around to continue the struggle.   One guy said, "It's kind of scary, but for sure, you're serious. "

WE'RE GONNA KEEP ON FIGHTING

We're trying to get the bail lowered for the folks who are in jail, and we're going to open up a storefront soon. The pig press has given us a lot of publicity.   And the black community--with its militancy and commitment to struggle-- has given us still another kick in the ass.   Back to work.

LONG LIVE THE VICTORY OF PEOPLES' WAR

(Distributed by SDS September 16 and 17, 1969 at Ohio State University.   Collected October 2, 1969.)

28. SUBSCRIBE TO NEW LEFT NOTES

find what sds is about
learn our plans for the future
read the ongoing debates inside the organization
read about your brothers and sisters in other parts of the
    country

$5. 00 for members ($1 for sub, $4 for dues)
$10. 00 for non-members

write to new left notes - sds
    1608 W. Madison St.
    Chicago, Ill.   60612

JOIN US

sds   students for a democratic society

1608 West Madison, Chicago 60612 (312-666-3874)

___ I would like to join sds and receive
    New Left Notes (dues $5/yr)
___ Send me a complete list of sds pub-
    lications
___ Send me further info on sds

(name) _____

(address) _____

(city, state, and zip) _____

(Collected February 10, 1969 at the University of California
at San Diego)

29. THREE AMERICAN UNIVERSITY PROFESSORS HAD THE AUDACITY TO REACT POSITIVELY TO THE STUDENTS' VOICES

1.) Two professors have had their contracts terminated and one has been demoted through arbitrary action on the part of Dean Pietrow and <u>selected</u> tenured faculty members.

Do you believe that students should have control over the structuring of the educational community including the hiring and firing of Professors?

2.) Don't you think students' control should extend beyond this singular instance?

What has happened to the three professors is just an example of arbitrary authority.

Not only was that authority arbitrary--but upon what basis was that authority exercised? Was the decision influenced by:

a.) A racist reaction to Gary Weaver's bringing Eldridge Cleaver, the Minister of Information of the Black Panther Party, to American University?

b.) Tom Reeves' support of Weaver's action?

c.) The fact that all three faculty members have political viewpoints which are further to the left than those of the Dean and tenured faculty members who control granting of tenure and termination of contracts?

Students for a Democratic Society

(Distributed by SDS at American University during March, 1969. Collected by the compiler June 22, 1969.)

30. A MEANINGFUL ALTERNATIVE

The American University Chapter of the Students for a Democratic Society offers the following as its alternative to those of the candidates for Student Association offices, especially those for the presidency. We believe that this platform offers a real challenge to the do-nothing, care-nothing attitude of the American University Student Association and the Administration, as well as to the superficial criticisms of the candidates for student office. We believe that the Administration and the leadership of the student organizations have overlooked the rights, the desires, and the needs of the students of the American University. Therefore, we offer these proposals.

I. Resident students should determine curfew hours and open house policy.

II. Students should be allowed more flexibility and more room for negotiation in their housing contracts; such obvious invasions of privacy as compulsory room searches should be abandoned. Students should have the real ability to move off campus. Furthermore, facilities on campus for married students should be provided at reasonable rates.

III. The residence associations should be reorganized so as to allow meaningful participation by students in their operation. Specifically we demand direct election of all officers of the MRA and the WRA.

IV. The ICC and other student organizations should be restructured to involve truly democratic procedures in order to prevent usurpation of power by individuals and cliques, especially since these organizations have strong power over tens of thousands of dollars of student funds.

V. Infirmary facilities should be provided 24 hours a day. Doctor service throughout the day should be provided now. Infirmary services should be available in both male and female dormitories. Adequate transportation to Sibley hospital should be provided for non-ambulance cases. Birth control information should be provided for both married and unmarried students.

VI.   The ARA Slater monopoly on catering campus events, indeed, their monopoly on all food used on campus must be ended now.   Competition must be allowed.   Fraternities should be allowed to provide whatever eating facilities they desire.

VII.   Drinking should be allowed at any and all campus functions, in the fraternity houses and in the dormitories, if the students so desire.

VIII.   A joint student-administration-faculty planning commission should be established to consider university expenditures. We demand full itemization of university expenditures.   We demand that these figures be made available to all students.

IX.   The scholarship program should be expanded, rationalized, and itemized.   There is no reason why students with full tuition scholarships should not have their scholarships increased with tuition increases.

X.   The American University Book and Gift store should be made a student-faculty owned and controlled cooperative. The atrocious price of books on this campus is an impediment to learning.

XI.   Real student representation in a student-faculty senate must be established now, if planning by both groups is to be effective.   We demand real not token representation.

THE AMERICAN UNIVERSITY CHAPTER
STUDENTS FOR A DEMOCRATIC SOCIETY

(Distributed by SDS at American University February 21-24, 1969.   Collected by the compiler March 22, 1969.)

31. ARBITRARY AUTHORITY !!!

Because of the dismissal and/or demotion of three popular professors, broader issues must be raised. These issues concern all students; and all students should discuss them now.

The issues of the three professors is a question of arbitrary authority. Not only arbitrary authority in hiring and firing, but also in;

1. The determination of racist policies at A. U. It is not only the probable connection between Weaver's demotion and his part in bringing Eldridge Cleaver to A. U. It involves the treatment of demands by the University administration. It involves the administration's decision to have A. U. train D. C. police to better suppress Black people in the ghetto (see its list of extension courses).

2. Maintaining the Center for Research in Social Systems (CRESS). This is the A. U. institution which researches better ways to control the people of Vietnam and the rest of the Third World. Its job is pacification and counter-insurgency in an attempt to stop movements for social change.

3. A budget which is not available to all members of the University. Why should not everybody have the opportunity to see the budget? Because it is used as an excuse for firing professors and raising tuition; because the CIA money which exists in that budget should be known to all.

One of our goals must be the reinstatement of the three professors who questioned some of the above policies. As well, we must discuss and act to change these policies.

S. D. S.

(Distributed by SDS during March, 1969 at American University, Washington, D. C. Collected by the compiler June 22, 1969.)

32. WOMEN, RISE UP!!!

<u>SEE</u>

See little girl
See girl cook
Cook girl cook
See girl grow
Cook girl cook
See girl type
Type girl type
See girl date
Marry girl marry
See girl work
Slave for man

We all know how women are supposed to be second-best to
men, and we all know what a drag it is. But it takes guts
to be different, and in this society women are taught to be
inferior human beings and non-resistent slaves. They even
teach women to dig it.

But a lot of women aren't digging it. They're fed-up with
being messed over, and they've got good ideas as to what
else is wrong. We know what's gotta be changed, and we're
gonna do it. That means we gotta fight back, and we gotta
start now. We need your ideas and your help in the struggle.

We're SDS women fighters and we're part of the Revolutionary Army that's gonna take this country away from the few,
and give it back to all the people including women. We need
women fighting to win this battle, and we can't let women
remain slaves under and to capitalism.

JOIN US-------ALL POWER TO THE PEOPLE!

ON MONDAY AUGUST 4 AT 7 PM, SDS WILL BE
SHOWING SOME RADICAL FILMS ABOUT THE WOM-
EN'S LIBERATION MOVEMENT, AND WE'LL BE
TALKING ABOUT WHAT WE CAN DO. SO COME TO:

St. Joseph's Episcopal Church

On Woodward between Holbrook & King
At 7 pm August 4, 1969

SDS

(Collected in the Special Collections/Archives Division, Regenstein Library, University of Chicago, January 17, 1974.)

33. BRING THE WAR HOME!

CHICAGO, OCT 8-11

SDS IS CALLING THE ACTION THIS FALL

We're going back to Chicago, tougher and more together than ever. The American Racist Pig Power Structure is under world attack, led by the Vietnamese and the blacks. Our fights on the campuses, in the high schools, and in the streets are part of that struggle. The war's on and everybody's got to take sides!

Four Days of Action

WED. --the day Ché was murdered by the CIA in Bolivia two years ago. We'll be marching through the black, brown, and white communities in solidarity with the international struggle and in tribute to Ché.

THURS. --liberate the high schools, bust our brothers and sisters out of jail, so they can join us in the streets.

FRI. --tear up the fascist courts. The Black Panthers and the Conspiracy 8, who led the struggle last summer in Chicago will be on trial, that is, unless we stop this shit.

SAT. --a huge march, a show of force. We can't be fucked with cause we're part of the world struggle!

JOIN US!!!!

ALL POWER TO THE PEOPLE!!!!

SDS

Dig it! Free!
REVOLUTIONARY FILMS
--come and rap
every Monday nite 7 pm
St. Joseph's Church at
Woodward & Gladstone

phones: 983-1415,   832-4191

JOIN US!!!!

(Collected in the Special Collections/Archives Division, Regenstein Library, University of Chicago, January 17, 1974.)

34. OCCUPATION TROOPS OUT!

CHICAGO OCT. 8-11

It has been almost a year since the Democratic Convention, when thousands of young people came together in Chicago and tore up pig city for five days. The action was a response to the crisis this system is facing as a result of the war. The demand by black people for liberation, and the ever-growing reality that this system just can't make it.

This fall, people are coming back to Chicago: more powerful, better organized, and more together than we were last August.

SDS is calling for a National Action in Chicago October 8-11. We are coming back to Chicago, and we are going to bring those we left behind last year.

The United States has occupational troops in over 60 foreign countries. From Puerto Rico to Thailand. From West Germany to India. From Guantanamo to South Korea. All over the world, the United States has guns, bombs, missiles, and men to defend our "national security" and protect our "freedom."

And at home, in the black and brown communities, the pig patrols the streets defending white-owned property against black people. Pigs occupy black and brown communities just like troops occupy Vietnam. Busting heads whenever they can. Arresting people on trumped-up charges just for trying to stay alive. And coming down hardest on the black and brown liberation struggles--on the people who are fighting the hardest for the freedom of their people, and all the oppressed people of the world.

And in the working class communities, the schools and the shops of the cities, the pig stands six feet tall to protect the boss against the worker, the principal against the student. Whenever there's trouble, the pig is there to defend the interests of the few against the needs of the many.

The only people the troops abroad and the pigs at home defend are the rich people--the ruling class--who own

and run this country. The giant corporation executives. The
people who pay for the Democratic and Republican parties
and make the laws of the land. The international businessmen who stay alive off the labor of poor and working people
all over the world, who profit off of military spending and
"space research," who profit off of Vietnam.

Behind all the pigs in the world are a few millionaires.
Behind the "riot squad" riding four deep through Watts, or the
"tactical unit" busting up a wildcat picket line, behind the
National Guard and the U.S. Army stand the rich people who
run every large company you can name.

It's got to be the truth. Because one thing that's
absolutely for sure is that those pigs aren't around to defend
YOU. They enforce the laws that mess you over. They
"keep you in your place." When you rebel, when you fight
for what you need, they try to crack your head.

The soldiers, the pigs, and the laws that they defend
make OUTLAWS of every black person, every poor person,
and every young person in this country and in the world.

Of course, it's not that the soldiers in Vietnam want
to be there killing the Vietnamese and getting themselves
killed. Those soldiers were drafted to do the job--the people who make all the money don't even have the guts to do
their own fighting. And it isn't that pigs in this country are
pigs because they're all bad people. Most have families and
kids, and just want to get along "like everybody else." The
difference is that THE JOB THEY HAVE MAKES THEM
PIGS. The job of keeping the people down. Of being sure
that everything in this country stays the same so that the
rich can go on getting richer and the poor can go on dying.

At different times, pigs act in different ways. Sometimes. Those soldiers were drafted to do the job. Poor and
working people--and particularly black and brown people--are
sent to Vietnam to demand their "freedom." "Freedom" that
is really the way for rich Americans to get richer off the
Vietnamese people. And it isn't that pigs in this country
are pigs because they're all bad people. Everybody knows
that they have families and kids, and just want to get along
"like everybody else." The difference is that THE JOB
THEY HAVE MAKES THEM PIGS. The job of keeping the
people down. Of being sure that everything in this country
stays the same so that the rich can go on getting richer and
the poor can go on dying.

Rich people need lots of different kinds of pigs. Sometimes their job is to train others to keep the people down. Like the U. S. Green Berets, who try to teach a Guatemalan traitor army how to fight against revolutionary guerrillas, the leaders of the Guatemalan people's movement.

"The world is round.
Only one third of
its people are asleep
at any one time.
The other two thirds
are awake and causing
mischief somewhere. "
--Dean Rusk

High school principals and guidance counselors and college administrators are also pigs, trying to bribe people and make them believe that one day they'll really get ahead. And, in the end, they'll use all the force they've got to stop things from changing.

There is a saying that political power grows out of the barrel of a gun. Think about it. The people who run this country know that it's true. The only reason they've been able to mess over Vietnam for so long is that they have guns, bombs, and troops. The only reason they've been able to rule over black people for 300 years is that they've got pigs to keep all black people down. And the only reason kids don't always tear up the schools they're in-- schools that teach kids lies and train them for the slaughter-house of fucking jobs that really benefit no one but the boss-- is that the pig is always just down the corridor or roaming around nearby.

But we can't let the pigs keep us down any longer. In almost all the countries of the world, in the black and brown communities, and in many schools and shops, people are getting together to fight and defeat the pigs and the people the pigs defend. In Vietnam 500, 000 U. S. troops are being defeated by a people's army, led by the National Liberation Front and the Provisional Revolutionary Government. The Vietnamese have shown us that the pig can be beaten.

All around the world the barricades are going up.
And you're either on one side or the other.

The people who want freedom are all on one side.

The pigs of the world are on the other.

On October 8-11, tens of thousands of people will
come to Chicago. During those days there will be a series
of actions aimed at exposing the real nature of the pig power
structure and taking a price for all of the suffering, misery,
and death that imperialism causes to the peoples of the
world. A memorial rally for Che Guevara, murdered by
CIA pigs two years ago October 8 in Bolivia. An action at
schools all over the city, carried out in co-ordination with
local high school, community college, and trade school people in Chicago. A women's action, with women from all
over the country breaking out of their old roles by fighting
together on the side of the people of the world. A march
on the courts demanding freedom for all political prisoners--
viciously jailed by the pigs and like the Chicago "Conspiracy
8," used as scapegoats for the pig violence that dominates
this country. A youth-rock festival. And a mass march demanding that U.S. troops get out of Vietnam, Latin America,
and all foreign countries, and that the pigs get out of black
and brown communities, out of the schools, and out of the
streets.

Join us.

BRING THE WAR HOME!

--U.S. Occupation Troops Out Of Vietnam, All Foreign Countries, The Black And Brown Communities, And The
   Schools!

--Free All Political Prisoners!

--Support The National Liberation Front And The Provisional
   Revolutionary Government of South Vietnam!

--Support the Black Liberation Struggle!

--Independence For Puerto Rico!

--End The Surtax!

--Solidarity With The "Conspiracy 8"!

--Support GIs' Rights And GIs' Rebellions!

SDS 1608 West Madison, Chicago 60612 (312-666-3874)

(Distributed by SDS at the University of Pittsburgh, Pittsburgh, Pennsylvania, September, 1969. Collected November 11, 1969.)

35. SDS HANDWRITING ON THE WALL

BRING THE WAR HOME

OCTOBER 8-11

This Wednesday through Saturday, October 8 through 11, we're bringing it all back to Chicago. Last year the Democratic Convention was important because we began to fight back against the pigs. But we've changed a whole lot since then.

Last year we were against the war. We knew that the elections were a shuck, that it didn't make any difference which fool was sitting on top of the shit. When you get down to it, Amerika is a totalitarianism built on fucking most of the people in the world. Amerikan businesses rip off the people's wealth, keeping most of the world in total poverty. When the people get pissed and rise up against the imperialists, like the Vietnamese have done, the military is sent in to crush the struggle. Rip off the thin, kick them while they're down...

But the people of the world don't dig it any longer. The war's not just in Vietnam. It's everywhere--in Latin America, Africa, Asia, and in the black colony within this country. The people know who their enemy is. They are demanding that the Amerikan imperialist pigs get out of their countries. Huey P. Newton, of the Black Panther Party, said, "The spirit of the people is greater than the man's technology." And the Vietnamese have shown us all that the biggest guns in the world couldn't do shit against a People's War of liberation.

White kids are moving against this racist decadent system too. We move because we're messed over--in school, on the job, in the courts, the army and on the streets. We're caught in a trap: fucked over because we're young, but at the same time a lot better off than Black people and oppressed people around the world. If we accept the honkey lives that Amerika forces on us--accept the privileges that come with being white--and don't move on the side of the people of the world, we are keeping their struggle

374

down. But we refuse to be the good nazi, to "follow orders." The orders are criminal, history is the judge, the world's people are the jury, and the generals have been sentenced to die!

When we move with the people of the world, to seize power from those who now rule, we can expect their pig lackeys to come down on us. We've got to be ready for that. This is a war we can't resist. We've got to actively fight. We're going to bring the war home to the mother country of imperialism. AMERIKA: THE FINAL FRONT.

STICK EM UP!

Stick this paper up all over town so everyone will see it. Put one poster up frontwards and another, next to it, backwards. Evaporated milk--lots of it--will stick it to smooth surfaces like windows, and on top of other posters. It's almost impossible to rip down a poster put up with evaporated milk. Or use wallpaper paste. Carry some mixed with water in a plastic bag and take along a sponge or rag to spread it with. Tape and staples are a lot quicker, but the paper can be ripped down with no trouble.

Take along a can of spray paint, too. Painting slogans is fast, easy, and an out of sight way of letting people feel our presence. Use your imagination for what to write.

We've got to paint the town red... But be as careful in this as you would be any other time. Never move alone, always have one person on lookout, etc. Remember: GOOD GUERRILLAS DON'T GET CAUGHT!

MOVEMENT CENTERS

People from Illinois, Indiana, Colorado, the Pacific Northwest, Washington DC, and the South should report to St. Luke's Lutheran Church, 1500 W. Belmont.

People from Wisconsin, Michigan, New York State, and New England should report to Garret Theological Seminary, 2121 Sheridan Road in Evanston.

People from New York City, Ohio, and Pennsylvania should report to University Disciple Church, 5655 S. University in Hyde Park.

People from any other areas of the country should call the central information number to be assigned to a movement center.

PHONE NUMBERS

When you arrive in town, get lost, need general information, the Central Communication numbers are 664-1185
                                                            664-1186

When you or someone you know gets busted, the legal communication number is: 641-7133

If you or someone around you is seriously hurt and cannot be adequately cared for by a medic on the street and cannot locate a safe medical center, immediately contact the medical communication number: 929-1424.

Everybody should remember these numbers.

BRINGIN IT ALL BACK HOME

Chicago is the heaviest city in Amerika.   To win this battle, we're going to have to do it in tight groups running and fighting together, and as thousands moving in the streets as one.   We have to go on the offensive--not just fight back. Offensive action means survival, and victory.

We live behind enemy lines, and we have got to move accordingly.   Never move alone.   Alone we get harassed, picked off.   There's no one to fight with us, or to know what's coming down.

Come to the action with kids you know and trust, the people you move with all the time.   Together you form an affinity group.   An affinity group can protect each of its members and at the same time move out aggressively because you know you're not alone.   To be revolutionary people have to dig on how fucked it is to be isolated, and how basic getting together is if we're going to win.   And winning is what we're about.

During the action people will be living in and working out of movement centers.   The centers are the base areas where we will assemble, discuss tactics, break into affinity

groups, eat and sleep. Many people have been through these
scenes before, and their experience is vital. They will provide tactical leadership in the streets, where a lot of us
might be less sure of ourselves. They have the responsibility of running the movement centers, getting our basic information on first aid, legal hassles, etc. They will help those
who haven't been into heavy actions before form themselves
into affinity groups and learn how to move.

People who come from a region where there is a city
wide SDS movement, will be assigned to centers under the
leadership of that collective. Other people should check the
list of movement centers in this poster to find out where
they should be. PEOPLE FROM THE CHICAGO AREA should
work out of the movement center at ST. LUKES LUTHERAN
CHURCH, 1500 W. BELMONT.

SISTER STOMP

ON THURSDAY, OCTOBER 9, THOUSANDS OF YOUNG
WOMEN WILL DESTROY THE ARMED FORCES INDUCTION
CENTER AT 165 W. VAN BUREN IN CHICAGO.

IN BRAZIL, an American ambassador was held hostage until
fifteen political prisoners were freed.

DURING ROCKEFELLER'S LAST "good will" visit to Latin
America, people in every country destroyed US owned busi-
nesses and fought savagely with the pigs who were protecting
Rocky.

IN OAKLAND, DETROIT, CORNELL, black people have
picked up the gun to fight for their national liberation.

IN VIETNAM, the Vietnamese people, led by the Viet-cong,
have liberated four-fifths of their territory and defeated US
armed forces and technology.

ALL THESE WARS ARE REALLY ONE BIG WAR.

People refuse to have their countries run by the US any
more, and that is what the war is all about. White Americans are living behind enemy lines. Either you fight or you
are part of the enemy. From Wednesday to Saturday, this
week, there will be a battle against the enemy in Chicago.
We are bringing the war home.

WHAT IS IT LIKE TO BE A GIRL BEHIND ENEMY LINES?

It's sitting behind a typewriter, standing behind a counter, waiting around with nothing to do until a guy drops by. It's growing up to take care of kids, clean the house, nurse the old man. It's taking orders, asking no questions, having no opinions--and trying to be nice, to be pleasant, to smile, be dull, and look "pretty. " A boring rotten life. And worse, much worse because we are kept from seeing that there is a war going on around us. And even if we know about the war, we are afraid to fight. We try to be neutral and nice to everyone. But because we are neutral, the fighting force is cut in half. The lines that are drawn between men and women in this society are similar to the lines that are drawn between blacks and whites. They are drawn for the same reasons--to divide the people--and by the same folks--the few, rich pigs who rule this country and most of the world.

THERE IS NO MIDDLE IN THE MIDDLE OF A WAR.

If you think you are in the middle, then you are on the wrong side. When you participate in and benefit from the Amerikan system, you are helping to keep it together.

More and more women are fighting on the right side now. They are realizing the strength within themselves and in women who are free and complete human beings, fighting out of love for all the people.

CALENDAR

WEDNESDAY--OCTOBER 8

DAY OF THE HEROIC GUERRILLA

On October 8, 1967, Ché Guevara was murdered by CIA pigs in Bolivia. A rally in Lincoln Park this night will commemorate Ché and Nguyen Van Troi, a Vietnamese hero who was executed on October 15, 1964 for trying to assassinate Secretary of Defense McNamara.

We rally our support for all the People's Guerrilla movements in the world.

THURSDAY--OCTOBER 9

The women's militia will strike the Armed Forces

Induction Center in the morning and show the strength of a
women's fighting force.   Meet at the Logan Statue (across
from the Hilton Hotel, Balbo and Michigan) in Grant Park,
at 9:30 a. m.

Jailbreak!   In the afternoon we move on some of Chicago's high schools to liberate kids from the racist pig lies
which are forced on them in the jails known as 'schools.'

Wargasm!   At night, we come together in celebration
of the struggle.   Details will be announced at the movement
centers.

FRIDAY--OCTOBER 10

We move on the courts to expose the racist, illegitimate nature of the pig judicial system.   Only through brute,
oppressive force will the pigs be able to hold their Freak
Show Conspiracy Trial, which is just one more attempt to
vamp on people who have fought back.

SATURDAY--OCTOBER 11

BRING THE WAR HOME!

A massive march in support of the Vietnamese, Black,
and Third World liberation struggles will follow a route from
Pig to Pig.   Assemble at the statue of a pig commemorating
the slaughter of striking workers at the Haymarket Massacre
in 1886 (Halsted and Randolph Streets) at 12:00 noon.   March
through the loop, power center of Pig City, to the Col. Logan
Statue in Grant Park, scene of the Battle of Michigan Avenue
during last year's Democratic Convention.

WANTED

ENEMY OF THE PEOPLE
JULIUS J. HOFFMAN

ALIASES: Hoofmouth, Fuckhead, Pigface, Jowl Jaws, Shiny-
head, Slopgut, Judge.

CRIMES: Killer, racist, exploiter, pig, oppressor, extor-
tionist, pervert, motherfucker, lackey.

UPON APPREHENSION, THIS ARCH-PIG WILL RECEIVE

THE REVOLUTIONARY JUSTICE OF THE PEOPLE.   FREE
ALL POLITICAL PRISONERS!

(Distributed by SDS at Loyola University, Chicago, October
6, 1969.   Collected the same day.)

36. DID YOU DIG THE WRITING ON THE WALL?

> Off the Pig
> Ho Lives
> Vive Ché
> Viet Cong
> Power to the People

Somebody put it there to tell you what's happening--
that people are getting together to bust up this system. We
all know what's wrong--lousy schools, worse universities
and jobs, and racism everywhere. Pigs in Vietnam, in the
Black community, in drive-ins, in schools--pigs everywhere.
What to do about it?

Lots of us think that the only way we can change
things is by revolution--that means power--not peace, but
war--a people's war to overthrow the rich capitalist hogs
who own and run the world for their own gain. And after
that to start a socialist state, where the riches belong to
everybody, not just a few.

Ché said that in revolution one wins or dies--that's
true--so you'd better have a real good idea on how to do it.
We do: we're going to win.

SDS fights alongside of winners. And the winners are
going to be the people of the Third World--the people of
Vietnam, of Guatemala, of Africa, and the Black colony of
the U.S.--they will win. China has won, Cuba has won, the
Vietnamese have driven the Americans into a few heavily
fortified cities. And the Black people here will be the vic-
tors. We support them totally in their struggle--not just because they are right but because if they win, this country
will crumble. If they lose--we all lose.

SDS is building a revolutionary youth movement to
start to open another front against U.S. imperialism--go to
Chicago on October 8-11. On these days hundreds of thousands of us from high schools, colleges, factories and the
streets from every city, town, and village in Amerika are
going to attack the centers of racism and imperialism in
Chicago--the schools, the courts, and the pigs. We are

going to make the rulers of Amerika pay a price for their profiteering off the people of the world.

JOIN US

SDS

(Collected in the Special Collections, University of Illinois, Champaign-Urbana on November 27, 1972. The demonstration referred to in the document occurred October 8-11, 1969.)

37. "SUMMER'S HERE AND THE TIME IS RIGHT
FOR FIGHTING IN STREETS, BOY"--Stones

This is the summer of the **PIG**. We must turn it into the
summer of the **PEOPLE**. The same goes from now on.

This **ROCK REVIVAL** is an example of our culture and our
times. So is the military takeover of Berkeley in which pigs
and the guard fired into a crowd of us who had built a "People's Park" on land the University "owned." 147 were
wounded, one brother killed, another blinded from ammo
ranging from rock salt to .30 cal. rifle slugs. The next
day a black student was shot dead in the back of the head
by pigs in Greensboro, South Carolina. In the past year,
over 20 Black Panthers have been killed or exiled. The
Man is everywhere--In our schools, on our streets, at our
meetings, in our parties--the Principals, our parents and
teachers, the neighbors, they all help him police our minds.
And we're gonna have to stop him.

We're gonna have a city-wide high school SDS next fall. If
you want to find out about it, contact us now. It will take
a while to learn what we're about and we're going to be doing things over the summer.

What we need to do:

The Grande--costs too damn much. Capitalism pimps us all.
We need a **FREE** "People's Night," and lower $

High School Defense--We need strength to beat the bullshit
political suspensions. We get that from knowing what's
coming down outside school in the real world so that we
know what we're up against. That's politics. SDS is no
club.

A High School Paper--done by high school students, that con-
nects us to the real world and helps us see what we're
up against.

IF YOU DON'T KNOW, LEARN   DETROIT HIGH SCHOOLS SDS
P.O. BOX 9571 N. END STA-
IF YOU KNOW, TEACH   TION DETROIT

383

SEND $1

People's Park Bail Fund:
Free Church, 2200 Parker
Berkeley, Calif.

It will free our people and get
the fascist bullets from their bodies

Every man, woman and child on the face of the
planet earth has the right to the highest and the
best and the most beautiful life that technology and
human knowledge and wisdom is able to produce.
Period!   So we start from there. --Eldridge Cleaver

(Collected in Detroit, Michigan during late August, 1969.
Collected August 28, 1969 by the Wayne State University Special Collections.   Collected by the compiler September 4,
1974.)

38. SECRET LEAFLET   SECRET LEAFLET   SECRET
     LEAFLET

WEATHER REPORTS:
> Just then a bolt of lightning struck the courthouse
> out of shape, And while everybody knelt to pray
> the drifter did escape.
>   --Bob Dylan

We have a weatherman strategy for the courts--the same
strategy we use in the streets.   The courts expect us to be
afraid and ask for delays, to be isolated from each other
and ask for drawn out, individual treatment.   We are together.   We are ready for our hearing today and we want to
defend ourselves in court, with the advice and help of our
lawyers.   Here is the basic information.   Hang on to this
page.   Don't use it while you're up in front of the judge and
don't leave it lying around for the pigs to get their hands on.
Read it and listen carefully to the proceedings in the court-
room.

**THIS IS A COLLECTIVE OFFENSIVE.   WE ARE ALL DE-
MANDING TRIALS.   WE ARE READY FOR TRIAL TODAY.**

The law says they have to try you within 120 days of your
demand for a trial.   But you can't in any way ask for or
agree to a delay (continuance).   They will ask for one, and
will try to trick you into agreeing, maybe by urging you to
wait till you get a lawyer.   But we want to defend ourselves
and we want a speedy trial and we want a trial by jury.
We are catching them off guard and forcing their hand now,
before they've prepared the pig tales.

DEMAND A TRIAL TODAY

If you are charged with a felony, you must say you
DEMAND a trial.   Say you are ready for trial and use
the word "demand."   If the cop is there, the court may
either postpone it or hold a preliminary hearing today.
There are no convictions or sentences to worry about at
this stage--there are still trials and appeals and more
appeals to go through before that.   There will not be
trials today, just preliminary hearings.

IN A PRELIMINARY HEARING, only the enemy has to show
his hand.   He must prove that there is enough evidence
against you to hold you for indictment and eventually this
leads to trial.   We have to play it tough but close to the
chest.   You are not testifying about what happened.   You
should not be under oath!   You can cross-examine the
prosecution witness (the arresting officer, probably), but
you should not cross-examine unless you are completely
cool and you can't stand to keep quiet.   The judge will do
some cross-examining of the witness himself.   If you do
cross-examine, DON'T ADMIT ANYTHING.   Some questions involve damaging admissions about things you did,
like "Did you grab me while I WAS RUNNING AWAY."
Never mention any other people in your questions.   You
want the cop to go on record about what happened.   Then
you have him tied down to a version of the facts and he
can't go back on it.   The judge will then decide whether
or not to send the case to the Grand Jury for indictment.
Some of us with lots of felony charges may have them
dropped or reduced to misdemeanors (maximum sentence
one year in Cook County Jail).

DEMAND A JURY

You are entitled to a jury of twelve red-blooded true
Americans free of any prejudice against us.   We will be
able to question jurors extensively about their feelings
about our politics, publicity, looks, anything, and can dis-
qualify them on these grounds.   But we won't have jury
trials today or even very soon.

Be polite to the judge, but firm.   Ask him to explain
anything that you don't understand, even if you have a
lawyer standing with you.   Be naive if that looks effective.   Or be aggressive.   Ask the judge specifically to
make sure that the written record shows that you demanded immediate trial by jury.

ASK FOR PERMISSION TO LEAVE THE STATE and go home,
to work or to school or to your family.   You have a
right to free travel.

IF YOU ARE STILL IN JAIL, ask that your bail be reduced.
The grounds for reduction of bail are that you are coming
back for your trial, that you are a respectable citizen
back home, that you just can't raise the bread and its unfair.   You can't prepare your own defense while you're

in jail.   High bail is a political weapon against you.   They
may try to raise your bail--you must argue against this
on the same grounds.

IF YOU ARE STILL IN JAIL, THERE IS ALL THE MORE
REASON TO GIVE YOU A SPEEDY TRIAL.

IF YOU ARE NOT OUT ON BAIL, ask for a free copy of the
record on the grounds that you are indigent--that is,
broke.

We are all doing this together.   We will not allow the
courts to scare and separate us.   Stick to our guns.

BRING THE
        ACTION HOME!

(Distributed in Chicago by SDS on October 14 and 15, 1969.
Collected October 14, 1969.)

39. PRESS RELEASE
CHICAGO AREA STUDENTS FOR A DEMOCRATIC SO-
CIETY
For more information contact 472-8745

SDS National Headquarters
1734 Massachusetts Avenue
Boston, Mass. 02115 (617) 267-6152

SDS CONDEMNS WEATHERMEN PROVOCATEURS

For the last two days a group of provocateurs claiming to be from SDS have attacked students and working people in Chicago. Wednesday night they broke windows of people's homes and cars and attacked cab drivers. Similar incidents have occurred in other parts of the country. In Detroit, nine women broke into an exam at Macomb Community
College declaring that it was over and the students should
listen to them. When two students got up to leave they were
attacked with karate. At Boston English High School they
fought students and teachers.

These actions are all the work of a group of police
agents and hate-the-people lunatics who walked out of SDS
at the June Convention because their ideas had been rejected.
Led nationally by Mark Rudd, this gang calling itself SDS-
Revolutionary Youth Movement-Weatherman has absolutely
nothing to do with SDS. They have been running all around
the country attacking people. NO SDS CHAPTER SUPPORTS
THEM!

Another faction of the Revolutionary Youth Movement
that split from SDS--called RYM II-is also calling for
marches and rallies this week. While claiming in rhetoric
to disassociate themselves from the Weathermen they are
actually allied with them! Their leadership, Mike Klonsky
and Les Coleman, originally invented the anti-people "Wild
in the Streets" strategy that Rudd's clique is now putting into
practice. They have never led any student struggles in alliance with workers. While claiming to support the Black
Liberation Movement they have not led one anti-racist struggle.

388

It is not true as the media is trying to portray that the difference between SDS and Weatherman is that they are militant and that we are pacifist or moderates.   Weatherman has total distortion of the concept of militancy: they see it as attacking the people.   SDS sees real militancy as workers striking and wildcatting against the bosses for better conditions, and students fighting against University expansion that throws workers out of their homes like at Howard or University of Chicago.   Last year SDS at San Francisco State College helped lead 14,000 students in a truly militant strike against racism--the longest student strike in U.S. history.

In the past year SDS has been moving toward building an alliance with working people.   Workers are hurt the worst by the U.S. bosses' war in Viet Nam which is causing inflation, falling real wages, and cutbacks in hospital care, education and welfare.   We also want to ally with workers to oppose racism which divides white from black workers and prevents them from seeing their common enemy: the corporation bosses and the government.   In Chicago, SDS has led students to support workers' strikes at United Parcel Service, C.T.A., Folletts' Warehouse, to name only a few.

At this time SDS' main program is to organize students to support campus workers' struggles like the ones at IIT, Normal and DeKalb, Illinois.   We support workers' demands for decent wages and working conditions, the right to unionize, an end to racist hiring and upgrading practices and an end to the use of students as scabs.

We want to build a movement that sides with the masses of American people against the boss class that runs this country.   The bosses have used the tiny Weathermen gang of provocateurs as an excuse to call in the 2500 National Guards.   They want to do two things: smear and discredit SDS, smash the honest student movement which is beginning to involve thousands of students in allying with workers.   The bosses want to take peoples' minds away from seeing the bosses as their enemy and focus on the student movement as a scapegoat, while at the same time carrying through an attack on working peoples' living and working conditions. This is the oldest trick in the book.   The facts cannot be hidden for long though.   We have confidence that the vast majority of people will see through this trick and repudiate Weatherman and RYMII--who have nothing to do with SDS--

and build a united movement of workers and students to fight against racism and imperialism.

SDS

(Distributed by the Progressive Labor Party-controlled Worker-Student Alliance, SDS, in Chicago on November 29, 1969. Collected the same day.)

40. SDS NATIONAL CONSTITUTION

(as amended at the 1967 National Convention, Ann Arbor, Michigan)

PREAMBLE

Students for a Democratic Society is an association of young people on the left. It seeks to create a sustained community of educational and political concern; one bringing together liberals and radicals, activists and scholars, students and faculty.

It maintains a vision of a democratic society, where at all levels the people have control of the decisions which affect them and the resources on which they are dependent. It seeks a relevance through the continual focus on realities and on the programs necessary to effect change at the most basic levels of economic, political, and social organization. It feels the urgency to put forth a radical, democratic program whose methods embody the democratic vision.

ARTICLE I: NAME

The name of the organization shall be Students for a Democratic Society.

ARTICLE II: MEMBERSHIP

Section 1: Membership is open to all who share the commitment of the organization to democracy as a means and as a social goal.

Section 2: SDS is an organization of and for democrats. It is civil libertarian in its treatment of those with whom it disagrees, but clear in its opposition to any antidemocratic principle as a basis for governmental, social, or political organization.

Section 3: DUES: The amount and period of national dues shall be determined by the National Council.

391

Section 4: ASSOCIATES: Individuals who do not wish to join SDS, but who share the major concerns of the organization, may become associates, with rights and responsibilities as defined by the National Council.

ARTICLE III: CHAPTERS AND AFFILIATES

Section 1: Any group of five or more members may apply to the National Office for charter as a chapter.

Section 2: A chapter may be chartered by the regional council of the area in which it is organized, or by the National Council. The chapter shall submit a membership list, a constitution or statement of principles, and notification of officers or regional representatives. Chapters may be provisionally recognized by the Secretaries or appropriate regional officer pending the meeting of the National Council or regional council respectively.

Section 3: Chapters are expected to operate within the broad terms of policy set by the National Convention and the National Council. Points of conflict should be referred to the National Council and a procedure established to make the issue public to the organization. In matters judged to be detrimental to the interests of the organization, the National Council shall have the power to cease whatever activity has been brought into question. The matter shall be finally resolved by the National Council in meeting or referendum.

Section 4: ASSOCIATED GROUPS: Independent groups can affiliate as associates of SDS by vote of their membership and designation of a liaison representative to sit on the National Council with consultative vote. The representative shall be a member of SDS. Such association is provisional until the approval of the National Council. The form of the relationship shall be worked out in each case between the group and the National Council.

Section 5: FRATERNAL ORGANIZATIONS: National or regional organizations whose programs and purposes are consistent with the broad aims and principles of SDS can be invited by the National Council to be fraternal with SDS and have a fraternal vote on the National Council. Such organizations shall appoint a liaison representative who shall be a member of SDS.

Section 6: SDS welcomes the opportunity to co-operate

with other individuals and organizations in jointly sponsoring specific action programs and joint stands on specific issues. The National Council shall be empowered to determine specific co-operative activity. (Co-operation does not imply endorsement.)

ARTICLE IV: REGIONAL ORGANIZATION

Section 1: All or some of the chapters and/or members in a given geographical area may constitute themselves a region of SDS. New regions shall submit their constitutions and be recognized provisionally by the Secretaries pending the next regular NC meeting. All disputes over regional boundaries shall be resolved by the NC.

Section 2: Regions of SDS shall hold at least one membership Convention each year, and may establish regional officers as deemed necessary. Regional programs, staff, and offices shall be responsible to decisions arrived at by a democratically constituted regional council.

Section 3: While fundamentally responsible to their regional constituency, regions are expected to operate within the broad terms of policy set by the National Convention and National Council. Any points of conflict shall finally be resolved by the National Council.

Section 4: If one-third of the duly chartered chapters in the geographic area of a region so petition, the National Council shall immediately consider whether to declare the regional organization defunct and to prohibit it from speaking or acting on behalf of SDS.

ARTICLE V: CONVENTION

Section 1: SDS shall meet in convention annually, at a time and a place fixed by the National Council, with at least three months prior notice being given to all members.

Section 2: The Convention shall serve to debate major issues and orientation of the organization, to set program mandates to the national staff, and to elect national officers. The Convention shall not be the policy-making body on specific resolutions.

Section 3: REPRESENTATION: Chapters shall elect

Convention delegates on the basis of one delegate for every
five SDS members in the chapter, each delegate to have five
votes at the Convention.   However, in order to be seated as
a delegate with five votes, a written notice of the delegate's
election must be received by the National Office prior to the
Convention.   Members present at the Convention, but not as
delegates, have one vote on the floor of the Convention.   Delegates from associated and fraternal groups shall be elected
by a procedure determined by the National Council.   The National Council shall draft Convention rules, accreditation procedures, and other requirements.

ARTICLE VI: NATIONAL COUNCIL

        Section 1 (a): The National Council shall be composed
of (1) one representative from each chapter with from five to
twenty-five members, and one additional representative for
each additional twenty-five members or fraction thereof in
that chapter; (2) the eleven national officers; (3) elected liaison representatives from associated groups (with consultative
vote); (4) liaison representatives from fraternal organizations
(with fraternal vote); and (5) national staff (without vote).   In
all cases, National Council members and liaison representatives must be members of SDS.   No more than three members from one chapter or associated group may serve con-
currently as national officers.

        Section 1 (b): Five or more members residing in an
area where there is no organized chapter may meet together
to elect a delegate to the National Council or regional council,
provided that (1) a certification of the meeting and election,
bearing the signatures of at least five members, be sent to
the National Office or regional office prior to the National
Council or regional council meeting, and (2) evidence is offered that all SDS members in the area concerned received
prior notice of the meeting and election.

        Section 2: The National Council shall be the major
policy-making and program body of the organization.   It shall
determine policy in the form of resolutions on specific views
within the broad orientation of the organization; determine the
program priorities and action undertaken by the organization
consonant with the orientation and mandates set by the Convention; charter chapters, with the right of appeal to the Convention.   The National Council shall be responsible for the
drafting of a budget, administration of the budget, and organ-

ization of fund-raising; appointment of committee chairmen
and representatives to other organizations; overseeing the
functioning of the administrative committee; drafting an annual
report; and making arrangements for the Convention.

Section 3: The National Council shall have the power
to appoint standing committees to carry on its work between
its meetings.

Section 4: The National Council shall meet at least
four times a year. A quorum shall be 40% of the voting
members of whose election the National Council has been noti-
fied. National officers may designate specific alternates.
Chapter and liaison representatives may be represented by
designated alternates from their groups.

ARTICLE VII: NATIONAL INTERIM COMMITTEE

The Secretaries shall have the power to call a meeting
of a National Interim Committee, to be composed of all the
national officers, on a regular basis and in emergencies.
Decisions of this body shall be subject to National Council approval.

ARTICLE VIII: NATIONAL OFFICERS AND STAFF

Section 1: The national officers shall be: National
Secretary, Education Secretary, Inter-Organizational Secretary,
and eight other officers, all to be elected at the Convention
and to serve as members of the National Council.

Section 2: The national officers must have been members of SDS at least two months prior to election.

Section 3: The eleven national officers are the spokesmen of SDS. They shall be responsible for seeing that organizational and political policies are carried out and shall convene the National Council. Political responsibility lies with
the three secretaries in consultation with the other officers.
The three secretaries shall work out of the National Office(s).
Important decisions in any one area which are made between
meetings of the National Interim Council are to be made by
the three national secretaries together. The national officers
shall be responsible to the Convention and the National Council.

Section 4: The National Secretary shall have primary responsibility for the functioning of the National Office. The National Secretary shall also have primary responsibility for the implementation of national programs approved by the Convention or National Council.

Section 5: The Inter-Organizational Secretary shall have primary responsibility for liaison with other organizations, both national and international, and for informing the membership about these groups. He or she shall not attend congresses, accept money, or establish formal relationships with organizations without the approval of the Convention, the National Council, or in emergency, the National Interim Council.

Section 6: The Education Secretary shall have the primary responsibility for the functioning of the internal education program.

Section 7: The Secretaries shall appoint assistants as necessary, subject to the approval of the National Council.

Section 8: The National Council shall elect administrative bodies to review the administrative decisions of the secretaries. It shall also fill, for the duration of the term, positions vacated by the national officers.

ARTICLE IX: PARLIAMENTARY AUTHORITY

In all cases not covered by this constitution, Roberts' Rules of Order, Revised Edition, shall be the authority governing SDS business.

ARTICLE X: POLICY AND DISCIPLINE

Section 1: Any member of the organization, including the officers, may be expelled or relieved of duties by a two-thirds vote of the National Council. Due process shall be followed in all cases.

Section 2: Any two chapters, or one-third of the National Council, can initiate a national referendum on any question.

Section 3: All statements of organizational policy shall have the approval of the National Council.

ARTICLE XI: AMENDMENTS

This constitution may be amended by one of three procedures:

(1) by a two-thirds vote of the Convention in session on amendments introduced at the Convention, in which case the amendment will take effect at the following Convention;

(2) by a two-thirds vote of the Convention in session on amendments introduced by distribution to the membership at least a month before the Convention, in which case the amendment will take effect immediately upon adoption;

(3) by a two-thirds vote of the membership on referendum, in which case the amendment will take effect immediately upon adoption.

Originally adopted in Convention June 1962; amended in Convention June 1963, June 1964, June 1965, September 1966, June 1967.

(Collected June 12, 1968 from the Harvard University SDS, Cambridge, Massachusetts.)

V

BIBLIOGRAPHY

This bibliography has been compiled to enable the reader to interpret and clarify the history and documents presented in this book by referring directly to the sources specified. The bibliography incorporates entries for nine categories of material: A. Books; B. Periodicals and Articles; C. Pamphlets; D. Government Reports; E. Scholarly Papers; F. Reports of Private Groups; G. Films; H. Judicial Document; and I. Bibliography.

A. BOOKS

1. Abeles, Elvin. The Student and the University: A Background Book on the Campus Revolt. New York: Parents' Magazine Press, 1969.

2. Adelson, Alan. SDS: A Profile. New York: Scribner's, 1971.

3. Ali, Tariq (ed.). New Revolutionaries: A Handbook of the International Radical Left. New York: Morrow, 1969.

4. Altbach, Philip G. Student Politics and Higher Education in the U.S.: A Select Bibliography. Cambridge, Mass.: Harvard Center For International Affairs, 1968.

5. American Civil Liberties Union. Academic Freedom, Academic Responsibility, Academic Due Process in Institutions of Higher Learning. New York: ACLU, 1966.

6. American Council On Education. Campus Disruption During 1968-1969. Washington, D.C.: Publication Division, ACE, 1969.

7. _____. Faculty Role in Campus Unrest. Washington, D.C.: Publication ACE, 1969.

8. Anderson, Walt. The Age of Protest. Pacific Palisades, California: Goodyear Publishing Co., 1967.

9. Andrews, Harry J. The Book of Grass ... Anthology on Indian Hemp. New York: Grove Press, 1967.

10. Aptheker, Herbert. Marxism and Alienation. New York: Humanities Press, 1966.

11. Atlantic Monthly. Troubled Campus. New York: Little, Brown, and Co., 1966.

12. Avorn, J. L., and Andrew Crane. Up Against the Ivy

Wall: A History of the Columbia Crisis. New York: Atheneum, 1969.

13. Axelrod, Joseph. Search for Relevance: The Campus in Crisis. San Francisco: Jossey-Bass, 1969.

14. Barlow, Bill, and Peter Shapiro. An End to Silence: The San Francisco State Student Movement in the Sixties. New York: Pegasus, 1970.

15. Bayer, Alan E., and Alexander W. Astin. Campus Disruption During 1968-1969. Washington, D.C.: American Council on Education, 1969.

16. _____. and Robert F. Boruch. Social Issues and Protest Activity: Recent Student Trends. Washington, D.C.: American Council on Education, 1970.

17. Becker, Howard S. (ed.). Campus Power Struggle. Chicago: Aldine, 1970.

18. Bell, Daniel. The End of Ideology. New York: Free Press, 1960.

19. _____. and Irving Kristol. Confrontation: The Student Rebellion and the Universities. New York: Basic Books, 1969.

20. Benne, Kenneth D. Education for Tragedy: Essays in Disenchanted Hope for Modern Man. Lexington: University of Kentucky Press, 1967.

21. Benson, Dennis C. The Now Generation. Richmond, Va.: John Knox Press, 1969.

22. Berger, Peter L., and Richard John Neuhaus. Movement and Revolution. New York: Doubleday, 1970.

23. Bernstein, Saul. Alternatives to Violence: Alienated Youth and Riots, Race, and Poverty. New York: Association Press, 1967.

24. Birmingham, John (ed.). Our Time Is Now: Notes from the High School Underground. New York: Praeger, 1970.

25. Bloomquist, E. R. Marijuana. New York: Glencoe Press, 1968.

26. Bolton, Charles D., and Kenneth C. W. Kammeyer.
     The University Student: A Study of Student Behavior
     and Values. New Haven, Conn.: College and Univer-
     sity Press, 1967.

27. Bonachea, Rolando E., and Nelson P. Valdes (eds.).
     Che: Selected Writings of Ernesto Guevara. Cam-
     bridge, Mass.: MIT Press, 1970.

28. Boorstein, Daniel J. The Decline of Radicalism. New
     York: Random, 1969.

29. Bosch, Juan. Pentagonism: A Substitute for Imperial-
     ism. New York: Grove Press, 1969.

30. Bottomore, T. B. Critics of Society, Radical Thought
     in North America. New York: Pantheon, 1968.

31. Boulding, Kenneth E. Conflict and Defense: A General
     Theory. New York: Harper, 1962.

32. Bourges, Herne. The French Student Revolt. New
     York: Hill and Wang, 1968.

33. Braden, William. The Age of Aquarius: Technology
     and the Cultural Revolution. Chicago: Quadrangle,
     1970.

34. Breines, Paul. Critical Interruptions: New Left Per-
     spectives on Herbert Marcuse. New York: Herder
     and Herder, 1970.

35. Brickman, William W., and Stanley Lehrer (eds.).
     Conflict and Change on the Campus: The Response
     to Student Hyperactivism. New York: School and So-
     ciety Books, 1970.

36. Brown, Joe David. The Hippies. New York: Time-
     Life Books, 1967.

37. Brzezinski, Zbigniew. Between Two Ages: America's
     Role in the Technetronic Era. New York: Viking,
     1970.

38. Buckman, Peter. The Limits of Protest. Indianapolis:
     Bobbs-Merrill, 1970.

39. Butz, Otto (ed.). To Make a Difference: A Student Look at America, Its Society, and Its Systems of Education. New York: Harper, 1967.

40. Cain, Arthur H. Young People and Revolution. New York: Day, 1970.

41. Califano, Joseph A., Jr. The Student Revolution: A Global Confrontation. New York: Norton, 1970.

42. California, University of, Academic Senate. Senate Committee on Education. Education at Berkeley: Report of the Berkeley Faculty Senate. Berkeley, Calif.: University of California Press, 1965.

43. Calvert, Greg, and Carol Nieman. A Disrupted History: The New Left and the New Capitalism. New York: Random House, 1971.

44. Camus, Albert. Resistance, Rebellion and Death. New York: Knopf, 1969.

45. Cantelon, John E. College Education and the Campus Revolution. Philadelphia: Westminster Press, 1969.

46. Cantor, Norman F. The Age of Protest: Dissent and Rebellion in the Twentieth Century. New York: Hawthorn, 1970.

47. Carey, James T. The College Drug Scene. Englewood Cliffs, N.J.: Prentice-Hall, 1968.

48. Cashman, John. The LSD Story. Greenwich, Conn.: Fawcett, 1966.

49. Center for the Study of Democratic Institutions. The Establishment and All That: A Collection of Major Articles from the Center Magazine since Its Beginning in the Fall of 1967. Santa Barbara, Calif.: The Center, 1970.

50. Ché Guevara, Ernesto. Che: Selected Writings of Ernesto Guevara. Cambridge, Mass.: MIT Press, 1970.

51. _____. Complete Bolivian Diaries of Ché Guevara. New York: Stein and Day, 1969.

52. _____. Guerrilla Warfare. New York: Monthly Review Press, 1961.

53. _____. Venceremos! The Speeches and Writing of Ernesto Ché Guevara. New York: Macmillan, 1968.

54. Chomsky, Noam. American Power and the New Mandarins. New York: Pantheon, 1969.

55. Cohen, Mitchell, and Dennis Hale (eds.). The New Student Left: An Anthology. Boston: Beacon Press, 1966.

56. Cohen, Sidney. The Beyond Within: The LSD Story. New York: Atheneum, 1964.

57. Cohn-Bendit, Daniel. The French Student Revolt: The Leaders Speak. New York: Hill and Wang, 1968.

58. _____. and Gabriel Cohn-Bendit. Obsolete Communism: The Left Wing Alternative. New York: McGraw-Hill, 1968.

59. Columbia University. New York. Fact Finding Commission On Columbia Disturbances. Crisis at Columbia: Report of the Fact-Finding Commission Appointed to Investigate the Disturbances at Columbia University in April and May, 1968. New York: Vintage, 1968.

60. Cooper, John Charles. The New Mentality. Philadelphia: Westminster, 1969.

61. Coyne, John R., Jr. The Kumquat Statement: Anarchy in the Groves of Academe. New York: Cowles, 1969.

62. Crick, Bernard, and William A. Robson. Protest and Discontent. Baltimore: Penguin, 1970.

63. Cruse, Harold. Rebellion or Revolution? New York: Morrow, 1968.

64. Danforth Foundation, and the Ford Foundation. The School and the Democratic Environment. New York: Columbia University Press, 1970.

65. Davidson, Carl. The New Radicals in the Multiversity:

An Analysis and Strategy for the Student Movement. .
Chicago: Students for a Democratic Society, 1968.

66. Davis, David Brion (ed.). The Fear of Conspiracy:
     Images of Un-American Subversion from the Revolu-
     tion to the Present. New York: Cornell University
     Press, 1970.

67. De Jouvenal, Bertrand. Academic Youth and Social
     Revolution. Washington, D. C. : American Council on
     Education, 1969.

68. De Vane, William. Higher Education in Twentieth Cen-
     tury America. Cambridge, Mass. : Harvard Univer-
     sity Press, 1965.

69. Dietze, Gottfried. Youth, University, and Democracy.
     Baltimore: Johns Hopkins University Press, 1970.

70. Divoky, Diana (ed.). How Old Will You Be in 1984?
     Expressions of Student Outrage from the High School
     Free Press. New York: Avon, 1969.

71. Douglas, Bruce. Reflections on Protest. Richmond,
     Va. : John Knox, 1968.

72. Draper, Hal. Berkeley: The New Student Revolt. New
     York: Evergreen, 1969.

73. Dunlap, Riley. A Bibliography of Empirical Studies of
     Student Political Activism. Eugene, Ore. : University
     of Oregon, Department of Sociology, 1969. (Mimeo.)

74. Earisman, Delbert L. Hippies in Our Midst: The Re-
     bellion Beyond Rebellion. Philadelphia: Fortress
     Press, 1968.

75. Ehrenreich, John, and Barbara Ehrenreich. Long
     March, Short Spring: The Student Uprising at Home
     and Abroad. New York: Monthly Review Press,
     1969.

76. Eichel, Lawrence E. , Kenneth W. Jost, Robert Luskin,
     and Richard E. Neustadt. The Harvard Strike. Bos-
     ton: Houghton Mifflin, 1970.

77. Erikson, Erik (ed.). Challenge of Youth. New York:
     Doubleday, 1963.

78. Erikson, Erik. Identity, Youth and Crisis. New York:
     Norton, 1968.

79. _____. On The Origins of Militant Non-Violence.
     New York: Norton, 1969.

80. _____. Youth: Change and Challenge. New York:
     Basic Books, 1963.

81. Erlich, John, and Susan Erlich (eds.). Student Power,
     Participation and Revolution. New York: Association
     Press, 1970.

82. Eszterhas, Joe, and Michael D. Roberts. Thirteen
     Seconds: Confrontation at Kent State. New York:
     Dodd, Mead and Co., 1970.

83. Eurich, Alvin (ed.). Campus 1980: The Shape of the
     Future in American Higher Education. New York:
     Delacorte, 1968.

84. Feigelson, Naomi. The Underground Revolution: Hip-
     pies, Yippies, and Others. New York: Funk and
     Wagnalls, 1970.

85. Feldman, Kenneth A., and Theodore M. Newcomb.
     The Impact of College on Students. San Francisco,
     California: Jossey-Bass, 1969.

86. Ferber, Michael, and Staughton Lynd. The Resistance.
     Boston: Beacon Press, 1971.

87. Feuer, Lewis S. Conflict of Generations: The Char-
     acter and Significance of Student Movements. New
     York: Basic Books, 1969.

88. Finn, James. Protest: Pacifism and Politics; Some
     Passionate Views on War and Nonviolence. New
     York: Random House, 1968.

89. First, Wesley. University on the Heights. New York:
     Doubleday, 1969.

90. Foster, Julian, and Durwood Long (eds.). Protest!
     Student Activism in America. New York: Morrow,
     1970.

91. Frankel, Charles. Education and the Barricades. New York: Norton, 1968.

92. Freedman, Mervin. College Experience. San Francisco: Jossey-Bass, 1967.

93. Freedman, Morris. Chaos in Our Colleges. New York: McKay, 1963.

94. Freeman, Howard E., and Norman R. Kurtz. America's Troubles: A Casebook on Social Conflict. Englewood Cliffs, N. J.: Prentice-Hall, 1969.

95. Gerberding, William P., and Duane E. Smith (eds.). The Radical Left: The Abuse of Discontent. Boston: Houghton-Mifflin, 1970.

96. Gerzon, Mark. The Whole World Is Watching: A Young Man Looks at Youth's Dissent. New York: Viking, 1969.

97. Gish, Arthur G. The New Left and Christian Radicalism. Grand Rapids, Mich.: Eerdmans, 1970.

98. Glazer, Nathan. Remembering the Answers: Essays on the American Student Revolt. New York: Basic Books, 1969.

99. Goldberg, Harvey (ed.). American Radicals: Some Problems and Personalities. New York: Monthly Review Press, 1969.

100. Goldsen, Rose K. What College Students Think. Princeton, N. J.: Van Nostrand, 1960.

101. Goldstein, Richard. One in Seven: Drugs on Campus. New York: Walker and Co., 1966.

102. Goode, Erick. The Marijuana Smokers. New York: Basic Books, 1970.

103. Goodman, Mitchell. The Movement Toward a New America. Philadelphia: Pilgrim Press, 1970.

104. Goodman, Paul. Compulsory Mis-Education: Community of Scholars. New York: Random House, 1962.

105. _____ . Like a Conquered Province: The Moral
     Ambiguity of America. New York: Random House,
     1967.

106. _____ . New Reformation. New York: Random
     House, 1970.

107. Gorovitz, Samuel (ed.). Freedom and Order in the
     University. Cleveland, Ohio: Western Reserve,
     1967.

108. Gould, Samuel B. Today's Academic Condition. New
     York: McGraw-Hill, 1970.

109. Grant, Joanne. Confrontation on Campus: The Colum-
     bia Master Plan. New York: New American Li-
     brary, 1970.

110. Graubard, Stephen R., and Gene A. Ballotti (eds.).
     The Embattled University. New York: Braziller,
     1970.

111. Guerin, Daniel. Anarchism: From Theory to Practice.
     New York: Monthly Review Press, 1970.

112. Gustaitis, Rosa. Turning On. New York: Macmillan,
     1969.

113. Hamalian, Leo, and Frederick R. Karl (eds.). The
     Radical Vision: Essays for the Seventies. New
     York: Crowell, 1970.

114. Hampdem-Turner, Charles. Radical Man. Cambridge,
     Mass.: Schenkman, 1970.

115. Hansel, Robert R. Like Father, Like Son--Like Hell!
     New York: Seabury, 1969.

116. Hare, A. Paul, and Herbert A. Blumberg. Nonviolent
     Direct Action: American Cases; Social-Psychological
     Analyses. Washington, D.C.: Corpus Publications,
     1969.

117. Harrington, Michael. The Other America: Poverty in
     the U.S. New York: Macmillan, 1969.

118. _____ . Toward a Democratic Left: A Radical

Program for a New Majority. New York: Macmillan, 1968.

119. Hart, Jeffrey. The American Dissent: A Decade of Modern Conservatism. New York: Doubleday, 1966.

120. Hart, Richard L., and J. Galen Saylor (eds.). Student Unrest: Threat or Promise? Washington, D. C.: Association for Supervision and Curriculum Development, 1970.

121. Hayden, Tom. Rebellion and Repression: Testimony by Tom Hayden before The National Commission on the Causes and Prevention of Violence and the House Un-American Activities Committee. New York: World, 1969.

122. _____. Rebellion in Newark: Official Violence and Ghetto Response. New York: Vintage, 1967.

123. _____. Trial. New York: Holt, Rinehart, and Winston, 1969.

124. Hazen Foundation. Committee on the Student in Higher Education. The Student in Higher Education. New Haven, Conn.: Hazen Foundation, 1968.

125. Heath, G. Louis. The High School Rebel. New York: MSS Educational Publishers, 1969.

126. _____. The Hot Campus: The Politics that Impede Change in the Technoversity. Metuchen, N. J.: Scarecrow Press, 1973.

127. Heirich, Max. The Beginning: Berkeley, 1964. New York: Columbia University Press, 1970.

128. Heist, Paul. The Dynamics of Student Discontent and Protest. Berkeley, Calif.: University of California Center for the Study of Higher Education, 1965.

129. Hodgkinson, Harold L. Institutions in Transition: A Study of Change in Higher Education. Berkeley: Carnegie Commission on Higher Education, 1970.

130. Hoffman, Abbie. Revolution for the Hell of It. New York: Dial, 1968.

131.   . Woodstock Nation: A Talk-Rock Album.
       New York: Random-Vintage, 1970.

132. Hofstadter, Richard. Academic Freedom in the Age
       of the College. New York: Columbia University
       Press, 1969.

133. Hook, Sidney. Academic Freedom and Academic Anar-
       chy. New York: Cowles Education Corp., 1970.

134. Horowitz, David. Student. New York: Ballantine,
       1969.

135. Horowitz, Irving Louis (ed.). The Anarchists. New
       York: Dell, 1964.

136. Howe, Irving (ed.). Beyond the New Left. New York:
       McCall, 1970.

137.   . Radical Imagination: An Anthology from
       Dissent Magazine. New York: New American Li-
       brary, 1967.

138. Jacobs, Harold. Weatherman. New York: Ramparts
       Press, 1970.

139. Jacobs, Paul, and Saul Landau. The New Radicals.
       New York: Vintage Books, 1966.

140. Jaffe, Harold, and John Tytell. The American Ex-
       perience. New York: Harper and Row, 1970.

141. James, Daniel. Ché Guevara: A Biography. New
       York: Stein and Day, 1969.

142. Jencks, Christopher, and David Riesman. The Aca-
       demic Revolution. New York: Doubleday, 1968.

143. Kahn, Roger. The Battle for Morningside Heights.
       New York: Morrow, 1970.

144. Kane, John. Voices of Dissent: Positive Good or
       Disruptive Evil? Englewood Cliffs, N.J.: Prentice-
       Hall, 1969.

145. Kaplan, Morton A. Dissent and the State in Peace and
       War: An Essay on the Grounds of Public Morality.
       New York: Dunellen, 1970.

146. Katope, Christopher G., and Paul Zalbrod (eds.). Be-
      yond Berkeley: A Source Book in Student Values.
      New York: World, 1966.

147. Katz, Joseph. No Time for Youth: Growth and Con-
      straint in College Students. San Francisco: Jossey-
      Bass, 1968.

148. Kavanaugh, Robert. The Grim Generation. New York:
      Trident, 1970.

149. Kelman, Steven. Push Comes to Shove: The Escala-
      tion of Student Protest. Boston: Houghton-Mifflin,
      1970.

150. Keniston, Kenneth. The Uncommitted: Alienated Youth
      in American Society. New York: Harcourt, Brace
      and World, 1965.

151. _____. The Young Radicals. New York: Harcourt,
      Brace and World, 1968.

152. Kennan, George F. Democracy and the Student Left.
      Boston: Little, Brown and Co., 1968.

153. Kerr, Clark. The Uses of the University. Cambridge,
      Mass.: Harvard University Press, 1963.

154. Kolakowski, Leszak. Toward a Marxist Humanism:
      Essays on the Left Today. New York: Grove Press,
      1968.

155. Kornbluth, Jesse. Notes from the New Underground:
      An Anthology. New York: Viking Press, 1968.

156. Kostelanetz, Richard (ed.). Beyond Left and Right:
      Radical Thought for Our Times. New York: Mor-
      row, 1970.

157. Kriyinanda. Cooperative Communities: How to Start
      Them and Why. San Francisco, Calif.: Ananda
      Publications, 1969.

158. Kronovet, Esther, and Evelyn Shick (eds.). In Pursuit
      of Awareness: The College Student in the Modern
      World. New York: Appleton, 1967.

159. Kunen, James S. Strawberry Statement: Notes of a
     College Revolutionist. New York: Random House,
     1969.

160. Lasch, Christopher. The Agony of the American Left.
     New York: Knopf, 1969.

161. _____. The New Radicalism in America, 1889-
     1963. New York: Knopf, 1965.

162. Leary, Timothy. High Priest. New York: New
     American Library, 1968.

163. Lee, Calvin B. T. The Campus Scene: 1900-1970.
     New York: McKay, 1970.

164. Leiden, Carl, and Karl M. Schmitt. Politics of Vio-
     lence: Revolution in the Modern World. Englewood
     Cliffs, N.J.: Prentice-Hall, 1968.

165. Lens, Sidney. The Military-Industrial Complex.
     Philadelphia: Pilgrim Press, 1969.

166. _____. Radicalism in America. New York:
     Crowell, 1969.

167. Lester, Julius. Revolutionary Notes. New York:
     Grove-Evergreen-Black Cat, 1969.

168. Levitas, Mitchel. America in Crisis. New York:
     Holt, Rinehart, and Winston, 1969.

169. Liberation News Service. A Book for a Fighting Move-
     ment. New York: Liberation News Service, 1969.

170. Lichtheim, George. The Origins of Socialism. New
     York: Praeger, 1969.

171. Lineberry, William P. (ed.). Colleges at the Cross-
     roads. New York: Wilson, 1966.

172. Lipset, Seymour Martin, and Sheldon S. Wolin.
     Berkeley Student Revolt: Facts and Interpretations.
     California: Anchor Books, 1965.

173. Lipset, Seymour Martin. Revolution and Counter
     Revolution: Change and Persistence in Social Struc-
     tures. New York: Basic Books, 1968.

174. _____ (ed.). Student Politics. New York: Basic
     Books, 1967.

175. Lipset, Seymour Martin, and Philip G. Altbach (eds.).
     Students in Revolt. Boston: Houghton-Mifflin, 1969.

176. Lloyd-Jones, Esther, and Herman A. Estrin. The
     American Student and His College. Boston: Hough-
     ton-Mifflin, 1967.

177. Lombardi, John. Student Activism in Junior Colleges:
     An Administrator's Views. Washington, D. C. :
     American Association of Junior Colleges, 1969.

178. Long, Priscilla (ed.). The New Left. Boston: Porter
     Sargent, 1969.

179. Lorber, Richard, and Ernest Fladell. The Gap. New
     York: McGraw-Hill, 1968.

180. Lothstein, Arthur (ed.). All We Are Saying: The
     Philosophy of the New Left. New York: Putnam,
     1970.

181. Lubell, Samuel. The Hidden Crisis in American Poli-
     tics. New York: Norton, 1970.

182. Luce, Phillip Abbott. The New Left. New York:
     McKay, 1966.

183. Lynd, Staughton. Nonviolence in America: Documen-
     tary History. New York: Bobbs-Merrill, 1966.

184. McAfee, Kathy, and Myrna Wood. Bread and Roses.
     San Francisco: Bay Area Radical Education Project,
     1969.

185. McEvoy, James, and Abraham Miller. Black Power
     and Student Rebellion. Belmont, California: Wads-
     worth, 1969.

186. McGrath, Earl J. Should Students Share the Power?
     A Study of their Role in College and University
     Governance. Philadelphia: Temple University
     Press, 1970.

187. Magee, Bryan. The New Radicalism. New York:
     St. Martin's Press, 1963.

188.   Mallery, David. Ferment on the Campus: An En-
       counter with the New College Generation. New York:
       Harper, 1966.

189.   Mallin, Jay. Ché Guevara, on Revolution. Miami,
       Florida: University of Miami Press, 1969.

190.   Mao-Tse-Tung. Quotations from Chairman Mao-Tse-
       Tung. New York: Praeger, 1968.

191.   Marcuse, Herbert. Essay on Liberation. Boston:
       Beacon Press, 1969.

192.   _____. Negations: Essays in Critical Theory.
       Boston: Beacon Press, 1969.

193.   _____. One-Dimensional Man: Studies in the
       Ideology of Advanced Industrial Society. Boston:
       Beacon Press, 1964.

194.   Marek, Franz. Philosophy of World Revolution. New
       York: International Publishers, 1969.

195.   Martin, David (ed.). Anarchy and Culture: The Prob-
       lem of the Contemporary University. New York:
       Columbia University Press, 1969.

196.   Martin, Warren B. Alternative to Irrelevance: A
       Strategy for Reform in Higher Education. Nashville,
       Tenn.: Abingdon Press, 1968.

197.   Masters, R. E. L., and Jean Houston. The Varieties
       of Psychedelic Experience. New York: Dell, 1966.

198.   Mead, Margaret. Culture and Commitment. New
       York: Natural History Press, 1970.

199.   Menashe, Louis, and Ronald Radosh. Teach-ins U.S.A.
       New York: Praeger, 1967.

200.   Metzger, Walter P., Sanford Kadish, and Arthur De
       Bardeleban. Dimensions of Academic Freedom.
       Urbana, Ill.: University of Illinois Press, 1969.

201.   Michael, Donald N. The Next Generation: The Pros-
       pects Ahead for the Youth of Today and Tomorrow.
       New York: Vintage, 1965.

202. Miller, Michael V., and Susan Gilmore. Revolution at Berkeley: The Crisis in American Education. New York: Dell, 1969.

203. Millett, Kate. Sexual Politics: A Manifesto for Revolution. New York: Doubleday, 1970.

204. Momboisse, Raymond M. Blueprint of Revolution: The Rebel, the Party, the Techniques of Revolt. Massachusetts: C. C. Thomas, 1970.

205. _____. Control of Student Disorders. California: MSM Enterprises, 1968.

206. Moos, Malcolm, and Francis E. Rourke. The Campus and the State. Baltimore: Johns Hopkins Press, 1960.

207. Morgan, Robin. Sisterhood Is Powerful: An Anthology of Writings from the Women's Liberation Movement. New York: Vintage, 1970.

208. _____. Women in Revolt. New York: Random House, 1969.

209. Morison, Robert S. (ed.). Contemporary University: USA. Boston: Houghton-Mifflin, 1966.

210. Morison, Samuel Eliot, Frederick Merk, and Frank Freidel. Dissent in Three American Wars. Cambridge: Harvard University Press, 1970.

211. Mungo, Raymond. Famous Long Ago: My Life and Hard Times with Liberation News Service. Boston: Beacon Press, 1970.

212. National Conference on Higher Education. Smith, G. Kerry, editor. Stress and Campus Response. San Francisco: Jossey-Bass, 1968.

213. Nelson, Jack, and Jack Bass. The Orangeburg Massacre. Cleveland, Ohio: World, 1970.

214. Nelson, Truman. The Right of Revolution. Boston: Beacon Press, 1968.

215. Newfield, Jack. A Prophetic Minority. New York: New American Library, 1966.

216. Nowlis, Helen H. Drugs on the College Campus. New York: Doubleday, 1969.

217. O'Brien, James. A History of the New Left: 1960-1968. Boston: New England Free Press, 1968.

218. Oglesby, Carl. The New Left Reader. New York: Grove Press, 1969.

219. Oppenheimer, Martin. The Urban Guerrilla. Chicago: Quadrangle, 1969.

220. Orrick, William H. Colleges in Crisis. Tennessee: Aurora, 1970.

221. Otten, C. Michael. University Authority and the Student: The Berkeley Experience. Berkeley, Calif.: University of California Press, 1970.

222. Perkins, James A. University in Transition. Englewood Cliffs, N.J.: Princeton University Press, 1966.

223. Perry, Helen Swick. The Human Be-In. New York: Basic Books, 1970.

224. Pomeroy, William J. Guerrilla and Counter-Guerrilla Warfare. New York: International, 1964.

225. Potter, Paul. A Name for Ourselves. Boston: Little, Brown, and Co., 1971.

226. Powers, Thomas. Diana: The Making of a Terrorist. Boston: Houghton-Mifflin, 1971.

227. Proxmire, Sen. William. America's Military-Industrial Complex. New York: Praeger, 1970.

228. Rader, Dotson. I Ain't Marchin Anymore. New York: McKay, 1969.

229. Rapoport, Roger, and Lawrence J. Kirshbaum. Is The Library Burning? New York: Random House, 1969.

230. Record, Wilson. Race and Radicalism. Ithaca, N.Y.: Cornell University Press, 1964.

231. Reich, Charles A. The Greening of America: How
      The Youth Revolution Is Trying to Make America
      Livable. New York: Random House, 1970.

232. Resek, Carl. The New Radicalism in America: 1889-
      1963. New York: Knopf, 1963.

233. Ridgeway, James. The Closed Corporation: American
      Universities in Crisis. New York: Random House,
      1969.

234. Roberts, Myron. The Roots of Rebellion: A Study of
      Existential America. Dubuque, Iowa: William C.
      Brown, 1969.

235. Rogan, Donald L. Campus Apocalypse: The Student
      Search Today. New York: Seabury, 1969.

236. Romm, Ethel G. Open Conspiracy: What America's
      Angry Generation Is Saying. Harrisburg, Pa.:
      Stackpole, 1969.

237. Rosset, Barney (ed.). Evergreen Review Reader.
      New York: Grove, 1969.

238. Roszak, Theodore (ed.). The Dissenting Academy.
      New York: Random House, 1968.

239. Roszak, Theodore. The Making of a Counter Culture.
      New York: Doubleday, 1969.

240. Rubin, Jerry. Do It! Scenarios of the Revolution.
      New York: Simon and Schuster, 1970.

241. _____. Letter to the Movement. New York: New
      York Review of Books, 1969.

242. Sampson, Edward E., and Harold A. Korn (eds.).
      Student Activism and Protest. San Francisco, Calif.:
      Jossey-Bass, 1970.

243. Sanford, Nevitt (ed.) The American College: A Psy-
      chological and Social Interpretation of Higher Learn-
      ing. New York: Wiley, 1962.

244. Sanford, Nevitt. Where Colleges Fail: A Study of
      the Student as a Person. San Francisco, Calif.:
      Jossey-Bass, 1967.

245. Schaap, Richard. Turned On. New York: New American Library, 1967.

246. Schiller, Herbert I., and Joseph Dexter Phillips (comps.). Super-State: Readings in the Military-Industrial Complex. Urbana, Ill.: University of Illinois Press, 1970.

247. Schoenfeld, Eugene. Dear Doctor Hip Procrates. New York: Grove Press, 1968.

248. Schwab, Joseph J. College Curriculum and Student Protest. Chicago: University of Chicago Press, 1969.

249. Scimecca, Joseph, and Roland Damiano. Crisis at St. John's: Strike and Revolution on the Catholic Campus. New York: Random House, 1967.

250. Scott, M. B., and S. M. Lyman. Revolt of Students. New York: Charles E. Merrill, 1970.

251. Seale, Patrick, and Maureen McConville. Red Flag/Black Flag: French Revolution. New York: Putnam, 1968.

252. Segal, Ronald. The Americans: A Conflict of Greed and Reality. New York: Viking, 1969.

253. Servan, Schreiben J. J. The Spirit of May. New York: McGraw-Hill, 1969.

254. Shinto, William. The Drama of Student Revolt. Valley Forge, Pa.: Judson Press, 1970.

255. Skolnick, Jerome. The Politics of Protest: A Report of the National Commission on the Causes and Prevention of Violence. Task Force on Violent Aspects of Protest and Confrontation. New York: Simon and Schuster, 1969.

256. Slater, Philip E. The Pursuit of Loneliness: American Culture at the Breaking Point. Boston: Beacon Press, 1970.

257. Smith, David E. The New Social Drug: Cultural, Medical and Legal Perspectives on Marijuana. Englewood Cliffs, N.J.: Prentice-Hall, 1970.

258. Solomon, D. The Marijuana Papers. Indianapolis:
     Bobbs-Merrill, 1965.

259. Stapp, Andy. Up Against the Brass. New York:
     Simon and Schuster, 1970.

260. Stein, David L. Living the Revolution: The Yippies
     in Chicago. New York: Bobbs-Merrill, 1970.

261. Stone, I. F. The Killings at Kent State: How Murder
     Went Unpunished. New York: Random House, 1970.

262. Strout, Cushing, and David I. Grossvogel. Divided
     We Stand: Reflections on the Crisis at Cornell.
     New York: Doubleday, 1969.

263. Taylor, Harold. Students Without Teachers: The
     Crisis in the University. New York: McGraw-Hill,
     1969.

264. Taylor, Robert N. This Damned Campus. Philadel-
     phia: United Church Press, 1969.

265. Teodori, Massimo (ed.). The New Left: A Documen-
     tary History. Indianapolis: Bobbs-Merrill, 1969.

266. Thayer, George. The Farther Shores of Politics.
     New York: Simon and Schuster, 1967.

267. Thompson, Mary Lou (ed.). Voices of the New Femi-
     nism. Boston: Beacon Press, 1970.

268. Toffler, Alvin. Future Shock. New York: Random
     House, 1970.

269. Trials of the Resistance. Essays by Noam Chomsky
     et al. New York: Random House, 1970.

270. Tussman, Joseph. Experiment at Berkeley. New
     York: Oxford University Press, 1969.

271. Urban Research Corporation. On Strike ... Shut It
     Down! A Report of the First National Student Strike
     in U.S. History. Chicago: Urban Research Corpora-
     tion, 1970.

272. Von Hoffman, Nicholas. Left at the Post. Chicago:
     Quadrangle, 1970.

273. _____. The Multiversity: A Personal Report on What Happens to Today's Students at American Universities. New York: Holt, 1966.

274. _____. We Are the People Our Parents Warned Us Against. Chicago: Quadrangle, 1968.

275. Wagner, Stanley P. The End of Revolution: A New Assessment of Today's Rebellions. New York: A. S. Barnes, 1970.

276. Wallerstein, Immanuel, and Paul Starr (eds.). The University Crisis Reader, 2 vols. New York: Random House, Vintage edition, 1971.

277. Wallerstein, Immanuel M. University in Turmoil: The Politics of Change. New York: Atheneum, 1969.

278. Weaver, Gary R., and James H. Weaver (eds.). The University and Revolution. Englewood Cliffs, N. J.: Prentice-Hall, 1970.

279. Williams, Sylvia Berry. Hassling. Boston: Little, Brown and Co., 1970.

280. Williamson, E. G., and John L. Cowan. The American Student's Freedom of Expression: A Research Appraisal. Minneapolis: University of Minnesota Press, 1966.

281. Wittner, Lawrence S. Rebels Against War: The American Peace Movement, 1941-1960. New York: Columbia University Press, 1970.

282. Wolfe, Tom. The Electric Kool-Aid Acid Test. New York: Farrar, Straus, and Giroux, 1968.

283. Wolin, Sheldon S., and John H. Schaar. The Berkeley Rebellion and Beyond: Essays on Politics and Education in the Technological Society. New York: Random House, 1970.

284. Yablonsky, Lewis. The Hippie Trip. New York: Pegasus, 1968.

285. Young, Alfred F. Dissent: Explorations in the History of American Radicalism. DeKalb: Northern Illinois University Press, 1968.

286. Young, Warren, and Joseph Hixson. LSD on Campus.
      New York: Dell, 1966.

287. Zinn, Howard. SNCC: The New Abolitionists. Bos-
      ton: Beacon Press, 1969.

288. Zorsa, Richard. The Right to Say We: The Adven-
      tures of a Young Englishman at Harvard and in the
      Youth Movement. New York: Praeger, 1969.

289. Zweig, Ferdynand. The Student in the Age of Anxiety.
      New York: Free Press, 1964.

                    B. ARTICLES

1.   Abram, Morris B. "Eleven Days at Brandeis, as
     Seen from the President's Chair," New York Times
     Magazine, February 16, 1969, pp. 28-29.

2.   _____. "The Restless Campus," College and Uni-
     versity Journal, VIII (Fall, 1969), pp. 34-39.

3.   Agut, J. R. "Miami at War with Hippies," Florida
     Free Press, March 14, 1968.

4.   Aiken, Ellsworth N. "Moratorium!," Grok, February,
     1970.

5.   Albert, Stewart. "... Piss in the Voting Booths,"
     Fifth Estate, October 31, 1968.

6.   Alegria, Fernando. "Student Revolutions in U. S. A.,"
     Occident, Fall, 1964-1965.

7.   Allen, James N. "A Defense of Activism," Conscience,
     August, 1969.

8.   Allen, J. E., Jr. "Campus Activism and Unrest,"
     School & Society, XCVI (October 26, 1968), pp. 357-
     359.

9.   Allen, Jesse. "Newark Community Union," Studies on
     the Left, IV, No. 4 (1965), pp. 80-84.

10. Anderson, Barbara. "Ordeal at San Francisco State
     College," Library Journal, XC (April 1, 1970),
     pp. 1275-1280.

11. Anderson, Michael. "Defend Yourself," Berkeley Barb,
     October 17, 1969.

12. Andrews, James R. "Confrontation at Columbia: A
     Case Study in Coercive Rhetoric," Quarterly Journal
     of Speech, LV (February, 1969), pp. 9-16.

13. Anthony, Richard, and Philip W. Semas. "The Many
     Voices of the New Left," New Republic, CLX (June
     29, 1968), pp. 12-16.

14. Apostolides, Alex. "Governor Ronnie and College Board
     Overkill Summerskill," Los Angeles Free Press,
     January 22, 1967.

15. Aptheker, Bettina. "Berkeley's Meddlesome Regents,"
     Nation, CCXI (September 7, 1970), pp. 169-173.

16. Aron, Raymond. "Student Rebellion: Vision of the
     Future or Echo from the Past?" Political Science
     Quarterly, LXXXIV (June, 1969), pp. 289-310.

17. Aronowitz, Stanley. "New York City: After the Rent
     Strikes," Studies on the Left, IV, No. 4 (1965), pp.
     85-89.

18. Aronson, James. "Beyond Old and New Left: The
     Emergence of a Third Force," Liberation, XIV
     (August-September, 1969), pp. 22-25.

19. Aronson, Ronald. "The Movement and Its Critics,"
     Studies on the Left, VI, No. 1 (January-February,
     1966), pp. 3-19.

20. Ascheim, Skip. "Resistance: Boston Style," Avatar,
     October 27, 1967.

21. Atkins, Neil P. "What Do They Want?" Educational
     Leadership, XXVII (February, 1970), p. 441.

22. Auerill, L. I. "Ecology of Discontent," Christian Cen-
     tury, LXXXVI (June 18, 1969), pp. 835-838.

23. Austin, C. G. "Student Protests and the Establish-
     ment," Journal of Higher Education, April, 1968,
     pp. 223-225.

24. Avi, Zede. "What's in Store for State," Berkeley Barb, August 15, 1969.

25. Avorn, J. L. "Columbia: To Be a Revolutionary or Not to Be?" Look, XXXIV (May 13, 1969), pp. 13-14.

26. Bannowsky, Flip. "The Great Obscenity Bust," Heterodoxical Voice, June, 1968.

27. Barton, Allen H. "The Columbia Crisis: Campus, Vietnam and the Ghetto," Public Opinion Quarterly, XXXII (Fall, 1968), pp. 333-351.

28. Baxandall, Lee. "Camp and Community," Studies on the Left, V, No. 2 (1965), pp. 97-98.

29. Bay, Christian. "Comment: Academic Citizenship in a Time of Campus Revolt," Trans-action, VI (January, 1967), pp. 4-7.

30. _____. "Political and Apolitical Students: Facts in Search of Theory," Journal of Social Issues, XXIII (July, 1967), pp. 76-91.

31. Bayer, Alan E., and Alexander W. Astin. "Violence and Disruption on the U. S. Campus, 1968-1969," Educational Record, L (Fall, 1969), pp. 337-350.

32. Beichman, Arnold. "Battle of Columbia," Encounter, XXXI (July, 1968), pp. 23-39.

33. Bennett, John C. "Modes of Dissent in a Democracy, the United States: The Politics of Dissent," Social Action, XXXV (1969), pp. 3-48.

34. Bensky, Larry. "Conspiracy: A New Nation," Great Speckled Bird, December 1, 1969.

35. Berger, Dan. "Nixon's War," Distant Drummer, April 9, 1970.

36. _____. "Why Cambodia?" Distant Drummer, May 7, 1970.

37. Berger, Pauline. "Student Revolt at CCNY," Independent Socialist, January 14, 1967.

38. Berland, Oscar. "Radical Chains: The Marxian

Concept of Proletarian Mission," Studies on the Left, VI, No. 5 (September-October, 1966), pp. 27-51.

39. Bettelheim, Bruno. "College Student Rebellion: Explanations and Answers," Phi Delta Kappan, L (May, 1969), pp. 511-514.

40. Bickel, Alexander M. "The Tolerance of Violence on the Campus," New Republic, CLXII (June 13, 1970), pp. 15-17.

41. Bingler, John A., Jr. "We Need Justice and Disorder," Pittsburgh Point, February 19, 1970.

42. Bitten, Ron. "Chicago ... October 11," Old Mole, August 15, 1967.

43. Black, Vonda. "What Women's Liberation Really Means," Free You, June 17, 1970.

44. Blackburn, Dan. "Up Against the Marble Wall," Nation, CCX (June 15, 1970), pp. 719-721.

45. Blank, Blanche D. "Running the Campus," Nation, CCX (June 8, 1970), pp. 690-692.

46. Blank, Dennis. "John Sinclair: Victim of Repression," Grok, June 27, 1970.

47. Blazer, Sam. "Amplifying the 'Strawberry Statement,'" Los Angeles Free Press, July 24, 1970.

48. Bloustein, Edward J. "The New Student and His Role in American Colleges," Liberal Education, LIV (October, 1968), pp. 345-364.

49. Blum, Sam. "Marijuana Clouds the Generation Gap," New York Times Magazine, August 23, 1970, pp. 28-29.

50. Boorstein, Daniel J. "Dissent, Dissension and the News," Reference Shelf Series, XL, No. 5 (1968), pp. 199-213.

51. Booth, Paul. "Students and Workers," Ramparts, VIII (September, 1969), pp. 19-20.

52. Boskin, John, and R. A. Rosenstone (eds.). "Protest

in the Sixties: Symposium, " American Academy of
Political and Social Science, The Annals, CCCLXXXII
(1969), pp. 1-144.

53. Bottomore, T. B. "Students Observed, " University
Quarterly, September, 1968, pp. 425-433.

54. Bowen, H. R. "Student Unrest in the United States, "
International Bureau of Education Bulletin, Fourth
Quarter, 1968, pp. 236-240.

55. Brammer, Lawrence. "The Coming Revolt of High
School Students, " Bulletin of the National Association
of Secondary School Principals, LII (September, 1968),
pp. 13-21.

56. Brann, J. W. "Continued at Columbia, " Commonweal,
LXXXIX (October 4, 1968), pp. 7-8.

57. Brant, Pasha. "Are You Willing to Be a Nigger
Again?" High School Independent Press, November
18, 1968.

58. Brayman, Rick and Mary Schonover. "Massacre at
Kent State, " Daily Planet, May 25, 1970.

59. Brickman, William W. "Anarchy vs. Freedom in
Academia, " School & Society, XCVI (October 26,
1968), p. 346.

60. Brienberg, Elizabeth. "More on FSM, " Studies on the
Left, V, No. 2 (1965), pp. 95-97.

61. Brightman, Carol. "Vietnam: Hey! Folks, That War
Is Escalating, " Liberation News Service, December
19, 1968.

62. _____. "Vietnam: The War Escalates, " Hard Core,
December 20, 1968.

63. Brock, William E. III. "Gut Issues of Campus Unrest, "
College and University Journal, VIII (Fall, 1969),
pp. 45-48.

64. Brogan, D. W. "Student Revolt, " Encounter, XXXI
(July, 1968), pp. 20-25.

65. Brooks, T. R. "Metamorphosis in SDS. The New

Left Is Showing Its Age, " New York Times Magazine, June 15, 1969, pp. 14-15.

66. Broslawsky, Farrel. "What's Left of the Left since LBJ Left?" Los Angeles Free Press, April 5, 1968.

67. Brown, Connie. "Cleveland: Conference of the Poor, " Studies on the Left, V, No. 2 (1965), pp. 71-74.

68. Brown, Robert McAfee. "Mayday for America: Mobilizing the Outraged, " Commonweal, XCII (May 29, 1970), pp. 266-268.

69. Brustein, Robert. "Honest, Intelligible Radical Politics, " New Republic, CLXIII (September 26, 1970), pp. 15-17.

70. _____. "When the Panther Came to Yale, " New York Times Magazine, June 21, 1970, pp. 7-9.

71. _____. "Whose University? The Case for Professionalism, " New Republic, CLXII (April 26, 1969), pp. 16-18.

72. Buchanan, James M. "Student Revolts, Academic Liberalism, and Constitutional Attitudes, " Social Research, XXXV (Winter, 1968), pp. 666-680.

73. Buckley, Neil. "HUAC Struggle at Penn State, " Water Tunnel, February 20, 1967.

74. Bunzel, John H. "Costs of the Politicized College, " Educational Record, L (Spring, 1969), pp. 131-137.

75. "Busting the Ban on SDS, " Nola Express, September 12, 1969.

76. Cain, Edward R. "Conscientious Objection in France, Britain, and the U.S., " Comparative Politics, II (1970), pp. 275-307.

77. "Call for Civil Disobedience, " New Left Notes, December 9, 1966.

78. Callahan, Daniel. "Resistance and Technology: Theory of the New Left Versus Technological Man, " Commonweal, LXXXVII (December 22, 1967), pp. 377-381.

79. Callaway, Howard. "Fascist America?" Water Tunnel,
    May 12, 1969.

80. Calvert, Peter A. R. "Revolution: The Politics of
    Violence," Political Studies, XV (1967), pp. 1-11.

81. Cannon, Terence, and Reese Erlich. "The Oakland
    Seven," Ramparts, VII (April, 1969), pp. 34-37.

82. Cannon, Terry. "Law and Order in Amerika," Wash-
    ington Free Press, July 1, 1969.

83. Cantor, Paul. "End the War Now Mr. Nixon, or the
    People Will End Your Administration," Berkeley Barb,
    October 31, 1969.

84. Capouya, Emile. "After the Failure of Nerve," Studies
    on the Left, III (November 3, 1963), pp. 3-13.

85. Carliner, Mike. "Pot--Psychological Effects," Distant
    Drummer, April 3, 1969.

86. Casey, Thomas J. "Student Unrest: Roots and Solu-
    tions," Liberal Education, LV (May, 1969), pp. 244-
    254.

87. Charyn, Marlene. "Fascism," Peninsula Observer,
    July 28, 1969.

88. Ché Guevara, Ernesto. "Contemporary Documents:
    Commandante Ernesto Ché Guevara. From 'Notes for
    the Study of the Ideology of the Cuban Revolution,'
    Verde Olivo, October 8, 1960," Studies on the Left,
    I, No. 3 (1960), pp. 75-85.

89. _____. "Contemporary Documents: From Analysis
    of the Cuban Situation in La Guerra de Guerillas,
    Published in Early 1960," Studies on the Left, I, No.
    3 (1960), pp. 79-84.

90. Childs, Charles. "Guns Come to Cornell," Life, LXVI
    (May 2, 1969), pp. 20-28.

91. Chomsky, Noam. "Some Tasks for the Left," Libera-
    tion, XIV (August-September, 1969), pp. 38-43.

92. Christensen, Gayle. "Fascism and George Wallace,"
    Campus Underground, November 4, 1968.

93.   Clamage, Dena. "Women's Liberation: The Only Path Is Revolution," Fifth Estate, March 5, 1969.

94.   Clarkson, Paul. "When People Are Powerful the Schools Are Free," Peninsula Observer, June 30, 1969.

95.   Cleaver, Eldridge. "Revolution No Game," Los Angeles Free Press, June 11, 1969.

96.   Clecak, Peter. "Tom Hayden and the New Left," Nation, CCX (January 12, 1970), pp. 21-23.

97.   Coffin, Tom. "Underground Press Rising," Great Speckled Bird, June 28, 1969.

98.   Cohen, Carl. "Essence and Ethics of Civil Disobedience," Nation, CXCVIII (March 16, 1964), pp. 257-262.

99.   Cohen, E. E., and L. B. Mayhew. "The New Work Ethic," Electronic Age, XXX (Winter, 1970-1971), pp. 17-20.

100. Cohen, Fred, Marc Weiss, and Jeff Blum. "SDS Lesson: Radicals Must Analyze U.S.," Peninsula Observer, July 14, 1969.

101. Coles, Robert. "Still Hungry in America," Great Speckled Bird, June 30, 1969.

102. Commager, Henry S. "Problem of Dissent," Saturday Review, XLVIII (1965), pp. 21-23.

103. Conant, R. W. "Rioting, Insurrection and Civil Disobedience," American Scholar, XXXVII (1968), pp. 420-433.

104. Conner, Frederick W. "Anarchist Echoes in Academia," Improving College and University Teaching, XVII (Summer, 1969), p. 157.

105. Cooper, Richard T. "A Town Turns on Its Children," Nation, CCXI (November 23, 1970), pp. 517-519.

106. Covert, John. "More Killings, More Protests," Pittsburgh Point, May 21, 1970.

107. _____. "The Sun Was Hot, The Crowd Was Cool,"
     Pittsburgh Point, May 14, 1970.

108. _____. "The Trial Is Over, but Not the Danger,"
     Pittsburgh Point, February 19, 1970.

109. _____. "A Week of Pain and Outrage," Pittsburgh
     Point, May 7, 1970.

110. Cross, K. Patricia. "Some Correlates of Student
     Protest," National Association of Student Personnel
     Administrators Journal, VIII (July, 1970), pp. 38-48.

111. Crowley, Louise. "What's It All About--Anarchy?"
     Other Sciences, July 15, 1969.

112. Dana, Jane. "From Outer to Inner Space," Pittsburgh
     Point, July 31, 1969.

113. Daniels, John. "Eastern Michigan Student Action,"
     Fifth Estate, March 5, 1969.

114. Darlington, Sandy. "Revolution's Getting Groovy: Oak-
     land 7 Acquitted," Ann Arbor Argus, April 14, 1969.

115. Davidson, Carl. "Behind the 'Antiwar Amendment,'"
     Guardian, June 6, 1970.

116. _____. "Crime Laws Limit Democratic Rights,"
     Guardian, June 8, 1970.

117. _____. "Neutralizing Campus Radicals," Guardian,
     November 23, 1968.

118. Davis, B. H. "From the General Secretary; Campus
     Upheaval," American Association of University Pro-
     fessors Bulletin, LIV (September, 1968), pp. 292-
     294.

119. Dea, John. "The Generation Gap Is Only the Death
     Throes of Fascism," San Diego Free Press, June
     11, 1969.

120. Deakin, James. "Big Brass Bombs," Veterans Stars
     And Stripes Forever, January, 1968.

121. "Debacle at Columbia," America, May 18, 1968.

122. Dellinger, Dave. "Conversations with Ho, " Liberation,
      XIV (October, 1969), pp. 2-6.

123. _____. "The Future of Non-Violence, " Studies on
      the Left, IV, No. 4 (1965), pp. 90-96.

124. _____. "Memoir of Czechago, " Liberation, April,
      1970.

125. Demaio, Don. "You Were Not Wearing a Pink Garde-
      nia: So How Could I Tell It Was You, or, Should a
      Gentleman Offer a Typarillo to Jerry Rubin?" Dis-
      tant Drummer, May 9, 1969.

126. Demchak, J. M. "Pittsburgh Underground, " Los
      Angeles Free Press, September 13, 1968.

127. Denson, Ed. "What Happened at the Happening, "
      Berkeley Barb, January 1, 1967.

128. Deutscher, Isaac, A. J. Muste, and Dave Dellinger.
      "Marxism and Nonviolence, " Liberation, July, 1969,
      pp. 10-16.

129. Devine, J. Travers. "Revolution--American Style, "
      Grass Roots Forum, October 21, 1967.

130. Diamond, Edwin. "Class of '69: The Violent Years, "
      Newsweek, LXXIII (June 23, 1969), pp. 68-73.

131. Diamond, Steve. "The Columbia Revolution, " Los
      Angeles Free Press, May 10, 1968.

132. Dickie, Allan. "The New 'Breed' on the University
      Campus, " Educational Forum, XXXIII (November,
      1968), pp. 27-29.

133. Dickinson, John K. "Ideology and Prediction, " Studies
      on the Left, II, No. 3 (1962), pp. 26-34.

134. Didion, Joan. "A Generation Not for Barricades, "
      Life, LXVIII (June 5, 1970), p. 26.

135. Divoky, Diane. "The Way It's Going to Be, " Saturday
      Review, LII (February 15, 1969), pp. 83-84.

136. Doggett, David. "SDS Severs Ties with SSOC, "
      Kudza, April 5, 1969.

137. Donner, Frank. "HUAC: The Dossier-Keepers, "
      Studies on the Left, I, No. 4 (1961), pp. 7-25.

138. Donovan, Bernard. "Jailbreak: New York High
      School Shutting It Down, " Old Mole, May 23, 1969.

139. Dorsey, Ellie. "The 'Sexist' Society, " First Issue,
      February, 1969.

140. Draper, Hal. "In Defense of the New Radicals, " New
      Politics, IV (Summer, 1965), pp. 5-28.

141. _____. "On Marcuse: A Critique of Pure Elitism, "
      Independent Socialist, March, 1969.

142. Duberman, M. "On Misunderstanding Student Rebels, "
      Atlantic, CCXXIII (November, 1968), pp. 63-70.

143. Duerr, Edwin C. "Police on the Campus: Crisis at
      SFSC, " Educational Record, L (Spring, 1969), pp.
      126-130.

144. Eberle, Paul. "San Fernando Valley State--San Fran-
      cisco State, " Los Angeles Free Press, December
      13, 1968.

145. _____. "Silence Between the Generations, " Los
      Angeles Free Press, March 1, 1968.

146. _____. "This People's War Produces a People's
      Communism, " Los Angeles Free Press, October 16,
      1970.

147. _____. "Valley State Student Uprising, " Los Angel-
      es Free Press, November 8, 1968.

148. _____. "We Are 18 Months from Open Revolt in
      This Country, " Los Angeles Free Press, December
      15, 1967.

149. Eddy, E. D. "Scratching The Surface: Campus Un-
      rest in 1968, Adaption of an Address, June, 1968, "
      School & Society, XCVII (January, 1969), pp. 16-18.

150. Edgerton, Karl R. "UC Chancellor Says Don't Stop
      Dissent, " Argo, March, 1969.

151. Egan, Edmund J.   "Pacifism: The Dynamics of Dis-
      sent," Worldview, X (1967), pp. 8-11.

152. Egelson, Nick.   "Letter to the Movement: Re-crea-
      tion, Self-transformation, and Revolutionary Con-
      sciousness," Liberation, XV (April, 1970), pp. 45-
      50.

153. Eisen, Jonathan, and David Steinberg.   "The Student
      Revolt Against Liberalism," Annals of the American
      Academy, CCCLXXXII (March, 1969), pp. 83-84.

154. Elam, Stanley.   "Does Student Power Equal Democra-
      cy's Strength?" Phi Delta Kappan, L (September,
      1968), pp. 1-2.

155. Engo, Robert, and John Williams.   "Blacks on Cam-
      pus," Nation, CCIX (November 17, 1969), pp. 537-
      540.

156. Erlich, Reese.   "Convention Mayhem Splits SDS
      Forces," Los Angeles Free Press, June 11, 1969.

157. Etheridge, Eugene W.   "Student Rights and the Campus
      Riots," College and University, XL (Fall, 1969),
      pp. 15-23.

158. Etzioni, Amitai.   "Confessions of a Professor Caught
      in a Revolution," New York Times Magazine, Sep-
      tember 15, 1968, pp. 25-27.

159. Fager, Charles E.   "Demonstrate, Yes, but Not Futile-
      ly," Christian Century, LXXXV (February 28, 1968),
      pp. 259-262.

160. Fairfield, Dick.   "The New Dropout Creating an Al-
      ternative Life Style," Grok, June 27, 1970.

161. Farber, Jerry.   "Non-violent Defense Made in Court-
      room," Los Angeles Free Press, October 29, 1965.

162. _____.   "The Student as Nigger," Distant Drummer,
      January 8, 1970.

163. Fearon, Christopher P.   "Campus Protest and the
      Administrator," Bulletin of the National Association
      of Secondary School Principals, LIII (September,
      1969), pp. 28-35.

164. Feuer, Alan. "We Got the Fever; We're Hot...,"
     Fifth Estate, June 3, 1970.

165. Feuer, Lewis S. "Conflict of Generations," Saturday
     Review, LII (January 18, 1969), pp. 53-66.

166. Fine, David. "High School Movement," Heterodoxical
     Voice, April, 1968.

167. Fischer, John. "Case for the Rebellious Students and
     Their Counterrevolution," Harper's, CCXXXVII
     (August, 1968), pp. 9-12.

168. Flacks, Richard. "The Liberated Generation: Roots
     of Student Protest," Journal of Social Issues, XXIII
     (July, 1967), pp. 52-75.

169. _____. "Social and Cultural Meanings of Student
     Revolt," Social Problems, VII (Winter, 1970), pp.
     340-357.

170. Flash, J. Jack. "Frisco Moratorium," Berkeley Barb,
     October 17, 1969.

171. Foreman, Alex, and F. P. Salstrom. "Revolution,
     Diggers Style," Distant Drummer, October 3, 1969.

172. Foreman, Clark H. "In Defense of Robert F. Wil-
     liams," Studies on the Left, III, No. I (1962), pp.
     66-67.

173. Fox, Josef W. "Quest for Relevance," Campus Under-
     ground, December 9, 1968.

174. _____. "Thoughts on Campus Rebellion," Campus
     Underground, November 18, 1968.

175. Franklin, Ted. "Exploitation at Woodstock," Pitts-
     burgh Point, August 24, 1969.

176. Freemond, Jules. "Capitalist Hangout under Siege,"
     East Village Other, December 1, 1967.

177. Freistadt, Hans. "Modern Marxism and Scientific
     Knowledge: Any Common Ground?" Studies on the
     Left, I, No. 3 (1960), pp. 62-74.

178. Friedenberg, Edgar Z. "Current Patterns of Genera-
      tional Conflict," Journal of Social Issues, XXV (April,
      1969), pp. 21-30.

179. Friedland, William H., and Harry Edwards. "Confron-
      tation at Cornell," Trans-action, VI (June, 1969),
      pp. 29-36.

180. Fruchter, Norm. "Mississippi: Notes on SNCC,"
      Studies on the Left, IV (1965), pp. 74-80.

181. Frymier, Jack R. "Why Students Rebel," Educational
      Leadership, XXVII (January, 1970), pp. 346-350.

182. Furlong, William Barry. "The Guardsmen's View of
      the Tragedy at Kent State," New York Times Maga-
      zine, June 21, 1970, pp. 12-13.

183. Gans, Herbert J. "Rational Approach to Radicalism,"
      Studies on the Left, VI, No. 1 (January-February,
      1966), pp. 37-53.

184. Geerdes, Clay. "Berkeley Forecast: Haight Re-
      visited," Los Angeles Free Press, June 20, 1969.

185. _____. "Student-Worker Alliance: Viable or Naive--
      Will It Work?" Los Angeles Free Press, August 1,
      1969.

186. Gershman, Carl. "The New Left in the Nixon Era,"
      Pittsburgh Point, January 2, 1969.

187. _____. "SDS, or the New Thermidor," Pittsburgh
      Point, May 5, 1969.

188. Gerth, Hans H. "C. Wright Mills, 1916-1962,"
      Studies on the Left, II, No. 3 (1962), pp. 7-11.

189. Ginsberg, Allen. "Speed Is a No-No," Distant Drum-
      mer, April 2, 1970.

190. Gitlin, Todd. "New Left: Old Traps," Ramparts,
      VIII (September, 1969), p. 20.

191. Gitlin, Todd, and John Simon. "The Meaning of Peo-
      ple's Park," Liberation, XIV (July, 1969), pp. 17-
      21.

192. Gitlin, Todd. "Revolution in the Revolution," Los
      Angeles Free Press, December 5, 1968.

193. Glaberman, Martin. "Marxism, The Working Class
      and the Trade Unions," Studies on the Left, IV, No.
      3 (1964), pp. 65-70.

194. Glazer, Nathan. "The Campus Crucible, Part I; Stu-
      dent Politics and the University," Atlantic, CCXXIV
      (July, 1969), pp. 43-53.

195. _____. "Campus Rights and Responsibilities: A
      Rule for Lawyers," American Scholar, XXXIX (Sum-
      mer, 1970), pp. 445-462.

196. _____. "Student Politics in a Democratic Society,"
      American Scholar, XXXVI (September, 1967), pp.
      202-217.

197. _____. "Student Power in Berkeley," University
      Quarterly, September, 1968, pp. 404-425.

198. Glusman, Paul. "Behind the Chicago Conspiracy
      Trial," Ramparts, VIII (January, 1970), pp. 39-47.

199. _____. "Eldridge on Weatherman; Seale on Ice,"
      Berkeley Tribe, November 7, 1969.

200. _____. "One, Two, Three ... Many SDS's,"
      Ramparts, VII (September, 1969), pp. 6-16.

201. Gold, Elliot M. "New Left Concentration Camps--
      Fact or Fancy?" Los Angeles Free Press, Decem-
      ber 20, 1968.

202. Gold, Mike. "Chicago Conspiracy," Washington Free
      Press, August, 1969.

203. Goldberg, Art. "Oakland 7 Conspiracy Trial Opens,"
      Guardian, January 18, 1969.

204. Goldhaber, Nat. "The Streets Belong to Which Peo-
      ple?" East Village Other, August 6, 1969.

205. Goldman, Lawrence. "W. J. Ghent and the Left,"
      Studies On The Left, III, No. 3 (1963), pp. 21-40.

206.   Goodheart, Eugene. "The Rhetoric of Violence," Nation, CCX (April 6, 1970), pp. 399-402.

207.   Goodhue, T. "Report on the Two Cultures: Orange County, California," New Republic, CLXII (June 20, 1970), pp. 12-13.

208.   Goodman, Paul. "Black Flag of Anarchism," New York Times Magazine, July 14, 1968.

209.   _____. "Reflections on the Moon," Liberation, XIV (August-September, 1969), pp. 60-62.

210.   _____. "Three Types of Resistance," Los Angeles Free Press, March 15, 1968.

211.   Gould, Howard. "Miami's Rainy Day SDS," Daily Planet, May 11, 1970.

212.   Graubard, Stephen R. (ed.). "The Contemporary University: U.S.A.," Daedalus, XCIII (Fall, 1964), pp. 1027-1032.

213.   Greene, W. "Militants Who Play With Dynamite," New York Times Magazine, October 25, 1970, pp. 38-39.

214.   Greenwood, Frank. "Genocide Definition Fits America," Los Angeles Free Press, July 12, 1968.

215.   Griffith, W. "People's Park: 270' x 450' of Confrontation," New York Times Magazine, June 29, 1969, pp. 5-7.

216.   Griswald, Erwin N. "Dissent--1968 Style," Reference Shelf Series, XL, No. 5 (1968), pp. 141-160.

217.   Guerrero, Gene. "A Hip Community," Great Speckled Bird, February 9, 1970.

218.   Halleck, Seymour. "The Generation Gap: A Problem of Values," Think, XXXIV (September-October, 1968), pp. 3-7.

219.   Halstead, Ron. "Dow Chemical Target for Napalm Protest," Fifth Estate, July 30, 1966.

220. Hamburger, Hilary. "SF State College Strike Described
     by Participant, " San Diego Free Press, January 1,
     1969.

221. Harris, David. "The University's Tragedy, " Cauldron,
     October 10, 1967.

222. Harvey, William. "College Students Today: Extrem-
     ists or Activists?" Phi Delta Kappan, LII (October,
     1970), pp. 84-85.

223. Hayakawa, S. I. "Gangsters Cash in on Student Re-
     volt: Exclusive Interview with S. I. Hayakawa, "
     U. S. News and World Report, DCLXVIII (February
     24, 1969), pp. 38-41.

224. Hayden, Tom. "All for Vietnam, " Ramparts, IX
     (September, 1970), pp. 26-27.

225. _____. "Chicago--The Alternative Convention: Ad-
     dress by Tom Hayden at Alternative Convention in
     Grant Park, Thursday, August 29, " Los Angeles
     Free Press, September 13, 1968.

226. _____. "Hayden: The Walker Report, " Old Mole,
     January 13, 1969.

227. _____. "Two, Three, Many Columbias, " Ramparts,
     VI (June 15, 1968), p. 40.

228. Hays, Samuel P. "Right Face, Left Face: The
     Columbia Strike, " Political Science Quarterly, June,
     1969, pp. 311-327.

229. Heath, G. Louis. The Anti-Man Culture: Bureau-
     technocracy and the Schools, by Charles A. Tesconi,
     Jr. and Van Cleve Morris. Book Review. Educa-
     tion and Urban Society, V, No. 1 (November, 1972),
     pp. 121-125.

230. _____. "Berkeley's Educational Opportunity Pro-
     gram, " 14 pp. Disseminated through the ERIC Docu-
     ment Reproduction Service, the ERIC Clearinghouse
     on the Disadvantaged, Teachers College, Columbia
     University, New York, N. Y. 10027. ERIC # 041968.
     The document is available from the ERIC Document
     Reproduction Service, 4936 Fairmont Ave., Bethesda,
     Maryland 20014.

438   Vandals in the Bomb Factory

231. _____. "Berkeley's Ethnic Studies College," Integrated Education, VII, No. 4 (July-August, 1969),
pp. 17-23.

232. _____. "Berkeley Protest: A Mass Movement?"
University College Quarterly, XV, No. 1 (November, 1969), pp. 3-9.

233. _____. "Counter Culture as Counter Technoversity,"
Educational Forum, XXXVI, No. 2 (January, 1972),
pp. 247-253.

234. _____. "Counter Culture at Kickapoo Creek,"
School & Society, XCIX, No. 2333 (April, 1971),
pp. 247-250.

235. _____. Ecotactics, The Environmental Handbook,
and The Promised Land. Book Review. Harvard
Educational Review, XL, No. 3 (August, 1970), pp.
498-504.

236. _____. "Needed: A College of the Human Environment," Educational Leadership, XXIX, No. 3 (December, 1971), pp. 261-264.

237. _____. "Political Extra-Curricula at Uppsala and
California," School & Society, XCVII, No. 2317
(April, 1969), pp. 223-227.

238. _____. "The Sources of Berkeley Student Protest
and the Theory of Mass Society," School of Education, University of California, Berkeley, 1966, 21
pp. Mimeographed.

239. _____. "Student Activism at Berkeley after 1964"
in Brickman, William W. and Stanley Lehrer (eds.),
Conflict and Change on the Campus: The Response
to Student Hyperactivism, New York: Society for the
Advancement of Education, 1970, pp. 160-169.

240. _____. "Student Unionism at the University of Uppsala," Educational Forum, XXXIV, No. 2 (January,
1970), pp. 235-237.

241. _____. "Voucher-Financed Higher Education,"
College Student Journal, V, No. 3 (November-De-
cember, 1971), pp. 57-60.

242. "Heavy Time in Pig City," Fifth Estate, October 16, 1969, p. 3.

243. Heimel, Cynthia. "Crepe Paper Revolutionaries," Distant Drummer, April 17, 1969.

244. Heitzer, Art. "San Francisco State Students Continue Protest," Kaleidoscope, January 17, 1969.

245. Henderson, Algo D. "Brick Throwing at the Colleges," National Association of Student Personnel Administrators Journal, VIII (July, 1970), pp. 17-28.

246. Hentoff, Nat. "A Generation without a Future," Evergreen Review, XIII (June, 1969), p. 47.

247. Herbers, John. "Critical Test for the Nonviolent Way," New York Times Magazine, July 5, 1964, p. 5.

248. Herman, Edward S. "The Alice in Wonderland Economics of the SDS Labor Committee," Distant Drummer, October 11, 1969.

249. _____. "More on SDS: Labor Committee Economics," Distant Drummer, October 23, 1969.

250. Herman, Joseph. "Injunctive Control of Disruptive Student Demonstrations," Virginia Law Review, LVI (Spring, 1970), pp. 215-238.

251. Herrera, F. "Generation Gap and International Development, Youth Movement," Americas, XXII (April, 1970), pp. 13-20.

252. Hessen, Robert. "Campus or Battleground? Columbia Is a Warning to all American Universities," Son of Jabberwock, November 8, 1968.

253. Higby, Kirby. "The South Campus Caper," Berkeley Barb, May 20, 1969.

254. Himmelbauer, Sue. "War Tax Resistance," Pittsburgh Point, March 12, 1970.

255. Hinckle, Warren, Robert Scheer, and Sol Stern. "The University on the Make (Or How MSU Helped Arm

Madame Nhu)," Muckrakers Guide, Ramparts, Special Collector's edition, n. d., pp. 52-60.

256. Hitchcock, James. "The Romantic Rebel on the Campus," Yale Review, LVII (Autumn, 1957), pp. 31-37.

257. Hodges, Donald Clark. "Socialists in Search of an Ethic," Studies on the Left, III, No. 2 (1963), pp. 14-33.

258. Hoffman, Abbie. "How SDS Spurned the Yippies," Distant Drummer, April 24, 1969.

259. _____. "Revolution Can Be Fun," Pittsburgh Point, January 29, 1970.

260. _____. "The United States of Special Effects," Pittsburgh Point, July 31, 1969.

261. Hoffman, Fred. "San Francisco State: When Worlds Collide," Los Angeles Free Press, December 28, 1968.

262. Hoffman, Joan. "Interview with Mark Rudd," Los Angeles Free Press, October 11, 1968.

263. Hofstadter, Richard. "Columbia's Ordeal," Phi Delta Kappan, L (September, 1968), pp. 15-17.

264. _____. "The Future of American Violence," Harper's, CCXL (April, 1970), pp. 47-53.

265. Holland, Vincent. "The New Left," News from Nowhere, September, 1968.

266. Holtom, Gerald. "The Nuclear Disarmament Symbol," Win Peace and Freedom through Non-Violent Action, V, No. 17 (October 1, 1969), p. 27.

267. Hook, Sidney. "Neither Blind Obedience Nor Uncivil Disobedience," New York Times Magazine, LII (June 5, 1966), p. 3.

268. _____. "Social Protest and Civil Obedience," Humanist, XXVII (1967), pp. 157-159.

269. _____. "Students, Universities," Phi Delta Kappan, LI (December, 1969), pp. 195-198.

270. _____. "Trojan Horse in American Higher Educa-
     tion," Educational Record, Winter, 1969, pp. 21-29.

271. _____. "Who Is Responsible for Campus Violence,"
     Saturday Review, LII (April 19, 1969), pp. 22-25.

272. Hoover, John Edgar. "The SDS and the High Schools,"
     PTA Magazine, LXIV (January, 1970), pp. 2-5.
     (Part II--LXIV, February, 1970, pp. 8-9).

273. Horowitz, David. "Bertrand Russell: The Final Pas-
     sion," Ramparts, VIII (April, 1970), pp. 38-43.

274. _____. "Hand-me-down Marxism and the New Left,"
     Ramparts, VIII (September, 1969), pp. 16-19.

275. _____. "Sinews of Empire," Ramparts, VIII (Oc-
     tober, 1969), pp. 33-43.

276. Horowitz, Irving Louis (ed.). "Anti-American Genera-
     tion," Trans-action, VI (September, 1969), pp. 3-80.

277. Horowitz, Irving Louis. "The Unfinished Writings of
     C. Wright Mills: The Last Phase," Studies on the
     Left, III, No. 4 (1963), pp. 3-23.

278. "How SDS Will Stir up Workers," Nation's Business,
     LVII (July, 1969), pp. 74-79.

279. "How to Foil the SDS," Pittsburgh Point, July 31,
     1969.

280. Howe, Irving. "New Course for the New Left,"
     Saturday Review, LII (May 30, 1970), pp. 8-11.

281. _____. "Political Terrorism: Hysteria on the
     Left," New York Times Magazine, April 12, 1970,
     p. 25.

282. Hutchins, Francis G. "The Campus Crucible: Mor-
     alists against Managers," Atlantic, CCXXIV (July,
     1969), pp. 53-56.

283. Igletzin, Lynne B. "Violence and American Democra-
     cy," Journal of Social Issues, XXVI (Winter, 1970),
     pp. 165-186.

284. Ingerson, David. "Politics of Sacrifice," Burning River News, June 23, 1969.

285. Israeli, Phineas. "Student Masses Win: UC Battle," Berkeley Barb, January 31, 1969.

286. Ivey, Allen E., and Westen H. Morrill. "Confrontation, Communication and Encounter: A Conceptual Framework for Student Development," Journal of the Association of Deans and Administrators of Student Affairs, VII (April, 1970), pp. 226-234.

287. Jacobs, Paul. "Prelude to Riot--A View of Urban America from the Bottom," Los Angeles Free Press, January 12, 1968.

288. Jacobson, Jon. "Strike Supporters Ready for Campus Whenever It Blows," Berkeley Barb, January 3, 1969.

289. Jay, Martin. "Metapolitics of Utopianism," Dissent, XVII (July-August, 1970), p. 342.

290. Jenkins, Don. "A Non-Interview with Tom Hayden," Reconstruction, March 3, 1969.

291. Jensen, Pennfield. "A Student Manifesto on the Environment," Natural History, LXXIX (April, 1970), pp. 20-22.

292. "Jerry Farber Talks at SDSC--Knocks Grading," San Diego Free Press, November 30, 1968.

293. Jezer, Martin. "A Yippie History," Florida Free Press, June 30, 1968.

294. _____. "Earth Read-Out. How Many Harvests Have We Left?" East Village Other, February 4, 1970.

295. Johnson, Dale L. "On the Ideology of the Campus Revolution," Studies on the Left, I, No. 4 (1961), pp. 73-75.

296. Johnston, Art. "The Lesson of the Battle of the People's Park," Ann Arbor Argus, June 19, 1969.

297. Johnston, O. W. "Amnesty vs. Order on College
      Campuses," School & Society, XCVI (October 26,
      1968), pp. 364-365.

298. Johnstone, Billy. "Woodstock Is Beautiful," Grok,
      June, 1970.

299. Jones, Ruth M. "New Mobe Plans Fall Offensive,"
      Pittsburgh Point, July 7, 1969.

300. Josephson, Eric, and Geoffrey Bauman. "The Persecu-
      tion and Suicide of SDS," Pittsburgh Point, June 26,
      1969.

301. Kampf, Louis. "The Radical Faculty," Humanist,
      XXIX (December, 1969), pp. 9-10.

302. Katz, Joseph, and Nevitt Sanford. "Causes of the
      Student Revolution," Saturday Review, XLVIII (De-
      cember 18, 1965), pp. 64-66.

303. Katzman, Don. "The New Left as American as Apple
      Pie," East Village Other, February 7, 1969.

304. Kaufman, Arnold S. "Future for Dissidents: Radical
      Education and Conventional Politics," Commonweal,
      LXXXIX (November 29, 1968), pp. 314-317.

305. _____. "Teach-ins: New Force for the Times,"
      Nation, June 21, 1965, pp. 666-670.

306. Kaufman, Bob. "The Berkeley Liberation Program:
      Who Does It Speak For? Who Does It Speak To?"
      Peninsula Observer, July 14, 1969.

307. Kaufman, George. "Confrontation Politics New Radical
      Weapon," Berkeley Barb, February 18, 1966.

308. Kearn, Francis E. "Campus Activism," Yale Review,
      LVIII (Autumn, 1968), pp. 28-44.

309. Keating, Kenneth B. "The Nature of Responsible Dis-
      sent: An Analysis of the Responsibilities of Dis-
      senters and the Duties of the Ruling Majority," New
      York State Bar Journal, XLI (1967), pp. 52-58.

310. Kelman, S. "Beyond New Leftism," Commentary,
      XLVII (February, 1969), pp. 67-71.

311. Keniston, Kenneth. "Report Analysis: Fact-Finding
      Commission on Columbia Disturbances; Cox Commis-
      sion, " Harvard Educational Review (Spring, 1969),
      pp. 337-339.

312. _____. "Students, Drugs, and Protest, " Current
      (February, 1969), pp. 5-19.

313. _____. "What's Bugging the Students?" Educa-
      tional Record, LI (Spring, 1970), pp. 116-129.

314. _____. "You Have to Grow up in Scarsdale to Know
      How Bad Things Really Are, " New York Times
      Magazine, April 27, 1969, pp. 27-29.

315. _____. "Youth, Change and Violence, " American
      Scholar, Spring, 1968.

316. Kerpelman, Larry C. "Student Political Activism
      and Ideology: Comparative Characteristics of Activ-
      ists and Non-Activists, " Journal of Counseling Psy-
      chology, January, 1969, pp. 8-13.

317. Ketels, Violet, and Renee Weber. "The Student Re-
      volt, " Main Currents in Modern Thought, 1968,
      pp. 123-129.

318. King, Lawrence T. "Pickets in the Valley, " Common-
      weal, LXXIII (October 14, 1960), pp. 64-67.

319. King, Martin Luther Jr. "Declaration of Independence
      from the War in Vietnam, " Ramparts, V (May,
      1967), pp. 33-37.

320. _____. "Nonviolence and Racial Justice, " Christian
      Century, LXXIV (February 6, 1957), pp. 165-167.

321. _____. "Pilgrimage to Non-Violence, " Christian
      Century, LXXVI (April 13, 1960), pp. 439-441.

322. Kirk, Russell. "The University and Revolution: An
      Insane Conjunction, " Intercollegiate Review, Winter,
      1969-1970, p. 6.

323. Kissinger, Clark. "SDS Founder Attacked, " Fifth
      Estate, May 15, 1969.

324. Kittredge, Jack. "Community and Struggle at University of Wisconsin," New Left Notes, May 27, 1966.

325. Knox, G. H. C. "Notes of a Young Radical; Arts Festival at Columbia University to Benefit Political Prisoners," Saturday Review, LIII (August 15, 1970), pp. 48-51.

326. Kohn, Jaokoy. "I Saw the Best Minds of My Generation," East Village Other, March 14, 1969.

327. Kopkind, Andrew. "Hard Times: Up the Country," Ramparts, IX (December, 1970), pp. 8-9.

328. Kramer, Mark. "It's Happened to Their Youngsters Too," High School Independent Press, November 18, 1968.

329. Kramer, Mike. "Counter-Institution Turns to Counter Insurgency," Liberation News Service, April 10, 1969.

330. Kunen, James S. "Why Colleges Are Revolting," News From Nowhere, March, 1969.

331. Kunkin, Art. "Teach-out Organized Following UCLA Ban," Los Angeles Free Press, October 22, 1965.

332. Kurtz, Alan. "Drone Probe Zombie Public Narcotic #1," Grok, May, 1970.

333. Kurtz, Paul. "Misuses of Civil Disobedience," Dissent, January-February, 1970.

334. Lack, Lawrence. "The New Left: Too Cool for Marx?" Los Angeles Free Press, December 9, 1966.

335. Lamb, Robert. "New Reform Party Takes Roots," Campus Underground, December 9, 1968.

336. Lampe, Keith. "Earth Read-out: People's Park Ecology," Madison Kaleidoscope, II, May 20, 1969.

337. _____. "Ecology and the Movement," Win, August, 1969.

338. Lane, Lois. "Leary Love Rap," Berkeley Barb, December 26, 1969.

339.   Lane, R. E.   "Political Education in the Midst of
       Life's Struggles," Harvard Educational Review, Sum-
       mer, 1968, pp. 468-494.

340.   Lang, Berel.   "Civil Disobedience and Nonviolence:
       A Distinction with a Difference," Ethics, LXXX
       (January, 1970), pp. 156-159.

341.   Langston, Robert.   "Politics of Scum," Great Speckled
       Bird, March 2, 1970.

342.   Laqueur, Walter.   "Reflections on Youth Movements,"
       Commentary, XLVII (June, 1969), p. 33.

343.   Lasky, M. J.   "Revolution Diary," Encounter, XXXI
       (August, 1968), pp. 81-92.

344.   Lathrop, Peter (pseud.).   "Teach-ins: New Force or
       Isolated Phenomenon?" Studies On the Left, V, No.
       2 (1965), pp. 41-52.

345.   Leach, William Spencer.   "The White Left--Serious or
       Not?" Fifth Estate, January 9, 1969.

346.   Leary, Timothy, and Richard Alpert.   "The Politics
       of Consciousness Expansion," Harvard Review, I
       (Summer, 1963), pp. 33-37.

347.   Le Blanc, Paul.   "SDS--Past, Present, Future, "
       Pittsburgh Point, July 3, 1969.

348.   _____.   "Theory and Practice," Pittsburgh Fair
       Witness, November 4, 1970.

349.   _____. and Joseph White.   "The Splintering of
       SDS, " Pittsburgh Point, October 16, 1969.

350.   Lens, Sidney.   "Notes on the Chicago Trial," Libera-
       tion, XIV (November, 1969), p. 6.

351.   Lester, Julius.   "To Hell with Protest, " Liberation
       News Service, January 3, 1968.

352.   Levenstein, Chuck.   "The Democratic Convention and
       the New Left," Paper Tiger, May, 1968.

353.   Levin, B.   "... mare's nest," Spectator, CCIV (Jan-
       uary 29, 1960), pp. 131-132.

354. Levine, Herbert. "Common Front at Buffalo," Nation, CCX (May 4, 1970), pp. 520-522.

355. Levitt, Dennis, and Linda Gage. "The Manifesto of the National Front for Liberation," Los Angeles Free Press, December 25, 1970.

356. Levitt, Dennis. "Nixon's Security Act 1984," Los Angeles Free Press, August 14, 1970.

357. Lewis, Joseph. "Looking Back on the Laughable 60's," Pittsburgh Point, January 15, 1970.

358. Liberation News Service. "Abbie Hoffman Tells It Like It Is ... Speaking of Pigs," Los Angeles Free Press, October 4, 1968.

359. _____. "Against the American Grain: Confrontation in Berkeley," Distant Drummer, May 29, 1969.

360. _____. "Conspiracy Fights Government Spy Tactics," Distant Drummer, November 2, 1969.

361. _____. "Dave Dellinger Goes to Jail," Pittsburgh Point, February 12, 1970.

362. _____. "Law Commune," Great Speckled Bird, September 1, 1969.

363. Liberation News Service, and E. G. Crichton. "People's Park," News From Nowhere, I (Summer, 1969), p. 6.

364. Liberation News Service. "SDS Splits with Progressive Labor," Dallas Notes, July 2, 1969.

365. _____. "United Front against Fascism," Fifth Estate, July 10, 1969.

366. _____. "Why a United Front against Fascism?" Peninsula Observer, July 28, 1969.

367. Lifton, Robert J. "The Young and the Old: Notes on a New History," Atlantic, CCXXIV (October, 1969), pp. 83-88.

368. Lipow, Arthur. "Assault on Academic Freedom at UC," Independent Socialist, September, 1968.

369. Lipset, Seymour Martin. "Political Thrust Motivating Campus Turmoil," Saturday Review, LII (March, 1969), pp. 23-25.

370. _____. "Rebellion on Campus," American Education, IV (October, 1968), pp. 28-31.

371. _____. "Student Politics," Comparative Education Review, X, No. 2, 1966.

372. Lipton, Lawrence. "The Dick-Daley Revised History of CZechago," Los Angeles Free Press, September 20, 1968.

373. _____. "Politics of Ecstasy: Tim Leary, Parapolitics Plus Ecstasy," Los Angeles Free Press, June 11, 1969.

374. _____. "Yippies to Visit Hog Capital," Los Angeles Free Press, August 16, 1968.

375. "Local SDS Breaks with National Office," Northwest Passage, October 21, 1969.

376. Lockshin, Arnold. "The Movement and Suppression," Paper Tiger, November, 1967.

377. Loewenberg, Peter. "An Interview with Richard Drinnon," Studies on the Left, I, No. 4 (1961), pp. 76-81.

378. Lomax, Louis E. "Mississippi Eyewitness," Muckrakers Guide, Ramparts, Special Collector's Edition, n. d., pp. 20-24.

379. Long, Everett. "The Politics of Pot," Kudzu, August 2, 1969.

380. Lovin, Roger. "Crusin in the Concrete Commune," Los Angeles Free Press, July 3, 1970.

381. Lowenstein, Eddie. "Where Have All the Protestors Gone?" Distant Drummer, January 29, 1970.

382. Lukas, J. Anthony. "The Making of a Yippie," Esquire, LXXII (November, 1969), pp. 126-134.

383. _____. "The Second Confrontation in Chicago,"
New York Times Magazine, March 29, 1970, pp.
10-11.

384. Lusky, Louis, and Mary H. Lusky. "Columbia 1968:
The Wound Unhealed," Political Science Quarterly,
LXXXIV (June, 1969), pp. 169-288.

385. Lyman, Mel. "To All Who Would Know," Avatar,
July 21, 1966.

386. _____. "What Is the Underground?" Avatar, July
7, 1967.

387. Lynd, Staughton. "Guerrilla History in Gary," Liberation, XIV (October, 1969), pp. 17-20.

388. _____. "A Program for Post-Campus Radicals,"
Liberation, XIV (August-September, 1969), pp. 44-
45.

389. _____. "Radicals and White Racism," Liberation,
XIV (July, 1969), pp. 26-30.

390. _____. "So You Want a Revolution?" News from
Nowhere, December, 1968.

391. _____. "Socialism: The Forbidden Word," Studies
on the Left, III, No. 3 (1963), pp. 14-20.

392. _____. "Waiting for Righty: The Lessons of the
Oswald Case," Studies on the Left, IV, No. 2 (1964),
pp. 135-141.

393. Lynn, Conrad J. "We Must Disobey! Civil Disobedi-
ence: An Analysis and Rationale, Significant Cases
Involving Negro Rights as Compared with Cases that
Concern Draft Card Burning, Refusal of Induction
and Other Issues Relating to the Prosecution of the
War in Vietnam," New York University Law Review,
XLIII (October, 1968), pp. 648-720.

394. McDonald, Donald. "The American Dilemma: 1967.
An Interview with Gunnar Myrdal," Center Magazine,
Center for the Study of Democratic Institutions, I,
No. 1 (October-November, 1967), pp. 30-33.

395. McKelvey, Donald. "Some Notes on Participatory Democracy," New Left Notes, May 6, 1966.

396. McLaughlin, Joseph F. "Free Education," Pittsburgh Point, July 31, 1969.

397. McPeak, Alice. "Kent, Kent, Kent, Kent," Burning River News, April 26, 1969.

398. McWilliams, Wilson Carey. "Civil Disobedience and Contemporary Constitutionalism: The American Case," Comparative Politics, I (1969), pp. 211-227.

399. Maher, Michael. "War in Berkeley," Reconstruction, I, No. 8 (1969), p. 4.

400. Majdalany, Gebran. "Reflections on Racism, Anti-Semitism, and Zionism," Liberation, XIV (November, 1969), pp. 36-39.

401. Malone, D. H. "Testimony on Student Unrest before California Legislature Committee," American Association of University Professors Bulletin, LV (March, 1969), pp. 91-93.

402. Marcuse, Herbert. "The End of Utopia," Ramparts, VIII (April, 1970), pp. 28-34.

403. _____. "Marcuse on Class Conflict, Black Power, Universities," Guardian, November 16, 1968.

404. _____. "Marcuse on the Hippie Revolution," Berkeley Barb, August 4, 1967.

405. _____. "Marcuse on Radical Perspectives," Liberation News Service, December 12, 1968.

406. Marighella, Carlos. "The Job of an Urban Guerrilla," Los Angeles Free Press, November 6, 1970.

407. Marine, Gene. "America the Raped," Ramparts, V (April, 1967), pp. 34-45.

408. Marine, Gene, and Reese Erlich. "School's Out," Ramparts, December 14-28, 1968, pp. 19-25.

409. Marshall, Burke. "The Protest Movement and the Law," Virginia Law Review, LI (1965), pp. 785-803.

410. Marshall, Sue. "Genocide Petition Speed-up Called for," Los Angeles Free Press, October 23, 1970.

411. Martin, Rex. "Civil Disobedience," Ethics, LXXX (January, 1970), pp. 123-137.

412. Marx, Gary T. "Civil Disorder and the Agents of Social Control," Journal of Social Issues, XXVI (Winter, 1970), pp. 19-57.

413. Maxson, R. E. "Peace Ecology Coalition," Los Angeles Free Press, August 21, 1970.

414. May, Henry F. "Living with Crisis: A View from Berkeley," The American Scholar, XXXVIII (Autumn, 1969), pp. 588-605.

415. Mead, Margaret. "Why Students Are Angry," Redbook, CXXXII (April, 1969), p. 50.

416. _____. "Youth Revolt: The Future Is Now," Saturday Review, LIII (January 10, 1970), pp. 23-25.

417. Melman, S. "American Needs, and Limits on Resources: The Priorities Problem," Teachers College Record, LXVIII (March, 1967), pp. 493-498.

418. Meredith, Robert. "The New Left: An Introductory Bibliographical Commentary," Radical American Studies, I (May, 1970), pp. 3-8.

419. Metefsky, George. "Right On, Culture Freaks!" Miami Free Press, October 8, 1969.

420. Miles, Michael. "Whose University?" New Republic, April 12, 1969.

421. Miller, William G. "New Brunswick: Community Action Project," Studies on the Left, V, No. 2 (1965), pp. 74-79.

422. Millett, Kate. "Sexual Politics," New Republic, CLXIII (August 1, 1970), p. 26.

423. Mills, C. Wright. "On the New Left," Studies on the Left, I, No. 4 (1961), pp. 63-72.

424.   Mintz, Elliot.   "We Were Freed by a Great Network
       of Love," Los Angeles Free Press, October 23,
       1970.

425.   Mitchell, Bill.   "Coffee Houses Open across U.S. to
       Fulfill Social Needs of Young People," Old Market
       Press, February 1, 1968.

426.   Mitchell, Juliet.   "The Longest Revolution," New Left
       Review, XL, November-December, 1966.

427.   Mitzman, Arthur.   "The Campus Radical in 1960,"
       Dissent, VII (Spring, 1960), pp. 142-148.

428.   Moffett, Toby.   "High-School Students: Somebody's
       Stealing Their Future," Electronic Age, XXX (Winter,
       1970-1971), pp. 7-9.

429.   Moore, P. W.   "Wiretaps: Disclosed or Leaked?
       Trial of the Chicago 8," Nation, CCIX (October 27,
       1969), pp. 432-434.

430.   Morris, Peter.   "The Meaning of the Berkeley War,"
       New Society, July 10, 1969, pp. 47-49.

431.   Moses, Bob.   "Mississippi: 1961-1962," Liberation,
       XIV (January, 1970), pp. 6-17.

432.   Moss, Andrew.   "Student Movement Prepares for Revo-
       lutionary Work," Peninsula Observer, July 14, 1969.

433.   Mulherin, Cathy.   "The People Need Their Park,"
       Peninsula Observer, June 30, 1969.

434.   Mulherin, Cathy, and Jim Mulherin.   "People's Park:
       Living Socialism Is Killed," Peninsula Observer,
       May 26, 1969.

435.   Muller, Steven.   "Restructuring the University," Col-
       lege and University Journal, VIII (Fall, 1969), pp.
       49-54.

436.   Nachman, Larry David.   "The Marxist Romantics:
       Obituary for SDS," Nation, CCIX (November 24,
       1969), pp. 558-561.

437.   Nagler, Michael.   "Berkeley: The Demonstrations,"
       Studies on the Left, V, No. 1 (1965), pp. 55-62.

438. Naison, Mark. "In Defense of SDS," Liberation, XIV (August-September, 1969), pp. 31-34.

439. Naramore, John A. "ROTC Wounded!" Reconstruction, May 21, 1969.

440. Neff, C. B. "Administrative Challenge of the New Student Activism," Journal of Higher Education, February, 1968, pp. 69-76.

441. Neff, Richard. "Marihuana ... A Key Issue," Distant Drummer, May 2, 1970.

442. _____. "SDS, Rizzo, the VFW and the Plot to Destroy Nearly Everything," Distant Drummer, April 3, 1969.

443. Neumann, Harry. "The Permanent War of Students and Teachers," Journal of General Education, XXI (January, 1970), pp. 271-279.

444. New University Conference. "Degrading Education," Spectator, April 22, 1969.

445. Newcomb, Theodore. "University Heal Thyself," Political Science Quarterly, June, 1969, pp. 351-356.

446. Nobbs, Russ. "Spokane Freaked by Story of 10,000 Hippies to Come," Spokane Natural, May 9, 1969.

447. Novak, Michael. "Students and the University: The Vacuum," Christian Century, LXXXVII (April 8, 1970), p. 413.

448. O'Brien, Basil. "Gay Liberation Front Doesn't Want Your Acceptance," Distant Drummer, June 18, 1970.

449. O'Brien, Conor Cruise. "Contemporary Forms of Imperialism," Studies on the Left, V, No. 2 (1965), pp. 13-26.

450. Ofari, Earl. "The Legacy of Martin Luther King, Jr.: I Have a Dream," Liberation News Service, April 5, 1969.

451. Oglesby, Carl. "A Program for Liberals," Ramparts, VI (February, 1968), p. 20.

452. O'Loughlin, Ray. "Second U.S. Revolution," Burning River News, July 21, 1969.

453. Oppenheimer, Martin. "Alienation or Participation: The Sociology of Participatory Democracy," New Left Notes, November 25, 1966.

454. _____. "The Student Movement as a Response to Alienation," Journal of Human Relations, 1968, pp. 1-16.

455. Orbell, J. M. "Protest Participation among Southern Negro College Students," American Political Science Review, LXI (June, 1967), pp. 446-456.

456. Osborn, Jim. "High School Walkouts: Demonstrations Sweep L.A. Area, Students Protest Sub-Standard Facilities, Faulty Curriculum," Los Angeles Free Press, March 15, 1968.

457. Oslick, Alan. "Why Have Families?" Distant Drummer, October 11, 1969.

458. Our Man in Prague (Hard Times). "Counter-Revolution within the Counter-Revolution," Hard Times, November 10, 1969.

459. Padgett, I. F. "New Breed in Search of a New Morality," Liberal Education, October, 1968, pp. 435-442.

460. Paine, Tom. "Radical Press: More Hassle," Liberation News Service, January 16, 1969.

461. Parent, A. "The SDS and Student Unrest," Conscience, August, 1969.

462. Parkinson, Tom. "Berkeley Litany," Spectator, July 15, 1969.

463. Peck, Abe. "Two Thousand Scream at Seale Trial in Chicago," Los Angeles Free Press, June 19, 1970.

464. Peck, Sidney M. "The Political Consciousness of Rank-and-File Labor Leaders," Studies on the Left, I, No. 4 (1961), pp. 43-51.

465.   Peddle, Iris.   "A Word on our Commune, " San Diego
        Free Press, September 9, 1969.

466.   Peek, B. M.   "SDS: It's Too Bad, " Conscience,
        August, 1969.

467.   Pemberton, John Jr.   "War Protester, " Current His-
        tory, LV (July, 1968), pp. 23-27.

468.   Perkins, David.   "Picknicking with the Liberals, "
        Screw, August 1, 1969.

469.   Perkins, Emily, and Jay Sargeant.   "Ally with Campus
        Workers!" New Left Notes, July 30, 1969.

470.   Peters, C. F.   "Activism: The Message It Holds for
        Placement and Recruitment, " Journal of College
        Placement, February, 1969, pp. 49-52.

471.   Peterson, Dan.   "Hip Village--Fact and Fiction, "
        Kaleidoscope, March 15, 1968.

472.   Peterson, Richard E.   "The Student Left in American
        Higher Education, " Daedalus, I (Winter, 1968), pp.
        293-317.

473.   Petras, James.   "Confrontation Politics and Intellec-
        tuals in Retreat, " Liberation News Service, July 5,
        1969.

474.   Podhoretz, Norman.   "Like Fathers Like Sons, "
        Commentary, L (August, 1970), p. 21.

475.   _____.   "Revolutionary Suicide, " Commentary, L
        (September, 1970), p. 23.

476.   Pohlmann, Bruce.   "High School Action, " New Left
        Notes, February 3, 1967.

477.   Popkin, Richard.   "Thanatology: A Blossoming, " San
        Diego Free Press, June 13, 1969.

478.   Powell, Lewis F.   "Civil Disobedience: Prelude to
        Revolution, " New York State Bar Journal, XL (1968),
        pp. 161-188.

479.   Powell, R. S. Jr.   "Student Power and the Student

Role in Institutional Governance," Liberal Education, LV (March, 1969), pp. 24-31.

480. "Power at Cornell out of the Barrel of a Gun," Black Panther, May 11, 1969.

481. Pratt, Annis. "Abortion March," Great Speckled Bird, May 12, 1969.

482. Primula, Ron. "Computers Threaten Right to Privacy," Los Angeles Free Press, January 17, 1969.

483. Puner, Nicholas. "Civil Disobedience: An Analysis and Rationale," New York University Law Review, XLIII (1968), p. 720.

484. Rabinowitz, Dorothy. "The Radicalized Professor: A Portrait," Commentary, L (July, 1970), pp. 62-64.

485. Rabinowitz, Victor. "An Exchange on SNCC," Studies on the Left, V, No. 2 (1965), pp. 83-95.

486. Rader, Dotson. "More about Columbia," New Republic, CLVIII (June 8, 1961), pp. 23-25.

487. Rader, Dotson, and Craig Anderson. "Rebellion at Columbia: Report from the Barricades," New Republic, CLVIII (May 11, 1968), pp. 9-11.

488. Raleigh, Doug. "Alternative Education," Los Angeles Free Press, June 6, 1969.

489. Ransom, David. "Fascism," Peninsula Observer, July 28, 1969.

490. _____. "Federal Repression Hits SDS National Office," Peninsula Observer, May 26, 1969.

491. Raskin, Marcus G. "The Man Who Came in from the Cold (War)," Ramparts, VI (February, 1968), pp. 32-34.

492. Raup, Philip Jr. "An Activist Party for the New Left," Paper Tiger, May, 1967.

493. Recca, Ron. "Spaceship Earth ... Countdown to Death," Grok, April, 1970.

494. Redlich, Norman, and Kenneth R. Feinberg. "Individ-
      ual Conscience and the Selective Conscientious Ob-
      jector: The Right Not to Kill, " New York University
      Law Review, XLIV (1969), pp. 875-900.

495. Reinholz, Mary. "Violence Breeds Counter-Violence:
      Marcuse, " Los Angeles Free Press, May 23, 1969.

496. Richer, Ed. "Campus Liberation: Another Look at
      Academic Freedom, " Los Angeles Free Press,
      October 16, 1970.

497. _____. "The Student Strike: Collegiate Revolt In-
      evitable, " Los Angeles Free Press, May 29, 1970.

498. Richmond, Al. "Workers against the War, " Ramparts,
      IX (September, 1970), pp. 28-32.

499. Richter, Edward. "Peace Activism in Vietnam, "
      Studies on the Left, VI, No. 1 (January-February,
      1966), pp. 54-63.

500. Rieker, Richard. "The Issue Is Human Misery, "
      Pittsburgh Point, July 17, 1969.

501. _____. "Our Children Are Turning On, " Pittsburgh
      Point, June 26, 1969.

502. Riesman, David. "Changing Campus and a Changing
      Society, " School & Society, XCVII (April, 1969),
      pp. 215-222.

503. Robb, Charles C. "Attack of the Weatherwomen, "
      Pittsburgh Point, September 11, 1969.

504. Roberts, Thomas B. "Campus Explosion, " College
      and University Journal, IX (Spring, 1970), pp. 35-36.

505. Robinson, Chris. "But What Do the Students Really
      Want?" Guardian, June 7, 1969.

506. _____ (comp.). "A Week in the Life of ... The
      Campus Revolt, " Guardian, April 26, 1969.

507. Rose, William. "Hippy--I OKai AY, " Distant Drum-
      mer, September 25, 1969.

508. _____. "Which Way for Hippies in New Mexico?"
     Liberation News Service, September 11, 1969.

509. Rosen, Sumner M. "The Case for a Radical Politics,"
     Studies on the Left, IV, No. 3 (1964), pp. 32-38.

510. Rosenblum, Sue. "Fellowship Farm," New Hard
     Times, November 21, 1968.

511. Rossi, Alice. "Women--Terms of Liberation," Dis-
     sent, XVII (November-December, 1970), p. 531.

512. Rossof, Dave. "Report on Oakland United Front Con-
     ference," New Left Notes, July 30, 1969.

513. Roszak, Theodore. "The Making of a Counter Culture,"
     Horizon, XII (Spring, 1970), pp. 20-21.

514. Rothkrug, Barbara. "Women Resisters Destroy Hun-
     dreds of Draft Files," Liberation News Service,
     July 5, 1969.

515. Rowls, Betty M. "Student Unrest Justified," College
     and University Journal, VIII (Fall, 1969), pp. 40-44.

516. Rubenstein, Ben, and Morton Levitt. "Rebellion and
     Responsibility," Yale Review, LVII (August, 1969),
     pp. 16-30.

517. Rubin, Gayle. "Woman as Nigger," Ann Arbor Argus,
     March 28, 1969.

518. Rubin, Jerry. "The Academy Award of Protest,"
     Fifth Estate, April 3, 1969.

519. _____. "What a Day at White Haul," East Village
     Other, December 15, 1967.

520. _____. "The Yippies Are Coming," Florida Free
     Press, March 14, 1968.

521. Rudd, Mark. "Victorious Struggle," Nola Express,
     July 18, 1969.

522. Russell, Bertrand. "Civil Disobedience," New States-
     man, LXI (February, 1961), pp. 245-246.

523. _____. "On American Violence," Ramparts, VIII
(March, 1970), pp. 55-58.

524. Ryan, Sheila. "Violence: Who Do You Believe,"
Chicago Kaleidoscope, February 28, 1969.

525. Sale, J. Kirkpatrick. "Ted Gold: Education for Violence," Nation, CCX (April 13, 1970), pp. 423-429.

526. Salstrom, F. P. "And Peace: A Future in Post-
Urban Communal Living," Los Angeles Free Press,
August 1, 1969.

527. Sampson, Edward E. (ed.). "Stirrings out of Apathy:
Student Activism and the Decade of Protest," Journal
of Social Issues, XXIII, No. 3, July, 1967.

528. Sanford, David. "Kent State Gag," New Republic,
CLXIII (November 7, 1970), pp. 14-17.

529. _____. "Protest at Pennsylvania: A Model for
Campus Dissent?" New Republic, CLX (March 15,
1969), pp. 19-21.

530. Sapir, Marc, and Carrie Sapir. "Students Shut Counterinsurgency Center," Peninsula Observer, May 26,
1969.

531. Sartre, Jean-Paul. "Ideology and Revolution," Studies
On The Left, I (1960), pp. 7-16.

532. _____. "Intellectuals and Revolution: Interview
with Jean-Paul Sartre," Ramparts, IX (December,
1970), pp. 52-55.

533. _____. "On Genocide," Ramparts, VI (February,
1968), pp. 36-42.

534. _____. "A Psychoanalytic Dialogue with a Commentary," Ramparts, VIII (October, 1969), pp. 43-
49.

535. _____. "Sartre's Essay on Genocide," Burning
River News, December 16, 1969.

536. Schechter, Dan, Michael Ansara, and David Kolodney.
"The CIA as an Equal Opportunity Employer,"
Ramparts, VII (June, 1969), pp. 25-33.

537. Schechtman, Michael. "Holiday Commune a Thing to
      Groove," Berkeley Barb, August 25, 1967.

538. Scheer, Robert. "Lord Russell," Ramparts, XV (May,
      1967), pp. 16-23.

539. Schlesinger, Arthur M. Jr. "Existential Politics and
      the Cult of Violence," Phi Delta Kappan, L (Septem-
      ber, 1968), pp. 9-15.

540. Schrag, Peter. "After Kent State: The First Hundred
      Days," Saturday Review, LIII (August 29, 1970), pp.
      12-15.

541. Schroth, B. A. "Violence and Understanding: Campus
      Unrest and the Scranton Report," Catholic World,
      CCXII (December, 1970), pp. 119-122.

542. Schultz, Roy. "Kick Ass Junction," East Village Other,
      April 21, 1970.

543. Scorpio, Paul. "LSD and Me," Distant Drummer,
      February 5, 1970.

544. "S. D. S.," News from Nowhere, I (Summer, 1969),
      p. 8.

545. "SDS ... A Step Forward," Helix, July 4, 1969.

546. "SDS Battles Police," Fifth Estate, July 4, 1969.

547. "The SDS Convention: A Layman's Guide," Helix,
      July 4, 1969.

548. "SDS Five on Trial," Los Angeles Free Press, May
      29, 1970.

549. "SDS in Court," Pittsburgh Point, October 2, 1969.

550. "SDS Ousts Progressive Labor," Williamette Bridge,
      July 7, 1969.

551. "SDS Runs CIA off Duke Campus," North Carolin
      Anvil, February 14, 1970.

552. Seale, Bobby. "Revolutionary Action on Campus and
      Community," Black Panther, January 10, 1970.

Bibliography   461

553. Selkirk, Errol. "The Blood Runs Cold, " Berkeley
      Barb, October 10, 1969.

554. _____. "U. C. Moratorium, " Berkeley Barb, No-
      vember 21, 1969.

555. Semas, Philip W. "At Berkeley Where It All Began,
      Activism Has Become a Way of Life, " Chronicle of
      Higher Education, IV (January 24, 1970), p. 1.

556. _____. "Some Students Will Take up Guns: Panel
      on Campus Unrest Is Told, " Chronicle of Higher Edu-
      cation, IV (August 31, 1970), p. 1.

557. Seward, Becky. "Review of Utica Teach-in on War, "
      New Patriot, January 18, 1968.

558. Shenker, Alan. "Marijuana Causes Immortality, "
      Grok, June 27, 1970.

559. Sherrill, Robert. "Patriotism of Protest, " Nation,
      XIII (December 13, 1965), pp. 463-466.

560. Shoben, Edward J. Jr. "Students and Civil Disobedi-
      ence, " Journal of General Education, October, 1968,
      pp. 218-226.

561. _____. "Toward Remedies for Restlessness: Is-
      sues in Student Unrest, " Liberal Education, May,
      1968, pp. 221-230.

562. Shoben, Edward J. Jr., and P. R. Werdell. "SDS
      and SNCC: Profiles of Two Student Organizations, "
      School & Society, XCVI (October 26, 1968), pp. 365-
      372.

563. Shorris, Earl. "Doctor Hayakawa in Thought and Ac-
      tion, " Ramparts, VIII (November, 1969), pp. 39-42.

564. Shuba, George. "Presidio Mutiny Case: Partial Vic-
      tory, " Liberation News Service, March 22, 1969.

565. Sibley, Mulford Q. "Anonymity, Dissent, and Individual
      Integrity in America, with Questions and Answers, "
      American Academy of Political and Social Science,
      Annals, CCCLXX (1968), pp. 45-57.

566. _____. "Conscience, Law, and the Obligation to
        Obey," Monist, LIV (October, 1970), pp. 556-586.

567. Silber, Irwin. "Five Thousand March against War at
        Fort Dix," Guardian, October 18, 1969.

568. Simmons, Bob. "Yoga and the Psychic Mind," San
        Francisco Oracle, June, 1966.

569. Singer, Cris. "The Chicago Conspiracy," Fifth Estate,
        April 3, 1969.

570. Sisk, John P. "The Intolerable Allegories of Dissent,"
        Catholic World, CCX (November, 1969), pp. 55-58.

571. Sklar, Martin J., and James Weinstein. "Socialism and
        the New Left," Studies on the Left, VI, No. 2
        (March-April, 1966), pp. 62-70.

572. Skolnick, Jerome. "Comment: The Generation Gap,"
        Trans-action, VI (November, 1968), pp. 4-5.

573. _____. "Excerpts from the Politics of Protest,"
        Dallas Notes, February 19, 1969.

574. Slater, R. Giuseppi. "The San Francisco State Strike:
        Eclipse," Distant Drummer, March 13, 1969.

575. _____. "San Francisco State: Struggle Continues,"
        Dallas Notes, February 5, 1969.

576. Smith, Jack A. "Where the Revolution Is At," Guard-
        ian, June 22, 1968.

577. Smith, John. "The Anti-War Movement inside the
        Armed Forces," Independent Socialist, July, 1968.

578. Smith, Michael. "Analysis of a Victory: Free Speech
        for G. I. s," Fifth Estate, May 29, 1969.

579. Smith, Victoria. "Students Live to Fight Another Day:
        From the University of Connecticut," Liberation
        News Service, November 13, 1968.

580. Sontag, Susan. "Some Thoughts on the Right Way
        (for Us) to Love the Cuban Revolution," Ramparts,
        VII (April, 1969), pp. 6-19.

581. Sorel, Jules. "Education for Revolt," Independent So-
      cialist, January, 1967.

582. Spence, Larry D. "Berkeley: What It Demonstrates,"
      Studies on the Left, IV, No. 4 (1965), pp. 63-68.

583. Spiegel, John P. "Campus Conflict and Professional
      Egos," Trans-action, VI (October, 1969), pp. 41-50.

584. _____. "Psychosocial Factors in Riots: Old and
      New," American Journal of Psychiatry, 1968, pp.
      281-285.

585. Spinard, Norman. "The American Revolution 1970--
      Not a Shot Away," Los Angeles Free Press, October
      23, 1970.

586. Starr, Paul. "Black Panthers and White Radicals,"
      Commonweal, June 12, 1970, pp. 294-297.

587. "The Steel City 26: SDS Women Vamp on Pittsburgh,"
      Liberation News Service, September 13, 1969.

588. Stern, Daniel J. "Defensive Reactions to Political
      Anxiety: The American Anti-Communist Liberal and
      the Invasion of Cuba," Studies on the Left, II, No.
      2 (1961), pp. 3-8.

589. Stern, Max. "On Being a Great Power," Los Angeles
      Free Press, December 17, 1966.

590. Stern, Peter S. "Stanford's Community of Consent,"
      Nation, CCXI (September 7, 1970), pp. 174-177.

591. Stern, Sol. "The Defense Intellectuals," Ramparts, V
      (February, 1967), pp. 32-37.

592. _____. "On Herbert Marcuse: The Metaphysics
      of Rebellion," Ramparts, VI (June 29, 1968), pp. 55-
      60.

593. _____. "A Short Account of International Student
      Politics and the Cold War, with Particular Reference
      to the NSA, CIA, etc.," Muckrakers Guide, Ramparts,
      Special Collector's Edition, n.d., pp. 87-97.

594. Stone, Harvey. "G. I. Coffee Houses for Peace," Fifth
      Estate, August 1, 1968.

595.   "Student Activism Steers away from SDS and Toward
        Educational Reforms, " Nation's Schools, LXXXIV
        (July, 1969), p. 41.

596.   Students for a Democratic Society, Press Release.
        "Sculpture Censored, " Los Angeles Free Press,
        April 5, 1968.

597.   _____ . "SDS Calls Pueblo Incident Desperate Move, "
        Fifth Estate, February 15, 1968.

598.   "Student Power Movement, " America, September 28,
        1968.

599.   Such, Rod. "A New Constitution?" Guardian, Septem-
        ber 19, 1970.

600.   Tannenbaum, Abraham J. (ed.). "Alienated Youth, "
        Journal of Social Issues, XXV, No. 2, April, 1969.

601.   Taylor, Harold. "The Student Revolution, " Phi Delta
        Kappan, LI (October, 1969), pp. 62-67.

602.   Tepperman, Jean. "Communal Living--You Have to
        Start or You Won't Get It after the Revolution, "
        Old Mole, October 24, 1969.

603.   Tessler, Mark A., and Ronald D. Hedlund. "Students
        Aren't Crazies, " New Republic, CLXIII (September
        12, 1970), pp. 17-18.

604.   Thelwell, Michael. "From San Francisco State and
        Cornell: Two Black Radicals Report on Their Cam-
        pus Struggles, " Ramparts, VIII (July, 1969), pp.
        47-59.

605.   Thomas, Norman. "Toward Total Disarmament, "
        Dissent, VII (Spring, 1960), pp. 163-166.

606.   Thomas, Wendell. "Intentional Communities Make for
        Peace, " Modern Utopian, May 8, 1964.

607.   Thornburg, Richard L. "The Continuing American
        Revolution, " Pittsburgh Point, September 18, 1969.

608.   Tolstoy, Leo. "Advice to a Draftee, " Atlantic Month-
        ly, CCXXI (1968), pp. 56-57.

609. Tornquist, Elizabeth. "Causes of Stanford Violence
      Ignored," North Carolin Anvil, November 8, 1969.

610. _____. "Dope People in Raleigh, " North Carolin
      Anvil, April 18, 1970.

611. Trent, James W., and Judith L. Croise. "Commit-
      ment and Conformity in the American College, "
      Journal of Social Issues, XXIII (July, 1967), pp. 34-
      51.

612. Trilling, Diana. "On the Steps of Low Library, " Com-
      mentary, XLVI (November, 1968), pp. 29-55.

613. Trimberger, Ellen K. "Why a Rebellion at Columbia
      Was Inevitable, " Trans-action, V (September, 1968),
      pp. 28-38.

614. Trounstine, Phil. "Tricky Dick's Reinforced Protec-
      tive Reaction Strikes, " Free You, May 11, 1970.

615. Truskier, Andy. "Epilogue to People's Park, " Chinook,
      October 23, 1969.

616. Tumin, Melvin M. "Violence and Democracy, " Dis-
      sent, XVII (July-August, 1970), p. 321.

617. Urquhart, Mike. "State of Emergency, " Independent
      Socialist, March, 1969.

618. Vanocur, Sander. "The Public and Higher Education, "
      College and University Journal, VIII (Fall, 1969),
      pp. 59-63.

619. Vick, George R. "Confrontation in the University:
      Academic Freedom Versus Social Commitment, "
      Intercollegiate Review, VI, Spring, 1970.

620. Waibel, Terry. "Tenants Organize, " Pittsburgh
      Point, March 19, 1970.

621. Wald, George. "A Generation in Search of a Future, "
      Grinding Stone, April, 1969.

622. Wallace, Rue, Warren Friedman, and Linda Friedman.
      "The Movement at Work: The Community College
      Scene, " Liberation, XIV (October, 1969), pp. 34-37.

623. Waller, Joseph. "On Contradictions," Burning Spear, September 21, 1970.

624. Walzer, Michael. "Obligation to Disobey," Ethics, LXXVII (1967), pp. 163-175.

625. _____. "Politics of Non-Violent Resistance," Dissent, VII (Autumn, 1960), pp. 369-376.

626. "A Warning from the 'Weathermen,'" Pittsburgh Point, October 2, 1969.

627. Warren, Dave. "How the Berkeley 3 Won Their Acquittal," Militant, November 14, 1969.

628. Warwick, Dick. "The Rise of Fascist America," Conscience, August, 1969.

629. Waskow, Arthur I. "Business, Religion, and the Left," Liberation, XIV (August-September, 1969), pp. 46-48.

630. _____. "Nonviolence and Creative Disorder," Christian Century, LXXXII (October 13, 1965), pp. 1253-1255.

631. _____. "The Religious Upwelling of the New Left," Liberation, XIV (July, 1969), pp. 36-37.

632. Waters, Mary Alice. "Key Problems Facing Anti-war Forces," Militant, November 14, 1969.

633. Watts, Alan. "Wit's End: Alan Watts 'Talks'," Grok, May, 1970.

634. Watts, William A., Steve Lynch, and David Whittaker. "Alienation and Activism in Today's College Youth: Socialization Patterns and Current Family Relationships," Journal of Counseling Psychology, January, 1969, pp. 1-7.

635. Watts, William A., and David Whittaker. "Profile of a Non-Conformist Youth Culture: A Study of the Berkeley Non-Students," Sociology of Education, Spring, 1968, pp. 178-200.

636. Ways, Max. "University's Position Is Secure But,"

College and University Journal, VIII (Fall, 1969), pp. 55-58.

637. "Weathermen Hit Rough Weather," Pittsburgh Point, September 18, 1969.

638. "Weatherwomen," Pittsburgh Point, October 9, 1969.

639. Weaver, Donna. "Woman: One More Exploited...," Grinding Stone, November, 1969.

640. Webb, Marilyn. "Abortion," Washington Free Press, August 1, 1969.

641. _____. "America's Comic Culture," Grinding Stone, April 30, 1969.

642. Weber, Paul J. "The Revolution on American Campuses," Catholic World, CCX (March, 1970), pp. 248-252.

643. Weingartner, Rudolph H. "Justifying Civil Disobedience," Columbia University Forum, IX (1966), pp. 38-44.

644. Weinstein, James. "Nach Goldwasser Uns?" Studies on the Left, IV, No. 3 (1964), pp. 59-64.

645. _____. "Weathermen (Revolutionary Youth Movement), A Lot of Thunder but a Short Reign," Socialist Revolution, January-February, 1970, p. 1.

646. Weisberg, Barry. "The Politics of Ecology," Liberation, XIV (January, 1970), pp. 20-25.

647. Welles, Earl. "Politics of Disorientation," Berkeley Barb, October 3, 1969.

648. Wells, Lyn. "Sisters United: They Haven't Seen Anything Yet," Great Speckled Bird, February 23, 1970.

649. Wendt, Larry. "War Is Bullshit," San Jose Red Eye, November 20, 1969.

650. Wesley, S. M. "The Creative Visionary and the New Revolution," Berkeley Barb, August 22, 1969.

651. _____. "Disantiestablishmentarianism: The Radical
     Middle, Another Alternative," Berkeley Barb, October
     3, 1969.

652. West, Phyllis. "Student Group Grows after Typo Ap-
     pears," Los Angeles Free Press, October 29, 1965.

653. Westby, David L., and Richard G. Braungart. "Class
     and Politics in the Family Backgrounds of Student
     Activists," American Sociological Review, XXXI
     (October, 1966), pp. 690-692.

654. Widmer, Kingsley. "Living-Room Confrontation: The
     Rage against Violence," Nation, CCXI (July 20, 1970),
     pp. 45-48.

655. _____. "Why the Colleges Blew up: California
     State Colleges System," Nation, CCVIII (February
     24, 1969), pp. 237-241.

656. Wiener, Jon. "Woodstock Revisited," Pittsburgh
     Point, November 6, 1969.

657. Wilkinson, Bob. "Capital Confrontation," Connections,
     September 19, 1967.

658. Williams, William Appleman. "Historiography and
     Revolution: The Case of Cuba. A Commentary on
     a Polemic by Theodore Draper," Studies on the Left,
     III, No. 3 (1963), pp. 78-102.

659. Wills, Garry. "The Making of the Yippie Culture,"
     Esquire, LXXII (November, 1969), pp. 135-138.

660. Wilson, John. "A Coalition of Militants," Liberation
     News Service, January 23, 1969.

661. Winters, Stanley B. "Urban Renewal and Civil Rights,"
     Studies on the Left, IV, No. 3 (1964), pp. 16-31.

662. Wolfe, Alan. "Hard Times on Campus," Nation, CCX
     (May 25, 1970), pp. 623-627.

663. Wolfe, Robert. "American Imperialism and the Peace
     Movement," Studies on the Left, VI, No. 3 (May-
     June, 1966), pp. 28-43.

664. _____. "Intellectuals and Social Change, " Studies
on the Left, II, No. 3 (1962), pp. 63-68.

665. Wolfson, Dave. "Killings at Kent, " Pittsburgh Point,
May 7, 1970.

666. Woodring, Paul. "Campus Stress, " Saturday Review,
LII (March 15, 1969), p. 72.

667. _____. "A View from the Campus: The Struggle
for Black Identity, " Saturday Review, LII (January
18, 1969), p. 62.

668. Wrong, Dennis H. "Reflections on the End of Ideology, " Dissent, VII (Summer, 1960), pp. 286-291.

669. Yokell, Mike. "A Guide to Radical Boston, " Paper
Tiger, May, 1968.

670. _____. "The Student Radical: After Graduation
What?" Paper Tiger, December, 1967.

671. York, Frank A. "Revolutionary 4th in Berkeley, "
Pittsburgh Point, July 10, 1969.

672. Young, Allen. "Academia in Rebellion, " Chicago
Kaleidoscope, January 3, 1969.

673. _____. "S. D. S. on Drugs, " Abas, May, 1969.

674. _____. "SDS Takes New Turn, " Fifth Estate, July
10, 1969.

675. _____. "Senate Report on the New Left, " Liberation News Service, November 9, 1968.

676. _____. "The War for the Hearts and Minds of
G. I.'s, " Liberation News Service, November 7,
1968.

677. Youngblood, Gene. "Movies: Under and Overground, "
Los Angeles Free Press, March 29, 1968.

678. Zagoria, Donald S. "Mediation: A Path to Campus
Peace?" Monthly Labor Review, XCII (January,
1969), p. 9.

679. Zeitlin, Maurice. "Inside Cuba: Workers and Revolu-
      tion, " Ramparts, VIII (March, 1970), pp. 10-20.

680. Zetteler, Mike. "Walls Have Ears: Wire Tap, "
      Kaleidoscope, December 22, 1967.

681. Zinn, Howard. "Force of Nonviolence, " Nation, CXCIV
      (March 17, 1962), pp. 227-233.

682. Zogby, Jim. "Students and Slum Lords, " Distant Drum-
      mer, April 9, 1970.

                        C. PAMPHLETS

1.   Aber, Joel, et al. Germ Warfare Research for Viet-
      nam: Project Spicerack on the Pennsylvania Campus.
      Philadelphia, Pa. : Philadelphia Area Committee to
      End the War in Vietnam, 228 Buckingham Place,
      Philadelphia, 1965, 31 pp.

2.   Aptheker, Bettina, Robert Kaufman, and Michael Fol-
      som. FSM: The Free Speech Movement at Berkeley.
      San Francisco, Calif. : WEB DuBois Clubs of Amer-
      ica, 1965, 52 pp.

3.   Davidson, Carl. The New Radicals in the Multiversity--
      An Analysis and Strategy for the Student Movement.
      Chicago: Students for a Democratic Society, May,
      1968, 37 pp.

4.   _____ . Toward a Student Syndicalist Movement.
      Chicago: Students for a Democratic Society, August,
      1966, 7 pp.

5.   Draper, Hal, and Ann Draper. The Dirt on Califor-
      nia: Agribusiness and the University. Independent
      Socialist Club, Berkeley, California, 1968, 32 pp.

6.   Free Speech Movement, Steering Committee. We
      Want a University. Berkeley: University of Cali-
      fornia, December, 1964, 10 pp.

7.   Garson, Marvin. The Regents. Berkeley: Independent
      Socialist Club, 1967, 25 pp.

8.   Haber, R. Alan. Students and Labor. Chicago: Stu-
      dents for a Democratic Society, September, 1962, 19pp.

9. Hayden, Tom. Revolution in Mississippi. New York:
    Students for a Democratic Society, 1963, 28 pp.

10. Hayden, Tom, and Carl Wittman. An Interracial Move-
    ment of the Poor? New York: Students for a Demo-
    cratic Society, 1965, 26 pp.

11. Hayden, Tom. Student Social Action. Chicago: Stu-
    dents for a Democratic Society, 1965, 12 pp.

12. Jacobson, Tom. Unions and the Working Student. New
    York: Students for a Democratic Society, August,
    1963, 4 pp.

13. Kissinger, C. Clark. The Bruns Strike--A Case Study
    of Student Participation in Labor. New York: Stu-
    dents for a Democratic Society, October, 1963.

14. Nicolaus, Martin. The Iceberg Strategy: Universities
    and the Military-Industrial Complex. Ann Arbor,
    Mich.: Radical Education Project, 1967, 6 pp.

15. Peterson, Richard E. The Scope of Organized Student
    Protest in 1964-1965. Princeton, N. J.: Educational
    Testing Service, 1966.

16. Public Interest. The Universities. A Special Issue of
    The Public Interest. New York: National Affairs, Inc.,
    1968.

17. Radical Feminists of New York. Notes from the Second
    Year. New York: Radical Feminism of New York,
    n. d.

18. Radical Student Union. The Uses of U. C. Berkeley:
    Research. Berkeley: University of California, Radi-
    cal Student Union, February, 1969, 56 pp.

19. Research Organizing Cooperative. Strike at Frisco State.
    San Francisco: R. O. C., 1969.

20. Rudd, Mark. Columbia. Chicago: Students for a
    Democratic Society, 1969, 14 pp.

21. Sasajima, Masu, et al. Organized Student Protest and
    Institutional Climate. Princeton, N. J.: Educational
    Testing Service, March, 1967.

22. Students for a Democratic Society. Port Huron State-
     ment. New York: League for Industrial Democracy,
     Student Department, 1964.

23. Weissman, Stephen, and Doug Tuthill. Freedom and
     the University. Chicago: SDS, April, 1966, 7 pp.

24. Yokell, Michael. M. I. T. and the Warfare State. New
     York: SDS at MIT, 1967, 21 pp.

                    D. GOVERNMENT REPORTS

1.   Illinois Crime Investigating Commission (ICIC). Report
     on the SDS Riots. April, 1970.

2.   Lange, David L. Violence and the Media. National
     Commission on the Causes and Prevention of Violence.
     Washington, D. C.: Superintendent of Documents,
     Government Printing Office, 1969.

3.   Michigan State Senate. Report of the Michigan State
     Senate Committee to Investigate Campus Disorders
     and Student Unrest. East Lansing, Michigan: 1970.
     (Mimeographed)

4.   New York, State of, Albany. Temporary Commission
     to Study the Causes of Campus Unrest. The Academy
     in Turmoil. Albany, New York: 1970.

5.   Orrick, William H. Shut It Down: A College in Crisis
     --San Francisco State College, October, 1968-April,
     1969. A Report to the National Commission on the
     Causes and Prevention of Violence. Washington, D. C.:
     Government Printing Office, 1969.

6.   Robinson, Lora H., and Janet D. Schoenfeld. Student
     Participation in Academic Governance. Washington,
     D. C.: Eric Clearinghouse on Higher Education,
     George Washington University, 1969.

7.   U. S. House of Representatives. Hearings before the
     Committee on Internal Security. Investigation of Stu-
     dents for a Democratic Society. Parts 1-A through
     7-B, 1969.

8.   _____. Hearings before the Committee on Un-Amer-

ican Activities. Subversive Involvement in Disruption
of 1968 Democratic Party National Convention. Parts
1-3, 1968.

9. U.S. Library of Congress. Legislative Reference Service. The New Left: Students for a Democratic Society. By Richard S. Jones. Washington, D.C.:
1968. (Multilith)

10. U.S. Senate. Hearings before the Subcommittee to Investigate the Administration of the Internal Security
Act and Other Internal Security Laws of the Committee
on the Judiciary. Extent of Subversion in the "New
Left." Parts 4-9, 1970.

11. _____. Hearings before the Permanent Subcommittee
on Investigations of the Committee on Government Operations. Riots, Civil and Criminal Disorders.
Parts 18-25, 1969-1970.

12. _____. Committee on Government Operation. Permanent Subcommittee on Investigations. Staff Study
of Campus Riots and Disorders, October, 1967-May,
1969. Washington, D.C.: Government Printing Office, 1969.

E. SCHOLARLY PAPERS

1. Braungart, Richard G. "Family Status, Socialization
and Student Politics." Paper presented at the 64th
annual meeting of the American Sociological Association, 1969.

2. _____. "SDS and YAF: Backgrounds of Student
Political Activists." Paper presented at the 61st an-
nual meeting of the American Sociological Association,
August 31, 1966.

3. Kerpelman, Larry C. "Student Activism, Ideology, and
Personality." Proceedings of the 76th annual convention of the American Psychological Association, 1968,
pp. 377-378.

4. Mock, Kathleen R. "The Potential Activist and His
Perception of the University." Washington, D.C.:
American Psychological Association, September 2, 1968.

5. Peterson, Richard E. "Reform in Higher Education--
    Goals of the Right and of the Left." Washington,
    D. C.: Association of American Colleges, January 15,
    1969.

F.   REPORTS OF PRIVATE GROUPS

1. Kent State University Chapter of the American Association
    of University Professors. Special Committee of In-
    quiry. The Kent State Tragedy. Kent, Ohio: 1969.

2. National School Public Relations Association. Education
    U. S. A.: High School Student Unrest. Washington,
    D. C.: National School Public Relations Association,
    1969.

3. National Society of Professors. Campus Unrest: What
    to Do until the Riot Squad Comes. Washington, D. C.:
    National Society of Professors, November-December,
    1970.

4. Nichols, David C. (ed.). Perspectives on Campus Ten-
    sions. Washington, D. C.: American Council on Edu-
    cation, 1970.

5. Nichols, David C., and Olive Mills. The Campus and
    the Racial Crisis. Washington, D. C.: American
    Council on Education, 1970.

G.   FILMS

1. "Chicago, The Seasons Change." The demonstrations
    and police riots during the 1968 Chicago Democratic
    Convention. 45 minutes. American Documentary
    Films, 379 Bay Street, San Francisco, California
    94133.

2. "The Chicago Convention Challenge." A documentary of
    the student demonstrations in Chicago, in August,
    1968 during the Democratic Party Convention. News-
    reel, Box 302, Canal Street Station, New York, N. Y.
    10013.

3. "The Columbia Revolt." A documentary on the Columbia
    University uprising in April-May, 1968. Newsreel.

4. "Huey." Film of the Birthday Party for Huey P. Newton
    held in April, 1968. Film includes speeches by Car-
    michael, Cleaver, Forman, and Seale.   30 minutes.
    American Documentary Films.

5. "Sons and Daughters." A documentary of the Vietnam
    Day Committee demonstrations conducted by Berkeley
    students in October, 1965. 90 minutes. American
    Documentary Films.

H. JUDICIAL DOCUMENT

1. Burnstein, Malcolm, et al. Attorneys for Appellants,
    People of the State of California vs. Mario Savio and
    571 Others. An Appeal of Conviction to the Superior
    Court of Alameda County, Criminal No. 235, Septem-
    ber, 1965. This appeal is a brilliant legal and politi-
    cal defense of the Berkeley Free Speech Movement of
    the Fall of 1964.

I. BIBLIOGRAPHY

1. Segal, Patricia. Annotated Bibliography on Student Re-
    bellion and Revolutionary Movements. Claremont,
    Calif.: Claremont Graduate School, Claremont, Cali-
    fornia, 1970. (Mimeographed)

INDEX

A. Major Developments

477

B. Names, Places, and Events